The Poetry of Richard Aldington

A Rider College Publication

RIDER COLLEGE
TRENTON, NEW JERSEY

THE POETRY OF
RICHARD ALDINGTON

A Critical Evaluation and
An Anthology of Uncollected Poems

NORMAN T. GATES

THE PENNSYLVANIA STATE UNIVERSITY PRESS

UNIVERSITY PARK AND LONDON

Library of Congress Cataloging in Publication Data

Gates, Norman T
    The poetry of Richard Aldington.

    "A Rider College publication."
    Bibliography: p. 348.
    1.   Aldington, Richard, 1892-1962.   I.   Aldington,
Richard, 1892-1962.   II.   Title.
PR6001.L4Z6   821'.9'12   73-6877
ISBN 0-271-01119-X

In memory of
Herbert Howarth

Contents

Preface

The purpose of this book can be briefly set forth as descriptive, critical, and redemptive.

The Complete Poems of Richard Aldington may be familiar to scholars of modern British poetry, but the thirty-two British and American individual volumes, from which the final collection is drawn, are probably not. I have sought out and examined each, and here I give an account of them for the first time (to my knowledge) since the appearance of the bibliographies by Snow, Kershaw, and Schlueter—even these I have had sometimes to correct. I narrate all details pertinent to the publications that I have been able to find, and I give an account of the critical reception of each work. I have also carefully described how the final collection was made from the earlier editions and collections: why the poems were arranged as they were, what poems were omitted and why, what revisions were made in the individual poems, and, if possible, why the changes were made.

The critical task has been approached from three angles. First, I have reviewed the criticism of Aldington's poetry from about 1910 up to this time, and have given an account of any work now under way. Secondly, I have dealt critically with each of the individual volumes by discussing poems within the volume and by appraising the thrust of the total of the poetry collected there. Finally, as a result of a close and constant perusal of all of his poetry, I have attempted to assess Aldington's position as a poet and as a speaker for his times, and his contribution to English poetry.

When he came to make up his final collection, Aldington ignored—may even have forgotten or been unable to obtain—many poems which he had sold to newspapers and magazines or left in manuscript form. He also omitted, sometimes for no apparent reason, many poems from the early editions. I have found one hundred and twenty-nine uncollected poems in newspapers, periodicals, and unpublished manuscripts, and have added to these all of the eighty-seven poems that appeared in early books of his poetry but were omitted from *The Complete Poems*. Many of these poems are of great interest. I give the texts of all of them.

Acknowledgments

First I would like to thank the faculty of the English Department of the University of Pennsylvania, whose help and encouragement to a "late- blooming" undergraduate and graduate student have made this work possible. Of course this book would not have been completed without the help and advice of the distinguished scholar and teacher, Herbert Howarth, whose recent death has cost me a rare friend.

I have been delighted with the cooperation received from libraries and librarians in what has literally been a world-wide search for Aldington material. I wish to extend my sincere thanks to the following libraries and their staffs: The University Libraries of the University of Pennsylvania; The Free Library of Philadelphia; Manuscript Collection, Temple University; Rutgers University Library; Franklin P. Moore Library of Rider College; the Library of State Teacher's College at West Chester, Pennsylvania; Muhlenburg College Library; The Poetry Collection of the Lockwood Memorial Library, State University of New York at Buffalo; *Poetry Magazine Papers*, The General Library of the University of California at Berkeley; Humanities Research Center, University of Texas at Austin; University Research Library, The University of California, Los Angeles; The Morris Library of Southern Illinois University; Beineke Rare Book and Manuscript Library, Yale University; Harvard College Library; The University of Washington Library; University College Library, London; and the British Museum.

I also wish to thank the Rider College Faculty Research Program for a Grant-in-Aid that helped make possible a trip to England to investigate British holdings of Aldington materials.

Permission to quote from unpublished letters and to reproduce unpublished poems, for which Madame Catherine Guillaume holds the copyright, was granted by Richard Aldington's literary executor, Mr. Alister Kershaw, and the owners of these documents: Southern Illinois University; the University of Texas; the State University of New York at Buffalo; the University of Chicago; the University of California, Los Angeles; Harvard University; the University of Washington; Yale University; Temple University; and the British Museum.

And finally I am proud to acknowledge the constant and immeasurable support and encouragement I have received from my family; without them this task could never have been accomplished.

PART I

CRITICISM AND EVALUATION

1
Critical Views of Aldington's Poetry

The first professional criticism of Richard Aldington's work came from an excellent, if eccentric, source: Bernard Shaw. Sometime in 1908, when the young poet was sixteen or seventeen, he had his first poem published in a London periodical, and his proud mother sent a copy of it to Shaw. Aldington quotes Shaw's reply from memory:

> Madam,
> Your son obviously has too much literary talent to earn his living in an honest way.
>   I enclose a guinea which he is to spend in some thoroughly selfish manner.[1]

It was probably in 1911 that Aldington met Ezra Pound and showed him some of his poems. "Well, I don't think you need any help from me," Pound is supposed to have said.[2] Certainly Pound must have been considerably impressed with the work of Aldington and H.D. Wallace Martin says that "according to Flint, Pound may have originally conceived Imagism as a means of publicizing the poetry of his friends—H.D. and Richard Aldington in particlar." Martin goes on to quote from an unpublished poem of Robert Frost which joshes Pound for being "brought to bed" of "twins" who "came into the world prodigiously united in wedlock"—obviously a reference to Aldington and H.D.[3]

The years 1912-1914 were to prove the high-water mark of Pound's critical approval of Aldington's poetry. From that time on he seems to have cooled considerably. In 1915 Pound wrote to Harriet Monroe of *Poetry* magazine, in which Aldington's early Imagist poems had been published at Pound's suggestion in 1912:

> Aldington has his occasional concentrations, and for that reason it is always possible that he will do a fine thing. There is a superficial cleverness in him, then a great and lamentable gap, then the hard point, the true center, out of which a fine thing may come at any time. . . . H.D. and William C. Williams both better emotional equipment than Aldington, but lacking the superficial cleverness.

In the same year he wrote to H.L. Mencken: "Have sent word to various people that you want good stuff. Aldington for light verse. . . ." And the next year to Harriet Shaw Weaver, editor of *The Egoist*, where Aldington was still assistant editor: "I haven't read his [Aldington's] prose, but there may be more snap in it than in his verse." In 1917 Pound wrote to another lady editor, Margaret C. Anderson of *The Little Review*, about John Rodker:

> He will go further than Richard Aldington, though I don't expect anyone to believe that statement for some time. He has more invention, more guts. His father did not have a library full of classics, but he will learn.[4]

Obviously Pound's judgment was not infallible, and occasionally he let personal irritation with one or another of his protégés sway him for the moment. Writing in *The Little Review* in 1921, Pound had this to say about a piece that Aldington had written on Joyce:

> Mr. Aldington's article on Joyce in the English Review is the funniest thing that has appeared in England for some time; if he does not succeed in succeeding Edmund Gosse, he at any rate ousts Mr. Owen Seaman, and for this clever bit of sewer cleaning he should receive a pension from the ever just British Govt.[5]

But oddly enough, in the same issue there is an advertisement for Sylvia Beach's Paris publication of *Ulysses* that quotes Richard Aldington: "A most remarkable book . . . Bloom is a rags and tatters Hamlet, a proletarian Lear. . . ."

Pound, however, never completely gave up on his original Imagist; in 1929 he wrote to Harriet Monroe: "More cheering news items are that Aldington seems to have awakened from his slumbers. I may be sending you something of his, before long."[6] And in his *Literary Essays* Pound spoke with high regard for Aldington's early poetry:

> . . . Aldington's version of "Atthis," . . . . These have worn smooth in my head and I am not through with them, nor with Aldington's "In Via Sistina" nor his other poems in "Des Imagistes," though people have told me their flaws. It may be that their content is too much embedded in me for me to look back at the words.[7]

Amy Lowell, who took over from Pound the editorship of the last three Imagist anthologies, wrote a critique of Aldington's poetry in *The Little Review* in 1915. She called his poetry delicate, elusive, and suggestive; his quality was a "stark, unsentimental preoccupation with beauty." Miss Lowell characterized his poetry as consisting of intense feeling underlying astringent utterance, and called Aldington a highly civilized, sophisticated lyrist of unusual achievement and fine promise.[8]

Another fellow poet and a contributor to the second Imagist anthology, John Gould Fletcher, reviewed Aldington's first American edition, *Images Old and New* in April of 1916. Several years earlier Fletcher had urged Amy Lowell not to contribute to *Des Imagistes* because it was to be, he thought, simply a scheme to promote Aldington in the United States. Now his attitude had changed. Writing in *Poetry* under the title "Mr. Aldington's Images," he said, "Recently there have been in England signs of a return to that simplicity

and restraint which are the qualities of highest art. . . . Of this admirable tend-
ency Mr. Aldington is the precursor and the most shining example."[9] In the
May issue of *The Little Review* Fletcher began an article on "Three Imagist
Poets" which he concluded in the June-July issue. In the first part he said of
Aldington that he was a cultivated, sophisticated, bookish poet. Among
Fletcher's comments on specific poems was his suggestion that nothing in all
literature could be safely set beside "Choricos." He said that Aldington was a
pessimist who could be humorous, playful, and even fantastic, but who, at
bottom, was a romantic. In the second half of the article Fletcher compared
Aldington and his wife and fellow poet, H.D. Aldington was a skeptic, en-
amored of lost Greek beauty, who wrote about life, while H.D. was a nature
poet. Aldington's work raised questions about our life, while H.D.'s offered
eternal answers. Fletcher thought that, except for "Choricos," H.D.'s work
was superior in rhythm. Aldington, he said, had many unsolved problems
underlying his thought; he wrote on many themes, H.D. on only two or three.
H.D.'s art was perfect within its limits, but Aldington's was more interesting
because of its human imperfection.[10]

O.W. Firkins, in an article in the January 1917 issue of *The Nation*,
expressed displeasure with Richard Aldington's metaphors:

> I am not sure but the palm for delicacy and indelicacy alike goes to Mr.
> Richard Aldington, who has grace in his luckier moments, and who, in
> his backslidings, can compare the moon, that "Queen and Huntress,
> chaste and fair," whom even the coarseness of the Elizabethans re-
> spected, to an awkward Venus, "with a rag of gauze about her loins,"
> or a pregnant woman "walking cautiously over the slippery heavens."[11]

In 1919 in *The Little Review*, William Carlos Williams, another of the
original contributors to *Des Imagistes*, was critical of Aldington's war poems:

> I speak of the work of Aldington and D.H. Lawrence (as presented
> in the July issue of *Poetry*). . . . Aldington has decidedly gone back-
> wards in these poems. . . . It is perhaps the war that has reduced them
> . . . they are empty nonsense having no relation to the place or time they
> were written in. They have no existence. . . .
> What is this silly invocation to love and loveliness—of Aldington's
> especially,—this address to doves flying over the horrid trenches? . . . I
> prefer Aldington to all the "men" in the world. It is not that. I am ob-
> jecting to a certain work of art that it is not what it is not. . . . Poetry is
> not a despairing cry of defiance . . . . It is an assertion: I am here today
> in the midst of living hell![12]

Also in 1919 F.S. Flint, represented in *Des Imagistes*, wrote in *Coterie*
"On Richard Aldington." Flint said that Aldington's work was a record
of his own spiritual experiences, and that these were the experiences of a
man who lived fully in his own day. In a slap at the Pound-Eliot school, Flint
declared that Aldington's work was "no mere rearrangement of echoes of
bygone literature, chosen by the common ear of a clique, and tuned to its
common fads." Flint thought the vice of modern English poetry to be "the

pretty line and the fine-sounding word." Aldington, he contended, had not been taken in by this weakness, since he was careful of the sense of his words before he looked to their beauty. Flint suggested that the theme of *Images* was "the spiritual contest between imagined beauty and the outer ugliness that is thrust upon you." In *Images of Desire* the "passion of love is exalted as the only sanction for the weariness of human existence." *Images of War* expressed the emotions of a civilized man suddenly transplanted into "the barbarous and crushing circumstances of modern battle." Flint felt that the development of the poet had been continuous, and named two other poets, Catullus and Horace, who had left a record of their century in their verse as Aldington had done.[13]

Harold Monro, keeper of The Poetry Bookshop and publisher of Aldington's first volume of verse, wrote *Some Contemporary Poets* in 1920. He said of Aldington:

> His poverty of adjectival qualifications is conspicuous. . . . He relies also to excess on the mere mention of colors.
> There is brain behind his poetry, perhaps too much brain, too much "labour to appear skillful." Intellect is the servant of poetry, but it is a dangerous servant, apt to interfere.

Monro, however, praised Aldington's war poetry: "Except Siegfried Sassoon, no 'war poet' has represented the torments of military life with such candour and so entirely without bombastic rhetoric."[14]

In his autobiography Aldington records his gratitude to May Sinclair for helping him to become a life member of the London Library.[15] This must have made a great impression on the young poet because years later in his novel *Rejected Guest*, the hero, David Norris, is refused a membership, and the author writes bitterly in the episode.[16] In May of 1921 May Sinclair wrote an extensive critique in *The English Review* on "The Poems of Richard Aldington." On the whole Miss Sinclair's article was favorable; some of her insights were extemely perceptive: "Richard Aldington is possessed by the sense of beauty, the desire of beauty, the absolute emotion, as no English poet since Shelley has been yet possessed, with the solitary exception of H.D." After pointing out that he should have been young when Sappho or Anyte of Tegea was young, she added that one half of him was not Greek, and "it brings into his poetry an element which is not Greek, a pain, a dissatisfaction, a sadness that the purely Greek soul did not know." This was one of the reasons, she felt, that we get a sense of incompleteness from the poems of his period of transition.

> If we are to find his sources and affinities it is clear that Richard Aldington owes an immense debt to Walter Savage Landor. There is no other writer of "prose poetry" with whom he can be more fitly compared.

Miss Sinclair saw in Aldington a split personality: one half a poet of classical Greece and the other half a poet of modern times. At the time of her writing

(1921) she felt that "it was the Greek Richard Aldington who ripened to a precocious mastery; the modern poet that is no less surely in him has not even approached maturity."[17]

The publication in New York in 1928 of Aldington's *Collected Poems* was the occasion for reminiscence and a review by Harriet Monroe. She recalled *Poetry*'s first exciting years and the young Imagist movement of which Richard Aldington had been such an important part. Remembering his poems that had been published in the second issue of *Poetry* in 1912, and writing particularly of "Choricos," she said:

> And this poem is youth's glamorous vision of death, beautiful under its mask of terror. It was an ironic destiny which led this poet-youth, so soon after, into the front-line trenches of the world's worst war, and changed the glamour into horrible realism.

Miss Monroe felt that Aldington's reaction to the war was "cynicism—bitter disbelief in life, its values and its gods." On the whole, she thought, "he has followed with fair consistency the stern principles under which he and the other imagists began their revolution nearly seventeen years ago."[18]

The *Collected Poems* also provided the occasion for Paull F. Baum to review Aldington's position as a poet. Baum wrote in *South Atlantic Quarterly*: "He who would have lived happily in a pastoral of Theocritus finds himself at bay among the complexities of civilization and the brutalities of war." This reviewer was one of the very few who did not praise Aldington's love poems highly. He found that their "note is forced to shrillness, sometimes, which begets doubt." Baum praised the poet's prosody, declaring that "if for no other reason, Mr. Aldington's poetry would be important for its metrical mastery." The reviewer concluded by seeing the same sort of divided self in the poet that May Sinclair had called attention to, and hoping that "Mr. Aldington will complete the story with a satisfying resolution of his Arcadian-modernistic discord."[19]

The publication in 1929 of Aldington's *Death of a Hero* catapulted him from the relative obscurity of a poet and man of letters, known in literary circles but not to the public at large, into a best-seller novelist with an international reputation. Besides adding considerably to his circle of friends and to his financial security, the novel's publication stimulated the writing of the first book devoted entirely to study of his work. In *Life for Life's Sake* Aldington tells of Thomas McGreevy's joining him at a table outside the Closerie des Lilas in Paris the September when *Death of a Hero* was brought out:

> Presently a man came up to our table and joined us. This was Tom Mc-Greevy, an Irishman I had met once or twice at Joyce's. . . . Although, as our friend A.S. Frere once remarked, Tom McGreevy is five hundred per cent Irish, he had served as a gunner officer in the B.E.F. in France; and therefore was well disposed towards my little efforts at reviving common memories. Since he has more than his share of Irish wit and charm, and is highly literate, we spent a pleasant evening.[20]

Aldington calls McGreevy "the first and certainly one of the best beloved of the many friends made for me by *Death of a Hero.*" He describes their friendship in a reminiscence of some length, during which he says:

> He was a graduate of Trinity College and, when I first knew him, Lecteur d' Anglais at the École Normale Supérieure, the most highbrow establishment in France . . . . Though Tom spent so much of his time with sceptical young Frenchmen who riddled every prejudice and superstition with witty satire, and though he was as much a man of the world as one so pure in heart could be, he had some singular views. Thus he astounded me by declaring emphatically that the Gunpowder Plot never existed and was entirely invented by the Protestants—a piece of Jesuit propaganda long ago exploded by competent historians.[2][1]

Thomas McGreevy's *Richard Aldington*: *An Englishman* was published in London by Chatto and Windus in 1931 as Number 10 in the Dolphin Book series. The book is dedicated "For Brigit," probably meaning Brigit Patmore, who was Aldington's mistress at this time. Its epigraph is from Samuel Beckett:

> Yesterday is not a milestone that has been passed, but a daystone on the beaten track of the years, and irremediably part of us, within us, heavy and dangerous. We are not merely more weary because of yesterday, we are other, no longer what we were before the calamity of yesterday.

This little book contains only seventy-three pages. The first chapter is political in nature and deals with the war and the postwar conditions that provided the background for Aldington's first novel, which appeared, McGreevy says, because "it was time for a generation that had fought and thought and felt deeply to say its say." Chapter II discusses the Imagists: "They were aesthetes—in a safer, a more virile, way than the young men of the 'nineties, but the American Mr. Pound did know who constituted the *avant garde* in early twentieth-century French painting and sculpture as the American Mr. Whistler had known who constituted it in the late nineteenth" (p. 10). McGreevy writes attractively of the early circle in which the young poet moved: Yeats, Pound, Marinetti. At first, he says, Aldington wrote only of what he loved: "nature which was still living and lovely, civilisation which seemed dead but was still lovely to dream over" (p. 12). He says of the young poet's metrical skill (p. 16):

> Without in the least deserting the genius of his own language, he won something of the subtle Greek harmony that is independent of any such mechanical element as rhyme. By giving no special importance to the last word of each line, by labouring over all the words more carefully, he got a natural, unmechanical grace which is absent from Swinburne, and which is one of the miracles of the Hellenic method in all the arts.

Chapter III deals with Richard Aldington's war poetry. "He went ahead, and for all he was young and only wakening from a boy's dream of poetry to fumble with a reality more dreadful than he could ever have imagined, he succeeded in turning that reality into poetry many, many times" (p. 25). In this chapter McGreevy discusses quite a number of the war poems individually. The chapter concludes with the suggestion that Aldington, despite his proximity to death for many months, finally "was for life—and for quick life, not still life" (p. 35).

The fourth chapter of *Richard Aldington: An Englishman* covers the ten postwar years during which, McGreevy says somewhat inaccurately, Aldington "gave relatively little time to poetry." McGreevy makes an interesting observation (p. 39) concerning the poet's interest in Voltaire:

> It is obvious why Richard Aldington should have been drawn to the study of Voltaire at the time. Voltaire's scepticism, his distrust of the vested interests, his humanity, and his often malicious fancy were bound to appeal to the disillusionment and sense of pity of the returned soldier.

Chapter V is devoted to *Death of a Hero*. McGreevy points out the Greek structure of the novel, indicating that this important influence on Aldington's poetry also carried over to his prose. In the final chapter of McGreevy's book the short stories are discussed and a few sentences given to *A Dream in the Luxembourg*, which McGreevy calls a "gracious wanton idyll." The Irishman speaks very highly, too, of the fourth section of Aldington's "Passages Toward a Long Poem," which he saw, of course, only in the 1930 Imagist anthology and not in its later form.

As a criticism of Aldington's poetry, Thomas McGreevy's *Richard Aldington: An Englishman* has its weaknesses. A good share of this book is taken up by what Aldington called McGreevy's "singular views." We have no doubts about the author's being both Irish and Catholic, since he expresses his views on England and Protestantism quite freely. McGreevy strays far too much into a garrulous appraisal "of shoes—and ships—and sealing-wax—," but on the other hand he has some pertinent things to say about Aldington. His closeness to the poet and his knowledge of the milieu out of which the poet wrote make him a valuable commentator.

In the late 1920s Glenn Hughes was a professor of English at the University of Washington and editor of the University of Washington Chapbooks. Number 6 of these Chapbooks, published in 1927, was Richard Aldington's *D.H. Lawrence: An Indiscretion*, and Number 13, published the following year, his *Remy de Gourmont: A Modern Man of Letters*. Probably at Aldington's suggestion, Hughes wrote a foreword (following one by Ford Madox Ford) to the *Imagist Anthology 1930*. In this foreword, which is dated 6 July 1929, Hughes reviews the past of Imagism, discusses its impact on modern poetry, and lists those poets who might be considered to have been Imagists. Probably as the result of this first-hand contact, he wrote, and had published by Stanford University Press in 1931, *Imagism and the Imagists: A Study in Modern Poetry*. In his Preface to the book Professor Hughes says (p. vii):

It seemed to me, when I undertook this study, that a certain advantage can be obtained by chronicling a literary movement soon after its climax, before the principal participants forget the motives and the events essential to it.

He points out also, however, that a contemporary historian is severely hampered by having to withhold certain biographical details; no literary history can be perfect, "for the contemporary historian withholds facts and the later one cannot discover them" (p. viii).

Imagism and the Imagists is divided into two parts: the four chapters of Part I deal with "Imagism," and Part II devotes a separate chapter to each of the seven Imagists who contributed to Amy Lowell's three anthologies. Chapter 5, the one concerned with Aldington, consists of twenty-four pages (pp. 85-108) under the subtitle, "The Rebel." Hughes begins with biographical material and a discussion of Aldington's early work, including his editorship of *The Egoist* and his early prose writings. There is this general characterization (p. 86):

> The essence of Aldington's character, the key to his poetry, is rebellion. He cannot tolerate the status quo. That is why he admires Pound and Lawrence and Wyndham Lewis, and why his god is Voltaire. The youngest of the imagists, he proved one of the staunchest defenders of the faith, a warrior eager for battle, and armed with much learning, tremendous mental energy, and a mocking, biting wit. His headstrong enthusiasms result sometimes in inconsistency and exaggeration, but generally he is a sound and penetrating thinker.

Hughes then discusses the individual volumes of poetry up to and including *A Dream in the Luxembourg* and, of course, those of Aldington's poems included in the 1930 *Imagist Anthology*. The early *Images (1910-1915)* is considered and some of its poems; then *Images of War*. Professor Hughes speculates on what would have happened to the poet if there had been no war. "It is possible that without the experience of war he would have become as bitter and cynical as he did with the experience. At any rate, his two and a half years of service, with fifteen months spent at the actual front, left him a quite different poet" (p. 93). Hughes thinks that Aldington's war poems are a recognizable continuation of his earlier work, although their tone is sterner and their details more vivid. They are "some of the truest and most beautiful poems written by any soldier in modern times."

Hughes praises the love poems of *Images of Desire* and quotes May Sinclair's admiration of *Myrrhine and Konallis*; he sees *Exile and Other Poems* as "voicing the disillusionment and despair which besieged the poet in the post-war days." There is a careful analysis of *A Fool i' the Forest*, which Professor Hughes considers "Aldington's finest poetic achievement." Of *The Eaten Heart* he says (p. 106):

> The contemplation of this romantic story, with its tragic end, leads the modern poet to an analysis of love, to a contrast between old and new ideals, and thence to a semi-autobiographical rhapsody in which the

recurrent motif is the struggle of a romantic nature to adapt itself to the hardness and disillusionment of a deflowered age, a post-war, machine-governed world.

Imagism and the Imagists and Thomas McGreevy's little volume are the only book-length works that try in any way to cope directly with Richard Aldington's poetry. Like McGreevy's, Professor Hughes's book has the disadvantage, because of its publication date, of not dealing with the last two long poems and the collected editions. And of its two hundred and forty-nine pages, only a fraction are directly concerned with Aldington's work, with the result that not much space can be devoted to the individual volumes, to say nothing of the individual poems. Nevertheless this is a seminal work on Imagism and a valuable contribution to Aldington scholarship. Unlike McGreevy's book, *Imagism and the Imagists* includes an index and an excellent bibliography of the individual poets as well as of more general books and articles about Imagism. Professor Hughes's conclusions about some of the poems, and especially his final comment that, for Aldington, "rebellion is the mainspring of his life," should be, however, accepted only with reservations.

The 1934 publication of *The Poems of Richard Aldington*, which included almost all of the poems of *The Complete Poems* except *Life Quest* and *The Crystal World*, provided another opportunity for critical review. R.P. Blackmur, writing in *The Nation* in that year, has little that is affirmative to say of the poetry of Aldington or, for that matter, any of the Imagists: "his work is not poetry of a high order. The best evidence for this statement is that his poetry loses rather than gains when read all at one time." Mr. Blackmur thinks that the failure may in part be historical:

> Mr. Aldington began publishing with the imagist groups of 1912, and that—as it has turned out for everyone in the group—was a heavy weight to bear. The excitement of a fresh, superficial view coupled with an easy, not to say laxative, method of writing produced or encouraged a good many rather fluid talents to whom the finished, the solid, the mature seemed stale. Success was accidental and fragmentary, and no poet can expect a lifetime of accidents unless the life is short.

The reviewer suggests that the heirs of Imagism "have been unable either to sustain a tone or explore a subject in terms the reader can accept." Citing Eliot and Pound as examples of poets who deliberately obstruct by obscurity, he classes Aldington with Cummings as writers who use words as they find them without much effort to particularize them in their poems. He continues:

> Perhaps nothing more orderly, especially in the realm of poetry and feeling—nothing less fragmentary, nothing less heretical—could have been expected of a generation whose young manhood was interrupted by the war and demolished by the peace, and whose imagination was thus driven by the need of exile or escape from the dreadful order that was laid everywhere upon it.

Blackmur concludes that while Aldington often creates powerful personal documents of life, he does not often do the necessary work to make them powerful poetry. "The success of many fragments only adumbrates the size of the failure." Along with Aldington, Blackmur attacks other modern poets and what amounts to the whole of modern poetry that has grown out of Imagism.[22] Time has proved him wrong in the instances of poets such as Lawrence and Williams; it may also do so in the case of Aldington.

John Wheelwright also contributed a critical review of the 1934 collection under the title "A Poet of Three Persons." The point that Mr. Wheelwright makes is that the first half of the poems show Aldington as a leader of the group which rescued Anglo-American poetry from its slump at the turn of the century, while the next quarter show his work in a post-war decline, and the last quarter how it has "come back to mastery of the direct and elegant record of sensation and opinion."

> Slowly awakened to intellect, sympathetically richer than Pound or Eliot, Aldington has always written as good verse as they have dug out of themselves rather than out of other poets. Less rich than D.H. Lawrence though prosodically neater, strong in the struggle against whimsy to be honest, weakened by "Stoic" loyalty to the things that make him sad, Aldington and the British strain he exemplifies widen in prosodic resources and become more didactic while British culture ever grows more somber.[23]

Frank Swinnerton in *The Georgian Scene: A Literary Panorama*, published in the same year as Blackmur's and Wheelwright's articles, devotes five pages to Richard Aldington. He is, however, mostly concerned with him as a novelist—and even there the criticism is too much concerned with the individual rather than with his work. Swinnerton mentions the poems only in passing: "As these scenes show [in the novels], and as his poems and such passages in other novels as slip past his earnest jocularity show, he has great capacity for emotion."[24]

In a 1938 review of *The Crystal World*, Kerker Quinn precedes his discussion with some general criticism. He begins by speaking of the fierce competition for a place in the first line of minor poets in an age when major poets are rare, and he finds some, like Richard Aldington, buried deep in the ranks through unhappy circumstances. Quinn feels that Aldington's prime misfortune was his association with Imagism: "the movement was temporarily beneficial to him, and he casually forsook it when it ceased being so. Yet when Imagism slipped its moorings and drifted far from popular favor, most of us overlooked that he wasn't still aboard." He also thinks that Aldington's link with the British war poets told against him, though he admits that Aldington, in company with Wilfred Owen and Herbert Read, wrote the most powerful verse occasioned by the war.

In the middle twenties, Quinn says, Aldington did not receive the praise he deserved because he did not "obey the Eliotic canon which decreed that poetic emotion be de-personalized." In 1928 and again in 1934 his collections were damned by the critics because they lacked the technical finish of Eliot.

"No one honored his apparent conviction that formal control is less essential to poetry than the spurt and flare of imagination." Quinn says Aldington needs to be judged along with such impulsive poets as Lawrence, Emerson, and Shelley, "whose success is intermittent, but who can be read with as much pleasure as the more disciplined, uniform poets." He concludes:

> Nearly as common is the charge that Aldington has relied on too few themes and rehearsed them too ploddingly. True enough, he has dealt almost exclusively with the radiance of immediate love and of love in the memory, with the hideousness of immediate battle and of battle in the memory, and with the suppression suffered by imagination at the hands of materialistic civilization. But at least he has searched them deeply, sometimes in unforgettable language; furthermore, his approach to them and his tone have been remarkably varied.[25]

Sometime not long after 1938 (which is the date of the latest of Aldington's works that it lists) an undated booklet, *Richard Aldington: An Appreciation*, by C.P. Snow was published in London by William Heinemann as an introduction to a planned "Uniform Edition" of Aldington's writings. At the end there is "A list of the Works of Richard Aldington." A good deal of the contents of this undated booklet are reprinted in *Richard Aldington: An Intimate Portrait*, which is discussed later in this chapter. The criticism covers all of Aldington's work; not very much space is devoted to the poetry.

Snow emphasizes the fact that Aldington's writing is full of life, and mentions particularly *All Men Are Enemies*, the *Collected Poems* (1929), and *A Dream in the Luxembourg* as illustrations.

> The romantic ideal and its negative; the "finer fuller life" and its absence through human stupidity; the delight and purity of acceptance, and the bitterness at ugly-minded and hostile men; this is much of Aldington, but there is a great deal more.

Snow suggests that there is "a kind of Sancho Panza matter-of-factness, which is combined in his case with mental integrity and passion for the truth." Snow also feels that the publication of *The Crystal World* convinced many of what they had been suspecting for some time: "that Aldington has written some of the best love-poetry in English." This booklet was written as "an appreciation" to help promote an edition that Heinemann planned, but it would not have been necessary for Snow to have added to his comment on the love poems, if he did not wish to do so, this last sentence: "Most of us are not over-willing to commit ourselves to a literary judgment on a contemporary; but that statement I would make myself without feeling that I was risking anything at all."

In 1949 Alister Kershaw prepared *A Bibliography of the Works of Richard Aldington from 1915 to 1948.*[26] Although this does not include any works published between 1948 and Aldington's death in 1962, it provides an excellent basis for the study of the more than two hundred items credited to him. Aldington himself wrote an introduction for the book in which he noted that the only other attempts at a bibliography were the list prepared by C.P. Snow and an incomplete one attached to a German dissertation. He discussed the question of anthologies and the decision to omit all of them from Kershaw's work, even the Imagist anthologies which are listed in D.H. Lawrence's bibliography. Aldington pointed to the hopelessness of the task of the bibliographer of the living author, and mentioned a foreign edition which had arrived by post the day Kershaw mailed off his manuscript to the publishers. Kershaw wrote a short Preface in which he said:

> But Richard Aldington (along with Lawrence) is one of the two or three authors of our time who is to be *read*, really read, and that means, for anyone who cares at all about the written word, collected—his every publication collected.

In 1951 the University of Oklahoma Press published *Imagism: A Chapter for the History of Modern Poetry* by Stanley K. Coffman, Jr. As its title indicates, this is primarily a history of the Imagist movement, and a good one, which in its two hundred and twenty-five pages is able to go into greater depth than Glenn Hughes's book. Dr. Coffman does not include studies of the individual poets. Of the forty-five separate references to Richard Aldington (only Hulme and Pound are mentioned more often), many are historical rather than related to criticism of Aldington's poetry; nevertheless, this analysis is valuable to a study of the poet.

Coffman notes that Aldington was very effective in advancing the cause of Imagism in England because of his position on *The Egoist*, and that he was one of the three poets (the others were H.D. and Flint) who continued their allegiance to the movement from 1912 to 1917. Coffman also gives credit to Aldington for the critical comment that most clearly defines Imagism. Of his poetry Coffman says (p. 165):

> Aldington also shared Pound's admiration for the quality of "hardness" in poetry; the second of the principles he listed in "Modern Poetry and the Imagists" demanded of a poem a "hardness, as of cut stone. No slop, no sentimentality." His poems show a feeling for the beauty of natural objects, the human body, or physical passions, which he found best expressed through the art and mythology of classical Greece.

Coffman says further that Aldington did not confine his attention entirely to classical objects, "but when he turned to contemporary scenes he could not always adequately objectify in his attitude toward them."[2][7]

Much of Aldington's prose work, particularly his novels, has enjoyed an international reputation. Novels, short stories, and some poetry have been translated into Russian. In 1956 Mikhail Urnov wrote in the Russian English-language periodical, *News*, on "Richard Aldington and His Books." He began with a short summary of Imagism and a few words on the war poems. Most of his space was devoted to *Death of a Hero. The Crystal World, Very Heaven*, and *Life for Life's Sake* were seen as withdrawals, and Urnov urged Aldington's return to the people:

During World War I Aldington was plunged into the thick of events and rubbed shoulders with the common man. This contact did not, however, prove enduring, and this told fatally on the creative evolution of the author of "Death of a Hero."[28]

Writing in 1965, Sir William Haley, editor of the London *Times*, said:

In 1957 I felt detraction of Aldington was becoming so undiscriminating that his real achievements were being forgotten. I wrote an article to put what he had done into perspective. He was touched, and thanked me for "standing by an unpopular writer, who has some claims to being considered England's literary public enemy number one. It would be a kingly title but for the fact that it practically abolishes income."[29]

The article referred to was published in the *Times* under Haley's pseudonym, Oliver Edwards. It appeared in his column "Talking of Books" under the title "Richard Yea and Nay," and concluded:

He has a firm place among the writers of the interwar years. His message was less striking and less dynamic than D.H. Lawrence's but it was healthier. He pioneered the work of other writers, both English and French, as a generous and perceptive critic. He has two novels (*Death of a Hero* and *All Men Are Enemies*), two books of poems (*A Dream in the Luxembourg* and *Life Quest*), and two biographies (*Voltaire* and *Portrait of a Genius, But—*) that will stand. It is to them we must look if we wish to get Aldington's true measure.[30]

On 18 January 1957, Aldington wrote to Henry Rago, then editor of *Poetry*:

I venture to send you a note on my books from the London Times, written by the editor (Sir William Haley). Well, he makes many reservations and lets me down over the Colonel Lawrence business, but I'd rather have that than silence![31]

Richard Aldington died in the south of France in July of 1962. In 1965 Dr. Miriam J. Benkovitz edited a group of his letters under the title "Nine for Reeves: Letters from Richard Aldington." (The title is an allusion to Aldington's 1938 novel, *Seven Against Reeves*.) These nine letters were written by Aldington during the early 1930s to James Reeves, a young admirer then an undergraduate at Jesus College, Cambridge University. Reeves was excited by *A Dream in the Luxembourg*, wrote about it for the *Cambridge Review*, and sent a proof to Aldington, who acknowledged with the first letter, dated 13 May 1930. Describing the letters Dr. Benkovitz says:

Thus the letters convey much about Aldington. Most obviously they emphasize his obsession with the horrors of the war from which he never recovered. They show, too, his involvement in current literary affairs and his earnestness about his own writing.

The letters show the older writer trying to help the younger aspirant with advice about publishing, reviewing, and writing on commission. In Letter 5 he tells Reeves how he and his friends used to publish cheaply in the *Egoist* days by having an article set in type for magazine publication, and then using the same typesetting to print books. He also comments on McGreevy's book on Eliot, which was Number 4 in the Dolphin series:

> I liked McGreevy's Dolphin. I am so bored with the dessicated intellectualism and genuine poppycock of Richards and Eliot that I welcome any critic who writes like a human being. I thought McGreevy's criticism pretty deadly under its apparent respectful harmlessness. He is a master of innuendo, and many of those excursions on side topics were far more relevant than they appeared at first.[32]

These letters have been edited with excellence and precision. There are one hundred and fifty-nine notes to the nine letters. Reading these notes, which explain Aldington's references to people, places, and events, provides one with a miniature literary history of the period 1912-1931.

Also during 1965 the most important step to date was taken in Aldington scholarship with the publication by Southern Illinois University Press of *Richard Aldington: An Intimate Portrait*. Its editors were Alister Kershaw and Frédéric-Jacques Temple. Kershaw, whose bibliography was discussed above, is an Australian who settled in France in 1947 and for some years was Aldington's private secretary; Temple, a French poet and writer, was born in Montpellier, where Richard Aldington spent many years. The editors outline the purpose of their book in the Preface (p. viii):

> It is because they believe that one of the outstanding literary figures of our time has been unjustifiably neglected in the English-speaking world that the editors offer the present volume to the public.

Also in the Preface the editors note that Aldington was an " 'angry young man' long before today's self-pitying intellectuals bestowed the term on themselves, and his anger, greater than theirs and rooted in a deeper experience, was expressed with a passion that they have never equalled" (p. v). The Preface concludes with a brief biographical sketch, before which the editors make this critical appraisal: "The whole key to Aldington's work, indeed, lies in his unfashionable passion for truth: in his novels, poems, and biographies, it was always the 'image of integrity' which was paramount" (pp. vi-vii).

The book is made up of twenty-two sketches by men who knew Richard Aldington during his lifetime. The articles vary in length and usefulness. Samuel Beckett writes a short paragraph expressing gratitude for Aldington's help with his first two publications; Harry T. Moore contributes twenty-six pages of valuable biographical material. Most of the memoirs are of the type that will be most useful to Aldington's biographer; some also contain excellent critical material.

An interesting aspect of the contributors to *Richard Aldington: An Intimate Portrait* is the fact that three of them are Russian. One of these is

Mikhail Urnov who wrote the article in *News* referred to earlier. He describes (p. 161) the extent of Aldington's popularity in Russia:

> Richard Aldington has always been accepted in Russia. . . . Articles have been written about him as a poet and a novelist, a translator and a critic, a man and a writer. . . . Papers have been read about him, lectures given, and students have written essays on him. His books have reached every part of our large country. And—what is even more imprtant—his books are read.

A few weeks before his death Aldington spent a month in Russia as a guest of the Soviet Writers' Union, which wanted to honor a writer whose books were so widely read and loved in Soviet Russia. While some of this popularity is certainly explained by the fact that Aldington's writings attack the "establishment," this does not seem enough to account for the great demand for his novels: in 1961, 225,000 copies of *All Men Are Enemies* were printed. Urnov says, "These books did not lie around in the bookshops—they were sold literally in a few days, and now it is impossible to find them in the shops" (p. 157).

John Gawsworth and Morikimi Megata, from opposite sides of the world, offer selections from Aldington's letters. Neither man had ever met him, but both enjoyed close relationships with him by mail. Their letters from Aldington indicate the richness of the trove that awaits final editing; Aldington wrote letters that are mines of literary information, and, being an expatriate, he wrote a great many.

C.P. Snow's contribution is reprinted in part from his earlier booklet. Of the critical views on Aldington's poetry, Sir Herbert Read's article is the most helpful. He knew his fellow poet from the days of World War I, and was in touch with him on and off for the rest of Aldington's life. He quotes quite a few of Aldington's letters which express the author's ideas about his own poetry and about poetic theory. Read concludes (p. 132):

> Imagism was too limited in its ideals to survive as a poetic "movement," but it was a necessary stage in the evolution of English poetry, and Aldington, H. D., and Flint purified the literary atmosphere between 1910 and 1915 and prepared the way for the emergence of greater poets like Pound and Eliot.

Alec Waugh writes a short memoir. He prefers Aldington's poetry to his prose and says that he was at his best when he wrote of love. Aldington leaves, according to Waugh, "a body of poetry which surely will survive 'the chances and changes' of our distracted day."

A most helpful addition to *Richard Aldington: An Intimate Portrait* is "A Chronological Check List of the Books by Richard Aldington" provided by Professor Paul Schlueter. Taking up where Alister Kershaw left off in his bibliography, this checklist brings the earlier work up to date; it is also annotated by Kershaw. There are separate divisions for "Poetry"; "Novels, Stories, and Plays"; "Essays, Criticisms, Biography, and Autobiography";

"Translations"; and "Books Edited by and/or with Introductions by Richard Aldington."

Future Aldington scholars will be grateful for this "intimate portrait." Besides being a starting point for a biography, it also provides many avenues for critical approach and indicates where many of the letters may be sought. Part of its value is certainly in the fact that some of its contributors, who are now dead, were able to leave memories of Aldington that otherwise would have been lost. It is indeed fortunate that Alister Kershaw and Frédéric-Jacques Temple were able to gather these tributes to their old friend.

In 1967 "Crosscurrents/Modern Fiction," of which Harry T. Moore is General Editor and Matthew J. Bruccoli Textual Editor, was responsible for the publication of Richard Aldington's *Soft Answers*, a collection of six short stories. Professor Moore wrote a seven-page Preface for this edition which gives considerable biographical and critical material but does not discuss Aldington's poetry.[33]

In 1968, Cassell, the London publisher, brought out a new edition of Aldington's autobiography, *Life for Life's Sake*, originally published in 1941 by The Viking Press. This was given an anonymous review in *The Times Literary Supplement* of 26 December 1968.[34] As Professor Moore points out, the reviewer gives a general lecture on Aldington rather than a review of the book.[35] Of the poetry, the review says, "The *Complete Poems* of 1948 looked like a literary monument, but it has gone out of print, and one can scarcely imagine the circumstances that will call it back."

Some recent Aldington publications are of interest. David S. Thatcher edits a fine selection of Aldington's letters to Herbert Read in *The Malahat Review*, Number 15, July 1970. Alister Kershaw has edited *Richard Aldington: Selected Critical Writings, 1928-1960* (Carbondale: Southern Illinois University Press, 1970). Sidney Rosenthal contributed "Richard Aldington and the Excitement of Reason" to *Twenty-Seven to One* . . ., edited by Bradford Broughton (Ogdensburg, New York: Ryan Press, 1971).[36] Selwyn Kittredge's "Richard Aldington's Challenge to T.S. Eliot: Background of Their James Joyce Controversy" in *James Joyce Quarterly*, Vol. 10, No. 3 (Spring 1973), pp. 339-341, clarifies Aldington's critical position vis-a-vis Joyce and particularly *Ulysses*.

As for the scholarly work on Richard Aldington which is in progress, there is first a promised edition of additional letters to be published by Professor Benkovitz. If the excellent editing given Aldington's letters to James Reeves is any indication, the publication of this new group of letters will prove most helpful to scholars interested in Aldington or his peers.

We also have the promise from Professor Moore, given in his Preface to the *Soft Answers* edition, that "for some time I have been working co-operatively on a biography of Aldington. . . ." More recently he has said that this biography is still in the preliminary stages and threatens to remain so for a long time to come; he is still collecting material for the work. He adds that far more material than expected has turned up and that it will take years to classify all of this.[37]

The historical pattern of the critical reaction to Richard Aldington's poetry has been curiously irregular. As a very young man he enjoyed a considerable reputation, part of which was undoubtedly a result of his leadership in the Imagist movement. This reputation was sustained through the wartime period but began to fall off during the twenties. Part of the lapse was caused by the reaction against Imagism and the introduction of the Pound-Eliot school of poetics; part also was occasioned by Aldington's own struggle to regain his equilibrium following his wartime experience.

Aldington's great success as a novelist during the 1930s tended to distract attention from the fact that he was continuing to write good poetry— was in fact writing some of his best poetry. This success, however, probably made possible McGreevy's study, which is one of only two major critical works on Aldington's poetry. If he had not established an international reputation with *Death of a Hero* in 1929, it is doubtful that McGreevy would have been commissioned to do a Dolphin Book about him; and without Aldington's reputation to promote it, the *Imagist Anthology* of 1930 might not have found a publisher.

The fact that Richard Aldington ceased to publish poetry in 1938, almost twenty-five years before his death, may also have had an adverse influence on his poetic reputation. Certainly it tended to focus critical attention on his fiction and particularly on his biographical writings of the fifties. The biographies, especially the one of T.E. Lawrence, caused Aldington, as Professor Moore puts it,[38] to be "semiofficially" anathematized, with consequent harm to his reputation as a writer.

It is probable that, with the increasing attention now paid to the years in which Aldington made his first appearance in the world of letters, this politic, distinctive, yet too-little-read writer will be the subject of much scholarly work.

NOTES

1. *Life for Life's Sake: A Book of Reminiscences* (New York: The Viking Press, 1941), pp. 59-60.

2. Charles Norman, *Ezra Pound*, revised edition (New York: Funk and Wagnalls, 1969), p. 89.

3. " 'The Forgotten School of 1909' and the Origins of Imagism," in *A Catalogue of the Imagist Poets* (New York: J. Howard Woolmer, 1966), pp. 36-37.

4. The extracts from Pound's letters are taken from *The Letters of Ezra Pound, 1907-1941*, ed. D.D. Paige (New York: Harcourt, Brace and World, 1950). No. 60, to Harriet Monroe, January 1915, p. 49; no. 62, to H.L. Mencken, 18 February 1915, p. 51; no. 81, to Harriet Shaw Weaver, February 1916, p. 69; no. 135, to Margaret C. Anderson, September 1917, p. 122.

5. "Historical Survey," *The Little Review*, Vol. 7, No. 2 (Autumn 1921), pp. 39-42.

6. *The Letters of Ezra Pound*, p. 222 (no. 233, to Harriet Monroe, 30 December 1929). In January of 1929, Aldington wrote to Crosby Gaige: "Apropos, Ezra Pound has sent the MS of the Eaten Heart and the rest of Filings [Aldington's original name for the group of poems that initially became "Passages Toward a Long Poem" in *Imagist Anthology 1930*] to some editors he knows in America. He did this without telling me, and has put me in a very awkward position, as you can see. I ought to have told him that you had the MSS and were trying to dispose of them to periodicals, but he dashed them off in his impetuous way as soon as I sent them to Paris. Maybe his editors won't like them—the journals are The Dial and Poetry. It is almost impossible for me to make a fuss, since he meant well and has been exceedingly kind to me recently." (This letter is dated 14 January 1929 and is in The Beinecke Rare Book and Manuscript Library at Yale University.)

7. *Literary Essays of Ezra Pound*, ed. T.S. Eliot (Norfolk, Conn.: New Directions, 1954), p. 14.

8. "Richard Aldington's Poetry," *The Little Review*, Vol. 2, No. 6 (September 1915), pp. 11-16.

9. "Mr. Aldington's Images," *Poetry: A Magazine of Verse*, Vol. 8, No. 1 (April 1916), pp. 49-51.

10. "Three Imagist Poets," *The Little Review*, Vol. 3, No. 3 (May 1916), pp. 30-35, and Vol. 3, No. 4 (June-July 1916), pp. 32-41.

11. "Meteorites in Verse," *The Nation*, Vol. 104, No. 2689 (11 January 1917), pp. 43-45.

12. "Four Foreigners," *The Little Review*, Vol. 6, No. 5 (September 1919), pp. 36-39.

13. "On Richard Aldington," *Coterie*, No. 3 (December 1919), pp. 24-25.

14. *Some Contemporary Poets (1920)* (London: Leonard Parsons, 1920), pp. 98-101.

15. *Life for Life's Sake*, p. 264.

16. *Rejected Guest* (New York: The Viking Press, 1939), p. 114.

17. "The Poems of Richard Aldington," *The English Review*, Vol. 32, No. 5 (May 1921), pp. 397-410.

18. "An Imagist at War," *Poetry: A Magazine of Verse*, Vol. 34, No. 1 (April 1929), pp. 42-46.

19. "Mr. Richard Aldington," *South Atlantic Quarterly*, Vol. 28, No. 2 (April 1929), pp. 201-208.

20. *Life for Life's Sake*, p. 343.

21. *Ibid.*, pp. 350-351.

22. "Richard Aldington," *The Nation*, Vol. 138, No. 3595 (30 May 1934), p. 625.

23. "A Poet of Three Persons," *Poetry: A Magazine of Verse*, Vol. 45, No. 1 (October 1934), pp. 47-50.

24. *The Georgian Scene: A Literary Panorama* (New York: Farrar and Rinehart, 1934), pp. 451-455.

25. "Aldington 1938," *Poetry: A Magazine of Verse*, Vol. 52, No. 3 (June 1938), pp. 160-164.

26. Burlingame, Calif.: William P. Wredon, 1950; London: Quadrant Press, 1950.

27. *Imagism: A Chapter for the History of Modern Poetry* (Norman: University of Oklahoma Press, 1951), p. 165.

28. "Richard Aldington and His Books," *News*, No. 7 (1 April 1956), pp. 29-30.

29. In *Richard Aldington: An Intimate Portrait*, ed. Alister Kershaw and Frédéric-Jacques Temple (Carbondale: Southern Illinois University Press, 1965), p. 41.

30. Thursday, 3 January 1957, p. 11.

31. Unpublished letter in the *Poetry Magazine Papers*, The University of Chicago Library.

32. "Nine for Reeves: Letters from Richard Aldington," *Bulletin of the New York Public Library*, Vol. 69, No. 6 (June 1965), pp. 349-374.

33. *Soft Answers* (Carbondale: Southern Illinois University Press, 1967).

34. "Journeyman of Letters," *The Times Literary Supplement*, 26 December 1968, p. 1448.

35. Letter to the writer dated 23 January 1969.

36. My own "Richard Aldington and The Clerk's Press" appeared in *The Ohio Review*, Vol. 13, No. 1 (Fall 1971), pp. 21-27, and "Richard Aldington and F. S. Flint: Poets' Dialogue" in *Papers on Language and Literature*, Vol. 8, No. 1 (Winter 1972), pp. 63-69.

37. Letter to the writer dated 17 September 1968. The most recent Aldington work-in-progress of which I am aware is a proposed checklist for Aldington's letters which Professor Benkovitz and I have under way, and a new Aldington bibliography being prepared by Ms. Ann Bagnell of Temple University.

38. Preface to *Soft Answers*, p. viii.

2

Editions Prior to
"The Complete Poems"

The Imagist Anthologies

Aldington tells us that when he was fifteen (1907) he discovered Keats and began to write poetry. The following year his first poem was printed in a London periodical.[1] The poem may have appeared in *The New Age*, then edited by A. R. Orage, since Alun R. Jones writes that in 1908 Aldington was one of a group including Middleton Murry, Katherine Mansfield, J. C. Squire, Michael Arlen, and Herbert Read, who "all found themselves drawn into discussion at Orage's table in Chancery Lane or the Café Royal and all were encouraged to contribute to *The New Age*."[2]

    An examination of *The New Age* for 1908 and 1909, however, fails to show any poetry credited to Aldington. In the 7 October 1909 issue (No. 787 New Series, Vol. 5, No. 24) there are nine short poems published anonymously under the title "Unpleasant Poems" (compare Shaw's "Plays: Pleasant and Unpleasant" of a decade earlier). These could be Aldington's, but if so they are in the brash, self-consciously modern style of his "Penultimate Poetry" (see Part II, Chapter 2), rather than in the cool, Greek manner of the first Imagist poems published in the second issue of *Poetry* in November of 1912.

    The earliest published poem that I have been able to find, "Song of Freedom," was written when Aldington was eighteen and was published 28 October 1910 in *Justice*. Aldington writes of it in his autobiography, *Life for Life's Sake* (pp. 92-93): "Somewhere about this time a revolution occurred in Portugal, Dom Manoel was deposed from the throne, and a republic was proclaimed. At that time I knew rather less than nothing about Portugal. . . All I went on was an abstract and unfounded belief that monarchies are corrupt and republics perfect *per se*. So I celebrated this tremendous victory of good over evil in a poem. I sent this to a leftish journal called *Justice*. . . *Justice* printed my poem conspicuously. This filled me with joy, about seventy-five per cent of which was gratified vanity and about twenty-five per cent conviction that this finally clinched the whole matter for happy Portugal." See chapter 2 of the Uncollected Poems in the second part of this book for a reproduction of this poem.

    In his autobiography (*Life for Life's Sake*, p. 73) Aldington wrote of some of his University College friends:

. . . one of them, who was obviously gifted as a writer and amused us with his wit, was drowned in a bathing accident before he was twenty. It is easy to exaggerate the talents of those who die young especially when they were the friends of one's own youth, yet it seems to me even now that if Arthur Chapman had lived he would have succeeded as a writer. I wrote a poem on his death which was published in the university magazine. . . .

The poem, "In Memoriam," appeared in Volume 5, Number 3 (December 1911) of *Union Magazine* and must number among the poet's earliest published works. It is reproduced in Chapter 2 of the Uncollected Poems in the second part of this book.

By the time that Aldington went to Paris in the spring of 1912 he "was selling poems regularly to the evening papers."[3] A check of the seven evening newspapers publishing in London during the fall of 1911 and the spring of 1912—*The Evening News, The Evening Standard, The Star, The Evening Times, The Globe and Traveller, Pall Mall Gazette,* and *The Westminster Gazette*— turns up ten Aldington poems published between February and June 1912, in *The Evening Standard, Pall Mall Gazette,* and *The Westminster Gazette.* Although all but three of these very early poems seem to be translations, I have included all of them in the section of this work devoted to Uncollected Poems.[4]

By the end of 1912, Aldington, along with H.D., his future wife, had been selected by Ezra Pound as a shining exponent of the new Imagist movement which Pound had developed from the aesthetic theories of T E. Hulme. The first result of Pound's patronage was the publication of Aldington's original free-verse poems in Harriet Monroe's *Poetry;*[5] the second was his inclusion in the first Imagist anthology, *Des Imagistes: An Anthology,* published in 1914.

Wallace Martin says that "a chronological reading of the poems written in the years immediately before and after the appearance of *Des Imagistes* substantiates the conclusion that it was largely responsible for the birth of what we consider 'modern poetry.' "[6] Although there is considerable argument as to who was the father of the Imagist movement, there seems to be no question about the fact that Ezra Pound was the father of *Des Imagistes.* In "Stepping Heavenward," a short story which is a lampoon of T.S. Eliot, Richard Aldington may be describing the occasion fictionally:

> Sick of the eternal cold shoulder of the academic world and confident that their methods were the right ones, these young men were arranging for the publication of a joint work, to which each would contribute some characteristic specimen of historical analysis or interpretation. Cibber [Eliot?] did not join the enterprise, pleading that he had nothing good enough to add to their collection—an excuse which seemed more than reasonable. In private, however, he made a number of notes in which the faults of each of his new friends were brought out with masterly incisiveness.[7]

Again, in his autobiography (*Life for Life's Sake,* pp. 134-136) Aldington tells about the beginning of *Des Imagistes* as he recalls the circumstances:

Like other American expatriates, Ezra and H.D. developed an almost insane relish for afternoon tea. . . . Naturally, then, the Imagist *mouvemong* was born in a tea-shop—in the Royal Borough of Kensington. . . . I have no exact memory of what was said at this bun-shop meeting, but I do remember that H.D. looked very much pleased by the praise that Ezra generously gave her poems. I didn't like his insistence that the poems should be signed: "H.D. Imagist," because it sounded a little ridiculous. And I think H.D. disliked it too. But Ezra was a bit of a czar in a small but irritating way, and he had the bulge on us, because it was only through him that we could get our poems into Harriet Monroe's *Poetry*, and at that time nobody else would look at them. . . .

I believe it was at this same tea—though it may have been later—that Ezra proposed we should all three publish a book of our poems together. . . . Through the good offices of John Cournos and Alfred Kreymborg, Ezra's collection of Imagists appeared in New York in February 1914 under the fantastic title *Des Imagistes*.

John Cournos remembers his part in the publication of the first Imagist anthology as follows:

The first Imagist anthology was already out, published first by Boni & Boni. I was directly instrumental in its publication by this firm. It happened this way. Before leaving for America, I received a letter from Alfred Kreymborg, whom I had met in New York in my *Record* days. Kreymborg was editing the Glebe series of short books for the Bonis and he thought I might have a manuscript of my own to offer. I had nothing at the moment, but happened to mention Kreymborg's request to Ezra Pound, who was compiling *Des Imagistes: An Anthology*. Thus the first Imagist anthology came to be published.[8]

After appearing first as Volume 1, Number 5 (February 1914) of *The Glebe*, *Des Imagistes: An Anthology* was published in New York by Albert and Charles Boni and in London by The Poetry Bookshop. Since the Bonis evidently printed both the *Glebe* issue and their own edition of *Des Imagistes* from the same plates and with the same paper stock, the two are identical in every respect except for their covers. There is a yellow leaf inserted after the last page of *The Glebe*, advertising *Poetry* and two other periodicals on the verso. Both periodical and book have an inscription in Greek which is followed by the translation: "And she also was of Sikilia and was gay in the valleys of Aetna, and knew the Doric singing." The book is covered in blue cloth over boards and is stamped in gold with the title. There is a tipped-in slip making acknowledgment to *Poetry* for the poems of Aldington and some of the others.

Before *Des Imagistes* was published, John Gould Fletcher wrote Amy Lowell advising her not to contribute to it. Fletcher called it a scheme to boom Aldington, who was really the editor rather than Pound, described Aldington as a silly cub who needed a licking, and rated Miss Lowell's work higher than Pound's or Aldington's.[9]

Des Imagistes contains ten poems (twelve pages) by Richard Aldington, seven poems (eleven pages) by H.D., five poems (five pages) by F.S. Flint, one poem (two pages) by Skipwirth Cannell, one poem (one page) by Amy

Lowell, one poem (one page) by William Carlos Williams, one poem (one page) by James Joyce, six poems (six pages) by Ezra Pound, one poem (four pages) by Ford Madox Hueffer, nine poems (three pages) by Allen Upward, and one poem (one page) by John Cournos. Since the poets are arranged in alphabetical order in this and the subsequent Imagist anthologies, Aldington's contribution is first. It consists of the following poems: "Choricos," "To a Greek Marble," "Au Vieux Jardin," "Lesbia," "Beauty, Thou Hast Hurt Me Overmuch," "Argyria," "In the Via Sestina," "The River," "Bromios," and "To Atthis."

At the end of the alphabetical sequence in *Des Imagistes*, there is a section entitled "Documents," which contains three "poems" which are presumably by Pound, Aldington, and Hueffer. Aldington's poem, "Vates, the Social Reformer," appears to chaff Hueffer, but, of course, a great many of the topical allusions are lost and with them much of the fun of the poem, which is written in the form of a monologue addressing God in rather uncomplimentary terms. "Vates, the Social Reformer" was not collected and can be found in Chapter 3 of the second portion of this book. As we shall see, Aldington wrote many of these joking poems which he later discarded.

Despite the fact that it is now considered one of the milestones of modern poetry, there were very few good critical reviews of *Des Imagistes* soon after its publication in England and America. Aldington complains of this in an article in *The Egoist* in which he reviews three books of poetry including *Des Imagistes*:

> And now I come to the book which I oughtn't to review because there are some of my own poems in it. I think it very odd that no other competent person can be found to do it, but as the only decent critic in England [10] has already published two long articles on the book, it remains for me to praise my friends maliciously and to try and explain the aims and common sympathies and theories which have bound us together between two violent green covers. [11]

The newspaper reviewers evidently had something to say, however; in *Life for Life's Sake* (p. 138) Aldington says of the American edition: "Under that ridiculous ensign, *Des Imagistes*, our little boatful of poets was launched, only to come at once under fire from apparently the whole American fleet of critics."

And of the reaction to the English edition published by Harold Monro he writes (p. 148): ". . . except for the ultra-conservative *Morning Post*, which gave us a column of praise, all the newspapers, particularly the 'liberal' ones, were against us." One of the papers that Aldington thought was "against" them was *The Evening Standard*; he wrote Harriet Monroe at the time that this paper's review was "short and sweet: 'affectation is the note of this book from the title to F.M.H.'s poem in Greek characters at the end. . . .' " [12] The reason for the apathy on the part of the critics was probably that they did not quite know what to do with this strange new verse; by the time of the second anthology they were more outspoken.

Pound included Amy Lowell in *Des Imagistes* over the objections of some of the other Imagist poets. Ironically she was to replace him as the leader of the movement, although by that time Ezra, ever the initiator rather than the consolidator, was busy with *BLAST*, Wyndham Lewis, and Vorticism. In *Life for Life's Sake* (p. 139) Aldington remembers the events in this way:

> In the summer of 1914 Amy was again in London, occupying her usual suite in the Berkeley Hotel, with its view across Piccadilly to the Green Park. With her usual energy and vivacity she had been battling valiantly for us all, but was fed up with Ezra. So were the others. . . . Amy arrived with certain proposals, to which she had evidently given a good deal of thought. She proposed a Boston Tea Party for Ezra, the immediate abolition of his despotism and the substitution of a pure democracy. There was to be no more of the Duce business, with arbitrary inclusions and exclusions and a capricious censorship.

John Cournos, one of the poets of the original Imagist anthology who was left out of Amy Lowell's anthologies, sees things somewhat differently:

> Ezra knew almost every one worth knowing, and scarcely an American poet passed through London but found his way to Ezra's flat. If I remember aright, he did not get on very well with Amy Lowell; that may have been because she proposed to run a rival show, and did finally run it on Ezra's thunder but opposed in principle to his method; for she made her annual Imagist Anthology a closed corporation of six, permanently excluding all new blood.[13]

The second Imagist anthology, edited by Amy Lowell, was published in Boston by Houghton Mifflin under the title *Some Imagist Poets: An Anthology;* it appeared in 1915.[14] It contains an Imagist manifesto and the notice that "each poet has been permitted to represent himself by the work he considers best, the only stipulation being that it should not yet have appeared in book form." The poets represented were Richard Aldington, H.D., John Gould Fletcher, F. S. Flint, D. H. Lawrence, and Amy Lowell. It is probable that Aldington had more to say about this anthology than the first one. As Dr. Coffman suggests in his study of Imagism:

> For a time after Miss Lowell suddenly assumed the sponsorship of the movement, she tactfully relied on Aldington for her understanding of its aims. H. D. was no theorist, and Lawrence and Fletcher had not been associated with Pound's original program; Flint could have helped her and without doubt he did to some extent, but it was on Aldington that she chiefly depended.[15]

Each of the six poets in the 1915 anthology is represented by seven poems, with the exception of Fletcher, who has only two. Aldington has the largest number of pages, fifteen, and his poems are: "Childhood," "The Poplar," "Round-Pond," "Daisy," "Epigrams," "The Faun Sees Snow for the First Time," and "Lemures."

Aldington wrote to Miss Lowell about Constable's English edition[16] of *Some Imagist Poets* (1915):

I enclose a few press-cuttings. It is interesting to see that we are getting more reviews for this anthology than for the first [*Des Imagistes*]. Also, as you will see, opinion is beginning slightly to turn our way. The next anthology, if we can keep up to the mark, ought to turn the scale.[17]

One of the reviews was Harold Monro's in *The Egoist*:

All these poets are primarily impressionists. . . . Richard Aldington and the lady who writes under the initials H.D. both are content to derive most of their subjects from Greek origins. Mr. Aldington's rhythms, though arbitrary, are smooth. He does not use rhyme.[18]

Ford Madox Hueffer (Ford) reviewed the British edition in *The Outlook*: "Mr. John Gould Fletcher, Mr. Aldington, and Miss Lowell are all too preoccupied with themselves and their emotions to be really called Imagists."[19]

A look at two of Aldington's poems from the 1915 anthology can reveal some details of his progress as a poet. There is a tendency when thinking of the Imagists to conceive them as completely breaking with the older poetic conventions; their own "manifestoes" and critical writings lend substance to this conception, which, however, is only partially true. In "The Poplar," an early poem which was probably written in 1913 or before, since it was originally published in *Poetry* in January 1914, Aldington uses a series of fine figures that would have appealed to any Victorian ear. The poem, in fact, was one of his best-liked, and was reprinted in 1915 in *Some Imagist Poets* before its appearance in any of the collected editions. The poet chides a poplar tree for standing shivering by "the white stream and the road" when she could leave her "nonchalant idle lovers" and join the "beautiful beeches down beyond the hill." If we accept the entire poem as metaphor, as perhaps the poet intended, and conceive of the tree as truly representing a woman, too much of the emotional power of the poem is lost in the transfer. If on the other hand the poem is to be understood as addressed to a tree, it is too precious. Nevertheless, the third stanza of the poem contains as effective a series of tropes as one would be likely to encounter:

I know that the white wind loves you,
Is always kissing you, and turning up
The white lining of your green petticoat.
The sky darts through you like blue rain,
And the grey rain drips on your flanks
And loves you.
And I have seen the moon
Slip his silver penny into your pocket
As you straighten your hair;
And the white mist curling and hesitating
Like a bashful lover about your knees.

The selection of detail is excellent: the poet has chosen things about a tree in nature that are true to the tree but at the same time depict relationships between a woman and her lovers.

"Childhood" was one of Aldington's longest early poems. It was first printed in the 1 December 1914 issue of *The Egoist* and reprinted in *Some Imagist Poets*. Harold Monro, in a review of the anthology, takes a neutral attitude toward this poem: "Richard Aldington in his 'Childhood,' the longest poem in the book (some 120 lines), records the effects on a sensitive child of the civilization of a modern small town. . . ."[20] Amy Lowell, who certainly should have been a friendly reviewer since she was the editor of the 1915 collection, suggests, in a general article on Aldington's poetry, that "Childhood" is not as good as it ought to be and that the poet evidently has not mastered the form of a long poem.[21] Professor Hughes says:

> The poem brought a good deal of ridicule from critics, and it must be admitted that its self-commiseration is annoying, but its objective passages are vivid and of sufficient consequence to justify the whole.[22]

Dr. Coffman, writing twenty years later, directs the same criticism against "Childhood" that he does against a subsequent poem, "Eros and Psyche": ". . . 'Childhood,' which describes the dull, grimy town in which he was reared . . . is [not] a successful poetic statement because the poet never transcends his personal distaste for his material."[23]

The poem succeeds in making the statement that Aldington apparently wished to make about "the bitterness, the misery, the wretchedness of childhood." That is to say, the images, the scenes, and the details selected are convincing enough to justify poetically the author's avowed disbelief "in God's goodness." One cannot help but feel, however, that the poem is somehow insincere. Does the memory really select and retain only those details of the past, particularly of childhood, that would leave such a picture of unrelieved gray as the poem gives us? Is it not rather just the reverse—that fortunately we remember mostly the happy moments of the past and so are able to face the future? What we have in the poem is the author's looking back and giving unnecessary sympathy to the child he once was. It is interesting to see what Aldington had to say about D.H. Lawrence in this regard. After noting that "clearly the Lawrence children in their childhood never thought of their home as mean and did not suffer too much from the discord of their parents," he continues:

> In later life Lawrence stressed the dreadful ugliness of his childhood's surroundings and liked to harrow the feelings of his friends with tales of grinding poverty. One can perhaps reconcile this discrepancy by the fact that the child knew nothing else and the grown man had seen the world.[24]

In a sense the poem has two voices. The man speaks bitterly of his childhood, but as he does the child's voice breaks through to deny him. The memory "of a white dog staring into a gramophone" (the old "Victrola" trademark with the legend, "His Master's Voice") does not seem "dull and greasy and grey and sordid," but rather like something that would have appealed to a little boy. Surely "the little harbour" connoted more things to the boy than "a salt dirty smell." In one stanza in particular the boy's voice seems to be telling us of the things that fill boys' dreams with the wild longing for the faraway:

> There were also several packets of stamps
> Yellow and blue Guatemala parrots,
> Blue stags and red baboons and birds from Sarawak,
> Indians and Men-of-War
> From the United States,
> And the green and red portraits
> Of King Francobollo
> Of Italy.

The poem might have been a better poem if the man had remained silent and permitted the boy to speak. We might have heard much more clearly the pathos of his boyhood, if indeed it existed.

Although the poem may fail, its central metaphor is interesting:

> I've seen people put
> A chrysalis in a match-box,
> "To see," they told me, "what sort of moth would come."
> But when it broke its shell
> It slipped and stumbled and fell about its prison
> And tried to climb to the light
> For space to dry its wings.

Twenty-five years later Aldington was to use the same metaphor in his novel *Rejected Guest*:

> A child, grubbing about in the garden, finds the chrysalis of a tiger moth. An old boot box is begged from the kitchen, a crumpled pile of unnecessary leaves is arranged for the treasure, useless air-holes are punched. Every half-hour or so, the child peeps into the box to see the wonderful change it has been told about. Nothing happens, the box is forgotten, and then one day carelessly opened. The bright-winged creature may be lying dead, with the cream and black and scarlet all tarnished and scattered in dust. . . .[25]

An incident such as this must have happened when Aldington was a boy; it is from such vivid biographical details that poets construct their personal mythologies and their archetypal metaphors. Just as Yeats had collected moths at his grandfather's in Sligo when he was a boy and used moth imagery throughout his poetry (for example, "The Song of the Wandering Aengus"), so Aldington was an avid butterfly collector not only in his boyhood but in later life.[26] Thus the image of the forgotten chrysalis was a natural one for him to use to describe a lost childhood.

In 1916 a continuation of *Some Imagist Poets* appeared, with the sub-title *An Annual Anthology*. This volume includes the same six poets who had appeared in the previous anthology: Aldington contributed seven poems (ten pages), H. D. four poems (fourteen pages), Fletcher six poems (fourteen pages), Flint seven poems (thirteen pages), Lawrence five poems (eight pages), and Amy Lowell three poems (eleven pages). The bibliography of the poets printed at the end of the collection now shows two volumes of Aldington's: the 1915 *Images (1910-1915)* and the 1916 *Images Old and New*. Aldington's poems are: "Eros and Psyche," "After Two Years," "1915," "Whitechapel," "Sunsets," "People," and "Reflections: I and II."

As noted in connection with the 1915 anthology, Dr. Coffman feels that "Eros and Psyche," like "Childhood," is not a "successful poetic state-ment because the poet never transcends his personal distaste for his material." "Eros and Psyche" was first published in *The Egoist*, Vol. 2, No. 8 (2 August 1915), and it is the longest of Aldington's poems in the 1916 Imagist anthology, just as "Childhood" was in the 1915 collection. In the poem the author first describes a statue of Cobden in the Camden Town section of London, and comments that he "can understand very well indeed that Eng-land must honour its national heroes"; but what he can never understand is the statue of Eros and Psyche "in an old dull yard near Camden Town." He describes the statue and then asks what the two figures are doing "in the midst of all this clamour and filth?/ They, who should stand in a sun-lit room." A number of proper backgrounds are suggested for them and then compared in detail with their present surroundings.

"Eros and Psyche" is a poem very similar to "Church Walk, Kensington," discussed later, except that it is more elaborate and more de-tailed in its presentation. There is the juxtaposition of a desirable past with the unhappy present: the past is symbolized by the statue of the lovers whose "naked beauty" and "fresh lust" is contrasted with the "toil and sweat and filth" of the present, embodied in Camden Town. The poem fails in the same way that "Church Walk, Kensington" fails—the poet is merely a helpless observer: "I peer from a bus-top." He sees the tragedy and reports it to us, but he is not able to take a position sufficiently far away to enable him to view both the beauty of the Greek statue and the filth of Camden Town objectively. If he had been able to do this, he could have looked at them, for instance, with the tragic gaiety of Yeats's Chinamen in "Lapis Luzuli," know-ing that "All things fall and are built again, / And those that build them again are gay."

The little poem "Sunsets," which is the shortest of the seven Aldington poems in the 1916 anthology, may owe something to Eliot's famous lines, "When the evening is spread out against the sky/ Like a patient etherized upon a table":

> The white body of the evening
> Is torn into scarlet,
> Slashed and gouged and seared
> Into crimson,

And hung ironically
With garlands of mist.

The three-line second stanza tersely suggests the reason for his seeing sunsets as torn and bleeding bodies, and is the first realistic foreshadowing of his coming preoccupation with the Great War:

And the wind
Blowing over London from Flanders
Has a bitter taste.

The 1917 volume of *Some Imagist Poets: An Annual Anthology* contains ten poems by Aldington, four by H. D., five by Fletcher, five by Flint, and one each by Lawrence and Amy Lowell. Aldington's poems, which appear on pages 3-16, are: "Vicarious Atonement," "Bondage," "A Moment's Interlude," "Field Manoeuvres," "Dawn," "Inarticulate Grief," "Images," "Captive," "R.V. and Another," and "Prayer."

Thomas McGreevy, in his 1931 study of Richard Aldington, gives a good reading of one of the 1917 anthology poems:

"Captive" is a good-bye to all the dream of loveliness of the young poet, good-bye to the boyish dream of Greek serenity which has never existed in any, except artistic, reality, and which could never be as unreal as on the day that a young man put on a private soldier's uniform for the first time.[27]

H.D. may be the poet's "friend" of the second stanza:

They who have taken from me my friend
Who knew the holy wisdom of poets,
Who had drunk at the feast
Where Simonides sang.

The poem is not entirely disconsolate; the dream is not entirely abandoned. Its final two lines speak the hope of youth: "But afar off I dream that I see/ Bent poppies and the deathless asphodel."

In *The Chapbook*, No. 23, May 1921, Harold Monro, probably thinking that the day of the Imagist anthologies was over, poked fun at them with "Pathology des Dommagistes (being specimens for a projected Anthology to be issued in the U.S.A.)." The "poems" are humorous parodies of the type of poetry which appeared in *Des Imagistes*, and seemed to give the more orthodox Georgians the last word. But the Imagists were not subjugated; they had one more anthology to go.

Imagist Anthology 1930: New Poetry by the Imagists makes clear its intentions in a prefatory note:

To prevent any possible misunderstanding the announcement is here made that this volume is not intended as an attempt to revive Imagism as an avant-garde movement. In 1912 [sic] certain young and almost unknown authors, who felt friendly towards each other, published their poems together in the "Imagist" anthology. They have developed along varying lines, but still feel friendly. The present anthology is intended to give specimens of their recent work.[28]

Aldington explained the purpose of the 1930 anthology to John Cournos in similar terms: "The idea of the Anthology is to show that the original Imagists are by no means dead as poets, and to give examples of their latest work."[29] Glenn Hughes contributes to the volume a short foreword on Imagism and the Imagists, and Ford Madox Ford,[30] writes delightfully if somewhat idiosyncratically in a section entitled "Those Were the Days":

What exactly VORTICISM was—though its most loyal champion—I never knew. That was probably because of Mr. Pound's singularly incomprehensible—because so pre-deluvian [sic] —American accent and Mr. Lewis's almost inaudible mumbles. I would be led along the narrow streets of the Transatlantic down-town region, poor Mr. Pound holding one arm and Mr. Lewis the other, and Mr. Pound with an extreme rapidity of diction would into my one ear yawp admirable doctrine, in the dialect and with the gestures of a pre-war nigger-daddy who had passed the greater part of his life in Camden, Pa. [sic] under the shadow of the good grey poet. And Mr. Lewis, into the other ear, would be letting drop vitriolic but inaudible denunciations of the Other Side. . . . And as a by-product of VORTICISM there evolved itself . . . Imagism.

This collection includes poetry by Richard Aldington, John Cournos, H.D., John Gould Fletcher, F.S. Flint, Ford Madox Ford, James Joyce, D.H. Lawrence, and William Carlos Williams. The volume begins with three long poems of Aldington's on pages 29 to 64. His poems are: "The Eaten Heart," "Passages Toward a Long Poem," and "Sepads: A Modern Poem."

Of "Passages Toward a Long Poem" Thomas McGreevy said: "But of all his more recent poetry I think nothing of Richard Aldington's is so simply beautiful as the fourth section of *Passages Toward a Long Poem*, published in the *Imagist Anthology* last year."[31] It is probable that "Passages Toward a Long Poem" was originally titled "Filings." (See above Part I, Chapter 1, note 6, and the poem "Additional Filings or Hour-Glass Grains" reproduced below in Part II, Chapter 2.)

"The Eaten Heart" was the title of a separate volume printed in France in 1929, and the poem of this name was to become the title poem of a 1933 volume published in England. Glenn Hughes says of Aldington's third poem in this anthology: "In 'Sepads: A Modern Poem' . . . he constructs an amusing poem from *Saturday Evening Post* advertisements."[32] This poem, which is dedicated to Walter Lowenfels, is one of Aldington's "joking" poems which, like "Vates, the Social Reformer," he did not put in his collected poems. (It is included in Chapter 3 in the second part of this book.)

Aldington's own recollection (*Life for Life's Sake*, p. 143) of the genesis of *Imagist Anthology 1930* explains his dedication of "Sepads: A Modern Poem":

In 1929 my modernistic friend, Walter Lowenfels, suggested to me in Paris that I ought to get out another Imagist anthology. Of course I knew Walter thought the Imagists were as dead as Shelley, and that the suggestion was ironical.[33] By way of snubbing him I promptly took a taxi to the cable office, and as I had just published a successful novel [*Death of a Hero*] I had no difficulty in selling the non-existent anthology to London and New York within two days. When I got the cables of acceptance I confess I was a little perturbed at what I had done. Suppose I couldn't collect any poems? However, I got to work, Ford and H. D. laboured nobly, and the *Imagist Anthology, 1930*, contained poems from everyone who had ever contributed (including James Joyce and Carlos Williams) except poor Amy who was dead, Skipwirth Cannell whom we couldn't trace, and Ezra who was sulky. Ford wrote one of his genially discursive introductions, and we sold several thousand copies between the two countries.

Despite his offhand manner in writing about this project some ten years later, Aldington actually worked hard to make the 1930 anthology a success, a fact which can easily be seen by examining the letters he wrote to William Carlos Williams about the difficulties he was encountering.[34]

The impact on modern poetry of the Imagist anthologies (especially the first one) was great. Curiously, most of the poets represented were not true Imagists, and those who were often contributed poems that could not truly be called imagistic. The Imagist anthologies were, therefore, more of a catalyst than a model for modern British and American poetry. Because of their unique position in twentieth-century poetry, one can hardly discuss the poetry of Richard Aldington without taking them into consideration.

The Individual Volumes

Since Aldington's first publication in book form was his contribution to the 1914 *Des Imagistes*, I have considered this, and the other anthologies that logically follow it, before dealing with his own individual volumes. In this section, the poet's first editions will be discussed in chronological order.

Aldington was only twenty-three the year his first volume of poetry was published. It was a pretty little book; and even though the youthful assistant editor of *The Egoist* was by this time accustomed to seeing himself in print, he must have been proud of this slim volume. The cover of the original *Images*, subtitled *(1910-1915)*, is of the same heavy cream-colored stock that is used for the body of the book. The title and the author's name are printed in black in the upper left above an apparently hand-colored line drawing of trees in green, yellow, and blue. The initials "JN" in the lower left-hand corner of the drawing indicate that it was done by John Nash, brother of Paul Nash, who in 1919 would do the woodcuts for the Beaumont edition of Aldington's *Images of War* volume. Beneath the drawing, at the lower left, is the price, "8d. net." Today, if you are lucky enough to find a copy of this book, which dealers list as exceedingly rare, its cost will be at least $25. In the lower right is listed the publisher, "The Poetry Bookshop, 35 Devonshire Street, Theobalds Road, W.C."

In the November 1912 issue of *Poetry Review*, Harold Monro, its editor, had announced: "On January 1, 1913, we shall open, at 35 Devonshire Street, Theobalds Road, in the heart of old London, five minutes walk from the British Museum, a Bookshop for the sale of poetry, and of all books, pamphlets and periodicals connected directly or indirectly with poetry."[35] Amy Lowell writes engagingly about her first visit to Harold Monro's Poetry Bookshop.[36] She tells how she spent so much time looking in the window before she went in, that she was surrounded by a group of London urchins anxious to see what the strange lady found so interesting in the window. Inside she was impressed by the shelf-lined walls which offered both the classics and the newest publications of poetry. Monro dealt exclusively in poetry, and not only sold it but also published it. Miss Lowell's visit to The Poetry Bookshop took place in July of 1913, which was some time before the publication of Aldington's *Images*. The husky, cigar-smoking Amy was soon to be in the middle of the poetic movement of which Aldington was a part, and to be instrumental in the publication of the three anthologies titled *Some Imagist Poets*; but this was in the future—for the moment she was charmed that there should be a bookstore devoted only to poetry.

Years later, Aldington was to say unkindly of Monro that he "had been the Marshal Joffre of contemporary English poetry—always ten minutes late and two divisions short" (*Life for Life's Sake*, p. 264). But in justice it should be added that if it had not been for Harold Monro in London and that brave young lady in Chicago whose name is so similar, Harriet Monroe, the birth of modern poetry would have been much more difficult.[37] In any event, in the 1 December 1915 issue of *The Egoist* The Poetry Bookshop advertised, "Ready December 1st, *Images* by Richard Aldington."

Images (1910-1915) contains thirty poems, all but two of which are later reprinted in *The Complete Poems*. The two that are not collected are the prose poems "Night Piece" and "Dawn," which I have reproduced in Chapter 3 of Part II. Aldington notes on the inside cover of the volume,

> A number of these poems have already appeared: some in "Des Imagistes" (The Poetry Bookshop; New York, Boni); some in "Some Imagist Poets" (Constable & Co.; Boston & New York, Houghton Mifflin Co.); others in "The Egoist," and one in "Poetry and Drama." Others have appeared in American periodicals: "Poetry" (Chicago), "The Little Review" (Chicago), "The Poetry Journal" (Boston), and "Greenwich Village" (New York).

In Appendix 1, I have tried, whenever possible, to show the original publication data for the poems from this edition that Aldington later collected. Publication data for the uncollected poems are given along with the poems themselves in Chapter 3 of Part II.

The titles of the poems in *Images (1910-1915)* and their order of appearance are as follows: "Part I: To a Greek Marble; The River; In the Old Garden; Beauty, Thou Hast Hurt Me Overmuch; Argyria; In the Via Sestina; Choricos; Images; A Girl; October; New Love; The Faun Sees Snow for the First Time; Lemures; Amalfi; At Mitylene; Hermes, Leader of the Dead; Part II: Summer;

At the British Museum; June Rain; In the Tube; Cinema Exit; Interlude; Evening; Hempstead Heath (Easter Monday, 1915); St. Mary's, Kensington; At Nights; Night Piece; Dawn; London (May, 1915); After Two Years."

"Choricos" is Aldington's best-known poem in his early manner; anyone who has had anything to say about his poetry has generally commented on it. Harriet Monroe said that "No later lyric by Aldington can ever dim the Greek-marble-like beauty of *Choricos*. . . ."[38] Hughes sees the poem as "one of Aldington's most effective efforts to recapture the Hellenic mood,"[39] and Coffman suggests that it "personifies death as a cold, chaste woman who brings rest and forgetfullness."[40] McGreevy shrewdly notes that "the poem is not purely Greek in its origins. There is plenty of Swinburnism in it." Moreover, says McGreevy, "the cold lips and regretful eyes and dropping breasts Mr. Aldington probably found on the wind among the reeds"[41]—an apparent reference to Yeats.

McGreevy is probably right about the Swinburne influence. As he says, "death in a purple robe and red shoes is a horribly Pre-Raphaelite piece of imagining." In Aldington's novel, *All Men Are Enemies*, the hero, young Anthony Clarendon, is much taken with Swinburne and quotes from *Atalanta* in admiration.[42] Furthermore, in *Life for Life's Sake* (p. 132) Aldington writes of a visit to Alice Meynell:

> All went well until I said something in mild praise of Swinburne. The lady bridled—I think that is the right word—and said she couldn't admire a man who started a poem "Before the beginning of years" and then went on to talk of "sand from under the feet of years." I pointed out that this was a trifling blemish in a long and magnificently rhetorical poem like "Atalanta." Whereupon she asked me if I admired Coventry Patmore, and I said cheerfully: "Not a bit."
>
> The temperature was rapidly approaching zero, and she then asked sarcastically what poets I did admire. I said, Swinburne for one, but at the moment I was very much interested in modern French poets and their interesting experiments in form.[43]

Despite the possibility of the Swinburnian influence, most of the commentators on "Choricos" have praised its recapture of the Greek tone; besides this, very little has been said about the poem itself. It begins by stating its thesis in the first two lines: "The ancient songs/ Pass deathward mournfully." In the second stanza the songs are personified and become "Symbols of ancient songs" who come to the ocean's edge to keep an appointment with death. They are unobserved save by "The frail sea-birds/ And the lithe pale girls." This is a powerful couplet that satsifies both by its rhythmic mating and its graphic depiction of the ocean's surf as "Daughters of Oceanus."

The songs move from "The green land" and "from the waters" toward "the quiet level lands" that Proserpina has made ready for all of us. In the fourth stanza the poet has become one of those "silently winging through soft Cimmerian dusk"; the "they" of the first part of stanza three now becomes "we." The transition is made possible by the "us" of lines twenty and twenty-one. Just as Keats joins the nightingale in the wood, Aldington has become one of the band who are "symbols of ancient songs."

In stanza four "we" abandon love ("The Cyprian's breasts"), and art ("Phoebus Apollo"), and the natural world that we have loved, because Death has "come upon us."

> And of all the ancient songs
> Passing to the swallow-blue halls
> By the dark streams of Persephone,
> This only remains—
> That in the end we turn to thee,
> Death,
> We turn to thee, singing
> One last song.

The internal logic of the poem becomes somewhat difficult here. The "symbols of ancient songs" have now become both songs and singers. The "cold lips that sing no more" of stanza two are unsealed for "one last song."

Stanza five is the hymn to Death, who is "an healing wind," "the lips of love mournfully smiling," and "the silence of beauty." It is a view of death that was only possible to the young, romantic poet. In his late fifties, Aldington wrote of D.H. Lawrence: "In lassitude and discouragement, death—a mere figment of rhetoric to the immortal young—seems not only desirable but the only hope."[44] We will look back to this youthful view when Aldington writes of his experiences in the trenches of World War I, where the face of death is something very different.

In the last stanza the singers kneel before Death, who crowns them with her "slim colourless poppies" and "smiling as a chaste woman/ Knowing love in her heart" seals their eyes so that the "illimitable quietude" may come upon them.

The poem begins as a lament for "ancient songs," by which Aldington possibly means all things Greek; these are brought to life as "symbols" and become a band of singers that the poet joins in their rendezvous with Death; they sing a last hymn to Death before she gives them "illimitable quietude." It may be destructive to try to pin down such a frail, moth-like poem; however, we can summarize Aldington's poetic statement in this way: since Greek art is dying out, in my love for it I will join its dwindling ranks and in my poetry sing one last song which will be in praise of that death which effaces both ancient art and my art—both ancient singers and today's poets.

Although some critics, Yvor Winters for example,[45] have attempted to establish a partial metric pattern in "Choricos," essentially it is without rhyme or meter—true *vers libre*. Like the Greek poetry that Aldington knew and loved, it depends on the cadences of the lines for poetic form to reinforce its language. It seems to me that the long swinging cadences are particularly suited to the subject matter of the poem. I agree with McGreevy that death with red-shod feet and purple robe in Swinburnian, but generally the diction of the poem is effective. I have mentioned "frail sea-birds" and "lithe pale girls"; "searing the grass as with a sudden flame" is another good phrase; and "healing wind," "pallid chaplets," and "colourless poppies"—all attributes of death—are also effective word choices. The imagery of "Choricos" is rich:

> And the songs pass from the green land
> Which lies upon the waves as a leaf
> On the flowers of hyacinths. . . .

Finally, however, it is to a mood or tone or atmosphere which it creates that the poem owes its power. There is an acceptance of the inevitable without whimpering, an almost sad joy in the final act of life's drama, an austerity and cold beauty in visualizing the inevitable end of all things, that gives "Choricos" its reputation of being Aldington's best poem in the "Greek manner."

"To a Greek Marble" is also one of Aldington's good early poems. Coffman suggests that the poet

> recreates the intense reaction to physical beauty which must have moved the sculptor of this piece. . . . "To a Greek Marble" presents a succession of images which make not only pictorial, but aural and tactile appeals: fragile pipes, cicada song, brown fingers moving over slim shoulders, the "sun upon thy breasts." The poem does not rely upon metaphor but bases its appeal upon the cumulative effect of a succession of separate images.[46]

I think also that the "white grave goddess" may have represented to Aldington all that was Greece, which by the warmth of his love, as expressed in his poetry, he tried to restore to that "far ecstasy." It was part of Aldington's tragedy, as it is of every man's, that the past cannot be permanently restored and that all attempts to breathe life into it are fruitless. Finally, as Aldington did, we must come to grips with the present, however much less desirable it may seem to us. The poem is a lament for the unattainable—the lost lover, the lost past, Aldington's beloved Greece. The second stanza expresses this clearly:

> I am not of these about thy feet
> These garments and decorum;
> I am thy brother,
> Thy lover of aforetime crying to thee,
> And thou hearest me not.

The poet pleads his special position: my love is warm, living, and passionate, not the respectful deference of the classicist; but Potnia, the Queen, who survives now only in marble, hears him not.

The third stanza of "To a Greek Marble" is a fine example not only of the general tonal qualities that can be achieved by free verse at its best, but also of the deftness with which the poet uses sound to support content:

I have whispered thee in thy solitudes
Of our loves in Phrygia,
The far ecstasy of burning noons
When the fragile pipes
Ceased in the cypress shade,
And the brown fingers of the shepherd
Moved over slim shoulders;
And only the cicada sang.

The whispering of the first line moves to the cicada song of the last line on a series of "s" sounds in "solitudes," "loves," "ecstasy," "noons," "pipes," "ceased," "cypress," "shade," "fingers," "shepherd," "slim," "shoulders," "cicada," and "sang." Gradually the soft whisper of the lover blends into the memory of the music of "fragile pipes," which is in turn lost in the shrill cicada song. Because it is not tied down by the requirements of metrical structure, *vers libre* should be able to produce effects such as this more easily than regulated verse—and should be expected to do so.

One unpleasant winter morning in 1912 Richard Aldington sat in an apartment in London working on a verse translation.

The postman rat-tatted at the door, and I found a letter and a picture postcard in the box.
    The postcard came from a friend in Genoa, and showed a hillside of blossoming almond trees on the Italian Riviera. Underneath was scribbled: "These will be full out in a few weeks." The letter was from Chicago, with a draft in English currency for the equivalent of forty dollars, in payment of my first free verse poems, and a letter saying the editor would be glad to see more. This was entirely due to Ezra, who used all his influence with this periodical to make it publish what was then called the new poetry.[47]

The editor, of course, was Harriet Monroe of *Poetry* and the poems included the two we have just discussed. Years later, Aldington wrote Miss Monroe that she could never know what her publication of his work had meant to a friendless and unknown boy: "I could have embraced you as my fairy god-mother!"[48] The postcard giving him the idea and the check the means, the twenty-year-old poet bought a ticket to Rome. One of the places he visited in Italy was Amalfi, of which he writes: "At Amalfi the two-sailed fishing boats rested like dark moths on the calm sea, and there was a crescent moon."[49] His visit to this Italian town is recalled in his poem "Amalfi."

    Not only is "Amalfi" representative of those poems in *Images (1910-1915)* which deal with the beauty of Aldington's own world rather than that of classical Greece, but it is also a typical Imagist poem:

We will come down to you
O very deep sea,
And drift upon your pale green waves
Like scattered petals.

We will come down to you from the hills,
From the scented lemon-groves,
From the hot sun.
We will come down,
O Thalassa,
And drift upon
Your pale green waves
Like petals.

This is the entire poem. The scattered petals on the pale green waves are reminiscent of Pound's "petals on a wet, black bough."[50] In fact the poem is an image or picture with no movement but a promised one: "We will come down to you . . . and drift." This is the sort of poetry that the Imagists, and Aldington in particular, were trying to attain. In the 1 April 1914 *Egoist*, Aldington is replying to a letter about his article on "Le Latin Mystique":

> . . . the difficulty—the real problem of the artist—is to present the exact emotion, the exact vision, the exact *image*. All great poets are exact; they give their emotions, their experiences, their observations, in exact phraseology. . . .
> Personally I would rather make five new "images" than found a new religion of Abstractions with capital letters. . . . "To generalize is to be an idiot; to particularize is the distinction of Merit" (Blake).[51]

I suppose that one might argue that there are three images in "Amalfi." There are the "scented lemon-groves" in the hot sun, the view that the poet has from here of the "very deep sea" with its "pale green waves," and finally the image that the poet sees in his mind's eye of what "we" will look like drifting on these pale green waves.

On a miniature scale the goal of the Imagist poet foreshadowed what was more exactly stated later in T.S. Eliot's well-known phrase, "objective correlative." The Imagist poem tried to create a scene so vividly that the reader would feel the same emotions that the poet did when he saw it in actuality or in his mind. For "Amalfi" to succeed, the reader must feel himself among the lemon groves high above the pale green sea. As he stands in the hot sun and breathes the pungent scent of the groves around him, he visualizes what he will look like from this height drifting on the green waves far below. In this respect the Imagist poem, like all other poetry, requires active effort on the part of the reader to bring about its artistic success.

"Amalfi" is nicely structured to achieve its effect. The first line is repeated to open the second stanza, but with the added phrase "from the hills."

The next two lines of stanza two give the only other information about the place of the poem: "From the scented lemon-groves,/ From the hot sun." Line four of stanza two again repeats the first line of both stanzas, but now in shortened form, "We will come down." Line five of the second stanza echoes the second line of stanza one: the Greek "O Thalassa" is substituted for "O very deep sea." (I feel, by the way, that this "very," which Aldington uses in other poems too, is a weak poetic word.) The third line of the first stanza becomes the sixth and seventh lines of stanza two, and the final line of the poem echoes the last line of stanza one in diminuendo: "Like scattered petals" reduces to "Like petals."

"Interlude" is an interesting poem because of the way in which it is able to connect the Greek world of Aldington's imagination with the real world around him. The poem tells a tiny narrative: the poet is outside a London pub when he hears a street musician playing; suddenly the "tin squeals" on the musician's "reedy whistle" bring girls from Attica "in linked dance":

> Gay girls dancing
>   in the frozen street,
> Hair streaming, and white raiment
> Flying,
> Red lips that first were
> Red in Ephesus.

Only when the dancers disappear does the poet realize that they have been conjured up in his mind by the organ man; he gives the man some pennies, but, more important, he recognizes him as a fellow poet, repeating Baudelaire's famous line: *"Mon semblable, mon frère!"*

The typography of the poem in the 1915 edition helps to suggest the linked dance of the Greek girls: line seven, for instance, is spaced from the end of the preceding line, that is to say, the lines "dance." The idea of "dance" was made even clearer in the original printing in *Poetry* (Vol. 5, No. 5, February 1915, p. 222), where "Interlude" is the second of two poems printed under the general heading "Dancers"; the first is entitled "Palace Music Hall—*(Les Sylphides)*" and subtitled *"To Nijinsky"* (reproduced in Chapter 2 of Part II). The diction of the poem is also "linked." The dancing girls have "Red lips that first were/ Red in Ephesus," and the street musician is "Red-nose, piping by the Red Lion."

The emotion of the poem lies in the poet's recognition of the possibility of a link between the past and the present—a link which is very like Proust's associations as he tastes the madeleine, except that here an imagined rather than a remembered past is being recaptured. Equally important is the poet's recognition of the fact that the link with the lost Greece can only be the artist: in this case, the lowly street musician whose "reedy" music brought the gay girls from Attica to dance for the poet in a frozen London. The poem itself, then, is a "linked dance," an illustration of how art can recreate the past in the imagination of the present.

The poem "After Two Years," first published in *Poetry and Drama*, No.

8, December 1914, and positioned last in *Images (1910-1915)*, helps to make the point (discussed earlier in connection with "The Poplar") that Aldington and the other Imagists did not break completely with the older poetic conventions. Certainly "After Two Years" is far from the Imagist ideal. Mary Aldis, reviewing *Some Imagist Poets* (1916)—where the poem was reprinted in spite of the stipulation that the 1915 anthology should contain only work which had not been printed in an earlier volume—said that "After Two Years" was "a short Elizabethan lyric,"[52] the finest of Aldington's seven poems. John Gould Fletcher moves the milieu back two centuries further when he speaks of its "fourteenth century feeling."[53] In any event, it is an excellent example of what Aldington can do in traditional meter and rhyme. This is the first stanza:

> She is all so slight
> And tender and white
>   As a May morning.
> She walks without hood
> At even. It is good
>   to hear her sing.[54]

The two poems in the *Images (1910-1915)* volume which are most opposite to "Greek" poems like "Choricos" and "To a Greek Marble" are "Cinema Exit" and "In the Tube," both from Part II. The first two poems are directly from the poet's Greek world of the imagination; the last pair represent the most radical attempt the early Aldington makes to confront the world around him.

"Cinema Exit" tries to tell what it feels like to come out of a cinema into the street when the movie is over. The transition from the world of the moving picture to the real world offers interesting material to the poet. Aldington deals with it in terms of light and darkness:

> Suddenly,
> A vast avalanche of greenish-yellow light
> Pours over the threshold;
> White globes darting vertical rays spot
>   the sombre buildings;
> The violent gloom of the night
> Battles with the radiance . . . .

He has just described the effect on the people of "the glimmering pictures," "the banal sentimentality of the films," "the tinkling piano"; now they must come out of this dream world and face reality again. To express this feeling in terms of the light battling "the violent gloom of the night" has possibilities—has not man always tried to hold back the darkness of reality by means of frail walls of light?

But Aldington has not been a part of the crowd in the cinema; instead he has been standing at one side observing them without sympathizing with them and without understanding that their visit to the cinema has been specifically a means of escaping the "violent gloom" of existence. In an ugly misanthropic ending to a poem that had interesting possibilities, he says:

> Millions of human vermin
> Swarm sweating
> Along the night-arched cavernous roads.
>
> (Happily rapid chemical processes
> Will disintegrate them all.)

"In the Tube" seems to have had fewer poetic possibilities than "Cinema Exit," but those that were present have been more carefully worked out. May Sinclair says of this poem:

> Richard Aldington presents his compartment in the Tube railway carriage with the most brutal directness. But the whole point of the presentation is in the last three lines:
>
> > I surprise the same thought
> > In the brasslike eyes:
> > *"What right have you to live?"*
>
> His mood is hostile to the Tube. And in his bitter poem it is the hostility, the mood that counts. It is the Tube *"à travers un temperament,"* in spite of the formula. Almost anybody else can do the "brown woodwork pitted with brass nails" and "the flickering background of fluted dingy tunnel" for him.[55]

I think that Miss Sinclair is right in saying that "it is the hostility, the mood that counts"; in being "hostile to the Tube" the poet is of course also hating the civilization that the Tube represents and in particular its representatives seated opposite to him.

Thomas McGreevy takes notice of "In the Tube" in this way:

> I cite this poem not so much as poetry as for the fact that it is the first of his poems that shows contact with discordant realities. It foreshadows the quality that was to mark his verse more and more during the years that followed, absolutely direct statement devoid of every kind of poetic "trimming."[56]

McGreevy's statement is correct only as a rough generalization. This is not the first poem that shows the realities of the present world intruding on the ideal world of Aldington's imagination ("Church Walk, Kensington," for instance, was written earlier, though not included in this first collection), nor is it quite right to speak of the quality of direct statement as marking "his verse more and more during the years that followed," unless we keep in mind that McGreevy was writing in 1930-1931. On the other hand, this poem is, as I have said, one of those diametrically opposed to the early "Greek" poems, and while I do not concede that all of Aldington's future poetry continues to go in the direction that McGreevy suggests, a change has indeed taken place from which the poet never fully recovers.

Miss Sinclair, in the passage quoted above, apparently took for granted that Aldington equates the Tube with the civilization which inspired it, and that he considers the people riding with him as that civilization's representatives. Within the poem itself the following takes place. The speaker falls into a seat as the car starts; he looks up and sees:

> A row of advertisements,
> A row of windows,
> Set in brown woodwork pitted with brass nails,
> A row of hard faces,
> Immobile,
> In the swaying train,
> Rush across the flickering background of fluted
>   Dingy tunnel;
> A row of eyes. . . .

What is happening, of course, is that the rows of advertisements, of windows, of brass nails, of hard faces, and of eyes are merged into one another. The man and the machine that he created have become a frightening unit whose intense hostility the speaker feels directed toward himself. In other words, the hostility is mutual; the speaker says that he feels antagonism, disgust, and immediate antipathy "cut his brain," and that

> I surprise the same thought
> In the brasslike eyes:
> *"What right have you to live?"*

In this connection it is interesting to note a possible link between this poem and Aldington's *Death of a Hero*, his war novel of 1929 that is ranked with *All Quiet on the Western Front* and *A Farewell to Arms* as one of the great novels of World War I. Aldington's hero, George Winterbourne, in a scene somewhat similar to the one in the poem, describes the hostility of civilians to him before his enlistment, including the look in their eyes that seemed to question his right to be alive when so many other young men were at the front, dead or dying. The concluding line of the poem—" '*What right have you to live?*' " in this context would have a more specific meaning.

At the time that Aldington was writing the poetry of the *Images (1910-1915)* volume, free verse was the center of a hot argument between the traditionalists and the new poets. Today the issues have been resolved by time, and we are as used to reading poetry in free verse as in traditional meter or meter and rhyme. What we have come to realize is that free verse is not free to the extent of being simply poetic prose printed in lines of arbitrary length. Its periods, generally, are longer than those of traditional poetry but shorter than those of prose; they must have what the Imagists themselves called "cadence." May Sinclair said of Aldington's prosody: "He has got more sheer music into his unrhymed cadence than any other contemporary writer of *vers libre*."[57] To write good poetry in free verse requires the utmost discipline on the part of the poet. He has no traditional frame to guide him, and any failure on his part to maintain firm control of his medium will result in what the enemies of the Imagists used to call "prose arranged in short lines." For the most part I agree with Miss Sinclair that Aldington does well in his chosen form. Lines like these from "Argyria" attest to his success:

> Swallow-fleet,
> Sea-child cold from waves;
> Slight reed that sang so blithely in the wind;
> White cloud the white sun kissed into the air;
> Pan mourns for you.

Aldington's failures in *Images (1910-1915)* are less attributable to faulty prosody than to an occasional inability to stand far enough off from his material. He succeeds when his poetry is able to heal the breach between the real and the ideal; he succeeds especially in a sensuousness of tone that is Keatsian in quality. This is his precious poetic heritage, and we will be especially concerned to see whether he is able to sustain this quality or whether it will be shattered by the horror of his wartime experiences.

Images Old and New was published in the United States in 1916, only one year after *Images (1910-1915)* was issued in England. The publisher was The Four Seas Company of Boston. The ability of this young poet (he was twenty-four in 1916) to publish his second volume in America, so soon after his first appeared in Britain, can be attributed to two circumstances. In the first place, Amy Lowell must have had an important hand in bringing about the acceptance of the work. In September of 1915 she wrote that a book of his was to appear bearing the imprint of an American publisher.[58] Second, and most important, the Imagist movement had brought about a cross-fertilization between British and American poetry to an extent never before realized.

Images Old and New is shown by Paul Schlueter in his "Check List"[59] as a "variant title," but since it contains poems not included in *Images (1910-1915)* and even excludes one poem that did appear in that volume, it should be treated as a separate edition. The contents of *Images Old and New*, listed in the order of the poems' appearance, are as follows: "To a Greek Marble; Argyria; The River; New Love; 'Beauty, Thou Hast Hurt Me Overmuch'; Stele; October; Lesbia; In the Old Garden; June Rain; In the Via Sestina; Choricos; A Girl; Images; Hyella; The Faun Sees Snow for the First Time; At Mitylene; Lemures; Amalfi; Hermes, Leader of the Dead; Summer; At the British Museum; Scents; Night Piece; Dawn; At Nights; Evening; Church Walk, Kensington; St. Mary's, Kensington; In the Tube; Cinema Exit; Interlude; A

New House; Hampstead Heath; London." Of the thirty-five poems in this book, twenty-nine had already appeared in *Images (1910-1915)*. The six that did not are: "Stele," "Lesbia," "Scents," "Church Walk, Kensington," "Hyella," and "A New House." "Lesbia" had previously been printed in the 1914 *Des Imagistes*.

In a "Note" of acknowledgment following the Contents are listed two publications (in addition to the first two anthologies) that were not listed in *Images (1910-1915)*: *The New Age* (London) and *Others* (New York).

The two prose poems "Night Piece" and "Dawn" are among the poems which also appear in the first British volume; they were printed in *The Poetry Journal* (also published by The Four Seas Company), Vol. 4, No. 3 (November 1915). "Dawn" is reprinted with only a spacing change, but "Night Piece" shows an interesting revision. The word "suddenly" in the last sentence of the original printing is now omitted, and the phrase "the post-horn of the coach of Romance" is added, following a dash (see the reproduction of the poem in Chapter 3 of Part II). In *The Little Review* of May 1916, John Gould Fletcher points to the conclusion of "Night Piece" to support his suggestion that Aldington is "at bottom a Romantic."⁶⁰

Of the five poems not previously printed in the first volume or in the anthologies, "Church Walk, Kensington" is one of the most interesting. Like "Interlude" and "Eros and Psyche," "Church Walk, Kensington," which is subtitled "Sunday Morning," is an attempt to make some kind of link between the Greek past of Aldington's imagination and the reality of his present. In this case, however, as in "Eros and Psyche," the attempt does not succeed as well as in "Interlude," and we have only the juxtaposition of the two elements and a bitterness over the resultant disparity.

> The cripples are going to church.
> Their crutches beat upon the stones,
> And they have clumsy iron boots.
>
> Their clothes are black, their faces peaked
>   And mean;
> Their legs are withered
> Like dried bean pods.
> Their eyes are stupid as frogs'.
>
> And the god, September,
> Has paused for a moment here
> Garlanded with crimson leaves.
> He held a branch of fruited oak.
> He smiled like Hermes the beautiful
> Cut in marble.

The poet's intentions are clear enough. Man today is crippled; his freedom restricted by "iron boots." "Going to church" may have a symptomatic or causal relationship to his condition. His whole appearance, "black," "peaked," "mean," "withered," "dried," and "stupid," is a travesty of the Grecian ideal. Only in nature—"the god, September"—does the poet see the old perfection that was epitomized in "Hermes the beautiful/ Cut in marble." While "Interlude" succeeds in joining the ideal and the real through the medium of the artist (the street musician's tune brings the Greek girls dancing to London's frozen streets), "Church Walk, Kensington" offers us no affirmation but only the bitter contrast between life in the mind and in the world.

John Gould Fletcher (who a few years earlier warned Amy Lowell not to publish in *Des Imagistes* with that "unlicked cub" Aldington!), writing a review of *Images Old and New*, holds "Church Walk, Kensington" up for admiration:

> Recently there has been in England signs of a return to that simplicity and restraint which are the qualities of highest art. . . . Of this admirable tendency Mr. Aldington is the precursor and the most shining example. . . . [He quotes "Church Walk."] There we have it all: a sense of the sordidness of existence, of the wayward and casual beauty with which nature decks that sordidness; irony and pity, concealed yet poignant. . . .[61]

But it is hardly enough to point out the antinomies of existence. They should be enveloped in the poetic vision so that we see them both as parts of the world. In "Church Walk, Kensington" Aldington regrets a paradox of life; in "Interlude" he derives value from what could be just a similar opposition.

In the "Poetry" section of Professor Schlueter's "Check List" of Aldington's books, *Reverie: A Little Book of Poems for H. D.* is shown as preceding *The Love of Myrrhine and Konallis, and Other Prose Poems*. Both of these volumes, according to Schlueter, were printed at Cleveland, Ohio, by The Clerk's Press in 1917.[62] The second volume is shown as being reprinted in Chicago by Pascal Covici in 1926. But an actual examination of these editions indicates the following: the first volume published by The Clerk's Press has the title *The Love Poems of Myrrhine and Konallis* and is dated 1 June 1917; *Reverie: A Little Book of Poems for H. D.* is the second volume to be published by The Clerk's Press and is dated 30 August 1917; *The Love of Myrrhine and Konallis, and Other Prose Poems* is the correct title of the 1926 volume published by Pascal Covici in Chicago.

The Love Poems of Myrrhine and Konallis is subtitled "A Cycle of Prose Poems Written after the Greek Manner." This dainty little book measures only about four by five inches, and is covered with a gray board, and printed on doubly deckle-edged paper. Its maker tells us proudly, "The Typography and Presswork done by Charles C. Bubb, Clerk in Holy Orders, at his Private Press, June the first 1917," and that "This edition consists of only forty copies printed upon Tuscany hand-made paper." Evidently the first contact between the youthful poet and the "Clerk in Holy Orders" was a letter written by the Reverend Bubb to Aldington inquiring about the possibility of printing privately some volumes of the Poets' Translation Series.

Aldington replied on 19 June 1916, and also sent Bubb a second, undated letter that must have been written at about the same time, suggesting six possible printings for Bubb, including "2. Reverie & other poems. A long poem & a few short ones, representing the best of my trench work."[63]

In his Forewords Charles C. Bubb writes:

> In a recent review of some of Richard Aldington's work, the writer says, "his unrhymed verses have a charm that reminds one of a well-cadenced translation from the Greek." This is especially true of the little cycle of poems herewith printed which are frankly imitations of the epigrams found in the Anthology. . . . These poems were first printed in "The Little Review" during the last two years and are now issued in this form by permission of the author.[64]

The Reverend Bubb, while approving of Aldington's poetry, does not feel the same way about its subject. He speaks of the decadence of this particular period of Greek civilization and compliments the poet on the appealing verse he has been able to make from this "midden" of the past. Aldington appreciated the paradox of having his Lesbian love poems printed by a "Clerk in Holy Orders." On 29 June 1917 he wrote Bubb:

> I wanted these little poems in a form which should be satisfactory while not public—I couldn't bear the idea of exposing these two spoiled children of mine to the uncomprehension & perhaps contempt of the public. I know that you must have felt some dislike to them, & I appreciate all the more your goodness in tolerating them.[65]

There are thirty-two poems in this little volume. The first fourteen are untitled; they celebrate the love of Konallis the goat-girl and Myrrhine the hetaira. The remaining eighteen poems are titled as follows and appear in this order: "The Lamp, The Wine Jar, Red and Black, After the Orgy, The Offering, The Wine of Lesbos, April, The Paktis, The Charioteer, White Rose, Her Voice, Antre of the Nymphs, Unfriendly Gods, The Old Love, Another Greater, The Last Song, Thanatos, Hermes-of-the-Dead."

On the whole it seems unfortunate that Aldington did not elect to preserve at least some of these poems in *The Complete Poems*. All of them are characterized by a limpid, sensuous beauty that is representative of the poet at his best. Aldington wrote Bubb that he had given the *Myrrhine* and *Reverie* volumes to Miss May Sinclair when he was in London and that she liked them and their printing "immensely."[66] Later she wrote of them: " . . . his *Myrrhine and Konallis*, a sequence of the most exquisite love poems in the language, poems that, if he had never written another line, ought to be enough to secure for him a high and permanent place in literature."[67]

The quality of the poems surely reflects the poet's own feelings for them:

> For I have lived with them & loved them and from shadows they became so real to me that human beings seemed only shadows by comparison. I wanted to express that intensity of passion of the Symposium

> & the Phaedrus; I wanted something sterile and passionate and lovely
> and melancholy—and Konallis & Myrrhine were born! Perhaps they are
> a perversion—but all excessive love of beauty is perhaps a perversion
> (which is the cause of my now enduring so much ugliness—the gods are
> just!) And then, in these poems, I have expressed more of myself than
> in "Images," which is tinged with influences foreign to myself.
> Myrrhine & Konallis are simply the love of beauty, too sensual to be
> abstract, too remote from biological affection to be anything but
> sterile.[68]

Many of the poems are arranged as dialogues between the two lovers and are
among the most beautiful of Aldington's love poems. Possible reasons for
their exclusion from *The Complete Poems* are discussed later.

In 1926, in Chicago, Pascal Covici printed *The Love of Myrrhine and
Konallis, and Other Prose Poems*. The Covici volume is quite different in
appearance and content from the original edition. It is almost twice the size
of the Clerk's Press booklet, and in hard covers of black cloth stamped in
gold. The end sheets are designed by Frank Mechau and consist of line draw-
ings of two nudes, printed in black on yellow paper, with an effect *á la* Beards-
ley. This edition was limited to "one thousand and ten copies of which five
hundred are for England and five hundred and ten for America. The first one
hundred and fifty copies are autographed by the author." There were now
forty poems in the Myrrhine and Konallis cycle of love poems. The first
fourteen of the previous volume were now titled and nine new poems had
been added. One poem, "White Rose," was deleted. The titles and the order
of the poems in the volume, including the "other prose poems," are as
follows: "Idyll, Myrrhine to Her Lovers, Morning, Noon, Evening, The Offer-
ing to Persephone, Her Voice, Prayer, The Storm, Memory, Konallis the
Epicurean, The Singer, Gifts, Festival, The Charioteer, Jealousy, The Offer-
ing, The Vigil, Unfriendly Gods, A Dialogue, The Paktis, Another Greater,
Antre of the Nymphs, The Three Aphrodites, The Old Love, The Oleander,
The Lamp, April, Two Goddesses, The Wine Jar, Konallis to Myrrhine,
Myrrhine to Konallis, Homer and Sappho, Red and Black, The Wine of
Lesbos, After the Orgy, The Last Song, Thanatos, Hermes-of-the-Dead, Epi-
taph, Discouragement, Fatigues, Sorcery of Words, Our Hands, Fantasy,
Stand-To, In an Old Battlefield, Reaction, Escape, Prayer, Landscape, The
Road, Dawns, Song, Lethe, The Return, In the Library, Bodies, The Last
Salute." The final poem of the Myrrhine and Konallis cycle, "Epitaph," is
followed by the dating "1914-1916," indicating that all of these love poems
were composed during the early war years.

The section following the Myrrhine and Konallis cycle is entitled "Nine-
teen Prose Poems,"[69] and has the epigraph, from Virgil's *Aeneid* (VI,268),
"Ibant obscuri sola sub nocte per umbram" ("Darkly they went through the
gloom of the lone night"). Professor Hughes said generally of the poems of
this volume: "They are rhetorical, archaic, and richly colored. The cadences
are long and voluptuous; the imagery weighted with ornament."[70]

A few months after its publication of *The Love Poems of Myrrhine and
Konallis*, The Clerk's Press printed *Reverie: A Little Book of Poems for H. D.*

The poems of *Myrrhine and Konallis* all were collected from the pages of *The Little Review*, but where did the poems of *Reverie* originate? Not from the periodicals, because those that were printed in magazines do not appear there until several years *after* the Clerk's Press volume. In *Life for Life's Sake* Aldington writes:

> I had jotted down poems in a small pocket-book during the war, for no other reason than the consolation of writing something; and unexpectedly I found I could sell them for five or six times as much as I got before the war. (That little note-book, which I carried through gas attacks, two battles, and many months of trench warfare, was given to Amy Lowell, and may now be reposing with the other papers she bequeathed to Harvard.)[71]

At this time it is only possible to conjecture that the poems published in *Reverie* were among those in the wartime notebook. In any event, these are the poems to which Aldington referred in his 1916 correspondence with Bubb as "A long poem & a few short ones, representing the best of my trench work."

The general appearance of *Reverie* is the same as that of the previous Clerk's Press booklet: gray cardboard covers with a tipped-on title label. The little book, twenty-eight pages, is the same four-inch by five-inch size, and the paper a fine-laid bond with a double deckle edge. Page [4] notes, "The typography and presswork done by Charles C. Bubb, Clerk in Holy Orders, at his Private Press, August 30th, 1917," and page [2] states that "This edition consists of only fifty copies printed upon Tuscany hand-made paper."

The Table of Contents on page [5] lists the nine poems of *Reverie* in the following order: "Proem, Reverie, The Wine Cup, Sorcery of Words, Ananke, Our Hands, Disdain, An Earth Goddess, Epilogue." Four of these poems, "Proem," "Sorcery of Words," "Our Hands," and "An Earth Goddess," which are dated individually between December 1916 and May 1917, were to become a part of Aldington's volume *Images of War: A Book of Poems*, printed by C. W. Beaumont in 1919. "Sorcery of Words" and "Our Hands" were also reprinted in the "Nineteen Prose Poems" of the second *Myrrhine and Konallis* volume.

Judging by his listings in the little books that he printed, the Reverend Bubb expected a type of relationship with Aldington that failed to materialize. At the end of the *Myrrhine and Konallis* booklet, he notes under the heading "Recent Publications of The Clerk's Press":

"Poets' Translation Series"
Latin Poems of the Renaissance
The Poems of Anyte of Tegea
The Garland of Months

The first two items were evidently intended as private reprints of the translations Aldington had done for The Egoist, Ltd. (the book-publishing adjunct to *The Egoist* magazine) in 1915; of these Professor Schlueter credits

The Clerk's Press with only the second one, which was published in 1917. *The Garland of Months* is credited solely to The Clerk's Press as "Poets' Translation Series, No. 5." Of the three booklets projected, then, only two materialized. Furthermore, at the end of *Reverie* the following appears under the heading "Announcement":

> The Clerk has in preparation and will issue at short intervals the following writings by Richard Aldington, the Imagist Poet.
> 1. Reverie, A Little Book of Poems for H. D. written in the trenches on the Western Front.
> 2. Latin Poems of the Renaissance, Second Series. Many translations printed for the first time.
> 3. The Saints of Paradise, by Remy de Gourmont. Authorized translation with French text.
> 4. Lament for Bion, by Moschus, with Greek text, and a prose piece "Theocritus on Capri."
> 5. Poems of Myrrhine and Konallis. Second edition with corrections and additions.
> 6. Latin text of Poems of the Renaissance, both series, with Italian and French translations and imitations.
> 7. The Poems of Meleager of Gadara, with the Greek text.
> 8. Neo-Hellenic Poems of Modern France.
>
> The edition of each will be strictly limited to fifty copies. A few copies remain unsubscribed.

It is sad to have to report that, according to Professor Schlueter's "Check List," none of these promised publications (except for the *Reverie* volume in which Bubb's list was printed) ever appeared under The Clerk's Press imprint, although a number of them were printed elsewhere. For bibliophiles this was unfortunate, because the two little booklets that I have examined (I have not seen copies of the translations) are fine examples of what the gifted amateur can do to raise bookmaking to an art.

The reason for the abrupt termination of this relationship between the private printer and the young poet is given in a letter written many years later by Aldington to Lawrence Clark Powell, then head librarian at the University of California, Los Angeles, who became a good friend of the poet during the latter's stay in that city:

> You may have a complete set of the Clerk's Press in Calif but you haven't got any more items of mine than Kershaw lists, for the simple reason that only two were issued. Rev. Bubb got mad with me about something he thought disrespectful to Jesus, and didn't issue the others, which he announced. Reverie and Renaissance Latins were issued (50 copies each, half of them destroyed in a bombing raid on London in 1918) and those I believe Kershaw listed.[72]

(Powell was being consulted at the time with regard to an American publisher for Kershaw's bibliography and had evidently questioned the listings under the Clerk's Press imprint. Kershaw's omissions must have been caused by the misinformation that Aldington gave Powell: as we have noted, Bubb issued two translations—*not* including "Renaissance Latins," according to

Schlueter—and the two editions of Aldington's own poems, *Reverie* and
Myrrhine and Konallis.)

In August of 1917 Aldington sent the Reverend Bubb the manuscript
for a second edition of *Myrrhine and Konallis*, this being one of the projects
announced in the back of the *Reverie* volume; but in December of 1918 the
poet wrote to ask whether Bubb intended to continue printing his booklets
and, if not, would he return the manuscripts for them.[73] This letter evidently
ended their relationship, whose importance to the young war poet is shown
clearly in an early letter to the Reverend: "I shall never forget how much
these little books meant when they came. (One of them lies buried under a
ruined house in France; luckily I was not there when the shell burst.)[74]

Harriet Monroe, the editor of *Poetry*, the periodical that in 1912 had
first published Aldington's poems, reviewed *Reverie* in an article titled "Ref-
uge from War." After transcribing a letter from an American soldier referring
to Aldington's "Choricos," she continued:

> No later lyric by Aldington can ever dim the Greek-marble-like beauty
> of *Choricos*, but neither can that poem dim the more tender and human
> beauty of *Reverie*. The contrast of moods in the two poems bridges the
> gulf between youth and manhood. *Choricos*, which was printed over
> five years ago in the second number of *POETRY*, was written while the
> poet was still in his teens. . . . This tiny book of nine brief poems contains
> "no murmur against Fate." . . . And out of his despair, out of his
> hunger for beauty, comes a lyric note clearer and richer than anything
> we have heard from him since those earliest poems. . . . [75]

Alec Waugh, writing many years later, had this to say about "Reverie,"
the title poem of the little booklet:

> *Reverie* describes how a soldier in a quiet part of the line in France
> broods over his wife in England. Written in rhythmed verse, it is tender,
> wistful, nostalgic, uncomplaining. I still think he is one of the best
> English war poets. There was no savagery, no resentment, not even the
> sting of satire in his war poems. They are love poems, rather than war
> poems.
>   He was at his best when he wrote of love. "Have I written too much
> or not enough of love?" he asks in *Epilogue*, one of his most quoted
> poems.[76]

Mr. Waugh's comments do not apply to all of Richard Aldington's war poems,
many of which are undeniably savage, resentful, and satirical, but what he
says is true of "Reverie."

I consider "Reverie" one of Aldington's best love poems, and definitely
agree with Mr. Waugh's estimate that "he was at his best when he wrote of
love." In "Church Walk, Kensington" and in "Eros and Psyche," the poet
contrasted the real of a sordid present with the ideal of a Greece of his imagi-
nation, but did not transmute the antithesis into anything finer. In addition
to juxtaposing the reality of trench warfare to the ideal of love, Aldington is

able to transcend the apparent conflict. He begins with vivid details of his all-too-real present:

> It is very hot in the chalk trench
> With its rusty iron pickets
> And shell-smashed crumbling traverses,
> Very hot and choking and full of evil smells
> So that my head and eyes ache
> And I am glad to crawl away
> And lie in the little shed I call mine.

In the second stanza he introduces the sustaining power of his love:

> But these things pass over, beyond and away from me,
> The voices of men fade into silence
> For I am burned with a sweet madness,
> Soothed also by the fire that burns me,
> Exalted and made happy in misery
> By love, by an unfaltering love.

The lover places this love above love of God, country, or gain, "Since it was for her sake only I was born/So that I should love her." Then he anticipates a battlefield death, and even though Reason and Despair have whispered to him "that we die and vanish utterly," he is

> . . . quite happy about Fate,
> For this is love's beauty
> That it does not die with lovers
> But lives on, like a flower born from a god's blood,
> Long after the lovers are dead.

Aldington, pagan of pagans, sees the promise of paradise in the bonds of lovers:

> For, since I do not know why love is
> Nor whence it comes, nor for what end,
> It may very well be that I am wrong about death,
> And that among the dead also there are lovers.

Now the poet wishes death for himself and his beloved, and in Dantesque fashion creates a heaven for his Beatrice:

> We would be together, always together
> Always in a land of many flowers,
> And bright sunshine and cool shade;
> We should not even need to kiss

Or join our hands;
It would be enough to be together.

She would stoop and gather a flower,
A pale, sweet-scented, fragile flower
(A flower whose name I will not tell,
The symbol of all love to us).

And I would watch her smile
And see the fair flowers of her breast
As the soft-coloured garment opened from her throat.

As Joyce and Nora had their seed-cake, Aldington and H. D. had "a flower" which was also "the symbol of all love."

In the final stanza the poet contemplates the possibility of his death on the morrow, but he is now secure in his vision of the future:

In the fair land I have built up
From the dreams of my love,
We two together, she bending by the pale flower
And I beside her:
We two together in a land of quiet
Inviolable behind the walls of death.

Aldington has succeeded in making his dream of the ideal stronger than the horrible reality of the battlefield around him. Because he has done so, the poem succeeds for us, too, and becomes, in my opinion, one of the finest soldier-love poems ever written.

In *Life for Life's Sake* (p. 209) Aldington writes of the period just after his return to London following the armistice:

Within a few weeks I had arranged with the Egoist Press to re-issue my translations and to add the Anacreontea to them; Elkin Mathews bought a small volume of my love poems; Allen and Unwin agreed to issue a popular edition of my war poems; C. W. Beaumont was at work on a limited edition of these war poems with illustrations by Paul Nash. . . .

Aldington makes a curious omission here: he neglects to mention the fourth of his volumes of poetry published in 1919, *War and Love (1915-1918)*. As we shall see, this was the edition projected first and it is the genesis of the others. Since the three British books of poetry apparently were published before this American edition, the effect in retrospect is that the American volume appears to be collected from them; in fact, Aldington had intended to publish the poems first in America.

Images of War: A Book of Poems was published in 1919 at Westminster by C. W. Beaumont. Although Aldington tells us nothing about Bubb in his autobiography, he does write about Beaumont (*Life for Life's Sake*, p. 210):

> Beaumont was an interesting character. He supported himself by
> running a small second-hand book shop in the Charing Cross Road;
> but his passion was for the Russian ballet, with hand-printed editions of
> new poets as a close second. He is an example of how much can be
> achieved by enthusiasm and pertinacious industry, in spite of strict
> limitations of time and opportunity. In his cellar he set up a hand-print-
> ing press on which he worked at night, and in time produced a very
> pleasant series of contemporary poets. Everything was hand-set and
> hand-printed, but it was necessary to look out sharply for misprints. At
> the last moment I caught a really terrible one in my book. A poem
> about the trenches had the line: "Out in those wire-fringed ditches,"
> and it was set up with a "b" instead of a "d".

The book, without the "terrible" misprint (actually it might have given the
critics an "image" to come to terms with), appeared in boards with
brick-colored cover papers printed with an allover abstract design by "Nash."
A printed title is tipped on, as is the spine title, "Images of War." The author's
name is abbreviated on the spine to "R. Aldington." The following appears
on the page facing the title page:

> This is the seventh book issued by The Beaumont Press and the third
> printed by hand 30 copies have been printed on Japanese vellum signed
> by the author and artist and numbered 1 to 30 50 copies on cartridge
> paper numbered 30 to 80 and 120 copies on hand-made paper
> numbered 81 to 200.

The poem "Proem" on page [5], printed under a woodcut of a World
War I battlefield, precedes the contents pages. This is the same poem that had
been printed in the *Reverie* volume; it is followed by the date "May, 1917."
Twenty-six poems are listed on the contents pages, [6], [7], and [8],
including the "Proem"; first lines are given for each one except the "Proem."
The order of the poems is as follows: "Proem, Vicarious Atonement, On the
March, Dawn, Sorcery of Words, Fatigues, Our Hands, In the Trenches, A
Ruined House, Battlefield, Daughter of Zeus/ For J. C., Living Sepulchres,
Trench Idyll, Three Little Girls/ For My Sisters, A Village, Barrage, A Young
Tree, [Bombardment], An Earth Goddess/ After the Advance 1917,
Soliloquy I, Soliloquy II, H.S.R./ (Died of wounds, April, 1917), E.T./ (Died
of wounds, May, 1917), Machine Guns, Picket, Terror, Apathy." As Alding-
ton tells us, "it was necessary to look out sharply for misprints" in Beau-
mont's work. Evidently the poet carefully checked the text, but he did not
scrutinize the contents pages so closely. The title "Bombardment" does not
appear in the contents pages of this edition, but the poem itself is to be found
on pages 30-31 between "A Young Tree" and "An Earth Goddess." There
are, therefore, twenty-seven poems in this volume although only twenty-six
are listed in the contents.
    In this attractive volume there are about a dozen woodcuts which are
usually illustrative of the poems with which they appear. For instance, "In

the Trenches" is accompanied by a cut depicting a typical trench scene; "A Ruined House" appears under the cut of a war-destroyed house; and "Living Sepulchres" under a woodcut of rats. All of the poems begin with a fancy capital letter four lines in height and the boldface printing of one or more words in the first line. The thirty copies printed on "Japanese vellum," besides being signed by the author and artist, have their woodcuts beautifully water-colored by hand.

The colophon of *Images of War* reads:

HERE ENDS IMAGES OF WAR A BOOK
of Poems by Richard Aldington the Cover and the Decorations designed
by Paul Nash the Typography and Binding arranged by Cyril William
Beaumont Printed by Hand on his Press at
75 Charing Cross Road in the City of Westminster Completed
on the evening of St. George's Day
MDCCCCXIX

Beneath is a cut of a sailing ship encircled with the motto "Simplex . Munditiis . The . Beaumont . Press"; and under this printer's device are two lines: "Pressman Charles Wright/ Compositor C. W. Beaumont."

In addition to the "Proem," three other poems of *Images of War* had appeared previously in *Reverie*: "Sorcery of Words," "Our Hands," and "An Earth Goddess." The remaining poems were new (except that some had been published in magazines) and probably represented the gleanings from the little notebook which Aldington says he carried with him during his service in France. There are poems in this volume that exhibit, as well as love and love of life, the savagery and resentment which Alec Waugh overlooked.

As we have noted, Aldington in his earlier poems recognizes the tension between the ideal of the Greek world of his imagination and the real of the sordid modern life around him. Placed now in the midst of the horror of the trench warfare of World War I, it is miraculous that he could sustain this tension and still write poetry. He seems to have depended for emotional survival on three touchstones: his Greek ideal, the memory of love, and a sensitivity to nature even on the ruined battlefields of France. Aldington's poems of the *Images of War* volume reveal his struggle for artistic as well as physical existence.

"In the Trenches," pages 16 and 17, is the eighth poem. Stanza one considers the havoc that war creates in nature:

. . . each rush and crash
Of mortar and shell,
Each bitter shriek of bullet
That tears the wind like a blade,
Each wound in the breast of earth,
Of Demeter, our Mother,
Wound us also,
Sever and rend the fine fabric
Of the wings of our frail souls,

Scatter into dust the bright wings
Of Psyche!

It is possible to speculate that behind the image of the last four lines lies the
memory of the abandoned chrysalis mentioned in the poem "Childhood" and
also in the novel *Rejected Guest*.

In the second part of "In the Trenches" the poet solaces himself with
the thought of the final impotency of "all this clamour,/ This destruction and
contest. . . ."

Soon the spring will drop flowers
And patient creeping stalk and leaf
Along these barren lines
Where the huge rats scuttle
And the hawk shrieks to the carrion crow.
Can you stay them with your noise?
Then kill the winter with your cannon,
Hold back Orion with your bayonets
And crush the spring leaf with your armies!

It is interesting to see how closely many of the poems of *Images of War*
were patterned on actual details of trench life rather than on the poet's
imagination, which was the basis for such early poems as "Choricos" and all
of the "Greek" poems.

The "huge rats" of the fourth line above recur in the poem with the
nasty-clever title "Living Sepulchres":

One frosty night when the guns were still
I leaned against the trench
Making myself *hokku*
Of the moon and flowers and of the snow.

But the ghostly scurrying of huge rats
Swollen with feeding upon men's flesh
Filled me with shrinking dread.

Aldington mentions "making . . . *hokku*"; in this connection the
following comment by Morikimi Megata, who exchanged letters with the
poet, is of interest:

There is no reference to the Japanese *Haiku* [the more familiar 19th
century form which developed from the older *hokku*] poems in his
letters to me, but that he has had some knowledge of them is indisput-
able. We may sense in some of his earlier poems the influence of
Haiku. I do not think, however, that Japanese art and literature
influenced him much; whatever strong attraction he might have found

in Japanese "culture and traditions, matured through so many centuries of civilisation". . . .[77]

Surely in "Living Sepulchres" (which is, however, a minor poem at best) art and reality are juxtaposed with a vengeance, and even Mr. Waugh would agree that "savagery" is apparent.

In his war novel, *Death of a Hero*, Aldington once more refers to the rats:

> Then he noticed that a legion of the fattest and largest rats he had ever seen were popping in and out the crevices between the sandbags. As far as he could see down the trench in the dusk, they were swarming over parapet and parados. Such well-fed rats! He shuddered, thinking of what they had probably fed upon.[78]

The emotion of the poem "A Village" is similar to that of "In the Trenches" but not quite the same. "A Village" is the fifteenth poem of the volume and one of the longer ones. The poem's speaker begins by recalling his own village:

> Now if you saw my village
> You'd not think it beautiful,
> But flat and commonplace—
> As I'd have called it half a year ago. . . .

The contractions reinforce the "flat and commonplace"; the tone is definitely Housman-like. Now the poet compares to his feeling for his home his changed attitude toward a similar French village where his company is evidently bivouacked for a rest from the trenches. He goes on:

> But when you've pondered
> Hour upon chilly hour in those damned trenches
> You get at the significance of things,
> Get to know clearer than before,
> What a tree means, what a pool,
> Or a black wet field in sunlight.

Thomas McGreevy objects to the "damned" in the second line above: "And I, at least, feel that the word 'damned' is prosaic, breaks in discordantly on the emotional essence as well as on the technical excellence of the passage."[79] It is true that we have destroyed the basic meaning of "damned" by using it as an expletive. I wonder, however, whether Aldington did not intend that we hear in this instance the classic meaning of the word.

The poet now gives us a catalogue of significant things, each of which, alone, is a fine example of Imagist poetics. He introduces them with an allusion to Theseus's "The lunatic, the lover, and the poet":

> So I go strolling, .
> Hands deep in pockets, head aslant,
> And eyes screwed up against the light,
> Just loving things
> Like any other lunatic or lover.
>
> .   .   .   .
>
> Pigeons and fowls upon a pointed haystack;
> The red-tiled barns we sleep in;
> The profile of the distant town
> Misty against the leaden-silver sky;
>
> .   .   .   .
>
> Then there's the rain pool where we wash,
> Skimming the film-ice with our tingling hands;
> The elm-fringed dykes and solemn placid fields
> Flat as slate and blacker.

Ten years later, the image of the pool appears again in *Death of a Hero* (p.
338): "There seemed to be no water supply in the village, and they had to
wash in thawing flood-pools, breaking the new thin ice with tingling fingers."

The final stanza of "A Village" makes the point of the poem, which is a
variation of the theme that death adds piquancy to life; in this case the
proximity to the horrors of the trenches peels the film of familiarity from the
poet's eyes when he looks about himself in the "dull village" where he is
quartered:

> And we have come from death,
> From the long weary nights and days
> Out in those frozen wire-fringed ditches;
> And this is life again, rich life—
> This poor drab village, lovely in our eyes
> As the prince city of Tuscany
> Or the crown of Asia, Damascus.

How nicely the phrase "wire-fringed ditches" echoes the "elm-fringed dykes"
of the earlier stanza, and what a disaster it would have been if Aldington had
not caught Beaumont's "typo"!

McGreevy describes "Bombardment," the eighteenth poem of *Images
of War*, in this manner:

> Technically, this poem is one of the most perfect Mr. Aldington has
> written, and it has none of the superfluous words that in accordance
> with his new transitional and later, as I have suggested, very English
> manner he preferred to leave in, rather than seem too self-consciously
> literary.[80]

The idea of not removing superfluous words from a poem to avoid seeming too self-consciously literary seems rather ridiculous; if McGreevy is repeating something that Aldington told him, which is possible, then I would think McGreevy naive to have believed it. But McGreevy is right in calling the poem a good one; it is particularly interesting as a further example of the way in which nature provided constant solace to the poet. This is the last stanza:

> The fifth day there came a hush;
> We left our holes
> And looked above the wreckage of the earth
> To where the white clouds moved in silent lines
> Across the untroubled blue.

"Machine Guns" provides another instance of a sharp image that so impressed itself on Aldington's mind that he used it again in his novel. Here is the first stanza of the poem:

> Gold flashes in the dark,
> And on the road
> Each side, behind, in front of us,
> Gold sparks
> Where the fierce bullets strike the stones.

and here the passage from *Death of a Hero* (p. 344):

> . . . while the shells crashed and the machine-gun bullets struck gold sparks from the road stones.

The purpose of the poem is to satirize wryly the enforced bravery of two officers who expose themselves to gunfire while the enlisted men "cower shrinkingly against the ground." This is the concluding stanza:

> Only we two stand upright:
> All differences of life and character smoothed out
> And nothing left
> Save that one foolish tie of caste
> That will not let us shrink.

Even this must be a remembered incident, since it also forms a part of Aldington's novel (p. 332):

> If the two men were exposed to shells or machine-gun fire, Evans walked more slowly, spoke more deliberately, seemed intentionally to linger.

I have called attention to a number of these instances in which Aldington uses a figure or idea or feeling first in his poetry and later in his war novel. In *Life for Life's Sake* (p. 331) he shows that he is aware of at least the more general types of borrowing:

> The complete detachment of the place [Port Cros] and almost complete leisure . . . enabled me to make a real start on my long-cherished project of a novel about the war, the old war of 1914-1918. Some of the main themes and emotions I had already put down in poems, but I wanted to do a prose book on a larger scale.

The two poems in *Images of War* closest to the earlier "Greek" style are really variations on the theme of nature as an escape from human despair. In a sense Aldington is amalgamating his Greek ideal with the reality of the war. This is "Daughter of Zeus":

> No!
> We will not slay the moon.
> For she is the fairest of the daughters of Zeus,
> Of the maidens of Olympus.
>
> And though she be pale and yet more pale
> Gazing upon dead men
> And fierce disastrous strife,
> Yet for us she is still a frail lily
> Floating upon a calm pool—still a tall lady
> Comforting our human despair.

The last three lines bring to mind both Imagism and *haiku* and the extent to which they are similar. The first lines of the second stanza echo Shelley's "Art thou pale for weariness/ Of climbing heaven and gazing on the earth." But what strikes us is the atmosphere, the rhythm, the suspending of the symbol across the changing length of line. The "tall lady" of the ninth line is of course a reference to the moon as it rides high in the sky, but John Cournos's description of H. D. gives it an added significance: "Hilda was good-looking and charming, a little too tall, perhaps, for a woman according to American standards but not so exceptional in England where tall women are more common."[81] In this edition (but not in *The Complete Poems*) this poem has for part of its title "For J. C.," probably meaning John Cournos.

The other poem in this volume which is reminiscent of Aldington's earlier poems is one of those reprinted from *Reverie*, "An Earth Goddess," which as the nineteenth poem appears on pages 44-46. In this poem also the speaker finds comfort in a nature which he has identified with a goddess in Demeter's hierarchy.

> You are not the august Mother
> Nor even one of her comely daughters,

> But you gave shelter to men,
> Hid birds and little beasts within your hands
> And twined flowers in your hair.

The poet uses the goddess to personify the battle-torn no man's land and the land immediately behind the trenches, and imagines her as being wracked like a woman in childbirth:

> Sister, you have been sick of a long fever,
> You have been torn with throes
> Fiercer than childbirth and yet barren;
> You are plague-marked;
> There are now no flowers in your hair.

A temporary quiet comes to the battlefield; the poet compares the earth goddess to Jocasta, who at the death of her sons felt only pity and anguish.

> And now since you have endured,
> Since for all your wrong and bitter pain
> There came no hatred upon you
> But only pity and anguish
> Such as the mother of King Eteocles felt
> Gazing upon her two angry sons—
> Because of this, your peace is wonderful.

In this patient acceptance by nature of even the holocaust of war, in her patient rebuilding of her ravaged beauty, the poet finds peace:

> Because of your old pain
> And long-suffering and sweetness,
> Because of the new peace
> Which lies so deeply upon you,
> The chains of my bitterness are broken,
> The weight of my despair leaves me.

It is easy in detachment to point out the fallacy in this kind of reasoning; what is important is that the poet did find this peace in nature, just as a much greater poet more than a century earlier, troubled by the excesses of the French Revolution, had found in the English countryside a similar peace. If the emotion is genuine, poetry need not be reasonable; if the emotion is false, being reasonable will not save the poetry.

Aldington carefully segregated most of the love poems which he wrote in France from the *Images of War* volume, although he did include four poems from *Reverie*. The majority of the love poems remained unpublished until the appearance of *Images of Desire*, which we will discuss later. Aldington closed *Images of War* with the poem "Apathy," which makes a sort of transition between the two books. While it is not really a love poem, it tells of a poet-soldier and his lover.

The setting for the poem is probably England, where the soldier could be home on leave or returned after the war's end. The speaker of the poem describes his state of mind, which is both bitter and apathetic:

> You do not speak, you do not look at me;
> Just walk in silence on the grey firm road
> Guessing my mood by instinct, not by thought—
> For there is no weapon of tongue or glance
> So keen that it can stir my apathy,
> Can stab that bitterness to hope,
> Can pierce that humour to despair.

In order to rid himself of his mental depression, he tries to go about his business as a poet: to observe the beauty about him.

> The bridge has three curved spans,
> Is made of weathered stones,
> And rests upon two diamond-pointed piers—
> Is picturesque.
> (I have not lost all touch and taste for life,
> See beauty just as keenly, relish things.)
> The water here is black and specked with white;
> Under that tree the shallows grow to brown,
> Light amber where the sunlight struggles through. . . .

He continues in this vein for another dozen lines, flexing his poetic muscles, but his outer eye is not able finally to suppress his inner vision.

> And yet there's always something else—
> The way one corpse held its stiff yellow fingers
> And pointed, pointed to the huge dark hole
> Gouged between ear and jaw right to the skull.

The emotion that the poem is trying to express—that of the soldier who has returned from the front and is on the edge of a breakdown—was the subject of a short story by another World War I soldier, Ernest Hemingway. In "Big Two-Hearted River" Hemingway tells how Nick Adams hangs on to his sanity for the moment by going through the ritualistic actions of a fishing and camping trip. In "Apathy" Aldington's soldier is a poet who tries to save himself from succumbing to the horror of his wartime memories by an almost ritualistic observation and description of nature.

When Aldington's *Literary Studies and Reviews* was issued by Allen and Unwin in 1924, its back pages contained, under the heading "By the Same

Author," a list of "blurbs" describing some of his previous books. The following ones advertised *Images of War*:

> A Poet of outstanding merit. —*New Outlook*. Mr. Aldington is an "Imagist," that is to say he endeavours to show to the reader with scrupulous exactness how the subject of the poem affected his mind at the time of writing. . . . "The Wine Cup" shows him at his best. —*Spectator*.
>
> Reveals the author, who was the best of our young Imagists in pre-war days, as a true poet. —*Illustrated London News*.
>
> His delicate love of quiet sophisticated harmonics is at tragic conflict with the filth and disorder of the trenches . . . there is a great ring about the last lines of Mr. Aldington's challenge to war. —*Manchester Guardian*.
>
> Mr. Aldington can always be relied upon to produce poetry worth while, and these poems . . . have the leisurely grace characteristic of his writing. . . . Delicate poems all, they are as ripe fruit gathered fresh from the orchard.—*Aberdeen Journal*.

Glenn Hughes wrote of the volume: "Almost never in these poems does the author allow self-pity to master him, and never does he indulge in heroics. He is consistently honest, and consistently an artist."[82] On the other hand, May Sinclair was not happy with *Images of War*:

> . . . I find myself disconcerted by some of his war poems (*Images of War*). They belong to the incomplete modern half of him so imperfectly fused with the other finished half. . . .[83]

Similarly, as I noted in Chapter 1, Harold Monro liked the poetry, while William Carlos Williams was severely critical.[84] McGreevy said: "The effect of the war on Aldington and Lurçat [Jean Lurçat, French designer] has been to bring their work closer to objective reality. . . ."[85]

One of the points that we need to keep clearly in mind when considering *Images of War* is that, in separating the war poems from most of the love poems by issuing two different volumes, Aldington has given us, in each case, only a partial view of his wartime poetry. Only the American edition, *War and Love* (discussed below), combined the two groups of poems. Having made this mental note, we can look at some of the differences between *Images of War* and the earlier *Images (1910-1915)*. I am overlooking, for the moment, the three intervening volumes, since *Images Old and New* is an expanded American edition of the first *Images*, and the two Clerk's Press private printings can be taken as previews of the love poetry of *Images of Desire*.

Images (1910-1915) revealed the increasing dichotomy that seemed to be developing between Aldington's ideal imaginings, as expressed by the earlier "Greek" poems such as "Argyria" and "At Mitylene," and his view of the reality of the world around him which he gives us in later poems like "Cinema Exit" and "In the Tube." In *Images of War* the real world, in one of its most horrifying aspects, threatens to overwhelm completely the young poet's idealism.[86] He is faced

with a situation which all of us encounter in one form or another. In Alding-
ton's case, however, the crisis is drastic and he must make an accommodation
not only to preserve his psychic stability but also to save his poetic life.

The soldier-poet seems to make this accommodation in the same way
that all men do: by a compromise that does not completely give up his earlier
position but which surrenders some of the outposts so that he may reinforce
and hold the core of his beliefs. Quite simply what he seems to do is to substi-
tute nature for the Greek ideal; or perhaps, more subtly, he permits a Greek
view of the real world to become his compromise between the idealistic
Greek world of his early imagination and the horror of the real world of
trench warfare in which he found himself.

The result is poems like "In the Trenches," "The Village," and, espe-
cially, "An Earth Goddess" in which Aldington peoples nature as the Greeks
did and thus builds a bridge between the real and the ideal to make man's
position on earth more tenable. In the short poem "Misery" (published in
the American edition) he tells us overtly about his reaction to his
dangerous position:

> Sometimes in bitter mood I mock myself:
> "Half ape, half ass, servant and slave,
> Where are your dreams gone now,
> Where your fierce pride?
> Whither goes your youth?
> And how will you dare touch again
> Dear slender women with those disfigured hands?
> Or bare your long-dishonoured body
> To the contemptuous sun?
> How live after this shame?"
>
> And all my answer:
> "So that hate poison not my days,
> And I still love the earth,
> Flowers and all living things,
> And my song still be keen and clear
> I can endure."

This is not a new answer, of course. To turn to nature as a solace for
human despair is to follow a well-worn path; Wordsworth did it and in so
doing gave us the finest of his poetry. There is a major difference, however,
between the approaches of these two poets: Wordsworth's Christian views
caused him to see in nature the garments of the unseen God; Aldington's
paganism suggested that he people nature with the old gods of Greece. Despite
the theological difference, psychically and aesthetically the result was the
same: both poets were able to maintain their mental balance and keep writing
poetry. In Aldington's case, the victory was not at first clean-cut, as
"Apathy" clearly shows. The memories of the horrors of the trenches would

never be completely gone; and at the time of *Images of War* he still needed to make a desperate effort to keep morbid recollections from overwhelming him.

How good, then, is this poetry written beneath the walls of the castle of Despair? To begin, it has lost some of the hard marble-like quality of the earlier poetry that many of Aldington's first admirers, like May Sinclair, liked so much. There are a few poems in which the terror of the battlefront conditions will not synthesize in the poetic imagination, with the result that in a poem like "Living Sepulchres" we have somewhat the same aesthetic problem as in the earlier "Eros and Psyche" and "Church Walk, Kensington." There is also occasionally, in spite of what Professor Hughes has said, an inclination to self-pity, which under the circumstances is understandable enough. What the poetry of Richard Aldington gains by the compromise made in *Images of War* between the impossible ideal and the unbearable real, is an increase in just that quality which to me seemed the most important attribute of his earlier work: a Keatsian sensuousness that is possible only to those who are willing to accept the beauty of life as its only truth.

Aldington called Allen and Unwin's 1919 edition of *Images of War* a "popular edition" as compared to Beaumont's "limited edition." It is also a considerably expanded edition. Of the twenty-seven poems of the Beaumont volume, the three prose poems "Sorcery of Words," "Fatigues," and "Our Hands" have been dropped, and eighteen new poems have been added to the remaining twenty-four to make up forty-one. The apparent discrepancy occurs because the two poems "H.S.R." and "E.T." are now arranged as one under the title "Two Epitaphs."

This is not nearly as attractive a book as the Beaumont edition. It is smaller, about four by seven inches; its boards are covered with gray paper and printed in gold on the front and the spine with the title and the author's name. On page 5 appears the following note:

> Some of these poems appeared in a limited edition (Beaumont Press) on hand-made paper under the title *Images of War*. Others have appeared in *The English Review, The Nation, New Paths* (an annual of new literature), *The Anglo-French Review, Art and Letters, The Egoist, Poetry* (Chicago). Others again were printed in the Imagist anthology for 1917.

The Contents on pages 7 and 8 lists the forty-one poems that appear on the book's sixty-four pages. The following eighteen poems are the ones that have been added to those of the Beaumont edition: "Leave-taking, Bondage, Field Manoeuvres, The Lover, A Moment's Interlude, Insouciance, Ananke, Misery, Time's Changes, The Wine Cup, Doubt, Disdain, Reverie, April Lieder, Concert, Taintignies, The Blood of Young Men, Epilogue." Five of these eighteen new poems are from the *Reverie* booklet; since the other four in *Reverie* are included in the poems carried over from the Beaumont edition, all nine of the poems of this little volume are reprinted in the expanded *Images of War*. In this connection I think that Alister Kershaw must have been mistaken when he wrote in the Preface to his bibliography of Aldington's works: "But how could I know of, say, *Reverie*, with one or two poems

nowhere else reprinted" (my italics).[87] Three others of the added eighteen
poems are from the 1917 volume of *Some Imagist Poets: An Annual
Anthology*: "Bondage," "Field Manoeuvres," and "A Moment's Interlude."
The remaining poems are reprinted from the sources that are listed in the
acknowledgment quoted above.

In writing of D. H. Lawrence, Aldington said that "flowers . . . to him
were always the loveliest symbol of the beautiful non-human world."[88] The
second stanza of "Leave-taking" sounds Lawrencian:

> Will the straight garden poppy
> Still spout blood from its green throat
> Before your feet?
> Will the five cleft petals of the campion
> Still be rose-coloured,
> Like five murdered senses, for you?

The poem is a series of questions which the departing lover asks his beloved as
he leaves her. It begins, "Will the world still live for you/ When I am gone?"
and concludes with another couplet, "Will the world die for you/ As it dies
for me?" The poet sees the world as but a mirror which reflects the beauty of
love; when the lovers are parted, the world of their love must die.

In another of the "new" poems of this volume, "The Lover," the
death-wish of the early "Choricos" is repeated.

> She will not come to me
> In the time of soft plum-blossoms
> When the air is gay with birds singing
> And the sky is a delicate caress;
> She will come
> From the midst of a vast clamour
> With a mist of stars about her
> And great beckoning plumes of smoke
> Upon her leaping horses.

This is not the cold, chaste death of the young man's imagination, but the
fierce, hot death of the real world of the war. The last stanza of the poem is,
however, reminiscent of "Choricos":

> But though she will hurt me at first
> In her strong gladness
> She will soon soothe me gently
> And cast upon me an unbreakable sleep
> Softly for ever.

"Insouciance" is the poem William Carlos Williams complained of:

> In and out of the dreary trenches
> Trudging cheerily under the stars
> I make for myself little poems
> Delicate as a flock of doves.
>
> They fly away like white-winged doves.

Possibly Williams was a little unfair. The metaphor of the doves is an emotionally rich way of describing the poems which all the war poets made for themselves, but which under the circumstances could not be set down for us, and thus were lost forever.

The last poem of the volume, except for "Epilogue," is "The Blood of Young Men." Aldington says it was "written in March, 1918, when we began to learn about the disaster on the Somme."[89] This poem had previously appeared in *New Paths, 1917-1918*, edited by C. W. Beaumont and M.T.H. Sadler, and published in London by Beaumont in 1918. Aldington refers to this book in his acknowledgment as "an annual of new literature." In corresponding with Harold Monro about some poems to be included in an anthology Monro was getting together, Aldington gave a list of his poems from which he wanted Monro to select. One of them was "The Blood of Young Men"; later, when Monro did not choose this poem, Aldington expressed his regret.[90]

I believe that Monro was right in choosing other poems over "The Blood of Young Men." The central idea of the poem is that the guilt and horror of war belong equally to the young men in the trenches and to the civilians at home. The poet makes his point by describing the blood of the soldiers as staining the home front as well as the battlefield:

> All the garments of all the people,
> All the wheels of all the traffic,
> All the cold indifferent faces,
> All the fronts of all the houses,
> All the stones of the street—
> Ghastly! Horribly smeared with blood-stains.

Essentially the weakness of the poem is that, as in the earlier "Living Sepulchres," too high a price is paid in shock value for the resultant revelation; today, especially, when most of us are only too aware of our guilt for the blood spilled by soldiers, the poem seems overwrought.

The third and final edition of Aldington's *Images of War* was published in the United States in 1921 by The Four Seas Company, which had previously published *Images Old and New*. This edition is an exact duplicate of the Allen and Unwin 1919 edition. The physical appearance of the book is the same, the acknowledgment and Contents are the same. That this American edition was produced from the same plates as the British one is suggested on the last page, which bears the notation "Printed in Great Britain by Unwin Brothers, Limited, Printers Woking and London."

Seven of Aldington's *Images of War* poems are printed on page 23 of *The Egoist*, Vol. 6, No. 2 (March-April 1919) with the following footnote: 'These poems are from two books which will appear in May: *Images of War* (12s. net), Beaumont Press, Charing Cross Road; and *Images of Desire* (2s. 6d. net), Elkin Mathews, Cork Street." One of the poems, however, "Doubt," while appearing in the Allen and Unwin edition, does *not* appear in the Beaumont edition. If even authors and editors confuse editions it is not surprising that bibliographers err.

As a final point in connection with *Images of War*, it is interesting to note that in *An Anthology of War Poems*, compiled by Frederick Brereton with an Introduction by Edmund Blunden (London: W. Collins Sons, 1930) and printed as a limited edition of 200 signed copies on hand-made paper, the following four Aldington poems from *Images of War* were included: "Bombardment," "Barrage," "Machine Guns," and "A Moment's Interlude."

Along with the two English versions of *Images of War*, the year 1919 also saw the printing of *Images of Desire*, the volume of love poems published by Elkin Mathews. This little booklet of thirty-nine pages has a paper cover of smooth, red stock of the same weight as the interior pages. The cover is printed in black with the title and author's name above the publisher's trademark, which is a medallion containing the Latin phrase "Fructus Inter Folia" and the initials "EM"; beneath the medallion are two lines: "London/ Elkin Mathews, Cork Street." The title page repeats the front cover, except that the date MCMXIX appears at the bottom and the following quotation is substituted for the medallion:

> . . . le peuple des hommes ne pense que des pensées déjà exhalées, ne sent que des sentiments déjà usés et des sensations fanées comme de vieux gants.
>
> Remy de Gourmont.

The acknowledgment is printed on page [4] :

> Some of these poems have already been printed in the following periodicals:—*Egoist, Art and Letters, Sphere, To-Day* and *Poetry*, and my thanks are due to their several editors for permission to reprint them.

The contents are printed on pages 5 and 6 as follows: "Dedication, Prelude, An Old Song, Epigrams, Possession, An Interlude, Ella, Her Mouth, Portrait, Daybreak, Sleep, Reserve, Images of Desire, Before Parting, Prayer, Loss, A Soldier's Song, Absence, Gain, Cynthia, The Winter Park, Meditation, Odelette, Epilogue." On page [39] the printers are indicated: "The Riverside Press Limited, Edinburgh."

Writing in August of 1919, Mary Butts sums up a review of the little book of love poems in these words:

But in the epilogue the most sincere and competent poet of his group has summarized with an emotional sincerity that gives beauty, his realisation that this is a very bad universe whose chief mitigation is love. It is something to say of love poetry that there is not a poem in the book which has not the same quality of sincerity.[91]

F. S. Flint says of this volume: "*Images of Desire* is a book of love-poems, in which the human and fallible passion of love is exalted as the only sanction for the weariness of human existence."[92] Professor Hughes adds: "Apart from their emotional content these poems are interesting to us because they indicate Aldington's transition from pure imagism to a less prescribed technique."[93]

The twenty-four poems of *Images of Desire* are probably more homogeneous than those in any of Aldington's other books of poetry. The moods vary, but they are all a lover's moods: he is lonely, he is jealous, he is far from his mistress, he is afraid to lose her love. We are conscious that a soldier is writing these poems, but war does not intrude as it does in the previous volume.

"Prelude," the first poem after the introductory "Dedication," expresses the lover's usual complaint that he cannot give his beloved such gifts as she deserves:

Alas, how poor the gifts that lovers give—
I can but give you of my flesh and strength,
I can but give you these few passing days
And passionate words that since our speech began
All lovers whisper in all women's ears.

A fine stanza from "An Interlude" recalls the last lines of Wordsworth's "The World Is Too Much with Us":

I wait,
And glide upon the crested surge of days
Like some sea-god, with tangled, dripping beard
And smooth hard skin, who glimpses from the sea
An earth-girl naked by the long foam fringe,
And, utterly forgetting all his life,
Hurries toward her, glad with sudden love.

The short poem "Sleep" illustrates Aldington's ability to deal with conventional prosody:

Ah, it were good to cease and die
    So sweet a way,
Never to waken from our bed
    To the chill day,
But sleep for ever in a dream,

> Head beside head,
> Warm in a golden swoon of love—
> Divinely dead.

This poem has a sexual connotation, deriving from the Elizabethan equation of death and the consummation of love.

The ninth stanza of "Images of Desire," the title poem, suggests Byron's unconventional ideas of love:

> Earth of the earth, body of the earth,
> Flesh of our mother, life of all things,
> A flower, a bird, a rock, a tree,
> Thus I love you, sister and lover,
> Would that we had one mother indeed
> That we might be bound closer by shame.

First the poet sees his beloved, like himself, as a child of earth, a relationship which makes them both lovers and siblings. This metaphor suggests the wish that they were brother and sister in fact, so that, like Byron and Augusta, their love could be intensified by its guilt.

The second stanza of "Before Parting" tells of the intensification of love that the war brings the poet and his mistress:

> Tonight there shall be no tears, no wearing sorrow,
> No drawn-out agony of hope, no cold despairing,
> Only we two together in a sudden glory
> Of infinite delight and sharp sweet yearning,
> Shutting out for a space the world's harsh horror.

These lines, and the whole of *Images of Desire*, express a philosophy of life very close to Arnold's in the last stanza of "Dover Beach." In "Epilogue," the poem to which Mary Butts refers in her review and which Alec Waugh calls "one of his most quoted poems,"[94] Aldington sums up this volume of his poetry and gives even fuller expression to his humanism:

> But we who do not drug ourselves with lies
> Know, with how deep a pathos, that we have
> Only the warmth and beauty of this life
> Before the blankness of the unending gloom.

This is one of Aldington's key poems and I will return to it later when I attempt a final evaluation of the man and his work.

Images of Desire is, I believe, one of Aldington's best volumes of poetry because, like *Reverie* and *Myrrhine and Konallis*, it deals with the "life of sensations." In this type of poetry lies Aldington's great strength, and, indeed, that of all those artists who find value only in "the warmth and beauty of this life."

The year 1919 was Aldington's *annus mirabilis* for the publication of his poetry.[95] The fourth volume published that year is the one planned first: *War and Love (1915-1918)*, issued by The Four Seas Company in Boston. In a foreword addressed to F. S. Flint, Aldington says in part:

> Like "Images" this little book comes out of conflict, but whereas the former conflict was of the spirit here it is of the flesh. "Images" consisted of short-hand notes, as it were, to illustrate the moods of a spirit torn between the beauty one imagines and the ugliness that is thrust upon one. . . . Here I have written . . . more for the kind of men I lived with in camp and in the line . . . this is a book by a common soldier for common soldiers.

Aldington adds that the conflict expressed in these later poems is that between the delight of the flesh and the agony of the flesh. He speaks of the second part of the book as articulating "a yearning of the flesh, a wild grasping for life" and adds that "the passion of love becomes almost unendurable in its piercing beauty." This foreword is dated February 1918, indicating how early this book was planned.

A note gives the following information about the poems that make up the volume:

> A few of these poems have appeared in books and periodicals, as follows: *Some Imagist Poets*, 1917 (Houghton Mifflin Co., & Constable); *New Paths* (1918) C. W. Beaumont London; *Reverie*, 1917, Privately printed, Cleveland, Ohio; *The Dial; The Seven Arts; The Egoist*.

Though the book seems to have come off the press later than the British editions, Aldington evidently conceived it before *Images of War* and *Images of Desire*, because on 2 January 1918 he wrote Amy Lowell:

> I am thinking of collecting all my war poems—I have about 60 or 70—into a book. . . . They are not popular— I mean they are bitter, anguish-stricken, realistic, not like Brooke or Noyes or anybody like that. They are stern truth. . . .[96]

And on 8 February 1918 he wrote the Reverend Charles C. Bubb:

> I may be getting out a new book of poems soon—to be called "War & Love." They will be something like those in Reverie, but I shall include some of my more sombre war-poems—which I have refrained from publishing—& include love poems which may perhaps shock people accustomed merely to conventional expressions of emotion.[97]

Later that year, on 12 July, the poet wrote Bubb of the two British editions:

Beaumont is printing one half of my new book under the title of "Images of War." If that is successful he will print the second half under the title of "Images of Love." The American edition which contains the whole book—about 60 poems—will be called just "War & Love."[98]

Of course "Images of Love" turned into *Images of Desire* and was not printed by Beaumont but by Elkin Mathews—possibly because of too many of the "misprints" of which Aldington wrote in the passage from his autobiography quoted earlier.

Aldington may have felt, because of his experiences with previous American publications, that it would be better for him to publish his war poems there first. As it happened, he was disappointed and continually wrote to Amy Lowell for help in expediting the publication of manuscripts placed with The Four Seas Company, and in collecting monies due him. He was even dissatisfied with the firm's marketing: Four Seas sold only 291 copies of *Images Old and New*, he says, and 211 of *War and Love* (when it was finally published), whereas *Images (1910-1915)* sold 650 copies in England and *Images of Desire* 300 copies in the first six months, why were American sales so small? he asked Miss Lowell.[99]

Although the publication of the British editions seems to have overlapped the appearance of the American *War and Love*, Aldington considered the latter volume the base work. On 8 December 1918 he wrote Amy Lowell:

I am going most carefully through the poems of "War & Love" & have rejected a number. Beaumont's edition of "Images of War" will contain only 26 poems & "Images of Desire" is down to four poems only since my drastic revision! I may re-write some of the others.[100]

The poems in *War and Love* are presented in two sections; Part I bears the simple title "War," and the epigraph:

They said that this mystery never shall cease:
The priest promotes war, and the solider peace.

                                                                    Blake

An analysis of the contents of Part I indicates that it is made up of one poem from the 1916 *Some Imagist Poets*, "People" (but here called "Civilians"), two poems from the 1917 *Some Imagist Poets*, "Prayer" and "Captive"; all of the twenty-seven poems of the Beaumont limited edition of *Images of War* (though, because of a typographical error on the contents page, "Battlefield" is listed as "Rattle-Field"), eleven poems of the expanded Allen and Unwin edition of *Images of War*: "Leave-taking, Bondage, A Moment's Interlude, The Wine Cup, The Lover, April Lieder, Misery, Time's Changes, Disdain, Doubt, The Blood of Young Men"; and three poems not previously published in book form: "Genius Loci, The Faun Complains, Defeat."

Part II is titled "Love" and is preceded by the epigraph:

Amor si dolce mi sa fa sentire
Che, s'io allora non perdessi ardire,
Farei, parlando, innamorar la gente

Dante

This section contains fourteen of the twenty-four poems used in the *Images of Desire* book: "Prelude, An Old Song, Possession, An Interlude, Before Parting, Prayer, Images of Desire, Absence, Her Mouth, Daybreak, Sleep, A Soldier's Song, Gain, Epilogue"; and four poems not elsewhere published in book form: "Song, Song for Her, Nights of Love, Epilogue." The second "Epilogue" is a different poem from the first.

In May of 1919 an anonymous reviewer in *The Dial* said of Aldington's *War and Love*:

> Whatever he has lost of the cold fire and chiseled form of the Images is richly returned in a warmer passion, a new humanity. Always the honest artist, he is now the honest reporter of war—and of love in war-time, though it drives him to meter and rhyme and an intensification of sex that recalls Donne. There is an ecstasy and exquisite suffering in these poems, but not sentimentality. The war has produced no more genuine poetry.[101]

In September of the same year Marjorie Allen Seiffert in *Poetry* gave a considerably less favorable review of *War and Love*. She particularly disliked the war poems:

> . . . he does not make great poetry, and he fails of being understood by the audience for which he is writing [i e., his fellow soldiers] . . . . The clearest cry of the spirit reaches ears we imagine to be deaf. But the war poems in this book are only bitter, muffled plaints of rebellion. . . . Aldington's genius could not use the crude, painful and bitter experiences he was made to undergo. Not many poets have been able to mould into beauty such material.[102]

An anonymous reviewer in *The American Review of Reviews* wrote one month later:

> "War and Love," by Richard Aldington, lieutenant in the British Army, contains the finest poetry of its kind published since the war. As a whole, the poems enclose one principal truth, namely, that in the final issue flesh and spirit are one and indivisible. Lieutenant Aldington has written the thoughts and emotions of the infantrymen of the line. . . . He offers this book as a memoir of two years of the war. In every poem of the collection one feels the maturity of his genius, the widening and deepening of his poetic power.[103]

Aldington's own view of the poems that make up this volume is interesting:

Some people like the poems I wrote in the trenches, others hint that they are badly written. I can't help feeling that this is a true criticism. Often I had no real time to put down what I wanted and it is now too late to tinker with these poems.[104]

Surely we ought to judge this passage as too self-critical, especially when we consider that not only all of the poems of this volume but the *Myrrhine and Konallis* poems were written in France. However, his suggestion that "it is now too late to tinker with these poems" is revealing. Yeats "tinkered" with his poems all his life; possibly Aldington felt that he wrote best at the moment of inspiration. Later, writing to Amy Lowell, the poet had some second thoughts on his war poems:

Personally I think I have lost a delicacy of technique, a sureness of form, but that I've gained a wider outlook & a more direct appeal to people who are not enthusiasts for poetry. . . . I've written honestly what I've seen, what I've felt. There is no lie, no sort of pose in the book.[105]

One poem in this collection reflects with particular appropriateness the despair the poet feels as a result of his war experience. "Doubt" expresses the poet's fear that the hostility of the world is too much for the strength of man:

Can we, by any strength of ours
Thrust back this hostile world
That tears us from ourselves,
As a child from the womb,
A weak lover from light breasts?

But if from somewhere man were able to gather the strength to "hurl back this menace on itself":

Why, it would be as if some tall god
Unburdened of his age-long apathy,
Took in his hand the thin horn of the moon
And set it to his lips
And blew sharp wild shrill notes
Such as our hearts, our lonely hearts,
Have yearned for in the dumb bleak silences.

The poem, however, ends on a note of despair:

Ah! Weak as wax against their bronze are we,
Ah! Faint as reed-pipes by the water's roar,
And driven as land-birds by the vast sea wind.

The desperateness of the human condition, which Aldington only began to glimpse in some of the final poems of the early *Images* has been brought home to the poet by his two years in the war. To resolve his position Aldington must find value in something or someone outside life, or else he must commit himself fully to some form of humanism, the path of his poetry seems to lead in the latter direction.

In *The Egoist* of July 1919 the following appears under the heading "Announcements":

> Later in July we are publishing, under the title *Images*, a collection of poems by our former assistant editor, Mr. Richard Aldington. The book will include the poems printed in *Images* (published in 1915 by the Poetry Bookshop, and now out of print), and in four Imagist anthologies (1914, 1915, 1916, and 1917), and a few not yet published in any book. The price will be 3s. 6d. net (by post 3s. 9d.).[106]

An enclosed leaflet contained particulars of a new set of the "Poets' Translation Series" also being issued. This issue of *The Egoist* was printed by a new printer, Pelican Press, whose work was obviously inferior to that of the former printer, The Complete Press. Two numbers later, in December 1919, on pages 70 and 71, *The Egoist* announced its demise as a journal. The problems of *Ulysses* were discussed and the decision reached to concentrate henceforth on book production. New publications announced included two more numbers in the Poets' Translation Series, one of which was *The Latin Poets of the Renaissance [sic]*, translated by Richard Aldington. The last page of this last issue advertised Aldington's *Images* and the Poets' Translation Series, including his contributions. So died *The Egoist*, one of the best friends of Aldington and of all the artists of this decade.

Images (London: The Egoist, Ltd., 1919) is not an attractive volume. Its boards are covered with dark brown paper and the back is bound with a tan cloth. On the cover the title and author's name are tabbed on, as is the title on the spine. The copy I have seen is a signed one, number 39.

There is a note opposite the contents page which reads as follows:

> These poems are taken from "Images" (Published 1915 and now out of print), and the various Imagist anthologies which are also being allowed to lapse. I have rescued one or two poems from periodicals. There are also one or two newer poems which did not quite fit into my other two books.

This note is somewhat mystifying since the contents of *Images* are taken from *Images (1910-1915)*, *Images Old and New*, and the four Imagist anthologies, with the exception of just one new poem. It could be that, since *Images Old and New* was an American edition, Aldington considered it to be in a separate category and chose not to list it as one of the sources. In any event, the poems listed are now the same ones, in the same order, as in the "Images" section of *The Complete Poems*, except that the positions of "Cinema Exit" and "In the Tube" are reversed.

The final poem of *Images*, "The Faun Captive," the only one not taken from an earlier book, is one of Aldington's best. Aldington "rescued" it from *The Nation*, where it had been printed (in Vol. 25, No. 9, 31 May 1919, p. 265) under the title "The Captive Faun" with only two minor differences in punctuation. In the month after the appearance of *Images* it would be reprinted (and credited to *The Nation*) in *The Living Age*, Vol. 302 (9 August 1919), p. 384, with some eight differences in punctuation. Another interesting thing about "The Faun Captive" is that in terms of its probable composition date, it belongs with the *Images of War* poems; the fact that the poet chose to place it where he did is significant.

One of the reasons that the poem is successful is that it is able to integrate the idea and symbol so well. The captive faun is the speaker of the poem. He tells of the loss of his strength, which for a god "lies/ More in the fervour of his worshippers/ Than in his own divinity." He relates the story of his capture:

> I lay asleep under Zeus-holy oaks
> Heavy with syrupy wine and tired
> With the close embraces
> Of some sweet wearer of the leopard-skin—
> That noon they snared and bound me as I slept. . . .

The faun finds most intolerable the degradation of his capture:

> I that should have been dreaded in wan recesses,
> Worshipped in high woods, a striker of terror
> To the wayfarer in lonely places,
> I, lord of golden flesh and dim music,
> I, a captive and coarsely derided!

The faun dreams of "the gay life of the half-god/ Who had no dread of death or sorrow." He longs for the "wooded silences," "the nymph-rapt hours," and the "clean brown streams." But he sees his captors growing careless and promises that one night he will break his thongs and "kill, kill, kill in sharp revenge" before escaping "to the wild-rose kisses of the deathless girls."

The emotion that the poem develops is valid both on the level of the faun and on the level of the poet. Civilization has torn both from everything they hold dear and is subjecting them to everything they hate. Standing at the dividing point between the *Images* and *Images of War* poems—at that period in the poet's life when his youthful struggle between Greek dream and present reality must give way to a total immersion in the most sordid and horrible reality—"The Faun Captive" is both a fine poem and a significant statement. Its most important line is, "But one night I shall break these thongs." We may imagine that the faun did break them; part of our business will be to determine if the poet did. .

After being busy, for a year or so following his demobilization, with the various 1919 books discussed above, Aldington began to tire of London[107] and to think "longingly of a country cottage, with woods and fields and the quiet sky and the immortal company of great books." The quotation is from *Life for Life's Sake*, in which he goes on to say (pp. 228-229):

> But when I came to look for a country cottage I found to my dismay that they were, if possible, even more difficult to obtain then apartments in London. . . .
>   I had almost resigned myself to a dreary existence of rented rooms in London when unexpectedly Lawrence turned up on his way to Italy and offered to hand over his cottage. It was in a place romantically called Hermitage, in Berkshire. In my then state of mind you could have offered me nothing more attractive than a hermitage, and I accepted the offer without seeing the place. However, it was a safe bet, because Lawrence and Frieda were adepts at finding cheap places in beautiful surroundings.

After living in the Hermitage a short while, Aldington moved to another cottage about fifteen miles away in the valley of the Kennet, in Berkshire. In the course of describing his life there he says in the autobiography (p. 246):

> I suppose I must admit that the valley of the Kennet *is* tame and domestic, but it has the charm of pastoral poetry. If I didn't think it offensive for a man to quote his own verses, I should be tempted to cite some octosyllabic verses I wrote on this theme.

The poem to which he refers is the 108-line *The Berkshire Kennet*, which was published in London by The Curwen Press in 1923.

The limited edition of this single poem is one of the tiniest of Aldington's publications. It has a parchment cover printed with a brown weave design resembling burlap, and a tipped-on title-and-author label. A loose bookplate bearing the name of Holbrook Jackson and portraying a Roman charioteer is inserted inside the cover. The title page repeats the cover label, with the addition of "London 1923" at the bottom and a fancy rule that encloses all the words on the page. The verso of the title page reads: "Of fifty copies, printed on hand-made paper for HOLBROOK JACKSON by the CURWEN PRESS, this is No. 44 [number in ink]." There are only eight pages of deckle-edged, cream-colored laid paper in this little booklet, on the next to last of which is printed: "The Berkshire Kennet first appeared in *To-Day*, September, 1923" (No. 55, Vol. 10, pp. 27-29). In accordance with Aldington's policy of printing his poems, whenever possible, in periodicals of both England and the United States, the poem also appeared in *The Yale Review*, Vol. n.s. 13, No. 1 (October 1923), pp. 81-84, under the title "The River Kennet." The epigraph from Drayton's *Polyolbion* — "Amongst his hills and holts, as on his way he makes/ At Reading once arrived, clear Kennet overtakes/ His lord, the stately Thames" — appears in the book but was not used in the periodicals.

There was also a special printing of *The Berkshire Kennet* by The Peacocks Press of Hurst, near Reading in Berkshire. It is undated but was received by Lockwood Memorial Library (State University of New York at Buffalo) in December of 1955. This printing consists of a sheet of folded gray bond paper on which is the notation: "Printed in an edition of 310 copies, by kind permission of the author and Sir Stanley Unwin, for distribution to selected customers and friends by G. F. Sims (Rare Books)."

The poem is pleasant pastoral poetry that illustrates Aldington's ability to work in the forms of the earlier centuries. After the extreme stress of the war, the seven years that the poet was able to spend in the valley of the Kennet were exactly what his troubled spirit needed.[108]

> O solitude, O innocent peace,
> Silence, more precious than the Fleece
> That Jason and his fellows sought,
> Our greatest riches though unbought,
> And hard to find and ill to praise
> In noisy and mechanic days!
> Yet in these humble meadows they
> Have cleansed the wounds of war away,
> And brought to my long troubled mind
> The health that I despaired to find,
> And, while their touch eased the pain,
> Breathed the old raptures back again
> And in their kindness gave to me
> Almost that vanished purity.

"The Berkshire Kennet" was included in the volume *Exile and Other Poems* also published in 1923. The dust jacket of this first British volume of Aldington's verse to appear in four years is a brown kraft printed in red. It reads: "Exile/ and Other Poems/ Richard Aldington/ *Limited Edition*/ London: George Allen & Unwin Ltd./ Ruskin House, 40 Museum Street, W.C.I." The inside front flap is printed in red with the lines "Cash Price in Great Britain/ Five Shillings Net." The back of the dust jacket lists "New and Forthcoming Poetry," including "The Temple: And Other Poems. Translated by Arthur Waley, with an introductory essay on Early Chinese Poetry and an Appendix on the development of Different Metrical Forms." The face of the dust jacket is enclosed in a stock printed border.

The cover of the volume is blue cloth over boards, printed in gold with the lines "Exile/ Richard Aldington" on the face and spine. On page [4] are listed the three principal English editions of poetry "By the Same Author," along with *Literary Studies and Reviews*, which is said to be "in preparation." The title page, number [5], repeats the dust jacket exactly, except that the border is omitted and a medallion replaces "*Limited Edition*"; the medallion is an intricate design used as a trademark by the publishers. Page [6] gives publication information and page [7] the usual acknowledgment: "These poems have appeared in the following periodicals: *The Yale Review, The Dial, Literary Review, Poetry, To-Day, The Monthly Chapbook*. Acknowledgment is made to the editors." Page [8] indicates that the edition is limited to 750 copies.

The book's contents are listed on pages 9 and 10 and are divided into two parts: "Exile" and "Words for Music." The first part shows exactly the same poems, listed in the same order, as in the "Exile" section of *The Complete Poems*, except that the poem "The Parrot" does not appear. The "Words for Music" section (some ten years later Yeats was to use a similar title) lists the individual "Songs for Puritans" by Roman numerals I to X; the "Songs for Sensualists" are listed by name, and another poem, "From Tasso," appears. The two longer poems, "The Berkshire Kennet" and "A Winter Night," are listed under the heading, "Metrical Exercises."

The first letter of each poem is a three-line capital, and the remaining letters of all the first words are capitalized. The paper of this 1923 edition is whiter and of a much better quality than that of *The Complete Poems*.

Again the contemporary appraisals from the back of Aldington's *Literary Studies and Reviews* are interesting:

> Impeccable in craftsmanship. . . . A book of poetry worthy of the highest commendation. *Morning Post.*
>
> His beautiful waterpiece, "The Berkshire Kennet" . . . glides on with an admirable solacing strength. . . . This is the poet who can drive away our pains and lead beside still waters. . . . Mr. Aldington's "Words for Music" and "Metrical Exercises" already represent perfections of picture and harmony. *Times.*
>
> The main part is in rhymed verse and of a quality which should silence all who believe that free verse is written only by those who are incompetent in rhyme. *Spectator.*
>
> Poems are wrought with the craftsman's skill. . . . One of the few books of poetry published this year that is likely to matter. *Aberdeen Press and Journal.*

Professor Hughes's views were written eight years after the poetry's publication. Of the volume generally he says:

> This book, though small, contains three sections. The first is composed of poems chiefly in free verse and blank verse, all of them voicing the disillusionment and despair which besieged the poet in the post-war days, when memories of horror were still fresh, and when it seemed impossible to make a readjustment of life along the lines of peace.[109]

Of the title poem Aldington said in 1933: "Who, for example, would know that 'Exile' was intended (in 1919) to express a contrast between brutal Nationalism and an ideal of civilization and culture?"[110] The epigraph to this poem, *"Do you dwell on the snowy promontory of Mimas?,"* is addressed to the goddess of "civilization and culture." She is contrasted with the one worshipped by the "Alien, brutish/ Base seed of Earth's ravished womb"; the latter goddess is

A boastful woman, a whore,
One greasy of flesh, stale
With hot musty perfume—
While ours—

> Firm-fleshed as the treeless hills
> With her rigid breasts and hard thighs,
> Cold and perfect and fresh—
> Fields crisp with new frost—
> Sets the violet-crown in her hair,
> Turns an unstained brow to the sky.

Without the cue from the poet it is true that one could not translate the metaphor into an opposition so specific as the one that he suggests was in his mind when he wrote the poem. However, it is not difficult to see clearly in the poem the old opposition between the real and the ideal. The contrast of "Church Walk, Kensington" is still evident in this later poem, and its tension is still as unresolved.

In "Eumenides" the poet tries to decide exactly what is troubling him. He recalls the way he has tried to live calmly during the months since the end of the war, and tells us that it has been to no avail; the horrors of the war cannot be dismissed. He attempts to answer the question "What is it I agonize for?":

> The dead? They are quiet;
> They can have no complaint.
> No, it is my own murdered self—
> A self which has its passion for beauty,
> Some moment's touch with immortality—
> Violently slain, which rises up like a ghost
> To torment my nights,
> To pain me.
> It is myself that is the Eumenides . . . .

This is one of the poems that Aldington hoped Harold Monro might include in his anthology.[111] Possibly Monro was wise to select, as he did, the poem "Interlude" instead. There is something in "Eumenides" that touches on self-pity. As with the earlier "Childhood," a greater degree of objectivity could have made "Eumenides" a much better poem.

Some of the best poems in this volume are those that draw their subject and strength from the Berkshire countryside. "At a Gate by the Way" presents a graphic picture of the poet and a friend looking over rolling fields in the fall:

> Stand here a moment, friend,
> And look across the silent garnered fields;
> See how they turn like huge-limbed country gods,
> Their labour ended to a solemn rest. . . .

The speaker compares the "labour" of the fields with that of his friend and himself:

> The shadows we pursue may not be shadows,
> The dreams we live with may be more than dreams . . .
> All this I hope; but when the autumn comes
> And heavy carts sway loaded to the barns,
> And swallows gather to be gone, and rooks
> Flock to the fields for scattered grain,
> O friend, I am filled with musing and distrust,
> So poor my harvest to this golden wealth,
> So teased my spirit to this opulent peace.

The poem is satisfying because it deals with the temptation which many writers feel at one time or another to yield to the blandishments of nature, fit in with the rhythm of her cycles, and desert the "hunters of truth and wisdom."

Of the "Words for Music" section of *Exile and Other Poems* Aldington has this to say:

> The rhymed pieces at the end were really metrical exercises, arising partly from the conviction that I needed to steep myself in English poetry again after so long an exile—the choice of Waller and Marvell as models was quite fortuitous—and partly from the fact that short poems were no longer adequate to express what I wanted to say.[112]

Professor Hughes comments:

> All these poems are exquisitely modeled upon seventeenth-century patterns, and one hears in them the scarcely disguised accents of Herrick and Carew. They contain little originality, but they testify to the virtuosity of their author.[113]

The ten "Songs for Puritans" are mostly in iambic tetrameter with various rhyme schemes. They are very reminiscent of the Cavalier poets and are delightfully sensuous. May Sinclair said of Aldington that "he should have ben born some centuries B.C.; been young when Sappho or Anyte of Tegea were young";[114] these poems show that he might have been content in the court of Charles II. We should not be surprised at Aldington's facility with this type of poetry. He writes:

> The reader may be amused to know that between the ages of fifteen and eighteen I produced a mass of "poems" at least twice the size of this book. . . . No doubt they had no more serious basis than the desire to reproduce the poetry I had read with such intense delight, but at least they provided a certain discipline in the study of metrical form. I tried my hand at everything from blank verse and rhymed couplets to Spenserian stanzas, ballades, sirventes and villanelles, with fatal facility.[115]

As Professor Hughes suggests, the "Songs for Puritans" are reminiscent of Herrick and Carew:

> But when that rose-tipped breast I see,
> Or the white splendour of your knee,
> I covet a more precious fleece
> Than ever Jason brought to Greece.

The "Songs for Sensualists"[116] (both titles are satiric) sound more like Marvell, whom Aldington himself mentioned as a model, although in this one the idea belongs to Shakespeare's sonnets:

> If all my senses still conspire,
>   Ere their meridian be past,
> To set the blossoms of desire,
>   The worm shall not exult at last;
> Her children and my words I trust
> Shall speak her grace when we are dust.

Of the two poems in the "Metrical Exercises" division of "Words for Music"—"The Berkshire Kennet" and "A Winter Night"—Glenn Hughes says:

> Both are written in rimed couplets, in rather an eighteenth-century manner, and both are in praise of country life. Apart from their intrinsic beauty they are interesting because of their biographical and psychological significance.[117]

Just as he described in the first of these poems the pleasures of the summer countryside, the poet celebrates in "A Winter Night" the joys of the warm hearth, his "noble books," and "Eliza's wits." Aldington was wise to consider these poems as "exercises." They are very pleasing—very well executed—but they are openly imitative and not representative of his own work. The entire "Words for Music" section of *Exile and Other Poems* has its greatest value as proof that Aldington was perfectly competent to write in the traditional styles, though he chose instead to develop his own way of writing poetry. As he tells us himself:

> At length I grew disgusted with copying and (influenced by Greek Choruses and, strangely enough, Henley) began to write what I called "rhythms," i.e., unrhymed pieces with no formal metrical scheme where the rhythm was created by a kind of inner chant. Was this merely the result of a surfeit of formal meter? Possibly, though I still think it was a legitimate development *after* considerable practice with the traditional forms.[118]

Certainly this should indicate how silly were the charges made by some critics of the Imagists, to the effect that the practitioners of free verse wrote in that manner because they could not meet the requirements of traditional forms.

The Four Seas Company published an American edition of *Exile and Other Poems*, limited to 750 copies, in Boston in 1924. Its contents are in all respects identical to those of the 1923 British edition.

On 22 September 1924, Richard Aldington wrote Harriet Monroe of *Poetry* a letter which was to be his last to her for ten years. In this letter he tells about his newest book of poetry:

> At the same time Allen and Unwin will publish a 1400 lines poem (chiefly in vers libres) by me called "A Fool i' the Forest; A Phantasmagoria." It is not to be published anywhere in periodicals—or I would have sent it to you— but will be sprung as a surprise, since it is a new departure. Only four people besides myself and the publisher have seen it . . . and all agree it is by far the best thing I have done.[119]

In 1925 Aldington's long poem *A Fool i' the Forest: A Phantasmagoria* was published. The dust jacket of this edition was a heavy, ribbed (Swedish) kraft printed with one color, red. The face is printed with the title, author's name, and publisher; the spine is printed with the title and author's name. The back of the dust jacket advertises "The Works of J.M. Synge" in a four-volume "New Collected Edition" and an eight-volume "Pocket Edition." The inside of the front flap reads:

> In this fantasy, under the guise of a fantastic pilgrimage with symbolical characters, Mr. Aldington mirrors the spiritual disarray and mental incoherence of our time. We are shown, in fantastic quickly changing vignettes, like the illogical pictures of a dream, the contest between the ideals of the old Art civilization and the new Trade civilization.
>
> The piece changes from vers libre to hexameters, from quatrains to rag-time, is satiric, ironic, lyric and tragic, runs from the merest fooling to passages of intense meditation, such as the tragic brooding over sleeping London. The poem breaks through many conventional boundaries but it is held into a sort of unity by the philosophical ideas behind it.

I have quoted this in full because it was undoubtedly written by or with the approval of Aldington and thus is a good guide to his intentions in the poem.

This volume is bound in green cloth over boards. It is embossed in gold with the title and author's name; the spine is embossed in gold with the title and "Aldington." The book size is approximately five by eight inches. On page [5], following the title page, is the epigraph from *As You Like It* (II, vii, 12) "A fool! a fool! I met a fool i' the forest." The "Note" on page [7] includes a one-sentence paragraph that does not appear in *The Complete Poems*: "Several quotations are woven into the piece; the two longest are from Aristophanes and Anatole France."

The American edition of *A Fool i' the Forest: A Phantasmagoria* was published in New York, in 1925, by Lincoln MacVeagh, The Dial Press. Since the sheets were printed in Great Britain by Unwin Brothers, this edition is identical with the British one except for the title page. Even the binding is the same, except that in some cases margins may have been trimmed; I have seen a finished book about three-and-a-half by eight inches in size as well as one in the same size as the British edition.

In *Life for Life's Sake* Aldington tells of his mental state when he wrote *A Fool*. He writes of expending "a good deal of nervous and emotional energy" (p. 292), and says that "the writing of this poem had been accompanied by moods of depression which were quite alarming" (p. 295).

McGreevy comments as follows:

> During these years also he published one long poem called *A Fool i' the Forest*, but as it is a statement in ideal terms of the theme of post-war disillusionment that was treated more realistically and elaborately in *Death of a Hero*, it does not call for detailed analysis here. One may, however, note the Shakespearian influence in some of the outstanding passages. . . . There is a Lear-like bitterness, for instance, in the dismissal of Scaramouche, the professional jester . . . and there are obvious echoes from Ophelia's song in the beautiful lament for Byron.
> . . .

Mr. McGreevy also suggests that "Mr. Aldington, though as a literary temperament he is almost the complete opposite of Mr. Eliot, shows in at least one short passage in *A Fool i' the Forest* that he has been reading *The Waste Land* and *Cousin Harriet* as well as Sappho and Byron."[120]

Glenn Hughes, too, sees a connection with *The Waste Land*:

> In fact, it has already been remarked by critics that *A Fool i' the Forest* owes much to *The Waste Land*. Humbert Wolfe's comment is that "Aldington . . . could only see life darkly in T. S. Eliot's looking-glass." But he adds that "that half-glimpse was worth the whole of the Imagist philanderings with verse which was only free in the sense that a bolting horse is free." His point is that in this poem the poet has allowed life itself to dedicate form, whereas in the earlier imagist poems an attempt was made to impose order upon a living organism. I cannot entirely agree with this generalization, but I do agree that *A Fool i' the Forest* is Aldington's finest poetic achievement.[121]

In his preface to *Death of a Hero* (p. x) Aldington writes to Halcott Glover:

> The technique of this book, if it can be said to have one, is that which I evolved for myself in writing a longish modern poem (which you liked) called "A Fool i' th' Forest." Some people said that was "jazz poetry"; so I suppose this is a jazz novel. You will see how appropriate that is to the theme.

And in a contemporary review of the poem in *The Criterion*, Humbert Wolfe says: "Why shouldn't poetry happen the same way, with a snatch of tune running through, and binding together buses, voices, fiddling beggars, guardsmen, churchgoers and their church?"[122]

And reviewing the 1929 *Collected Poems*, Harriet Monroe, in her article "An Imagist at War," recalls *Poetry*'s first exciting years and the young

Imagist movement, and comments on Aldington's latest poem:

> *A Fool i' the Forest* has been catalogued with the *Waste Land* as a
> revelation of civilization defeating itself and destroying with its own
> excess the spirit of man. . . . On the whole, he has followed with fair
> consistency the stern principles under which he and other imagists
> began their revolution nearly seventeen years ago.[123]

I do not agree with Professor Hughes that *A Fool i' the Forest* is
Aldington's "finest poetic achievement," but it is a fine poem. As for its
similarity to *The Waste Land*, this does not seem so important today, when
we have seen a whole half-century of poetry which could be described in the
same way. It was only because Aldington's poem appeared so soon after
Eliot's that the family likeness was noticeable; now that we are down to the
great-grandchildren it is much less apparent.

In his "Note" Richard Aldington clarifies his "phantasmagoria" by
telling us of the symbolic nature of the three speaking characters. They are
one person split into three: the "I" is a typical man of "our own time";
Mezzetin symbolizes the imaginative faculties—art, youth, satire, irresponsible
gaiety, liberty; the Conjuror symbolizes the intellectual faculties—age,
science, righteous cant, solemnity, and authority.

After its two introductory sections (all of the sections are named,
which is a helpful quality) *A Fool i' the Forest* has three settings: the
Acropolis in Greece, the battlefields of France, and London. There are a
number of dream sequences, including "The Vision of Hell" and "The
Church," in the latter of which the characters wander about, lost in a desert.
The poem is about the human condition, as Aldington saw it in the immedi-
ate post-World War I years. In a sense *A Fool i' the Forest* is an expansion of
the short poem "Exile," which itself was a restatement of the problem of
Aldington's earliest work—the age-old attempt to resolve the real and the
ideal.

It will be recalled that in the *Exile and Other Poems* volume of two
years earlier (and even in some of the later *Images of War* poems), the poet
laments what in "Eumenides" he refers to as his "own murdered self." In the
central twenty-sixth poem of *A Fool*, the Conjuror murders Mezzetin, in
effect, by exposing him to German shell fire; later the "I" character pitches
the Conjuror off London Bridge and settles down to become "a loyal English
husband" with three children—John, James, and Mary—and a fourth on the
way. Aldington is writing, as Eliot was, about the miserable position into
which modern man has gotten himself. Both are lamenting the loss of what
Aldington, in discussing "Exile," called an "ideal of civilization and culture."
But additionally, for Aldington, there is the personal reference. Like the three
characters in *A Fool*, the poet spent a considerable period of his life in a
"visit" to Greece; and he thought that some part of him, which he symbolizes
here by Mezzetin, had been "murdered" in France. As for the ending, possi-
bly Aldington thought that the Everyman of the poem might retreat to be-
coming a dissatisfied "loyal English husband," but I am sure he did not ex-
pect this of himself.

There are some interesting incidental and topical references in *A Fool*. After the war Aldington had dinner with Sir John Ellerman, reputed to be one of the richest men in England. Over port, Sir John complained to the poet about the hardships of civilians during the recent war: "it appeared that among other horrors the government had only allowed him one ton of coal a week from his own mines" (*Life for Life's Sake*, p. 212). This must have made quite an impression on Aldington, for besides mentioning it in his auto-biography he remembered it in the first verse of poem 30:

> Once we met a wealthy tradesman,
> Strong and cruel as an Assyrian King.
> The Conjuror said something about soldiers' hardships;
> But the rich man caught him up:
> "Hardships? We had hardships, too, in England.
> One winter—can it be believed?—the government
> Rationed my coal, allowed me only one ton a week,
> Coal from my own mines too."

Then there are the lines that may have annoyed one of England's senior poets:

> Then he quoted some insulting verses
> With a lot of "ifs" and ended
> With his favorite piece of cant:
> "We'll make a man of you, my son,
> Now Mezzetin is dead".

In her "Bibliography of Hours Press Publications" Nancy Cunard describes Aldington's next publication as follows:

> 1928
> Aldington, Richard. *Hark the Herald*. December. 5½ by 7½. 2 pp.
> 100 hand-set, signed copies, Vergé de Rives, 17 pt. Caslon Old Face.
> Mary blue wrappers. Title in gold letters on front wrapper. A present
> to the author; not for sale.

Miss Cunard remembers its printing:

> . . . an urgent request came from Richard Aldington, whom I had met
> in Rome for the first time the previous October, for 150 copies of a
> special Christmas message he wished to send to his friends. Somehow I
> managed to set the type for *Hark the Herald*, which was Aldington's
> title, print the 150 copies, and return them to him in time for
> Christmas mailings. Though no doubt capable of offending many, the
> little "satire on Christmas greetings," which Aldington called it, was
> amusing and succeeded, in his words, in "getting rid of a lot of rather
> tiresome acquaintances."[124]

Hark the Herald is printed on a single sheet of paper, on the verso of which the publication data are given. On the copy I have seen, after the words "This is number" the phrase "2nd edition" is written in ink, indicating possibly that Aldington used these "cards" for two Christmases. On this copy the words "for Ralph Stevens" are written in ink after the words "Printed for." This thirty-three line poem may be found in Chapter 3 of Part II. It is a highly irreverent treatment of the virgin birth which manages to be amusing without being offensive. Aldington evidently did not take the poem seriously, since he did not include it in any of his collections, although he did reprint it in *Movietones* four years later. Like "Vates, the Social Reformer" from *Des Imagistes*, and quite a few others of his uncollected poems, it falls into the category of humorous poetry which he wrote for his own pleasure, or to amuse his friends, without any idea of its having value.

In 1929 The Hours Press, still at Chapelle-Réanville, Eure (it would move to Paris that winter), published Aldington's *The Eaten Heart*. This small book is described in the "Bibliography of Hours Press Publications" as follows:

1929
Aldington, Richard. *The Eaten Heart*. Late Winter. 7 by 11. 28 pp. 200 hand-set, signed copies, Cason-Montgolfier. 16pt. Caslon Old Face. Title on front, gilt lettering on green marble paper. £I Is.

I have examined two copies of this folio-sized volume. The smooth dark-green cover stock seems to have been printed in gold in a bubble design. Since pagination begins and ends with the single poem itself, there are only seventeen numbered pages. Following the title page [3], "The Legend of the Eaten Heart" is told on pages [5] and [6]. The paper is deckle-edged and may be hand-laid. On the recto of the unnumbered page before the flyleaf [27], is the following:

This is the fourth book
issued by the Hours Press
200 signed copies have been printed
and the type distributed.
This is No

My own copy of this volume shows the number "71" and Aldington's signature; the other copy I have seen was evidently a gift, since it is inscribed in the poet's hand (somewhat illegibly), "Hors Commerce, Sylvia Beach from Richard Aldington."

Nancy Cunard reminisces:

My edition of *The Eaten Heart* came out about a year and a half before his greatly acclaimed war novel, *Death of a Hero* appeared. [She is wrong here; both were issued in 1929.] All went smoothly with the production of *The Eaten Heart*, which was printed on handsome Haut Vidalon paper on the Mathieu press, which responded as well as with *St. George* to the in-octavo jésus format. . . . The binding of *The Eaten*

Heart was better in idea than in execution, for the gold lettering of the title did not stamp well on to the dark green marble paper boards. [This is quite correct, since on my copy the book's title and the author's name can scarcely be read.]

Miss Cunard's critical comments are interesting:

To reread certain works after they have lain for years in memory surrounded by admiration is sometimes to discover something as fresh and beautiful as at first reading. And this (although I had reread it several times after publication), is the case with Richard Aldington's long romantic, philosophical poem *The Eaten Heart*. . . . One proof of its excellence surely lies in the fact that it is as moving as when Aldington first gave it me to print.

She also comments on contemporary reviews:

But sales were steady and excellent, and I remember good reviews, such as this one from the *Morning Post*: "This profound poem on the true significance of true love is a worthy sequel and supplement to Donne's 'Ecstasy' and the poems on the same theme by Meredith, Coventry Patmore and Lascelles Abercrombie. It well deserves the fine format of the limited edition in which it appears."[125]

Professor Hughes describes this poem as

. . . a single piece of some three hundred lines of free verse, with a theme drawn from the medieval legend of the beautiful lady who is tricked by her husband into eating the heart of her slain troubadour lover. . . . The recurrent motif is the struggle of a romantic nature to adapt itself to the hardness and disillusionment of a deflowered age, a post-war, machine-governed world. The conclusion . . . is that the soul of the poet survives.[126]

It seems to me that this is an oversimplification of the poem. What the poet is attempting to deal with is the essential loneliness of human existence[127] and the possible alleviation of that loneliness by means of the love of another human being.

The poem begins by asking:

Under the reign of Mr. Bloom
When the loud machines beat on our minds,
. . . What do we know of love?

The poet differentiates between sex and love:

But I say there is more in all this
Than the delicate friction of two skins . . . .

Do you know you live in a prison?
Do you know your own loneliness?

This loneliness is defined as "only a vague mysterious yearning,/ A dim
malaise, a something wanting," which can be eased only by love.

Most lives are monologues, and so grow poorer;
But conceive the riches if the response is there,
. . . .
If there is some response, a reaching-out,
Either to the full extent of a lesser world
Or the partial extent of an equal or greater world,
There remains a poignant memory, a dream—
Laura or Beatrice.

In part V the poet contemplates what the postwar period has done to
the old Europe he and his generation knew. He feels that they have been right
in turning away from "The false idealities of the last age,"

But, gazing back at the old dead Europe,
I think perhaps there is one thing worth achieving—
Escape the fate of Philoctetes, the essential solitude,
Achieve release, so that one's total nature
At all points meets another's
Whereby life becomes positive and immeasurably enriched.

Then he tells "the old Provence tale of the Eaten Heart," to illustrate both
the kind of love that rescues from loneliness and the tragic response it will
bring if thwarted. There is no escape in any case from the final tragedy of life,
but this at least is positive tragedy:

We have lost or thrown away
The power to live in this positive intensity—
For if life is not a tragedy it is nothing.

And even if the release takes place
And the dialogue of the two natures is perfect,
Still, the end must be tragic. It is easy to see that.

In the final sections of the poem Aldington seems to attempt to under-
cut himself by denying his ability to say what he means. The poem, however,
speaks for itself; it gives the essential message of the humanist, of Arnold in
"Dover Beach," of all lonely men who have not been able to accept the solace
of a metaphysical belief: "love," the complete touching of two selves, will
make positive the inevitable tragedy.

Paul Schlueter, in his "Chronological Check List," shows an edition of
The Eaten Heart by William Heinemann Ltd., 1931. Neither C. P. Snow nor
Alister Kershaw shows this edition; both list instead a 1933 edition in Lon-
don by Chatto and Windus.[128] Since I was able to locate the latter volume
but not the former, Professor Schlueter's entry may well be a printer's error.

The cover of the 1933 Chatto and Windus limited edition consists of a
red printed abstract design on paper over boards; the same design appears on
front and back. The spine is covered with a maroon cloth printed in gold with
the title and the author's name. The contents page lists not only "The Eaten
Heart" poem but also eleven short poems, numbered simply I to XI, and the
poem "In Memory of Wilfred Owen," bringing the total number of pages up
to fifty, considerably more than the nineteen of the Hours Press edition. Most
of the short poems were originally printed in the *Imagist Anthology 1930*
under the title "Passages Toward a Long Poem." Since this anthology also
included "The Eaten Heart," this poem had three printings before it appeared
in the first collection: by itself in the 1929 Hours Press edition, as part of the
1930 anthology, and in the 1933 English edition.

There was also a "popular" edition of *The Eaten Heart* in Chatto's
standard 5½-inch by 7¾-inch blue cloth-bound format, which was used as
well for the "popular" edition of *A Dream in the Luxembourg* and for *Life
Quest*. These are neat, good-looking little volumes that present the poems to
much better advantage than *The Complete Poems*: the type is better-looking,
there is more space between the lines and on the page, and the paper is far
superior, being a cream-colored stock with a distinct wire marking. These
books provide the beginning of a uniform set of the poet's works.

Of the eleven shorter poems of the 1933 Chatto and Windus editions,
eight came from "Passages Toward a Long Poem" in the 1930 anthology,
while two of those in that earlier sequence were dropped. Poem VIII of the
anthology, which is printed as "The Parrot" in *Collected Poems* (British
edition only), does not appear here; neither does poem IX, which is in French
(see below, Part II, Chapter 3, where it is reproduced under the title originally
given to all of the poems). Poem X of the anthology becomes poem VIII in
the Chatto and Windus edition. Poems IX, X, and XI of these editions are the
three that did not appear in the anthology. These three would have been
entirely new, if they had not been included in *Movietones*, a volume that was
issued after the French edition of *The Eaten Heart* but before the English
editions.

As noted in the first section of this chapter, Thomas McGreevy was
much impressed with "Passages Toward a Long Poem," which he could have
seen only in the anthology of 1930, since his comments were published in
1931, before the British editions of *The Eaten Heart* were published. He says:

There is unforgotten bitterness in it, but no indignation, only tender-
ness and pity in love. A stanza in the section that follows throws
further light in the direction of the poem:

> Think well of me but not too well.
> I would not seem to fail you,
> As I must,
> If you esteem me overmuch;
> But love me more than well,
> For too much love
> Was never known beneath the sun,
> And only your great love
> Can soothe that shame
> Of knowing me unworthy of your love.

It is this quality of humility before the benedictions of existence, love,
art, the beauty of nature, evident all through his work but not so clear-
ly since the boyish poems of the pre-war years, that made me say earlier
that at the end of the war Richard Aldington chose life instead of death
and quick life rather than still life. Without being at all worldly he is
interested in the world, eagerly interested.[129]

These little poems are, appropriately for accompaniments to "The
Eaten Heart," love poems. In the first Electra tells of the death of Helen of
Troy:

> She with her eyes, and hair
> red as the blood on her slender hands,
> and swift eddy of passions,
> dust in the rock-tomb under the gold garments.

"III" tells of two lovers in terms of the myth of Dionysus. "Gold head by
black head/ laid close on the pillow" become "ripe yellow muscat grapes"
and "dark shy clusters/ of cool black grapes" which must be "crushed in the
hot wine-press."

> This is the mystic sacrifice
> of the Dionysiac tearing of the flesh
> and crushing of the grape-clusters.
> The old gods are the most living,
> the primitive mysteries the most purifying,
> the most ancient symbols the truest.

It is tempting to see the influence of Aldington's editing of Lawrence's *Last
Poems* in these Lawrencian lines, but this poem was first published in *The
Nation and Athenaeum*, Vol. 46, No. 23 (8 March 1930), p. 764. Lawrence

died on 10 March 1930, and the *Last Poems* which Aldington prepared along with Guiseppe Orioli was published in 1932.[130] The entire question of influence between Aldington and Lawrence is a delicate one with which I try to deal in my next chapter. It is natural to attribute the influence to the major poet, but it can be pointed out that Aldington was using the Persephone myth, for instance, as early as 1912 in "Choricos." In Greek themes, both H.D. and Aldington anticipate Lawrence's later (and fuller) treatments.

With its mask and winding stairs, "VIII" suggests Yeats:

> up those winding stairs
> so long and tedious to mount alone
> always the mosaic mask
> that nothing says and says too much
> there is no way out
> except the inevitable final plunge. . . .

The ambivalence of the symbols of this poem gives it an interest that some of Aldington's other poems lack. As Yeats found, the revelation of the poetic vision is more powerful for reaching men's hearts than any poetic argument can ever be. The poem concludes:

> entered? well the mask said enter
> so beautiful a mask
> I forgot the blood
> so beautifully like a god
> said enter I forgot the blood
> ran stumbling upwards too eagerly
> then the mask changed
> and yes there is no way out.

"In Memory of Wilfred Owen," the book's last poem, is dated 1931 and is addressed to all the war dead. The speaker says that in the beauty of the world, in the struggles of life, and in love he had half-forgotten

> All you who lie there so lonely, and never stir
> When the hired buglers call unheeded to you,
> Whom the sun shall never warm nor the frost chill.

But finally the dead are blessed; nothing more can vex them, and "memory and forgetfulness are one."

Although Richard Aldington had occasionally been reprinting poems from older editions in his newer ones, it was not until 1928 that he made his first collection. *Collected Poems*, published in New York by Covici, Friede, bears the dedication, "This collected edition is dedicated to VALENTINE AND

BONAMY DOBREE." The epigraph from *Bucolic Fragments* is printed in
Greek and is translated as follows:

> (If my little poems have any beauty, those
> The Muse has granted me are enough for fame.
> And if they are worthless, why should I
> labour to compose more?)

The acknowledgment reads:

> The author wishes to thank the Four Seas Company for the permission
> to include in this collected edition poems published by them under the
> titles of *Images* and *War and Love*, and also for the transfer of
> anthology rights.
>
> The author also thanks the Dial Press for permission to include *Exile*
> and *A Fool i' the Forest*.
>
> This edition contains several poems which have not yet appeared in
> the United States, and in all cases gives the final, revised text.

The contents listed in this first collection are the same as those of
The Complete Poems, up to and including *A Fool*, except for the
following: "In the Tube" and "Cinema Exit" are reversed in order; "On
the March" and "Insouciance" are in reverse order; "The Faun Com-
plains" is included in this collection; "The Blood of Young Men" and
"The Parrot" are omitted. There are, however, no divisions, as in *The
Complete Poems*, on the contents pages; instead the sections are indi-
cated by half-title pages bearing the legends "From Images," "From
Images of War," and so forth. The "Bibliographical Note" is identical to
that in *The Complete Poems* for those works up to and including *A
Fool*.

Paull F. Baum reviewed *Collected Poems* in *South Atlantic
Quarterly*:

> He who would have lived happily in a pastoral of Theocritus finds
> himself at bay among the complexities of civilization and the brutalities
> of war. . . .
>
> But in the love poems the note is forced to shrillness, sometimes,
> which begets doubt. . . . Most of the poems are in free-verse, part of
> which is plain prose of assorted lengths, that is, of discontinuous
> rhythms, and part is very delicately modulated patterns. Often the lines
> will scan readily, though the rhythm may seem to shift from line to
> line. Often there is an approach to blank verse. Always in the best
> poems there is a true melody, not formal, but the more subtle for being
> continuously varied. . . . If for no other reason, Mr. Aldington's poetry
> would be important for its metrical mastery. . . . To call it decadent and
> Alexandrian is fair enough, provided one remembers that decadence
> and Alexandrianism are not altogether bad; and that there is enough of
> the *vrai beau*, along with the *faux bon*, to make one hope that Mr.
> Aldington will complete the story with a satisfying resolution of his
> Arcadian-modernistic discord.[131]

The only poem included in this collection that does not appear in *The Complete Poems* is "The Faun Complains." The analogy made in this poem is the same as that in "The Faun Captive," which I have called a fine poem. The reason that the present poem is not successful, and that Aldington was wise to omit it from his final collection, is its excessive overtness. A faun captured by men, as in the first poem, is a fine image of the sensitive artist in the trenches, but a faun's speaking of "aeroplanes," "mud holes," "breaking metal," and "bursts of flame" produces a metaphor in which only one referent functions; it also makes the poet sound precious and like a "complainer" indeed. I have included a copy of this poem in Chapter 3 of Part II; it was, as I previously noted, originally included in *War and Love (1915-1918)*.

George Allen and Unwin Ltd. published the English edition of *Collected Poems* in London in 1929. C.P. Snow, in his "A List of the Works of Richard Aldington" (included in *Richard Aldington: An Appreciation*), calls this edition "uniform with the American edition of Covici, Friede"; Alister Kershaw, in his bibliography, while he lists the English edition, says that "it has not been possible to trace a copy of the American edition of the foregoing item." Paul Schlueter does not show the American edition at all. Actually, a comparison of the two editions indicates that they are uniform as to contents, pagination, and all other details *except* that in the English edition the poem "The Parrot," absent from the American version, precedes the contents page. "The Parrot" was also printed as part VIII of "Passages Toward a Long Poem" in the *Imagist Anthology 1930*; possibly Aldington completed it after the 1928 American edition, and, as its position indicates, included it in the 1929 British edition at the last minute. This seems to be confirmed in a letter dated 21 December 1928, which Aldington wrote to Crosby Gaige: "I keep forgetting to tell you that my poem The Parrot was accepted by The Bookman several months ago, before I sent you the collection of new poems." (Unpublished letter in The Beinecke Rare Book and Manuscript Library at Yale University.)

In "The Parrot" the poet says he plans to buy a parrot that will act as his cynical companion to remind him of his failings.

> When I air my witless folly,
> When I dogmatise in print,
> When I lull the shuddering terrors
> With a cradle-tune of cant;
> Snap loud, parrot.

Perhaps Aldington, like Graves, had been reading Skelton's "Speke Parrot." In any event, the cynical, sardonic tone of this poem makes it very different from its fellows, those other poems of "Passages Toward a Long Poem" that Aldington elected to take from the 1930 anthology for his 1933 edition of *The Eaten Heart*. But it made a good introductory poem for his first English edition of his collected poems.

In the Preface to his bibliography, Alister Kershaw says: "But how could I know of, say, *Reverie*, with one or two poems nowhere else reprinted or *Movietones*, the contents of which have, with very few exceptions, also been nowhere else reprinted."[132] Though he was wrong about *Reverie*, he was right about the poems in *Movietones*. Professor Schlueter makes the following entry on this Aldington publication: *"Movietones. Invented and Set Down by Richard Aldington. 1928-1929.* Privately printed, 1932." The volume is described as item 17 in the Kershaw bibliography as follows:

> (Design) / MOVIETONES/ INVENTED AND SET DOWN/
> BY RICHARD ALDINGTON/ 1928-1929/ PRIVATELY PRINTED/
> 9 x 11¼ in.; pp. 19
> "Only ten copies of this book have been printed for the C.L.S. The decorations and the etchings under vellum for the binding are by Kenneth Hobson 1932"
> Printed on Van Gelden Zonen paper.
> Most of the poems in this book have never been published elsewhere.

More recently Mr. Kershaw wrote about *Movietones*:

> "Movietones" was a sumptuous production—produced by A. S. Frere (then Managing Director of Heinemann's) who showed me his copy. It was limited to 10 copies for a mock society—the Canterbury Literary Society—consisting of Frere, R. A., Thomas McGreevy, Norman Douglas, Pino Orioli: I can't remember—if I ever knew—who the others were.[133]

The purpose of the "society" was to accept in membership "someone who had been refused membership of an English Literary Society."[134] A year earlier, in 1931, a note in the Florence edition of Aldington's *Stepping Heavenward: A Record* had said: "This edition is printed on Pescia handmade paper, and limited to eight hundred and eight copies numbered and signed by the author; eight hundred being for sale and eight (printed on yellow paper) for members of the C.L.S."

I was able to examine the galley proofs of *Movietones*, which contain holograph corrections by the author. Aldington appears to have intended to omit three of the poems which are untitled. Their first lines are "not to define nor plan too far not," "to you o poet," and "we'll have no stories of dead women." They appeared the next year in the 1933 Chatto and Windus edition of *The Eaten Heart*, where they are poems IX, X, and XI respectively. Since they do not fit in precisely with the satiric tone of *Movietones* and are more in the nature of love poems, Aldington probably wanted to save them for the later volume; but, either through error or because he changed his mind, they are printed in the finished volume despite the slash he ran through the copy and the "X" he put on each page. Even the poet's handwritten numbering of the poems indicated that he intended these omissions.

On the first sheet of these galley proofs, above the printing, Aldington has written:

Ten beautifully printed copies of this work were produced by my dear friend, A.S. Frere. Several were destroyed by a fanaticed [probably *sic* but illegible] Roman Catholic, who objected to naked women. I think Frere has one copy; T. McGreevy had one; Charles Prentice had one; perhaps Orioli. I merely wrote them. [signed "Richard Aldington"]

It seems probable that this note was written many years after the printing of *Movietones*, at a time when the poet turned the galley proofs over to Lawrence Clark Powell. From his last sentence one gathers that he no longer had, or possibly never had, a copy of the finished volume.

Movietones is a handsome book. The cover is a cream-colored vellum with a drawing of a warrior, preparing to rest, printed in gray ink over the words "inverte me." The copy that I saw was signed by Aldington and Kenneth Hobson; since there were only ten copies, presumably all were signed. There is no pagination; three blank pages precede a page printed with a considerably smaller repetition of the cover design in maroon ink, beneath which is the copy that Kershaw quotes explaining that the book has been printed for the C.L.S. and decorated by Hobson. On the next page, recto, is a sketch of a girl with a lyre, the title of the volume being given beneath. The dedication to C.L.S. is printed on the recto of the next page over a line drawing of a girl in a transparent dress washing clothes. Another line drawing of a nude follows the poem "all art aspires. . ."; these are presumably the "naked women" Aldington refers to in his note.

Following the dedicatory poem:

> dedication
>   to the pessimist thomist
> Well, anyhow, it's something to have had
> The glad
> Eye from a few bad
> Girls, Dad.

there are thirteen poems of which only four are titled: "Debate, 'down in the city of,' 'unlike mr ezra pound I do not,' 'the carlylean hero-worship of,' 'not to define nor plan too far not,' 'we'll have no stories of dead women,' 'to you o poet,' 'the first political duty of a,' 'the second political duty of a,' 'all art aspires to the condition of,' 'Hark the Herald,' 'The Power and the Glory,' '*to the gentle and corteous* [sic] *reader-critic.*'" "Hark the Herald" is reprinted from its original 1928 "Christmas card" edition; otherwise all of these poems are new. Except for the three poems that are reprinted in *The Eaten Heart* and *The Complete Poems*, all of these poems from *Movietones* may be found in Chapter 3 of Part II of this book.

In *Life for Life's Sake* Aldington writes (p. 321):

One result of idling in Paris that spring [1928] —by which I mean I didn't work more than four hours a day, which, all said and done, is idling from the point of view of the real working world—was a sudden and unpremeditated access of writing poetry. One of the things I wrote pleased me. I enjoyed writing it; it was long enough to make a book by itself; it was constructed; it broke all the rules for modern poetry by having a beginning, a middle, and an end and by being comprehensible. It could not without injustice have the label of any school or clique pinned on it.

The poet says that all of his friends advised him not to publish it if he wished to retain any reputation he had. He hid it away for a couple of years and one day "fired it off to Chatto's and Pat Covici." It was called *A Dream in the Luxembourg*. On 9 June 1929 Aldington wrote Crosby Gaige, "I have also finished a poem of 1200 lines, which I call 'Love and the Luxembourg, A Novel in Free Verse.' It's a sort of dime novel, and a break away from the 'incomprehensible' school of modern poetry" (Unpublished letter in The Beinecke Rare Book and Manuscript Library of Yale University).

Covici, Friede, Inc. published the poem in New York in 1930, under the title *Love and the Luxembourg*, in a handsome volume bound in maroon cloth that was embossed in gold with a flower design framed with a double rule. The spine is decorated in gold with an allover design enclosing the title, author's name, and publisher's name. The title page, besides the title, author's name, and publication information, has an etching in green of two cupids kissing. Page [3] repeats the title and has the epigraph, "Si Vis Amari, Ama."; the dedication is "(For B.)."

On the reverse of page 53 the following appears:

This edition of LOVE AND THE LUXEMBOURG by Richard Aldington has been designed by Frederic Warde and printed by William Edwin Rudge, and consists of four hundred and seventy-five numbered copies, each signed by the author and the designer.

"Richard Aldington" is signed in ink and "Frederic Warde" in pencil. A beautiful pure white-rag, doubly deckle-edged paper stock is used; there are very wide margins; the printing is in italic with foreign words, and other words that would normally be italicized, in regular type.

The British edition published by Chatto and Windus in the same year bore the title Aldington used in referring to this poem in his autobiography: *A Dream in the Luxembourg*. This is also a fine edition. The covers are printed with an allover snowflake design in white on an orange-rust background. The cloth spine is gold embossed with the title and "Aldington." The page before the title page reads:

This special edition of
A DREAM IN THE LUXEMBOURG
consists of three hundred and eight
copies, of which three hundred are
for sale. No 233 [numerals in ink]
[signed] Richard Aldington

The epigraph and dedication are the same as in the American edition; again the poem is made much more attractive to the eye by fine typography and paper.

C.P. Snow says in "A List of the Works of Richard Aldington" that in addition to the limited signed edition, Chatto and Windus made four impressions of a cheap edition. The first impression of this "popular" edition was made on 10 April 1930; the second sometime later in April 1930; the third in August 1932; and the fourth in January 1935. The books of the last imprint are bound in blue cloth over boards with the title and author's name stamped in gold on the spine. These volumes are smaller in size than those of the limited edition, and the paper and typography are inferior; they are, nevertheless, handsome little books. Snow also notes that another fine limited edition was published from New Haven, Connecticut, in 1935.[135] Alister Kershaw adds to the entry from Schlueter's "Check List" the following: "Also published in Czech and French." Of this latter translation Sir William Haley says, "He [Aldington] was pleased with Gustave Cohen's translation, *Un Songe dans le Jardin de Luxembourg*, of his loveliest poem."[136]

In 1928 Richard Aldington had translated selections from the works of Remy de Gourmont. In his Introduction to the first of the two volumes Aldington said:

> During this period (1900-1910) Gourmont was in full maturity and produced much of his best work. His excursions into classical Latin poetry (Ovid, Lucretius) and a somewhat fanciful passion for Epicurus produced the admirable *Nuit au Luxembourg.*

Aldington includes in this work of translation "thirty-six unpublished letters from Remy de Gourmont to Richard Aldington (July 1913-August 1915)" and in a "Note" that precedes them says: "Miss Amy Lowell came to the rescue [of de Gourmont] with two hundred dollars, for which she afterwards received the complete MS of the *Nuit au Luxembourg*." A letter from Gourmont (translated by Aldington), dated 22 December 1914, confirms the involvement of Miss Lowell:

> I have not yet sent the manuscript to the American lady, fearing that I had not read the address exactly. I want to send her the MS of a *Night in the Luxembourg*. Do you think that will please her? It is the only complete thing I possess.
> I read your nice verses in *The Egoist*. You have a fine freedom of mind. All my compliments.[137]

Remy de Gourmont's *A Night in the Luxembourg (Une Nuit au Luxembourg)*, published in 1906, probably influences Aldington's *Love and the Luxembourg* or *A Dream in the Luxembourg*, if only in the title. Gourmont's work, however, is of a different nature from Aldington's, being the story of a journalist's "interview" with a "god" whom he discovers in the church of Saint-Sulpice in the Luxembourg. It is a type of philosophical dialogue that presents Gourmont's epicurean views. Aldington's poem uses the locality and the "dream" or "vision" idea; however, unless one equates Aldington's dream of love with Gourmont's "philosophy" of sensuality, the comparison cannot be carried further.

Glenn Hughes does not think highly of *Love and the Luxembourg*:

> [Aldington] has permitted himself an excursion into sentimental narrative. . . . Biographically the poem is interesting, because it chronicles the poet's flight from England to the Continent. Artistically, I should say, it is lacking in the merit belonging to *The Eaten Heart* and "Passages toward a Long Poem." Here and there a line flashes fire, but many passages are dull prose, and the intensity of emotion which evidently inspired the poem is by no means communicated to the reader. At best it exhales the perfume of a long-pressed flower.[138]

Thomas McGreevy is kinder but less specific:

> . . . a poem that in spirit if not in form recalled *Theocritus*, a gracious, wanton idyll, in which there was little or no bitterness, in which the author again indicated, in his own "British heretic" way, his conviction that *nature vivante* is of more importance than *nature morte*, if only men, and especially post-war men of genius, were honest enough and courageous to face the problems involved.[139]

As late as 1957 Oliver Edwards (Sir William Haley) was writing in his "Talking of Books" column in the London *Times*:

> *A Dream in the Luxembourg* is an adventure story, a fairy-tale for adults who will most certainly never, outside its pages, visit its particular Arcadia. . . .
> If there is a theme it is that the only way to live is to squeeze everything there is out of any momentary happiness that chance may throw in our way between disillusionment and annihilation. . . .
> It has, among his poems, the same place as *All Men Are Enemies* has among his prose works. The impression that remains is one of beauty and tenderness.[140]

It seems to me that Professor Hughes is looking at *A Dream in the Luxembourg* too literally in considering it "an excursion into sentimental narrative. . . . Biographically . . . interesting." The poet makes quite clear that this is a dream sequence which begins and ends with his sitting on "one of those uncomfortable iron chairs/ under the trees of the Luxembourg."

> And another thing troubles me about all this—
> Did it really happen?
> Was it only a dream in the Luxembourg?
> Was it a vision of what will be,
> My spirit brooding over her so intensely
> That for an hour I saw the future?

> For, though I know it all went on in my brain,
> Yet it was so vivid I seemed to behold it
> Clearly in a clear crystal glass.
> I saw her and I saw myself.
> And yet it all happened within myself.

The point is that the poem may very well be a recounting of an actual event in Aldington's life, and if that were all that it is we would be justified in considering it a "sentimental narrative." However, *A Dream in the Luxembourg* is a paean to that love between man and woman which, in *The Eaten Heart*, the poet suggests is the only answer to the essential loneliness of humanity. It seems to me that the emotion of the poet does communicate itself to the reader; in fact, as I have pointed out several times, Aldington's poetry is at its best when it is most sensuous.

There is, incidentally, a connection between this poem and *The Eaten Heart* in the analogies drawn here to the chivalrous love of Provence, including that of the principals of the legend which is told in the latter poem.

> Well, the Queen kissed Alain Chartier's lips
> (And he was no beauty among *trouvères*)
> And the Lady Marguerite,
> Who was the fairest of all the ladies of Provence,
> Loved Guilhem de Cabestanh, and died for his memory,
> And do you remember how Peire Vidal ran mad for his Wolf Lady. . . .

Structurally the poem is held together by a set of fine images that are skillfully united at the end of the poem. In section IV the poet introduces the image of the Luxembourg fountain:[141]

> In the distance I could see the wavering fountain jet,
> Always rising and always falling in foamy parabolas
> Like the path of a comet fixed in tremulous water.

In section VII he uses the fountain as a metaphor for his love:

> And the heart of at least one of them
> Pouring out tenderness and devotion and desire
> Like the tall fountain in the Luxembourg
> Perpetually pouring and never failing. . . .

Section X introduces an image for unrequited love:

Suppose you were a rather clumsy glass-maker
And one day a miracle happened,
From your breath grew a miraculous slender glass bowl
More exquisite than any Venetian glass.
And just as you were marvelling at its beauty
And thinking how your whole life would be changed,
Some invisible hand poured in the traditional poison
So that in a flash the miraculous cup collapsed
And crumbled to a little dust in your hand. . . .
"She does not love me" is the poison.—

In the last section of the poem the two images come together:

At that moment the tall white fountain jet
Fell from its height, crumbled like dust of water;
. . . .
The dream was broken, fallen into dust
Like the white fountain, like a Venetian glass
When the poison is poured in it.
. . . .
Crumbled into dust my dream like the dying fountain
Which collapsed in a dust of white water,
Dust like the crumbled Venetian glass,
Dusty like the dusty wind-whirls about me,
A world of grey-white dust.

Section VI of *A Dream in the Luxembourg* contains some lines that are interesting in connection with the two "faun" poems discussed earlier: "When I was younger they called me a faun/ Because I have pointed ears and tell the truth."

Aldington's next book of poetry seems to have caused a number of bibliographical problems. C.P. Snow says that *Collected Poems, 1915-1923* "contains the same books as the 1929 edition, but was re-set with a new introduction." This seems to be correct but is complicated by Alister Kershaw's note in his bibliography: "This cheap edition was first published in 1923. It does not include *A Fool i' the Forest*, which appeared in the 1929 edition." Schlueter, apparently following Kershaw, dates the volume 1923 and places it directly after *The Berkshire Kennet* and before *Exile and Other Poems*, although it does not seem reasonable to publish a collection *before* the edition of some of the poems which are collected.

I think what has happened is that the "1923" in Kershaw's bibliography is a typographical error for "1933," a mistake that appeared reasonable because of the "1915-1923" which is part of the collection's title. But of course what Aldington was doing was making logical the omission of *A Fool i' the Forest* from this cheaper edition, by using date limits which would exclude it. There is quite a bit of internal evidence to suggest that the proper date for *Collected Poems, 1915-1923* is 1933 and that a "1923" volume does not exist.

First, we have the publisher's dating: "London: George Allen & Unwin Ltd., 1929 [New and Cheaper Edition 1933] "; and opposite "Contents": "All rights reserved/ FIRST PUBLISHED IN GREAT BRITAIN 1929/ New and Cheaper Edition 1933." Under "Bibliographical Note" on page xiv both the London and New York editions of *Collected Poems* are shown, dated 1929; but there is no earlier collection shown, although all other trade editions of Aldington's poetry are listed here. Furthermore, the poem "The Parrot" is listed in the contents of the collection; this, it will be recalled, is a late poem that just made the London edition of *Collected Poems* and was not in the New York edition.

One of the most interesting things about this collection is Aldington's Introduction, which also helps to date the book. Lord Snow says, "This preface was written in 1929," but he must be wrong, since in it Aldington says, "Ten years have passed since the latest of these pieces was published . . ." —a comment obviously referring to the 1923 *Exile and Other Poems*. Aldington speaks in this Introduction of his concern for the way in which his poems were published:

> Moreover, this is the first time I have been able to issue them in England in the way I wanted. The last edition, under the title of Collected Poems, was far too expensive. It was not my fault or the fault of the English publisher; we had to collaborate with the American publisher who initiated the enterprise, and has his own ideas of production.

Considering that it was to be a "cheaper edition," this book is surprisingly attractive, particularly when it is compared to *The Complete Poems*. It is covered with light-blue cloth embossed in dark red on the face with the title, and on the spine with the title, the author's name, and the publisher's name. The contents of this collection are identical with those of the 1929 *Collected Poems* except that, as noted, *A Fool i' the Forest* is deleted and "The Parrot" is now included in the body of the book just before "Songs for Puritans."

The Poems of Richard Aldington (Garden City, N.Y.: Doubleday, Doran, 1934) is not, as might be expected, an American version of the 1933 *Collected Poems, 1915-1923*, but a collected edition that differs basically from the 1948 *Complete Poems* only in not containing the last two long poems, *Life Quest* and *The Crystal World*. There are also some minor points of difference: "In the Tube" and "Cinema Exit" are still in reverse order, and "The Faun Complains" is still included. "Epilogue to 'Death of a Hero'" is not yet included in this collection and "The Parrot" is still placed before "Songs for Puritans."

The Introduction to this collection is almost the same as that in *The Complete Poems*, with the exception that the latter was brought up to date. The following interesting section, however, was omitted in the final collection:

At the risk of ridicule, I will give two instances of this [the "moment of poetic ecstasy" referred to in the preceding paragraph]. A few mornings ago I was in my bath dreaming rather vaguely. Suddenly, for no apparent reason, a line of blank verse seemed to be spoken in my head:

And something dies each day that I may live.

It is not a good or original thought, and I did nothing more with it; but I swear there was nothing in my previous meditation to suggest such a line. Again, some years ago I was in a train going from London to the country, looking out of the window. Apropos nothing in particular I seemed to hear the words:

Court jester to an age that lacks a king.[142]

That not particularly distinguished line suggested the whole of "A Fool i' th' Forest." I was so much impressed by the feeling that the words didn't really belong to me that I have always printed them in inverted commas.

I can offer no explanation of this, rational or otherwise; I can only record the fact.

Besides collecting all of the poems of the 1929 *Collected Poems*, the 1934 edition includes *A Dream in the Luxembourg* and an added section, "New Poems," which contains the following: "A Place of Young Pines, A Grave, To One Dead, Dilemma, January Aconites, Morning in the South, Death of Another Hero, 1933: For Eric Remarque, Life Goes On."

The first of these nine poems, "A Place of Young Pines," seems to ask a question that the last poem, "Life Goes On," answers. His house, the poet says, is like a battlefield where he is forever struggling with himself, and is "only victorious by defeating myself." The struggle is presumably his creative effort, which is made more difficult by the "voices and passions" of the world outside himself. To avoid both the creative struggle and the rough contact with the world, the poet escapes to "a place of young pines." This is also the theme of "At a Gate by the Way" in *Exile and Other Poems*; it seems to have been a recurrent temptation for Aldington.

So for a little time I stand among the pines
Above the clean dry water-course
Where all sounds are hushed.
There I am at peace, there I am at one with all things.

But he is somehow aware that this is a dangerous escape, and he questions himself:

Asking if what I seek is not rather the peace of death,
The lapse, the going forth, the peace
After all the waters have passed under the young pines.

In "Life Goes On," the last of his collected short poems, Aldington characteristically affirms his acceptance of life and answers the doubt of "A Place of Young Pines." Do not let your life become a "Pharaoh's tomb/ Of buried memories, hopes embalmed," he says. Even though the "crystal dream and golden ecstasies" of youth are wrecked by time, there is still

> . . . rain-washed rock and tender fugitive water
> Under the old sky worshipped with new eyes,
> For life goes on.

The dryness and water imagery of the two poems links them as though they were written as a pair. As a matter of fact, since they were both published in periodicals in December of 1933, they could have been written at almost the same time.

In a poem which is related in emotion to these two, "Morning in the South," the poet considers mutability. He has described a morning so perfect that it is as if

> Some god has passed unseen
> Leaving an ecstasy in wave and land
> And fragrance of his body on the air. . . .

He wonders why it is not possible that time stand still, and

> Poise with unswerving wing at this one hour
> When life has stepped into immortal paths
> And beauty triumphs like a faultless rose.

And he gives the answer that we all must: "Because it passes it is beautiful."

The opinions of two critics whom I quoted in Chapter 1 bear repeating. R. P. Blackmur, in reviewing this collection, criticized Aldington's poetic work severely:

> Mr. Aldington is a type of the poet—in intention, in attitude toward life and toward past literature, in vocabulary, in the tone of his thinking, and in his wilful assertion of personal inspiration. But he is, on the whole, not an example: his work is not poetry of a high order. . . . while he presents us with a fund of substance and a talent for feeling, Mr. Aldington lacks either the genius or the arduous will for persistent execution. . . .[143]

But John Wheelwright was favorable in his review:

> Half of these poems present him as a leader in his twenties, during the reclamation of Anglo-American poetry from its slump at the turn of the century. The middle quarter show how his work slumped after the war; the last quarter, how it has come back to mastery of the direct and elegant record of sensation and opinion.[144]

In 1934, driving in Austria, Aldington had an automobile accident that resulted in a broken kneecap. During his convalescence from this mishap and from a subsequent fall that rebroke the kneecap, he worked on and finished his long poem *Life Quest*.

> . . . I thought it rather a nice poem, about the best thing I'd done in that line. Charles Prentice and Frere [his publishers from Chatto and Windus and Heinemann] thought so too; indeed, Frere liked it so much I gave him the manuscript. But in the literary football scrum it is considered a foul for anybody who writes novels which are read to write poetry as well, and the reviewing umpires blew disapproving whistles.

The poem is important because it expresses the poet's view of life:

> In its unsystematic way this poem expressed my views—I will not try to dignify them with the term "philosophy"— on the subject of life for life's sake. Far from considering this life as a painful test of worthiness for future lives, we should look on it as a short holiday from nothingness, a unique opportunity to enjoy the singular prerogative of consciousness.[145]

Although Aldington says that he gave his manuscript to Frere of Heinemann's, *Life Quest* was actually published in London in 1935 by Chatto and Windus. The book is bound with dark blue cloth on boards; the spine is stamped in gold with the title and the author's last name. A cream-colored, watermarked paper is used. The first edition contains the following "Author's Note":

> The following pages are not intended to be a narrative or the exposition of a philosophy. There is no argument, but a loose string of moods and meditations, variations on the theme of the "Life Quest". For the historical description of the life quest, see pages 23-35 of Sir G. Elliot Smith's *Human History* (1934).[146]

An examination of Smith's book shows that although the introductory chapter contains a division with the title "Life Quest," the material covered cannot be credited with giving Aldington any more than background for his poem. The pages that Smith writes under this title deal with early man's efforts to preserve his life and to attain new life.

In the same year that *Life Quest* was published in England it was also published in Garden City, New York, by Doubleday, Doran and Company, Inc. The American edition is covered with black cloth over boards. The spine is embossed in gold with the title, the author's name, and the publisher's name. There is an embossed design on the face of the book which is probably intended to represent a walled city on a hill. The poem in this volume, as in the English edition, is more effective than in *The Complete Poems*, because of better typography and paper and particularly because of larger spaces between lines.

As Aldington suggests, contemporary criticism was "disapproving." The Boston *Transcript* seemed to be criticizing Imagism rather than *Life Quest*:

> While they produced sometimes rhythmical lines, much of their product is in reality prose written with broken lines that make it look like poetry. This group of poems is in the truly imagist style, with perhaps a little more of thought centered around one idea, than is usual with such poets.[147]

And *Christian Science Monitor* criticized the poet as much as the poem:

> If a poet is not to be bound to society by active participation in national or community life, he must all the more have roots in a familiar patch of earth.
>
> Because the poet of "Life Quest" has not assumed such a partnership with its responsibilities, his verse, sincere and intensely felt as it is, is episodic and disjointed.[148]

Michael Roberts in the *Spectator* dealt more directly with the poem itself:

> Mr. Aldington . . . is an old campaigner for vigour, intelligence and accuracy in poetry: he insists, too, upon a contemporary accent, and he knows very clearly what he thinks is wrong with the world, and consequently what is right. . . . Here are clear visual images, but the lines are memorable for visual rather than verbal reasons, and the end of each section of the poem tends to disconnect the reader by a sudden raising of the emotional pitch which makes the whole thing seem, for the moment, as banal as some of Mr. Aldington's rather commonplace similes.[149]

The first section of *Life Quest* considers the living as "the diamond point of living light,/ Cresting the shadowy pyramid of the dead." Next the poet surveys the world of the dead and, in a direct answer to D.H. Lawrence's "The Ship of Death," which Aldington had edited in *Last Poems* a few years before, declares that there is no life after death: "The Ship of the Dead has never come to port,/ It never started." Then he considers all of the old religions that have promised a life after this one and concludes:

> The earth is haggard with our ruined shrines,
> With crumbling temples, dusty tombs,
> Dead bibles teaching the way of life
> And many a saviour who never saved. . . .

In section XII the poet faces the devil, who wrestles him in the form of a foggy death-serpent:

> Sometimes in the evening
> Through the mountain gorge below

An enormous ghost comes creeping,
Lifting a flat head on a sinuous neck,
Peering above the highest peaks, and after
Slowly pulls its huge and misty bulk.

He sits "in the belly of the mist ghost," weighing human fate, and concludes that:

The stuff of the body is immortal;
Before birth it was and after death it is.
But the soul
The evil or lovely soul is mortal
As a flower or a rainbow.

This being so: *carpe diem*. Once again Aldington repeats the message of all of his postwar poetry—of "Exile," *The Eaten Heart*, and *A Dream in the Luxembourg*: love while there is time.

In section XVI, filled with a lust for life, he sees the body of a dead snake floating in the water of the river along which he is walking. He recalls the dead soldiers he has seen; he sees his own body lying white and helpless—but he is not afraid:

I saw that which was the snake
And myself and those others
Softly dissolve and drift with the stream
Down to the Dordogne
Down to the Gironde
Down to the great rollers of the sea,
And return as rain or cloud or air
But never again as a crisp-gliding snake
Rustling its way over dried grasses,
Never again as a human soul
Avid for much living. . . .

In section XIX the poet stands at the Pillars of Hercules and sees "the last mountains of Europe" and "the first mountains of Africa." He sees the Atlantic and the "mid-earth sea" shining in the sunlight.

I was swept speechless
By a huge choking wave of life.
I knew it was folly and wickedness
To worship Christs and abstractions
And never to revere the real holy ones
Sun Sea and Earth.

In 1932 Richard Aldington had written an Introduction to the first
English edition of D.H. Lawrence's *Apocalypse*. In this essay Aldington
quoted from Lawrence's conclusion:

> For man, as for flower and beast and bird, the supreme triumph
> is to be most vividly, most perfectly alive. Whatever the unborn
> and the dead may know, they cannot know the beauty, the
> marvel of being alive in the flesh. The dead may look after the
> afterwards. But the magnificent here and now of life in the flesh
> is ours, and ours only for a time. We ought to dance with rapture
> that we should be alive and in the flesh, and part of the living,
> incarnate cosmos. I am part of the sun as my eye is part of me.
> That I am part of the earth my feet know perfectly, and my
> blood is part of the sea.[150]

Aldington was a great friend and admirer of D. H. Lawrence. He defended
Lawrence's work from the very beginning and considered him "the most
interesting human being I have known."[151] His love and admiration for
Lawrence is not surprising: in many respects their life-views were identical. It
is also not surprising that, five years after the death of his friend, Aldington
should restate in *Life Quest* the views that the greater artist had put down for
the last time in *Apocalypse*, the work that was completed immediately before
his death. Close as the ideas of the two men were, there were important
differences. One of these is best exemplified by a comparison between the
first lines I quoted from *Life Quest*—"The Ship of the Dead has never come
to port,/ It never started"—and Lawrence's lines from "The Ship of Death":
"And the little ship wings home, faltering and lapsing on the pink flood. . . . "
Lawrence considered the possibility of the soul's immortality; Aldington
flatly denied it from his earliest poetry to his last. Moreover, Aldington's
ideas about love were based on a simple man-woman relationship, while
Lawrence, besides having more complex notions of heterosexual love, also
urged a curious blood relationship between men.

I have said that *Life Quest* is an important poem in the Aldington
canon because it so closely expresses his idea of "life for life's sake." It is not,
however, one of the best of the long poems. Too often the ideas that the
poem is trying to express overwhelm the poem itself, with the result that it
becomes a vehicle for other things rather than a structure important in itself.
The best parts of the poem are those in which the emotion thrusts aside the
message and we "feel" what the poem is saying; examples are the mist ghost
portion of section XII and the dead snake episode of section XVI. In other
parts of the poem, in which the poet is cerebrating rather than writing from
his solar plexus, as Lawrence would have said, we can be sympathetic to the ideas,
but we have the feeling that prose would have done as well.

Life Quest also seems to suffer from the lack of unity which is the
plague of many long poems. It gives the impression of a series of short poems
arbitrarily joined together. The structural unity which *A Dream in the
Luxembourg* gets from the fountain image, and which *The Eaten Heart* de-
rives from the legend of the love of Lady Marguerite and Guilhem de
Cabestanh, is missing.

Two years after the poem's publication, Aldington's novel *Very Heaven* appeared. The entire last chapter of *Very Heaven* is a repetition of the theme of *Life Quest*. Chris Heylin stands on the edge of a high cliff overlooking the ocean; he is discouraged with life and contemplates hurling himself onto the rocks at the base of the cliff. Suddenly he sees a little yellow butterfly sucked over the cliff and out towards the sea; the wind shifts and the butterfly is blown landward; he watches it struggle toward the woods and meadows inland:

> If I care so much for the death of so slight a creature, why so little for my own? On the edge of barren land and barren sea under this same sun, life was born. For millions of centuries life has struggled and perished under these great three powers. Yet it has always been passed on. The salt of the sea is in my blood, the radiance of the sun and the chemicals of earth in my cells. In all that unimaginable stretch of time what an infinity of chances against my ever existing![152]

Aldington's last volume of poetry before *The Complete Poems* was *The Crystal World*, published in London by William Heinemann, Ltd. in 1937. This is a good-looking volume bound in dark, blue-purple cloth embossed only on the spine: "Aldington: The Crystal World." The recto of the first page is printed with the title; the verso lists the works of the author. The second page recto displays the title, the author's name, and, under Heinemann's windmill trademark, the publisher's signature; the verso of the second page gives the publication date and the information that the book was "Printed in Great Britain at the Windmill Press, Kingswood, Surrey." On the verso of the third page the volume is dedicated to the poet's second wife: "For Netta."

The American edition of *The Crystal World* was published in Garden City, New York, by Doubleday, Doran and Company, Inc., in 1937 from the British sheets; it is identical to the Heinemann edition. The binding is maroon cloth over boards; a paper label lists title and author's name and bears the device of a naked girl riding a dragon.

Kerker Quinn, reviewing *The Crystal World* for *Poetry*, is severely critical:

> Intensely personal lyrics, which do not seem personal because of their utter commonplaceness. . . . In the past, Aldington has from time to time shown a bent for cloying lushness, but has checked himself. . . . But now he rides desperately through the quagmire, spreading clichés before him to make the path look solider. . . .
>
> Whether any of the failure of Aldington's new poem can be blamed on his increasing preoccupation with novels and sketches and articles, one cannot say. . . . Certainly Aldington's last novel, *Very Heaven*, and his last essays, *Artifax*, also betray a lack of concentration and of self-criticism, which subtracts a good deal from their potential excellence.[153]

C.P. Snow, in his pamphlet *Richard Aldington: An Appreciation* from which

I quoted in Chapter 1, sees *The Crystal World* much differently:

> ... his poetical output has gone steadily on, *A Dream in the Luxembourg, The Eaten Heart, Life Quest*; and then in 1937 *The Crystal World*. This last poem convinced many of what they had gradually been suspecting for some time: that Aldington has written some of the best love-poetry in English. Most of us are not over-willing to commit ourselves to a literary judgment on a contemporary; but that statement I would make myself without feeling that I was risking anything at all.[154]

The Crystal World is a love poem in twenty-two parts; the twenty-second part is, in turn, divided into eleven parts. The parts are numbered in arabic; the subdivisions of part twenty-two in roman. What the poet seems to be doing is telling the love story poetically in the first twenty-one sections or poems, and then dissecting what he has done. The last section of the poem seems, perversely, to undercut the rest. It is as though we are introduced to a beautiful woman and then shown how she functions biologically. In the first three short sections, for instance, the beloved is compared in turn to flowers, to the sea, and to a queen-goddess. Then in segment V of the last section, the poet analyzes what he has done:

> The passion at first is hardly sexual at all,
> But—by instinct or convention?—
> Speaks in terms of "this is beautiful".
> Not in the subtle forms of the artist
> Who is always seeking exact equivalents
> For the experiences of the sensibility,
> But in the common terms of common men—
> She is flowers, the sea, a young queen,
> Primitive symbols.

We are given the "Old Yellow Book" so that we may see the raw gold from which the ring was fashioned. *The Crystal World* can be seen as a love poem, a poem about the nature of poetry and of love, and a paradigm for poem-making.

The first section of the poem is the simple story of two lovers who are separated by the world's conventions, suffer alone, and then decide to be together regardless of the cost. Sections eight to sixteen tell of the lover's desolation. As an analysis of grief they are faintly reminiscent of *In Memoriam*.

> Punctual as waking comes my grief,
> And every solitary hour
> Hurts me with memories of you.

Section sixteen laments the children that will never be born to the pair. Its final stanza relates to the over-all theme of *Life Quest*, as well as to Aldington's war experiences, which, after more than twenty years, are still an emotional spring:

> O comrades lying in the fields of France,
> Strange is our fate; childless like me you died;
> For us the coloured flame of love fades out,
> The million generations have an end,
> The ship of life sinks in a dusky sea.[155]

In section seventeen the poet celebrates his beloved's decision to return to him; in nineteen he indulges in the fancy that, as his mistress, she will henceforth be "clad in my words and dreams"—her clothes literally deriving from the income he receives through writing; in twenty-one he is rushing over the ocean to her.

And then the curious twenty-second part, which begins, "What is poetry? And what is love?" and seems to analyze away the preceding parts of the poem. The poet retells the love story in flat terms and asks us to "admire the ingenuity of Sapiens/ Who can make biology into a life poem!" In one way this last section gives the poem an emotionally jolting effect that would otherwise be lacking; in addition, it provides a metaphysical ingenuity. But while tearing the veil aside may be salutary, it also has the effect of disturbing the organic structure of the poem.

This was Aldington's last volume of poetry until *The Complete Poems of Richard Aldington* in 1948. As far as can be determined, he composed little or no poetry after *The Crystal World*. He wrote John Gawsworth (who was editing *The Poetry Review*) on 6 December 1948: "I'm afraid I can't send you any poems: there were only a few unpublished and an edition of my *Complete Poems* now in the press has scooped those in too." And again on 24 November 1950 he told the editor:

> This is very kind of you, and I wish I could respond. Perhaps you noticed that the last edition of my poems was entitled *Complete Poems*—which was intended to convey that I shall publish no more verse. In fact I have not published any since 1938, and am far better content to be a reader than a would-be writer of poetry. It is always pleasant to belong to a minority.[156]

NOTES

1. *Life for Life's Sake: A Book of Reminiscences* (New York: The Viking Press, 1941), pp. 43, 59. This confirms a letter he wrote to Amy Lowell dated 20 November 1917, which is in The Houghton Library at Harvard.

2. *The Life and Opinions of T. E. Hulme* (London: Victor Gollancz, 1960), pp. 28-29.

3. *Life for Life's Sake*, p. 113.

4. While this is a breach of my own guidelines calling for the strict elimination of all admitted translations, the obvious interest of these very early poems in any appraisal of Aldington's work should be sufficient excuse for their inclusion.

5. "I only hope," he wrote Miss Monroe, "that my 'vers libre' will not bring down cascades of reproof upon you!" (Unpublished letter dated 24 November 1912, in the *Poetry Magazine Papers* at the University of Chicago Library.)

6. " 'The Forgotten School of 1909' and the Origins of Imagism," in *A Catalogue of the Imagist Poets* (New York: J. Howard Woolmer, 1966), p. 37.

7. *Soft Answers* (Carbondale: Southern Illinois University Press, 1967), p. 195.

8. *Autobiography* (New York: G. P. Putnam's Sons, 1935), pp. 269-270.

9. Charles Norman, *Ezra Pound*, revised edition (New York: Funk and Wagnalls, 1969), pp. 110-111.

10. Probably refers to Ford Madox Ford (then Hueffer). On 25 May 1914 Aldington wrote to Harriet Monroe that Hueffer had done two articles on *Des Imagistes*. (University of Chicago Library: unpublished letter in the *Poetry Magazine Papers*.)

11. "Modern Poetry and the Imagists," *The Egoist*, Vol. 1, No. 11 (1 June 1914), p. 202. The "green covers" Aldington refers to are those of the Poetry Bookshop edition; the Boni edition was bound in blue cloth.

12. Unpublished letter dated 25 May 1914, in the *Poetry Magazine Papers* collection of the University of Chicago Library.

13. *Autobiography*, p. 271.

14. Pound wrote Macmillan (who was evidently the first publisher approached) objecting to the new group's using the title *Some Imagist Poets*. Aldington suggested to Amy Lowell that they call their book "Some 20th Century Poets" if Macmillan would not use the original title. (Unpublished letter to Amy Lowell dated 6 November 1914, in The Houghton Library of Harvard University.)

15. *Imagism: A Chapter for the History of Modern Poetry* (Norman: University of Oklahoma Press, 1951), p. 163.

16. Constable published from the American sheets; Aldington complained to Amy Lowell that they were late arriving and might have gone down with the Lusitania. (Unpublished letter dated 11 May 1914, in The Houghton Library of Harvard University.)

17. Coffman, *Imagism*, p. 29.

18. "The Imagists Discussed," Vol. 2, No. 5 (1 May 1915), pp. 77-80.

19. "A Jubilee," Vol. 36, No. 910 (10 July 1915), pp. 46-48.

20. "The Imagists Discussed," pp. 77-80.

21. "Richard Aldington's Poetry," *The Little Review*, Vol. 2, No. 6 (September 1915), pp. 11-16.

22. *Imagism and the Imagists: A Study in Modern Poetry* (Stanford, Calif.: Stanford University Press, 1931), p. 92.

23. *Imagism*, p. 165.

24. *D. H. Lawrence: Portrait of a Genius But . . .* (New York: Collier Books, 1961; originally published in 1950), p. 15.

25. New York: The Viking Press, 1939, p. 21.

26. "Aldington was both bookman and entomologist. His letters are equally full of book talk to me and butterfly talk to Norman." Lawrence Clark Powell in *Richard Aldington: An Intimate Portrait*, ed. Alister Kershaw and Frédéric-Jacques Temple (Carbondale: Southern Illinois University Press, 1965), p. 107.

27. *Richard Aldington: An Englishman* (London: Chatto and Windus, 1931), p. 26.

28. *Imagist Anthology 1930: New Poetry by the Imagists* (New York: Covici, Friede, 1930), p. vii.

29. Unpublished letter dated 29 August 1929, in The Houghton Library of Harvard University.

30. Ford always liked to think of himself as the original Imagist or at least as a pre-Imagist. In 1915 he wrote: " . . . for a quarter of a century I have preached the doctrine that my young friends now inscribe on the banner of their movement" ("A Jubilee," pp. 46-48). In a 21 November 1914 letter to Amy Lowell, Aldington wrote about Ford: "And about a fortnight ago he said that he was after all the only real imagiste!" (Unpublished letter in The Houghton Library of Harvard University.)

31. *Richard Aldington: An Englishman*, p. 65.

32. *Imagism and the Imagists*, p. 107.

33. In an unpublished manuscript of his autobiography Walter Lowenfels admits that he hoaxed Aldington into the 1930 Imagist anthology so that he could get the job of typing the manuscript. (A copy of Lowenfels' manuscript is in the possession of the University Research Library of the University of California, Los Angeles.)

34. These are in the Poetry Collection of the Lockwood Memorial Library, State University of New York at Buffalo.

35. "The Bookshop," *Poetry Review*, No. 11 (November 1912), p. 498.

36. "The Poetry Bookshop: (35 Devonshire Street, London)," *The Little Review*, Vol. 2, No. 3 (May 1915), p. 19.

37. In 1956 Aldington wrote: "The fact cannot be disputed that *Poetry* was the head and center of the so-called 'revolution of 1912' partly because of Miss Monroe's skill and open-mindedness as editor, partly because Ezra Pound was in touch with young writers, but also because Chicago is away from the literary rackets of New York, London and Paris." (Unpublished letter dated 10 October 1956, in the University of Chicago *Poetry Magazine Papers*.)

38. "Refuge from War," *Poetry: A Magazine of Verse*, Vol. 12, No. 1 (April 1918), pp. 44-46.

39. *Imagism and the Imagists*, p. 88.

40. *Imagism*, p. 165.

41. *Richard Aldington: An Englishman*, p. 15.

42. *All Men Are Enemies: A Romance* (London: Chatto and Windus, 1933), pp. 28-29.

43. Aldington also wrote Harriet Monroe on 20 June 1915 that a friend of his took a brilliant degree at University College, London, while he (Aldington) was "messing about the courtyard reading Swinburne." (Unpublished letter in the University of Chicago *Poetry Magazine Papers*.) In this regard, see also Aldington's first published poem of record, "Song of Freedom," which was written several years prior to "Choricos." It is reproduced below in Part II, Chapter 2.

44. *D. H. Lawrence*, p. 65.

45. *Primitivism and Decadence: A Study of American Experimental Poetry* (New York: Arrow Editions, 1937), pp. 112-115.

46. *Imagism*, pp. 165-166.

47. *Life for Life's Sake*, pp. 121-122.

48. Unpublished letter dated 12 August 1922 in the *Poetry Magazine Papers* of the University of Chicago.

49. *Life for Life's Sake*, p. 128.

50. Aldington is obviously poking fun at Pound's "In a Station of the Metro" in section IX of his "Penultimate Poetry," which is reproduced in Chapter 2 of the second part of this book.

51. "Correspondence," Vol. 1, No. 7, pp. 138-139.

52. "Some Imagist Poets, 1916," *The Little Review*, Vol. 3, No. 4 (June-July 1916), pp. 26-31.

53. "Three Imagist Poets," *The Little Review*, Vol. 3, No. 3 (May 1916), pp. 30-35.

54. Critics might have had a different reaction to the poem if it had been printed with the original last stanza that appeared in the manuscript copy sent to Amy Lowell:

> Therefore sweet friends, I know,
>   By the splendour of Mary!
> Into innermost hell shall I go
>   For my sin with this lady.

(This manuscript copy, handwritten in ink, is in the Amy Lowell collection of The Houghton Library at Harvard University.)

55. "Two Notes," *The Egoist*, Vol. 2, No. 6 (1 June 1915), pp. 88-89.

56. *Richard Aldington: An Englishman*, p. 24.

57. "The Poems of Richard Aldington," *The English Review*, Vol. 32, No. 5 (May 1921), p. 409.

58. "Richard Aldington's Poetry," *The Little Review*, Vol. 2, No. 6 (September 1915), pp. 11-16.

59. In *Richard Aldington: An Intimate Portrait*, ed. Kershaw and Temple, p. 175.

60. "Three Imagist Poets," p. 35.

61. "Mr. Aldington's Images," *Poetry: A Magazine of Verse*, Vol. 8, No. 1 (April 1916), pp. 49-51.

62. See my "Richard Aldington and The Clerk's Press," *The Ohio Review*, Vol. 13, No. 1 (Fall 1971), pp. 21-27.

63. Unpublished letters in the University Research Library at the University of California, Los Angeles.

64. The first fourteen poems appeared in Vol. 2, No. 5 (August 1915), pp. 18-22 under the title "Poems: (*from the Greek of Myrrhine of Mitulene and Konallis, translated by Richard Aldington*)." The next sixteen were printed in Vol. 3, No. 7 (November 1916) as "Myrrhine and Konallis," and the last two in Vol. 3, No. 9 (March 1917).

65. Unpublished letter in the University Research Library at the University of California, Los Angeles.

66. Unpublished letter dated 14 October 1917 in the University Research Library at the University of California, Los Angeles.

67. "The Poems of Richard Aldington," *The English Review*, Vol. 32, No. 5 (May 1921), p. 403.

68. Unpublished letter dated 29 June 1917 in the University Research Library at the University of California, Los Angeles.

69. On 21 June 1918 Aldington wrote Harriet Monroe that he was sending her six or seven prose poems which were his newest work, all done at the front in France. (Unpublished letter in the University of Chicago *Poetry Magazine Papers*.)

70. *Imagism and the Imagists*, p. 96.

71. P. 209. The Houghton Library at Harvard has no record of this notebook in their Amy Lowell collection. There are several of Aldington's wartime notebooks in The Morris Library at Southern Illinois University (Carbondale) but none that seems to meet this description.

72. Unpublished letter dated 12 January 1949 in the University Research Library at the University of California, Los Angeles. But an unpublished Aldington letter of 20 April 1926 to Crosby Gaige in the Beinecke Rare Book and Manuscript Library at Yale University states that the two books Bubb printed other than reprints of the "Poets' Translation Series" were *The Garland of Months* and *The Love Poems of Myrrhine and Konallis*. This seems to ignore *Reverie. A Little Book of Poems for H. D.*

73. Unpublished letters of 6 August 1917 and 8 December 1918 in the University Research Library.

74. Unpublished letter dated 22 June 1917, from the collection in the University Research Library.

75. *Poetry*, Vol. 12, No. 1 (April 1918), pp. 44-46.

76. In *Richard Aldington: An Intimate Portrait*, pp. 162-163.

77. In *Richard Aldington: An Intimate Portrait*, p. 73.

78. *Death of a Hero* (London: Chatto and Windus, 1929), p. 324.

79. *Richard Aldington: An Englishman*, p. 30.

80. *Ibid.*, p. 29.

81. *Autobiography*, p. 269.

82. *Imagism and the Imagists*, p. 95.

83. "The Poems of Richard Aldington," pp. 397-410.

84. Williams's criticism upset Aldington, who wrote a three-page letter to Harriet Monroe pointing out the impossibility of writing the kind of poetry Williams wanted, given the conditions of trench warfare. (Unpublished letter dated 14 October 1919, in the University of Chicago *Poetry Magazine Papers*.)

85. *Richard Aldington: An Englishman*, p. 32.

86. After the war Aldington wrote: "Until I joined the Army I had lived with dreams books and love—the shock of change was too abrupt and I still feel like a man grasping vainly for breath after being kicked in the stomach!" (Unpublished letter of 29 June 1917, to the Reverend Charles C. Bubb, in the University Research Library at the University of California, Los Angeles.)

87. *A Bibliography of the Works of Richard Aldington from 1915 to 1948* (Burlingame, Calif.: William P. Wredon, 1950; London: Quadrant Press, 1950), p. xi.

88. *D.H. Lawrence*, p. 129.

89. Introduction to *Collected Poems, 1915-1923* (London: George Allen and Unwin, 1933), p. xii.

90. Unpublished letters dated 8 April and 15 June 1929 in Lockwood Memorial Library, State University of New York at Buffalo.

91. "Aldington's Images of Desire," *The Little Review*, Vol. 4, No. 4 (August 1919), pp. 35-36.

92. "On Richard Aldington," *Coterie*, No. 3 (December 1919), pp. 24-25.

93. *Imagism and the Imagists*, p. 96.

94. In *Richard Aldington: An Intimate Portrait*, p. 163.

95. On the day before Christmas of 1918, just demobilized, Aldington had written Harriet Monroe that he had been out of things for two or three years and was "anxious to get back!" (Unpublished letter in the University of Chicago *Poetry Magazine Papers*.)

96. Unpublished letter in the Amy Lowell collection of The Houghton Library of Harvard University.

97. Unpublished letter in the University Research Library of the University of California, Los Angeles.

98. Unpublished letter in the University Research Library.

99. Unpublished letter dated 17 June 1920 in the Amy Lowell collection.

100. Unpublished letter in the Amy Lowell collection.

101. "Books of the Fortnight," *The Dial*, Vol. 66, No. 791 (31 May 1919), p. 576.

102. "Soldier and Lover," *Poetry: A Magazine of Verse*, Vol. 14, No. 6 (September 1919), pp. 338-341.

103. "Volumes of Poetry," *The American Review of Reviews*, Vol. 60, No. 4 (October 1919), p. 446.

104. Unpublished letter to the Reverend Charles C. Bubb dated 22 June 1917, in the University Research Library of the University of California, Los Angeles.

105. Unpublished letter dated 2 February 1918, from the Amy Lowell collection in The Houghton Library of Harvard University.

106. Vol. 6, No. 3, p. 48.

107. He wrote Harriet Monroe, "I am hoping to get away from London & forget the bitterness in work & I think the next lot of poems will be sweeter and more happy." (Unpublished letter of 15 October 1919, in the University of Chicago *Poetry Magazine Papers*.)

108. Many years after its original publication, and probably referring to the Peacocks Press edition, Aldington wrote: "Willy Maugham thanks me for my Kennet poem, but wonders if I would really have been satisfied with the peace and untroubled life I prayed for. I should say that on the whole I've had it—there would have been no trouble at all if the silly political fools could have checked their quarrelsome greed and avoided wars. War and war only upset my apple-cart." (Unpublished letter to Netta Aldington dated 3 January 1956, in the collection of the British Museum.)

109. *Imagism and the Imagists*, p. 97.

110. Introduction to *Collected Poems, 1915-1923*, p. xii.

111. Unpublished letter dated 15 June 1929 in Lockwood Memorial Library, State University of New York at Buffalo. Harriet Monroe also turned down "Eumenides." (Unpublished letter from Aldington dated 2 August 1920, in the University of Chicago *Poetry Magazine Papers*.)

112. Introduction to *Collected Poems, 1915-1923*, p. xii.

113. *Imagism and the Imagists*, pp. 98-99.

114. "The Poems of Richard Aldington," p. 400.

115. Introduction to *Collected Poems, 1915-1923*, pp. x-xi.

116. In 1930 Nancy Cunard's Hours Press printed *Henry-Music* by Henry Crowder. This limited private press edition contained one poem each by Nancy Cunard, Richard Aldington, Walter Lowenfels, Samuel Beckett, and Harold Acton. All of the poems were set to music by Henry Crowder. Aldington's contribution was "Madrigal," which first appeared in this section of "Words for Music."

117. *Imagism and the Imagists*, p. 99.

118. Introduction to *Collected Poems, 1915-1923*, p. xi.

119. Unpublished letter in the *Poetry Magazine Papers* of the University of Chicago.

120. *Richard Aldington: An Englishman*, pp. 41-42, 42-43.

121. *Imagism and the Imagists*, pp. 100-101.

122. Vol. 3, No. 11 (April 1925), pp. 459-463.

123. *Poetry: A Magazine of Verse*, Vol. 34, No. 1 (April 1929), pp. 42-46.

124. *These Were The Hours*, ed. Hugh Ford (Carbondale: Southern Illinois University Press, 1969), p. 39. The "Bibliography of Hours Press Publications" also appears in this volume.

125. *These Were The Hours*, pp. 54, 57; 51; 57-58.

126. *Imagism and the Imagists*, p. 106.

127. Aldington himself seems to support this suggestion in a letter which he wrote a few years later: "When you get on to Sophocles, don't omit the Philoctetes—a strange but subtle drama about the essential loneliness of the human spirit." (Unpublished letter to Sydney Schiff dated 26 June 1931, in the collection of the British Museum.) Philoctetes and his predicament have an important role in the poem.

128. This is undoubtedly the edition to which Aldington referred when he wrote to Sidney Schiff: ". . . I am reissuing The Eaten Heart with a few other short poems at the end of this month." (Unpublished letter dated 19 January 1933, in the collection of the British Museum.)

129. *Richard Aldington: An Englishman*, p. 66.

130. Brigit Patmore wrote on 12 February 1932: "R is editing last poems of Lawrence for Orioli. There's a good bit of work because the MS is scrappy & worked over. But R feels so annoyed at the way all the stuff Lorenzo life [*sic*] has been carelessly treated by Frieda that he wants these poems to be done with the utmost care." (Unpublished letter to Sidney Schiff in the collection of the British Museum.)

131. "Mr. Richard Aldington," Vol. 28, No. 2 (April 1929), pp. 201-208.

132. *A Bibliography of the Works of Richard Aldington from 1915 to 1948*, p.xi.

133. Letter to the writer dated 30 August 1969.

134. Bibliographical description appended to the galley proofs of *Movietones*, which are in the University Research Library of the University of California, Los Angeles. This note also adds the names of D. H. Lawrence and Frieda Lawrence as members of "C. L. S."

135. Actually this is Stamford, Connecticut, where the Overbrook Press in 1935 printed a limited edition of 165 copies following the British text, although copyright acknowledgment is made to Doubleday, Doran and Company. The typography was done by T. M. Cleland. The book is bound in light green cloth over boards; the face and back are embossed in gold and there is a framing design with the title and author's name on the spine. The paper is watermarked "Bishopstoke, Freefolk English Handmade" and has a double deckle edge. This is a very handsome edition. A copy of it can be seen in the Graphics Arts Room of the Princeton University Library, Princeton, New Jersey.

136. In *Richard Aldington: An Intimate Portrait*, p. 42.

137. The three quotations are from *Remy de Gourmont: Selections from All His Works* (Chicago: Pascal Covici, 1928), pp. 30, 284, 305. In writing to Harriet Monroe Aldington said, "Owing to the generosity of editors & of a private individual—whom I cannot too highly praise—I have managed to get M. de Gourmont nearly £ 100. I feel a much higher regard for human nature!" (Unpublished letter dated 3 January 1915, in the *Poetry Magazine Papers* of the University of Chicago.)

138. *Imagism and the Imagists*, p. 108.

139. *Richard Aldington: An Englishman*, p. 65.

140. "Perchance To Dream," Thursday, 5 December 1957, p. 13.

141. There are two fountains in the Luxembourg Gardens. I spent a pleasant several hours during the summer of 1972 sitting before each trying to decide which Aldington refers to. The one that rises from a small pool before the palace seems the more likely, although the one at the other end of the gardens is the more beautiful.

142. Nearly the same line appears, however, in the poem "Prologue" included in a letter to Harriet Monroe dated 3 October 1922 and reproduced in Chapter 1 of Part II. It would seem that Aldington was remembering a line from this earlier, unpublished poem.

143. "Richard Aldington," *The Nation*, Vol. 138, No. 3595 (30 May 1934), p. 625.

144. "A Poet of Three Persons," *Poetry: A Magazine of Verse*, Vol. 45, No. 1 (October 1934), pp. 47-50.

145. The two quotations are from *Life for Life's Sake*, p. 399.

146. Sir G. Elliot Smith, according to the title page of the book, holds five degrees from the University of London, Aldington's school.

147. Issue of 11 September 1935, p. 3.

148. Issue of 6 September 1935, p. 16.

149. Vol. 154 (31 May 1935), p. 928.

150. Introduction to *Apocalypse* (London: Martin Secker, 1932), p. xli. Aldington also uses this quotation to close his biography of D. H. Lawrence, which was published in 1950.

151. *Life for Life's Sake*, p. 334.

152. *Very Heaven* (London: William Heinemann, 1937), p. 367.

153. "Aldington 1938," *Poetry: A Magazine of Verse*, Vol. 52, No. 3 (June 1938), pp. 160-164.

154. *Richard Aldington: An Appreciation* (London: William Heinemann, n.d.), p. 15; reprinted in *Richard Aldington: An Intimate Portrait*, p. 140.

155. Note the allusion to Lawrence's "The Ship of Death" which once more underscores the difference between the two poets' views.

156. *Richard Aldington: An Intimate Portrait*, pp. 28, 32.

3
Richard Aldington: An Evaluation

There are a number of obstacles to any just consideration of Aldington's poetry. Among these is the fact that his private life often blurs or distorts our vision of his art. Aldington's love-life attracted attention even in a circle in which amorality was not an exception. His fine love poetry is addressed to two wives and two mistresses; his romances are an important part of the plots of a number of *romans à clef*.[1]

Like Joyce and Lawrence, and many other artists of his time, Aldington was an expatriate. He lived in France and Italy, on the island of Tobago for a short time, in Jamaica, and in the United States during the Second World War. F.-J. Temple says of him:

> To be quite candid, I think that Richard Aldington was a disappointed lover. Like his friend D. H. Lawrence, his love for England had been rejected and betrayed but, far from his native land, he remained utterly, almost desperately English.[2]

As a disappointed lover he had some things to say about England that were bitter and satiric; they did not endear him to many of his countrymen, and they may have blinded some to the value of his work.

Willy-nilly, Aldington found himself thrust in the midst of the giant lights of his time; he was friend and associate, pupil and mentor, critic and patron of artists like Pound, Eliot, and Lawrence, in addition to many of the lesser figures of the first half of this century. It is difficult to emerge as a good minor artist against the background of such brilliance; it is easy to singe one's reputation by riding too close to the sun of a greater one.

As we have seen, Aldington stood right at the nerve center of Imagism. He and Hilda Doolittle were the young poets Ezra Pound promoted as the leaders of the new poetic movement. When Amy Lowell took over from Pound, she depended on Aldington's help in editing the Imagist anthologies, and his work was given the most space in them. Richard Aldington, from 1912 to 1920 in England and America, was a leading poet of the avant-garde. When Imagism had done its work by giving impetus to modern poetry, and began to fade into literary history along with the other "isms" of this century's second decade, Aldington's reputation faded with it.

A review of a recent edition of Aldington's autobiography, *Life for Life's Sake*, carries the headline "Journeyman of Letters."[3] It is true that Richard Aldington was a poet, novelist, translator, critic, biographer, essayist, and editor; as the anonymous reviewer says, except for the short period of his wartime service, he earned his livelihood with his pen. As noted earlier, Aldington himself pointed out, in connection with the reviews of *Life Quest*, that "in the literary football scrum it is considered a foul for anybody who writes novels which are read to write poetry as well. . . . "[4] If this holds for the novelist-poet, how much more can it affect the critic's judgment if the poet has been a jack-of-all-literary-trades as Aldington undoubtedly was?

The final, and probably most damaging, hurdle to a fair appraisal of Aldington's poetry has been the reputation, in fact the notoriety, earned by two of his prose works of the 1950s: *Pinorman: Personal Recollections of Norman Douglas, Pino Orioli, and Charles Prentice*, and *Lawrence of Arabia: A Biographical Enquiry*. The first damaged Aldington's reputation in literary circles; the second, by denigrating one of Britain's popular war heroes, to a large extent alienated his reading public. Lawrence Durrell suggests the seriousness of these blows:

> His books on T. E. Lawrence and Norman Douglas were responsible for this state of affairs; they had not only damaged him critically but had alienated him from the common reader, from his own public, from the libraries. With the trouble caused by these two volumes the whole of the rest of his admirable life work went out of print and out of public demand—some seventy titles in all![5]

These, then, are the facts that tend to obscure the vision of Aldington's critics; we will be least affected by them if we keep our eyes fixed as completely as possible on the poems themselves. It is at once apparent that Richard Aldington had at his command an extremely lucid poetic style. Of the more than one hundred and fifty short poems and the five long poems in *The Complete Poems*, there are scarcely any that present syntactical or verbal problems. This clarity of style traces back to his early Imagist poetry.[6] As the years passed, Aldington made it known that he did not like the direction in which some of his contemporaries were going, and that he knew exactly the kind of poetry that he wanted to write. In 1925 he wrote to Read:

> I am rebelling against a poetry which I think too self-conscious, too intellectual, too elliptic and alembique. This poetry is (selon moi) distinguished by over-elaboration of thought and expression and by a costiveness of production.[7]

The poetry he was particularly thinking of was, naturally, that of Eliot and Pound, and, despite what appear to be occasional desertions to the enemy camp, like *A Fool i' the Forest*, Aldington remained consistent in his position. In 1938, speaking of Housman, Aldington repeated his views:

> . . . it is quite clear that the lecture [Housman's] is a satire directed against the intellectualist school, represented in poetry by T.S. Eliot and in criticism by I.A. Richards. . . .
> Now, I agree with Housman in thinking that all this is "nonsense" (his word) which has had a "pernicious effect" on the writing of poetry

and the criticism of poetry. I had been hammering away on opposition lines for a long time, and you may imagine how delighted I was when a great poet and scholar carried the attack so effectively into the heart of the Cambridge stronghold.[8]

As late as 1950, Aldington held this position, and it is interesting to note that even Yeats, in his later work, did not escape Aldington's criticism:

> I speak of the new writers and artists—those already formed either stayed as they were or (like Yeats, for instance) tried gradually and cautiously to adapt themselves to changed tastes. Yeats succeeded where others failed; yet in his early work one finds a spontaneous charm and loveliness not present in the more pondered intellectualist work of his later years.[9]

Now the fact is that the two divergent schools of poetry, the one that Housman and Aldington were thinking of and the one that Pound and Eliot represent, are not mutually exclusive. They are not, for that matter, even at all new, but rather opposite tides of an ebb and flow in poetry that has continued for centuries between what one might call the classical and the renaissance views of poetic expression. If it had not been for the showmanship of Pound, there might never have been such a term as Imagism in our literary history; the critics might simply say that during the second decade of this century a revival of classical poetics helped to sweep away the cobwebs of Victorianism and bring about the birth of modern poetry. In this connection Aldington wrote in the Foreword of *Latin Poems of the Renaissance* about a similar period:

> . . . all are Italian humanists of the 15th and 16th centuries, so in love with classic culture that they used its language and form as well as its thought. Imitative as this movement was, it was the soil, so to speak, which produced the Pléiade and our own Elizabethan lyrists.[10]

Despite all of the furor about Imagism, Aldington himself must have realized that he and his group represented, in the final analysis, recent examples of a very old tradition. He writes of Landor:

> The poetry of the great Romantics and their successors is often merely "prismatic"; deficient in architectural qualities but abounding in picturesque details and irridescent language. . . . Now the style of Landor is deliberately architectural and "classic," perhaps the most classic (in intention) of all our poets; Landor is the most determined to reproduce in English the effects of earlier Greek poetry, the most consistent in his poetical ideal and the most ruthless expunger of every tendency and influence foreign to his ideal.[11]

It should not be necessary to "excuse" Aldington's lucid poetic style; however, it does help to put it into a living tradition for those of us who have become accustomed to dealing with the ambivalent and ambiguous poetics of the more representative twentieth-century poets. Certainly the clarity of his poetic approach should not prevent our hearing what he has to say.

It is curious that the second primary attribute of Aldington's poetry, which does not today strike us as being particularly unusual, was the very thing that caused all of the hue and cry in the halcyon days of Imagism. The simplicity of his diction and style was accepted by his early readers as their due, but his prosody (and that of his fellow Imagist poets) aroused their ire. Aldington's use of free verse originated in the same period as his lucid style:

> I began to write vers libre about the early part of 1911, partly because I was fatigued with rhyme & partly because of the interest I had in poetic experiment. I didn't know Heine or Patmore's "Unknown Eros," & never suspected the existence of the French vers librists. I got the idea from a chorus in the Hippolytus of Euripides.[12]

Walt Whitman may also have been an early influence, since Aldington says that "at London University I was invited to read a paper on some poet to the Literary Society. At that moment I was deep in Whitman, and was greatly excited about him."[13] While writing in 1920 about Thomas Campion's "Observations," Aldington called attention to the fact that free verse, like lucidity of expression, had a historical basis:

> Dissatisfaction with rhymed accented verse is not peculiar to our time; the most robust and flourishing period of English poetry, that of the Elizabethans, is marked among other things by a distinct effort to abolish mediaeval poetic forms which were based on somewhat cheap effects of alliteration, stress and rhyme, and to substitute a type of verse more satisfying to ears trained in music or familiar with Greek.[14]

Richard Aldington fought the battle of free verse long and earnestly. In *The Egoist* of 15 September 1914, he stated the credo of the new poets:

> For the essential difference between free verse and accented verse is just this: the old accented verse forced the poet to abandon some of his individuality, most of his accuracy and all his style in order to wedge his emotions into some preconceived and sometimes childish formality; free verse permits the poet all his individuality because he creates his cadence instead of copying other people's. . . .[15]

Eleven years later in *The Chapbook* he wrote in "A Note on Free Verse":

> The people who fought the first battles for free verse twelve years ago in England were always convinced that they would capture the sympathy of new poets. This has been proven to be true. It was never our claim that free verse would supersede all other poetic measures; we only claimed that it was an additional "vehicle" which had great possibilities for poets who cared for style and for modernity.[16]

Aldington's own verse is the best demonstration of the value of his arguments. T.S. Eliot writes of him as a poet "whose own accomplishments as a writer of vers libre qualify him to speak" about Pound's "Seafarer."[17] His free verse is finely cadenced and in perfect harmony with his clean, classic style. In the longer poems particularly, his individualistic rhythm plays a large part in conveying the emotion of the poem. He also wrote just enough poetry in traditional meter and rhyme to confound those critics who were anxious to convict all users of free verse of a subterfuge designed to conceal their inability to deal with the traditional prosody.

The two attributes of Aldington's poetry so far considered, lucidity of style and *vers libre*, are functions of form. The final and most important characteristic is concerned rather with content, although it is related to the use of free verse, as the poet himself points out. Writing in 1914 of the poetry of Amy Lowell and John Rodker, Aldington, again discussing cadence, says: "cadence, which is primarily the expression of individual emotion, may be ruined by inadequate technique as well as by insufficient emotion."[18] Later, writing of Sir Herbert Read in his autobiography, Aldington says:

> As a poet, Read lacks a something which I can only hint at by saying that while I admire the skill behind his poems I am never moved by them. They seem to me to lack the passion which gives life to even the worst splurgings of D. H. Lawrence, and the intellectual concentration which so effectively conceals Eliot's emotional sterility.[19]

Ten years afterwards, in a letter to Peter Russell, looking back on the "movement," Aldington says that from his point of view Lawrence and not Eliot followed the authentic line.[20] Certainly much of the emotion of Aldington's poetry is Lawrencian; indeed, Aldington never hid his admiration for his friend's ideas, as can be seen from his biography of Lawrence, his many introductions to Lawrence's books, and his editing of Lawrence's poems.

It is apparent from Aldington's own critical writings that the emotion, the passion of poetry was, in his view, the ingredient that counted most toward its success or failure. He also makes clear that he is not thinking of the cold passion of the intellect. In his Introduction to his *Complete Poems* he says:

> Obviously, poetry has intellectual elements, but it is not solely intellectual. Men and women are not distinguished from one another only by quality of mind, but also by the quality of their feelings and the quality of their senses.

And further:

> . . . the sensual and emotional qualities distinguish poetry from philosophy, for though philosophy undoubtedly takes account of both, it is not concerned directly with the life of the senses and the feelings, but with abstractions derived from them.[21]

Speaking of the conception of life that a novel should communicate, in his Author's Note to *All Men Are Enemies*, Aldington again emphasizes the sensual:

> It is the life of the here and now, the life of the senses, the life of the
> deep instinctive forces. If we do not live in these we scarcely live at all.
> We have been taught so long that life must have some exterior end and
> justification that we have forgotten that living is itself enough, that to
> be alive and conscious is itself an excellent and miraculous experience.

And in the novel itself Aldington speaks through Clarendon: "I saw life, not
as action but as experience, not as the exercise of power but as sensual com-
munion with living things, the mysterious forces behind them, the ideal ex-
pression of them in the arts."[22]

Mikhail Urnov, the Russian critic, reports on a discussion that took
place just days before the death of the British poet. "In one of his conversa-
tions, Aldington defined the underlying idea of his creative work in the short
and, at first sight, somewhat mysterious statement, 'To live here and
now.' "[23] C.P. Snow, writing of Aldington's early days, says, "It was also
natural that he should begin as an 'imagist'—for in that way he could express
the 'immediate life' which he has always instinctively felt to be his major task
as an artist."[24] Emotion, passion, sensuousness, life—these were the key-
stones of Richard Aldington's poetic art.

In a broad view of Aldington's poetical work, such as we have been
taking, we cannot overlook his importance as a unique spokesman for his
times. The most important single event in the affairs of humanity during the
first third of the present century was World War I. For all of Europe, certain-
ly for all English-speaking peoples, it is a line of demarcation between two
eras. For better or worse, the old world was lost in the battlefields of France
along with thousands of its young men, and a new world came into being. No
poet-novelist reflected this cataclysm in his work more completely than Rich-
ard Aldington.

Eliot's poetry largely ignores the war and deals with the problems of its
aftermath as they were reflected in the emptiness of the human soul and its
thirst for regeneration. Lawrence does write of the war but from the stand-
point of a harassed civilian. The two Irishmen, Joyce and Yeats, stood to one
side. Yeats, in all of his great body of poetry, hardly mentions the war except
peripherally in poems such as "In Memory of Major Robert Gregory," and
"An Irish Airman Foresees His Death." There are no war poems or novels in
Joyce's limited canon.

The practical reason for the omission of any treatment of the
1914-1918 war by these major figures of the time was that none of them, for
various reasons which are not important, took part in the war as Aldington
did. In Aldington's poetry, which covers the quarter-century from 1912 to
1937, we can trace the effect of the Great War on a sensitive writer who is
able to speak for the thousands of his generation who also endured this
holocaust and survived. We see the idealism of youth smashed on the battle-
fields of France, the long and bitter period of healing for a wound whose scar
will never be entirely erased, and finally the way in which one man came to
terms with a world that included this horror.

At various times in his writings Aldington spoke of his "conception of life." I have tried in the earlier chapters to show the position he reached in his poetry. Let me review this briefly, since it is an important consideration in any evaluation of Aldington's work. In the early "Greek" poems there is more yearning for a lost ideal of life than celebration of "the life of the senses." There can be no doubt of the young poet's being enamored of classical Greece:

> Youth, spring in a Mediterranean island, Greek poetry, idleness—these were the simple factors of an enchantment whose memory will only end with life. . . . Those were the days when Greek was an intoxication of delight. . . .[25]

It is always easier to idealize the unobtainable than to cope with reality, and so in the early poems such as "Choricos," "To a Greek Marble," and "Stele," Aldington dreams nostalgically of the perfect time and place.

During the period when he wrote many of the poems that make up his first volume, *Images (1910-1915)*, Aldington was in Italy. At age twenty in Italy in the springtime, it would be very difficult for any young man to remain in love only with an ideal of the cold, chaste past, being surrounded with so much warm beauty of a real present. In poems like "Amalfi," "June Rain," and "Images" the youthful poet writes of the loveliness of this time and place.

Aldington, however, would have considered finally that he was evading life if his poetry failed to deal with the real world in terms of both its beauty and its ugliness. Writing of the poetry of F.S. Flint, he said:

> "For the modern artist," says Georges Duhamel in one of his essays, "There can be only two methods: s'accepter ou s'évader." . . . that has been Mr. Flint's problem also, and though his resolution has evidently been to accept life, his century, his surroundings, the temptation "to evade" has sometimes overcome him. He is the strongest and finest when he accepts. . . .[26]

In many of the poems of his first volume Aldington tries to come to terms with the real world's darker face. There is some question, however, whether he has been able "to accept," because in many of these poems he seems only to be making a contrast between the ideal world of his imagination and the misery and ugliness he finds surrounding him.

Even the most casual reading of the *Images of War* poems will quickly reveal the sharp impact of the reality of trench warfare on the still-young poet who had not yet completely resolved the conflict between his Grecian ideal and the world of his own time. In the hell of the trenches of France, Aldington hammered out the shape of his "life quest"; the remaining body of his poetry is an extension of this first accommodation to reality. He began to substitute nature for his unattainable Grecian ideal, and by taking comfort in the beauty that nature offered even during war, as well as by keeping alive the memory of love, he saved his creative self from complete destruction (although not from a scar it was to carry for the rest of his life). In *Images of*

Desire, the volume of love poems written in the same years as the war poems, similar adjustments to reality occur, but here the power of passionate human love becomes the primary salvation.

Although Richard Aldington survived the war physically (which a great many of his fellow artists did not), and appeared in his poetry to have made an accommodation to it, he was in fact quite a number of years "healing" from its effects. The whole of his *Exile and Other Poems* reveals a period of convalescence during which he is striving to regain his psychological and also his poetic balance. In an article for *Poetry* magazine in 1921 he asks: "How can poetry, which is essentially order, affirmation, achievement, be created in an age, a *milieu*, of profound doubt and discouragement?"[27] All of the poems of the "Words for Music" part of *Exile* are, as the poet quite frankly tells us, an effort to steep himself again in poetic tradition—to rehabilitate his craft while he is restoring his spirit.

In *A Fool i' the Forest* Aldington returns once more to a consideration of the schism between the world as it is and the world as it might be. In a "Note" to the poem he identifies the dichotomy as that between an artistic and a scientific civilization. The poem is inconclusive, however, since the poet leads us into the wasteland without Eliot's promise of regenerative fire and water. It is in the four long poems of the last ten years of his poetic work that Aldington gives final shape to the "conception of life" that he first glimpsed on the battlefields of France.

Life Quest expands the concept of the godhead in nature that Aldington first wrote of in his war poems; it urges man to "revere the real holy ones/ Sun Sea and Earth." In Aldington's novel *All Men Are Enemies* (p. 301), Antony Clarendon says, on seeing the palace at Blois:

> It symbolized, he thought, the moment when the real degeneration had started, when men began to believe that a crass tyrannizing of nature was the ideal, when they began to lose touch with the sky, earth and water as mysterious god-like things and to think of them only as forces to be exploited for an immediate gain, and when all the splendor and beauty came to be used only for self-glorification.

This glorification of nature is one facet of Aldington's vision of life which was built up through the early poems like those in *Images of War*, and culminated in *Life Quest*. Besides being a part of his resolution of the conflict between ideal and real that troubled him even before the war, it is a bringing together of the classical vision and the beauty of his own world so that he never quite needs to relinquish the dream of his youth.

The other and more important facet of the poet's "conception of life," the power of love, is expressed in the three long love poems. *The Eaten Heart* marks the close of the ten years of "exile" during which the poet was trying to make himself whole again. The poem is first an assertion of the essential human condition: "The dreadful inevitable loneliness of the human soul." For this loneliness the poet, like D.H. Lawrence, prescribes quite simply the love of man for woman:

> I think perhaps there is one thing worth achieving—
> Escape the fate of Philoctetes, the essential solitude,
> Achieve release, so that one's total nature
> At all points meets another's
> Whereby life becomes positive and immeasurably enriched.

In the other two long love poems, *A Dream in the Luxembourg* and *The Crystal World*, the poet provides exempla for his text—he tries to prove on our senses the point he has argued reasonably in *The Eaten Heart*.

What Richard Aldington has to say to us in the body of his poetry is not new; his "conception of life" is not unique. It was said before by the classical Greek writers in the age he admired so much; it was said in part by Remy de Gourmont, the Frenchman whose works he edited and translated; and it is central to the message left by his friend and contemporary, D. H. Lawrence. Of Aldington's novels, *All Men Are Enemies* comes the closest to his poetry in the expression of his life-view. It is written in the sensuous style which is his best, and is for this reason his finest novel. But it is to his poetry that we should turn for the clearest statement of his creed—to the "Epilogue" of *Images of Desire*, for instance, a poem that was probably written in 1917-1918 and to whose theme Aldington returned again and again in his poetry of the next twenty years.

> Have I spoken too much or not enough of love?
> Who can tell?
>
> But we who do not drug ourselves with lies
> Know, with how deep a pathos, that we have
> Only the warmth and beauty of this life
> Before the blankness of the unending gloom.
> Here for a little while we see the sun
> And smell the grape-vines on the terraced hills,
> And sing and weep, fight, starve and feast, and love
> Lips and soft breasts too sweet for innocence.
> And in this little glow of mortal life—
> Faint as one candle in a large cold room—
> We know the clearest light is shed by love,
> That when we kiss with life-blood in our lips,
> Then we are nearest to the dreamed-of gods.

Richard Aldington was a better poet than his present reputation indicates. One of the things that has damaged his permanent reputation was the tendency, early in his career, to associate him with poets such as Eliot and Lawrence whose work is of a different order. Equally detrimental was his position as a leading Imagist poet which gave him, while still young, a station he could not maintain. There is also the question of the effect of his wartime service on his poetic art. While it made him a more representative poet of his period, it may also have hurt his poetry. It is possible that as a novelist Aldington used as a spring the traumatic shock of a wartime experience that proved injurious to him as a poet.[28]

NOTES

1. See, for instance, H.D.'s *Bid Me To Live* (*A Madrigal*) (New York: Grove Press, 1960), and John Cournos's *Miranda Masters* (New York: Alfred A. Knopf, 1926).

2. In *Richard Aldington: An Intimate Portrait*, ed. Alister Kershaw and Frédéric-Jacques Temple (Carbondale: Southern Illinois University Press, 1965), p. 142.

3. *The Times Literary Supplement*, 26 December 1968, p. 1448.

4. *Life for Life's Sake: A Book of Reminiscences* (New York: The Viking Press, 1941), p. 399.

5. In *Richard Aldington: An Intimate Portrait*, ed. Kershaw and Temple, p. 20.

6. Although Sir Herbert Read says that "sometime between the publication of the second Imagist Anthology (1916) and the end of the war Aldington had abandoned his imagist ideals" (in *Richard Aldington: An Intimate Portrait*, pp. 123-124), this is not exactly the case. No one, except possibly H. D., remained an Imagist poet in the full sense of the "manifesto." Imagism was a breath of fresh air which blew away the staleness of the prevailing tradition that was stifling the poetry of the century. It was not a school that was destined to be propagated to new poets of succeeding generations, but a seedbed which promoted the growth of poets. One did not abandon Imagism but rather grew from it toward something else.

7. *Ibid.*, p. 126.

8. *A.E. Housman and W. B. Yeats: Two Lectures* (Hurst, Berkshire: The Peacocks Press, 1955), p. 11.

9. Introduction to *The Religion of Beauty: Selections from the Aesthetes* (London: William Heinemann, 1950), p. 5.

10. Foreword, *Latin Poems of the Renaissance* (London: The Egoist, Ltd., 1919).

11. "Landor's Hellenics," *Literary Studies and Reviews* (First published by George Allen and Unwin in 1924; Freeport, N. Y.: Books for Libraries Press, reprint ed., 1968), pp. 143-144.

12. Unpublished letter to Amy Lowell dated 20 November 1917, in The Houghton Library of Harvard University.

13. *Life for Life's Sake*, pp. 119-120.

14. "Campion's 'Observations,' " *Poetry: A Magazine of Verse*, Vol. 15, No. 5 (February 1920), pp. 267-271.

15. "Free Verse in England," Vol. 1, No. 18, pp. 351-352.

16. *The Chapbook: A Miscellany*, No. 40 (1925), pp. 36-41.

17. *Ezra Pound: His Metric and His Poetry* (New York: Alfred A. Knopf, 1917). Reprinted in *To Criticize the Critic, and Other Writings* (New York: Farrar, Straus and Giroux, 1965). The quotation appears on p. 173 of the latter edition.

18. "Two Poets, " *The Egoist*, Vol. 1, No. 22 (16 November 1914), pp. 422-423.

19. *Life for Life's Sake*, p. 222.

20. Unpublished letter dated 18 December 1951, in Lockwood Memorial Library, State University of New York at Buffalo.

21. *The Complete Poems of Richard Aldington* (London: Allan Wingate, 1948), p. 15.

22. *All Men Are Enemies: A Romance* (London: Chatto and Windus, 1933), pp. ix-x, 308.
23. In *Richard Aldington: An Intimate Portrait*, p. 159.

24. *Richard Aldington: An Appreciation* (London: William Heinemann, n.d.), pp. 17-18.

25. *Literary Studies and Reviews* (London: George Allen and Unwin, 1924), p. 241.

26. "The Poetry of F. S. Flint," *The Egoist*, Vol. 2, No. 5 (1 May 1915), pp. 80-81.

27. "The Poet and Modern Life," *Poetry: A Magazine of Verse*, Vol. 18, No. 2 (May 1921), pp. 99-100.

28. "Somehow I have never recovered from those war years—it was too long, and I still think it would have been better to have stopped a bullet in 1916 than to struggle on with a shattered life." Aldington included these lines in a letter written to Crosby Gaige on 31 May 1927, which is now in the Beinecke Rare Book and Manuscript Library at Yale University.

4

"The Complete Poems": A Commentary

"Images"

The Complete Poems is arranged in sections that correspond approximately to original editions of Aldington's poetry. Thus the "Images" section, which is the first, draws almost half of its poems from the 1915 edition of *Images (1910-1915)*; with the exception of one poem, the remainder are from the 1916 *Images Old and New* and the four Imagist anthologies. This does not mean that the 1948 *Complete Poems* was compiled directly from these earlier editions; as we have noted, there were a number of intermediate steps: between the original editions listed above and the "Images" section of *The Complete Poems* are the 1919 *Images, Collected Poems* (1928), *Collected Poems, 1915-1923*, published in 1933, and *The Poems of Richard Aldington* (1934). The 1948 collection, therefore, is at the top of a pyramid that grew gradually from scattered periodical publications, to first editions, to enlarged editions, and through a series of collections that preceded the final one.

Fortunately Aldington, a scholar as well as poet, provides a Bibliographical Note to the 1948 *Complete Poems* in which he lists the original editions from which he selected its contents. (He also makes acknowledgments for those poems in the "New Poems" section which, prior to the 1934 collection, had appeared only in periodicals.) We have, therefore, good directions leading us to the first book publications of the poems in the "Images" section. Moreover, since *Images (1910-1915)* lists on its inside cover the anthologies and magazines in which "a number of these poems have already appeared," and the three later Imagist anthologies supply similar information, many of the poems can be traced back to their original publications.

As noted in Chapter 2, all thirty poems of *Images (1910-1915)*, with the exception of the two prose poems "Night Piece" and "Dawn," are reprinted in the 1948 volume in the "Images" section. This section contains a total of forty-six poems of which twenty are *not* from Aldington's first book of poetry. The apparent discrepancy is caused by the fact that three of the 1915 poems are printed together in the collected volume under the title "Epigrams."

The general arrangement of the "Images" section of *The Complete Poems* seems to be simple enough: the poems from *Images (1910-1915)*, interspersed with four additional poems from the later *Images Old and New* volume, are followed by poems from the Imagist anthologies. But examined more closely, the actual arrangement of the poems in this section is somewhat more complex. For instance, the first poem in this part, "Choricos," is the seventh poem in the *Images (1910-1915)* edition; the third and fourth poems of the collected edition are the fifth and fifteenth of the early edition. The sixteenth poem is from the first Imagist anthology, *Des Imagistes: An Anthology*, the nineteenth poem from the third Imagist anthology, *Some Imagist Poets* (1916), and the twenty-second poem from the second anthology. Appendix A lists all of the poems of the "Images" section in the order in which they appear in *The Complete Poems*, indicates the original edition or editions in which they were first printed, and shows their order of appearance there. Prior periodical publication is also indicated when possible. Before attempting to suggest a rationale for Aldington's arrangement of his poems in this part of his collected edition, I shall examine revisions in the poems themselves. Tentatively, however, the arrangement may be thought of as basically chronological but altered somewhat to reflect the poet's idea of his own emotional development.

In his Introduction to *The Complete Poems*, written presumably in 1947, Richard Aldington has this to say about the poems he selected to begin the "Images" section: "More than thirty-five years have passed since the first three poems in this book were published in Chicago by Miss Harriet Monroe in her magazine *Poetry*."[1] This would be reason enough to place these poems first; in addition, they are acutely representative of the poet's early "Greek" mode. That "Choricos" is placed the very first may also be attributed to the fact that critics have always considered it one of Aldington's finest poems in his early style.

A comparison of the poems in the original editions with those in *The Complete Poems* indicates that Aldington was not, like Yeats for instance, a poet whose work underwent constant and extensive revision. In "Choricos," for example, there are some seventeen minor changes in a poem containing seventy-five lines. The number of revisions is approximately the same regardless of which of the early versions is considered: the source can be *Poetry*, the 1914 *Des Imagistes, Images (1910-1915)*, or the 1916 *Images Old and New*. We will therefore confine our discussion of textual differences to those existing between the *Images (1910-1915)* volume and the final collection.

Because most of the revisions made in "Choricos" are characteristic of those made throughout the "Images" section, we will look at them here in some detail. By far the majority of changes are minor revisions in punctuation. There are about ten of these in "Choricos," and most of them involve an omission or addition of commas which has little if any effect on the meaning of the lines. As a matter of fact, the original punctuation often seems preferable. Other punctuation revisions involve an interchanging of semi-colons and colons and the removal of some dashes which appeared in the original version. A number of compound words that were formerly separated are now hyphenated. In lines eleven, eighteen, and twenty-six the spelling of classical place and personal names is brought into conformity with modern usage.

One very characteristic change is the omission of a stanza break at line thirty-seven. Many of Aldington's poems, as they appear in *The Complete*

Poems, have been compressed by the omission of this extra spacing. Occasionally one suspects that typographical requirements may have influenced the change; that is to say, two or more stanzas will be joined in order to fit the poem on the page. This is not so in the case of "Choricos," which ends on a page three-quarters blank. Whatever the reason, it remains a fact that the spacing and marginal limitations imposed on many of the collected poems detract from their appearance. Even the type faces used in the original editions are usually much superior to that found in the collected edition. As to paper stock, there is, unfortunately, an even more unhappy decline. *The Complete Poems* was printed in 1948, when all the wartime restrictions on paper had perhaps not yet been relaxed. In any event, the paper must have had a high ground-wood content, since it is now considerably yellowed. The contrast to the still snow-white, crisp, high-rag-content paper of the *Images (1910-1915)* edition (at least of the copy which I have examined) is sad indeed.

The only change in "Choricos" which does not involve punctuation or orthography occurs in line fifty, where "far" has been substituted for "dark" in the phrase "Over dark leagues of lonely sea." Possibly Aldington did not like the echo of line thirty-nine's "By the dark streams of Persephone," or felt that the original phrase was too close to Homer's oft-repeated "wine-dark sea."

We can turn now to some other poems that provide examples of Aldington's revisions. Quite frequently he seems to have reversed intermediate changes and gone back to the version printed in an earlier publication. For instance, line five of "Argyria" now reads, "You have hidden away your hands." In *Des Imagistes* (1914), *Images (1910-1915)*, and *Images Old and New* (1916), the "away" was omitted, but in *Poetry*, where the poem was first published in January 1914, the printing was identical to the final version.

"The River" is a second example of this kind of change. Lines seven and eight now read as they did when the poem was first published in *Poetry* in January 1914, but in *Des Imagistes* and in *Images (1910-1915)* the same lines read, "She has come from beneath the trees/ Moving within the mist." The final (and original) version is much more effective, moving the poem toward the dramatic monologue and away from its impersonal viewpoint.

On the other hand, the poet sometimes retains intermediate changes, as in "At Mitylene," in which lines nine and ten of *The Complete Poems* did not appear in the original version which was published in *The Egoist* (1 May 1914) and reprinted in *Images (1910-1915)*. These lines were added to the poem by 1916, when they were present in *Images Old and New*. The three little poems now printed as "Epigrams" are another instance. In *Images (1910-1915)* and in *Images Old and New* they appeared as separate poems on individual pages. But by the time of the 1915 anthology, *Some Imagist Poets*, they were arranged as in *The Complete Poems*, except that the order was reversed. In line four of one of these little poems, "October," the 1915 anthology substituted the word "autumn" for the "silver" of the earlier versions. Aldington maintained this alteration in *The Complete Poems*, although it does not preserve the logic of the poem as well as the original term.

Occasionally Aldington changed the titles of poems from those used in the earliest versions. "In the Old Garden," when first printed in *Poetry* in November 1912, and later in *Des Imagistes* (1914), was entitled "Au Vieux Jardin," and only subsequently was the title anglicized. In his Introduction to *The Complete Poems* (p. 16), Aldington gives us a clue to his reason for this change:

> One more point. Though I believe that a poet should make use of any knowledge he may have, all parade of erudition is abhorrent to me. There are only one or two translations in this volume. My translations of foreign poets are collected in two books (in England) called *Medallions* and *Fifty Romance Poems*. There is one passage of "A Fool i' th' Forest", written in French because it happened to come that way, but otherwise there are only a few words of foreign language.

There are some interesting changes made in the six-stanza poem "Images." In the first place, roman numerals are used almost uniformly to number the stanzas throughout all editions except *The Complete Poems*, which uses arabic; I feel that the former look better. More importantly, the original version of "Images," as published in *Poetry* of October 1915, shows, in addition to four punctuation differences, two textual variations from the final version: line four of the third stanza reads, "Art thou to me," without the added "my beloved"; line three of stanza six reads, "So does my mind fill slowly with misgiving," compared to *The Complete Poems'* "So does my heart fill slowly with tears." In *Images (1910-1915)*, line three of stanza two has become "So my love leaps forth towards you"; "my beloved" is still missing from III, 4. In *Images Old and New*, an additional line* is added to stanza six so that it now reads:

> The flower that the wind has shaken
> Is soon filled again with rain:
> So does my heart fill slowly with tears
> *o Foam-Driver, Wind-of-the-Vineyards,
> Until you return.

These changes affect three of the poem's stanzas; let us consider them in more detail, beginning with the stanza quoted immediately above. Certainly we must agree that the final version of line three is a considerable improvement over the line as it first appeared in *Poetry*. The heart that fills with tears equates more logically with the flower filling with rain than does the mind that fills with misgiving. As for the extra line that was added to the stanza when it was printed in *Images Old and New*, I feel that it had a disastrous effect on the poem as a whole, since it impersonalized what is otherwise a fine love poem made up of a series of graceful compliments to the loved one. How the poet could have thought that the "You, O exquisite one" of stanza I, the "you" that his "love leaps toward" of stanza II, and the "you" who trembles like "a young beech-tree" of stanza IV could become the "Foam-Driver, Wind-of-the-Vineyards" is hard to understand. Perhaps he

began to think of the "Images" as separate poems, but obviously when pre-
paring their final version he saw them as interlocked and wisely eliminated
the incongruous line.

Stanza III, where another of the changes occurs, reads as follows in the
Poetry version:

> A rose-yellow moon in a pale sky
> When the sunset is faint vermilion
> In the mist among the tree-boughs
> Art thou to me.

In *Images (1910-1915)* the last line of this stanza reads "Are you to me," but
in *Images Old and New* the original line is restored and "my beloved" added
to it. This addition, as I noted, is retained in the final version. The added
words have the advantage of both filling out the cadence of the line, and
preserving the intimate relationship between the poet and his lover that is
suggested by the earlier stanzas. In the face of this "my beloved," Aldington's
addition of the extra line to the last stanza, creating just the reverse of an
intimate effect, is even more puzzling.

Stanza II in *Poetry* differs from the final version only in the use of a
period instead of a comma at the end of line two:

> The blue smoke leaps
> Like swirling clouds of birds vanishing.
> So my love leaps towards you,
> Vanishes and is renewed.

In *Images (1910-1915)* and in *Images Old and New,* the third line became "So
my love leaps forth towards you." One of the problems that Aldington was
wrestling with in this stanza was the double metaphor. The basic image of the
smoke which "leaps" towards the sky is compared with clouds of birds
"vanishing" skyward; then with a nice twist the poet's love is seen to "leap"
like the smoke, "vanish" like smoke and birds, and be "renewed" as the
smoke is by the fire from which it rises. The poet as fire sends his love as
smoke towards the beloved, who is properly affixed in the heavens. Thinking
of the metaphor in this way, we can see that the original and final version is
certainly the best. The "forth" confines the smoke (to a chimney, for
instance), restricting the metaphor. "To" implies that both smoke and love
reach their objectives, while "towards" fits better the idea that both never
quite obtain their goal but rather vanish and are renewed.

Images Old and New contains thirty-five of Aldington's poems:
twenty-nine that had already appeared in his first volume (of which all but
the prose poems "Night Piece" and "Dawn" were collected in *The Complete
Poems*) and six new poems of which only four found their way into the
collected edition.

The two new poems that were not finally included in *The Complete*

Poems are "Hyella" and "A New House." Both of these poems are repro-
duced in Chapter 3 of Part II of this book, and an examination of them gives
clues as to why they were omitted. "Hyella" is the fifteenth poem and
appears on page 26 of *Images Old and New*. Beneath the title the following is
printed in parentheses in italic: "From 'Acon,' written in Latin in the six-
teenth century by the Italian, Giovanni-Battista Amalteo." The fact that the
poem was a translation was sufficient reason for its exclusion. The reasons for
omitting the second poem, "A New House," are more subtle and we can only
guess at them. The emotion behind the poem is the same that Aldington's
friend Lawrence felt in *Lady Chatterley's Lover* when he wrote about the
motor trip that Constance Chatterley made through Derbyshire:

> The car ploughed uphill through the long squalid straggle of Tevershall,
> the blackened brick dwellings, the black slate roofs glistening their
> sharp edges, the mud black with coal-dust, the pavements wet and
> black. It was as if dismalness had soaked through and through every-
> thing. The utter negation of natural beauty, the utter negation of the
> gladness of life, the utter absence of the instinct for shapely beauty
> which every bird and beast has, the utter death of the human intuitive
> faculty was appalling.[2]

The difference is that Lawrence does give us Mellors and the forest, so that
his view is tinged less with bitterness than with compassion for the human
situation. Lawrence is the prophet who is trying to lead us out of the
wilderness. In "A New House," however, one feels only the bitterness over
the "trampled soil . . . felled trees . . . and naked flowers." Aldington may
have felt the negative quality of this poem and decided that its tone was not
one that he wished to make a permanent part of his poetry. Besides, the
poem is not quite successful in its juxtaposition of the "old earth-gods" with
the realistic description of a new house under construction.

   The four poems which appear in this edition and in *The Complete
Poems* but not in *Images (1910-1915)* are "Stele," "Lesbia," "Scents," and
"Church Walk, Kensington." "Scents" is made up of two little poems entitled
"White Jonquils" and "Yellow Jonquils"; the first one reads:

> Old cloisters where a hollow fountain drips
> And the brown church walls
> Are soft with summer sun.
>
> And the moist garden mould in March
> After the wind.

Aldington made an interesting change in the third line: in *Images Old and
New* this reads, "Are soft with winter sun." What this change does is to
separate the two images, making us see that the cloisters and the garden are
not together in time or space. The second little poem, "Yellow Jonquils,"
makes clear Aldington's intention to contrast both seasons and localities:

The moon
Low down the hills Sorrento sees about her—
The orange orchards sweet in May.
Again the soft wet earth
In English gardens
When rain and wind have passed.

Since in *Images Old and New* this second poem is divided into two tercets, there is no question that the poet is comparing England and Italy; with the change of the word "winter" to "summer" the two images of the first poem are clearly separated and the same comparison made apparent. This is a good example of the kind of care that Aldington exercised in his revisions. It is also an example of the manner in which the spacing of the poetry in *The Complete Poems* detracts from some of the individual poems. A space between the first and second three lines of "Yellow Jonquils" reinforces the poet's intention and clarifies his meaning.

"Stele," "Lesbia," and "Church Walk, Kensington" are reprinted in *The Complete Poems* almost exactly as they appear in *Images Old and New*, although "Lesbia" has changed since it first appeared in book form in the 1914 anthology, *Des Imagistes*.[3] The earlier version did not have the present first line: "Grow weary if you will, let me be sad." The poem is perhaps a better one without the new line, which seems gratuitous. The sadness of the poet is obvious in the other lines:

And Picus of Mirandola is dead;
And all the gods they dreamed and fabled of,
Hermes and Thoth and Christ are rotten now,
Rotten and dank . . . .
And through it all I see your pale Greek face;
Tenderness
Makes me as eager as a little child to love you,
You morsel left half-cold on Caesar's plate.

That the Greek girl has grown "weary" should somehow be conveyed through the lover's emotion toward his beloved rather than in a bald statement.

With a single exception ("The Faun Captive"), the remainder of the "Images" section of *The Complete Poems* is made up of verse that appears in the four Imagist anthologies. There is one poem from the first anthology, *Des Imagistes* (1914); four are from the 1915 volume of *Some Imagist Poets*, five from the 1916 volume, and five from 1917. When I speak of a poem in the "Images" section of *The Complete Poems* as being "from" these anthologies, I mean that the same poem did not also appear in either *Images (1910-1915)* or *Images Old and New*. The converse, of course, is not true; there are a number of poems that I have considered as being "from" the two individual works that also appeared in one of the anthologies.

Of the ten poems that Aldington contributed to the 1914 Imagist anthology, eight were reprinted in *Images (1910-1915)* and found their way from there to *The Complete Poems*. Since, of the two others, "To Atthis" was discarded, "Bromios" alone comes directly into the collected poetry without an intermediate printing.

The reason that "To Atthis" is excluded from *The Complete Poems* is made clear by the parenthetical note under its title: "After the Manuscript of Sappho now in Berlin." As usual, Aldington has rigidly excised a poem that he does not consider completely his own work. Possibly the poet has been too strict in this regard; here again is what Pound says of this poem and the others by Aldington in *Des Imagistes*:

> "Only emotion endures." Surely it is better for me to name over the few beautiful poems that still ring in my head than for me to search my flat for back numbers of periodicals and rearrange all that I have said about friendly and hostile writers. . . .
> Aldington's version of "Atthis". . . . These things have worn smooth in my head and I am not through with them, nor with Aldington's "In Via Sistina" nor his other poems in "Des Imagistes," though people have told me their flaws. It may be that their content is too much embedded in me for me to look back at the words.[4]

While there are nine minor changes of punctuation and spacing in "Bromios" from the version in *Des Imagistes* to the final version, the only significant change is the addition of a subtitle. This reads, "A Frieze in the Vatican," and thus makes explicit for the reader the poem's starting point, which otherwise might have been difficult to deduce.

In the 1915 Imagist anthology Aldington had seven poems, of which three came into *The Complete Poems* via *Images (1910-1915)*; four of these poems, however, do not appear in any of the intermediate editions of Aldington's poetry we have discussed in this chapter.

"Childhood," which was published first in *The Egoist*, shows only minor punctuation and spacing changes when the versions in the periodical and the anthology are compared to the final version. "The Poplar," which first appeared in *Poetry* numbered IV under the general heading "Poems," shows practically no change. "Round Pond" (the title is hyphenated in the anthology) has an additional line in the original version. The last line reads: "Even the cold wind is seeking a new mistress"; previously there was a line before it which read: "Too-hoo, this is brave." It seems to me that the poem misses this perky little line, which brought the poet closer. "Daisy" is unchanged except for the loss of its epigraph from Catullus: "Plus quam se atque suos amavit omnes,/ Nunc. . . ."

Of Aldington's seven poems in *Some Imagist Poets* of 1916, "After Two Years" had already appeared in *Images (1910-1915)*, and "People" is collected in the "Images of War" section of *The Complete Poems*; the other five poems are included in the "Images" section of the final collected edition.

"Eros and Psyche" shows practically no change in *The Complete Poems* from the ways it appeared in *The Egoist* and later in the 1916 anthology. In line sixty the old-fashioned "goods-train's" of *The Egoist* version was changed in the 1916 printing to the final "freight-train's." There are a number of similar instances in other poems in which the poet has modernized his language. "Fantasy" is reprinted in the "Images" section with no change except in the title; in the anthology it was simply "1915." This seems to be another instance, like that of "Bromios," in which Aldington felt the need to be more explicit. "Whitechapel," in both *The Egoist* and the anthology, appears exactly as it does in *The Complete Poems*; the other two poems show only minor changes.

Half of Aldington's poems from the 1917 volume of *Some Imagist Poets* are collected in the "Images" section: "Prayer," "R. V. and Another," "Captive," "Images," and "Inarticulate Grief." The only important change in these five poems is in "Inarticulate Grief," in which the last line is changed from the anthology's "For the sea is the cry of our sorrow" to "For the sea is the cry of sorrow." This seems a good change; the removal of "our" makes the "sorrow" more universal and swings the "s" sound of "sea" into that most lovely sounding of poetic words, "sorrow," without the extra blocking effect of the additional word. Beyond this slight change, the only other point worth noting is the fact that "R. V. and Another" was, in *The Egoist*, the second of two poems appearing under the general title "Two Poems"; the first poem, "The Days Pass," was not reprinted in *The Complete Poems* but is reproduced by me in Chapter 2 of Part II.

Of the forty-six poems in the "Images" section of *The Complete Poems*, we have now accounted for all except "The Faun Captive." This is the only poem in this section that did not originally appear in *Images (1910-1915)*, *Images Old and New*, or one of the four anthologies. "The Faun Captive" was printed in *The Living Age* (Vol. 302, 9 August 1919, p. 384) as "The Captive Faun." This version differs from the final one only in punctuation. *The Living Age*, all of whose poetry was evidently reprinted from other periodicals, credits this poem to *The Nation*. In *The Nation* the poem appears in Vol. 25, No. 9 (31 May 1919), p. 265; here the title is also "The Captive Faun," and there are only two very minor differences from the final version.[5]

From this examination of the original publications from which the poems in the "Images" section were drawn, we should be able to reach some general conclusions. What kind of revisions did Aldington make? Why did he select some poems and omit others? Are the poems he decided to include in this section of *The Complete Poems* arranged in any particular fashion?

By far the largest number of changes made between versions of poems in earlier publications and the same poems as printed in the final collected edition are in punctuation. Most of these punctuation changes seem only to reflect the poet's changing habits or general changes in usage and do not affect the poem's meaning or aesthetic appearance. Spelling is also modernized, and terms that have become archaic are brought up to date. Many of the spacing changes that were made seem to detract from the poems; it is probable that these were enforced by space limitations in *The Complete Poems* rather than put into effect by Aldington's wishes.

The changes made in the texts of poems are, for the most part, considerable improvements. The relative scarcity of such changes can be explained by Aldington's early retirement as a poet. His letters to John Gawsworth, saying that he stopped writing poetry in 1938, were noted at the end of Chapter 2. It can be argued that a poet who no longer considered himself an active practitioner of his craft, unlike Yeats, who wrote until the week of his death, would not be inclined to make the constant and extensive revisions in his work that Yeats did.

As will be readily seen from the second part of this book, Richard Aldington omitted from the final collection a great many of his poems that had been published earlier in periodicals or even in book form. The poems not carried over from those early volumes which supplied all but one of the poems in the "Images" section fall into three general categories: poems that the poet evidently thought did not come up to the standard of quality he was trying to maintain; prose poems; and translations.

In a sense, a poet is always selecting; this is one of the important bases of art. He selects from words to make a poem, he selects from his poems for periodical publication, he selects from periodical publications for editions, and, if time permits, he selects from these editions and from previous collections for a final collection. Once a poem has been published in any way, however, the critic has a right to consider it, whether or not the poet later rejects it for final collection. Although Aldington, in making up the contents of *Images (1910-1915)*, *Images Old and New*, and the four Imagist anthologies, rejected many of the verse poems he had published in periodicals, only "A New House" was included in one of those volumes but rejected later. It is the only poem in the "Images" section that fits into the first of the three categories mentioned above; and in discussing this poem earlier, I indicated that I thought its omission to be justified.

A great many prose poems never found their way from the periodicals in which they were published to the first editions. Of the two that did reach any of the volumes that were the sources of the "Images" section, neither appears in *The Complete Poems*. Despite his strong defense of the prose poem against Eliot and others, Aldington seems to have backed down by the time he came to make his own final selection from his work. It is unfortunate that he did not include at least some of his better prose poems in the final collection. In the first place, there are some whose inclusion would be justified on the basis of their value as poetry; and second, since freedom from orthodox form was a characteristic of the revolution in poetry of which Aldington was an important part, he would have done well to preserve some of the best examples of his most revolutionary experiments.

The question of "translations" is a touchy one. Aldington seems to take too stiff an attitude in his Introduction to *The Complete Poems*. All translations of poetry are in effect new poems, and the poet is the best judge of whether the resultant poem is really "his." Possibly Aldington was right in omitting a poem like "Hyella," but good poetry written "in the manner of" need not be excluded. This is particularly true of the two *Myrrhine and Konallis* editions; there is no question but that these poems were not collected because Aldington felt they were too close to being "translations," and because he considered some or all of them as "prose" poems. May Sinclair evidently did not think either point an objection, or she could not have said what she did about them. I agree with her opinion and feel that Aldington did himself a grave injustice by not collecting some of these sensuous love poems; they represent the kind of poetry in which Aldington's talents are shown to best advantage. The poet's decision is especially odd when one considers that much of the "Words for Music" section of *The Complete Poems* is made up of poetry written "in the manner of" the seventeenth-century Cavalier poets; these poems, however, are in verse rather than prose, and perhaps that was their saving grace to Aldington.

The arrangement of the poems in the "Images" section, as suggested earlier, is basically chronological. That is to say, the poems of *Images (1910-1915)* are placed first and followed by poems from the 1915, 1916, and 1917 anthologies. This order makes the poems tend to fall into a natural pattern, in which the "Greek" poems come first, followed by the poems that deal with the world of the poet's own time. This arrangement is emphasized by the placement of the poems from *Images Old and New*: those dealing with Greek themes, like "Stele" and "Lesbia," are placed among the early poems; those that touch on the poet's own environment, like "Church Walk, Kensington," are put later in the section.

This particular sequence, as we have seen in our earlier critical examination of some of the poems, reflects Aldington's growth from a young poet lost in his vision of the ideal beauty of Greek civilization to a man confronted with the reality of the world in which he lives, and finally jarred by experiences of the 1914-1918 World War in which he is eventually an active participant.

The first eight poems in the section are definitely Greek in theme; then the poet seems to consider the beauties of his own world in poems like "The River" and "In the Old Garden." In poems such as "Bromios" and "The Faun Sees Snow for the First Time," the Greek themes are still present; in the second half of the section, however, a new note is introduced in poems like "Church Walk, Kensington," "Cinema Exit," and "In the Tube." Now the poet is confronting the ugliness of his age as well as the beauty it shares with the past, and in "Sunsets" he hints at the great horror he will meet with in the "Images of War" section:

And the wind
Blowing over London from Flanders
Has a bitter taste.

The "Images" section is carefully arranged in an almost symphonic pattern which begins on the clear, cool note of the Greek poems, introduces the theme of the beauty of the poet's own world only to have this drowned out by a sordid view of the world, and then plays a short prelude to the next section. The Greek theme is restated in the closing poem, "The Faun Captive," but it is now in a minor key; the poet laments the loss of his ideals but, still young and hopeful, promises that he will somehow break out of the prison of ugliness in which he finds himself and regain his world of beauty.

"Images of War"

The music-like arrangement of the "Images" section of *The Complete Poems* illustrates the great care Aldington took when he began to rearrange his early poems into collections. But as might be expected, the make-up of the "Images of War" section is somewhat less complicated than that of the preceding one, and the revisions within the individual poems not as frequent. All the remaining sections are reprints of the first editions with little or no change. This is natural enough (given a poet who was not an extensive reviser in the first place) since the later poems were being collected at a time less distant from their original dates of publication. Furthermore, even though only four years elapsed between *Images (1910-1915)* and *Images of War*, this was a crucial period for Aldington, and it seems likely that earlier work would be more subject to change than that published after the war.

The easiest way to see how the "Images of War" section was put together is to note the sources of its poems. There are twenty-three poems from the original C.W. Beaumont 1919 edition. Of the twenty missing poems, eleven were added from the expanded Allen and Unwin 1919 edition. Of the remaining nine, *Reverie* supplied four, the 1917 anthology three, the American edition, *War and Love*, one, and the 1916 anthology one. Appendix A lists the poems in the "Images of War" section of *The Complete Poems*. It shows, as completely as could be ascertained, the first editions, anthologies, or periodicals in which these poems first appeared.

The poem from the 1916 anthology is "Resentment." Its title then was "People," and in *War and Love* it was called "Civilians." By the time of the first *Collected Poems*, the title had been changed to the final one, which describes the emotion of the poem; the previous titles name those against whom the feeling is directed. No changes were made in the original text of the poem except for the deletion of a hyphen.

Of the poems taken directly from *Reverie* (some of the *Reverie* poems were included in the Beaumont *Images of War* and I have counted them as deriving from that volume), two have changes worthy of note. "The Wine Cup" did not have its present last line, "As we to death," and was a better poem without it. One of Aldington's weaknesses is a tendency to be too overt; the emotion of the poem is clear enough without the last line. A more important change took place in the fine poem "Reverie," from which the following lines, originally occurring after line eighty-six, were excised:

All men love for a flash, a day,
As I love now,
But all men do not love so long
Nor find in love the excuse for life,
The sanction for the bitterness of death.

The transition from lines eighty-five and eighty-six

> She would be bending by the flower's face
> And I would stand beside and look and love

to the description of the trenches where the poet is writing, is now much more effective than it was when the philosophical lines intervened. On the other hand, these lines that Aldington left out of the poem are extremely important to an understanding of his whole outlook on life: the words "find in love the excuse for life,/ The sanction for the bitterness of death" express the major emotional impact of his body of poetry.

Of the poems from the 1917 anthology, only "Field Manoeuvres" shows any appreciable change. In line sixteen the phrase describing the shrill cry of a mosquito has been changed to "loud and close" from the cliché "loud and clear." In line nineteen the word "obsolete" has been deleted before "rifle"; possibly Aldington did not want to "needle" the War Department any longer. Otherwise the changes are only minor ones involving punctuation.

The eleven poems from the expanded Allen and Unwin edition of *Images of War* show no significant changes. In *War and Love* (Four Seas, 1919) "Misery" had the title "Ivy and Violet . . . " although when published in *The Nation* it had its final title. "Time's Changes" shows some interesting differences between its final version and those of the original magazine publications. In *The Anglo-French Review* of April 1919, there is a subtitle, "Loos"; line three, "Thick scented broom, wild sword-flowers," does not appear, and line five reads "frail-scented" rather than "frail-throated." Lines four, seven, and eight of the version found in *The Complete Poems* do not appear in the version published by *The Living Age* in July of 1919. One needs the whole poem to examine these changes in context:

> Four years ago in Italy
> I gathered wild flowers for a girl—
> Thick scented broom, wild sword-flowers,
> The red anemones that line the ways
> And the frail-throated freesia
> Which lives beneath the orange boughs
> And whose faint scent to me
> Is love's own breath, its kiss. . . . [6]
>
> Today in sunless barren fields
> I gather heads of shells,
> Splinters of shrapnel, cartridges. . . .
>
> What shall I gather
> Four years from today?

Once the third line is added, the "frail-scented" of line five must be changed

to avoid the harsh repetition. It is hard to say why the poet eliminated the
fourth line in the *Living Age* version unless he saw a dramatic value in bring-
ing "sword-flowers" as near as possible to the battlefield scene of the tercet.
The elimination of lines seven and eight would work toward this same end,
although their removal destroys some of the poem's emotional effect.

The twenty-three poems from the Beaumont edition of *Images of War*
also show relatively slight differences when they are compared to their
versions in the "Images of War" section of *The Complete Poems*. "Proem,"
the first poem, preceded the contents page in the first edition and was the
first poem in *Reverie*, where it was set in italics. In both of these earlier edi-
tions, and when it was published in *The Egoist* in the March-April issue of
1919, there was an additional line at the end of the first stanza which read,
"Some Attic gesture." Here is the present poem:

> Out of this turmoil and passion,
> This implacable contest,
> This vast sea of effort,
> I would gather something of repose,
> Some intuition of the inalterable gods.
>
> Each day I grow more restless,
> See the austere shape elude me,
> Gaze impotently upon a thousand miseries
> And still am dumb.

The elimination of the line improves the poem: it is incongruous to equate
"Attic" with the supernatural "intuition."

"Vicarious Atonement," the second poem of *Images of War*, which
appears in the "Images of War" section also as the second poem, has an
interesting one-word change. Addressing the god whom he holds responsible
for the war, the poet concludes, in the poem's present form, "Take, if thou
will, this bitter cup from us." In the original edition the line read, "Take,
if thou canst, this bitter cup from us."

The poem "Dawn" has a number of changes made which seem, as a
whole, to effect a subtle improvement in the music of the lines without great-
ly affecting their meaning. Here are the two versions, the original first:

> The grim dawn lightens thin bleak clouds;
> In the hill clefts beyond flooded meadows
> Lies **death-pale**, death-still mist.
>
> We trudge along wearily,
> Heavy with lack of sleep.
> Spiritless, yet with pretence of gaiety.

The sun brings crimson to the colourless sky;
Light gleams from brass and steel—
We trudge on wearily—

O God, end this bleak anguish
Soon, soon, with vivid crimson death,
End it in mist-pale sleep!

The grim dawn lightens thin bleak clouds;
In the hills beyond the flooded meadows
Lies death-pale, death-still mist.

We trudge along wearily,
Heavy with lack of sleep,
Spiritless, yet with pretense of gaiety.

The sun brings crimson to the colourless sky;
Light shines from brass and steel;
We trudge on wearily—
Our unspoken prayer:
"God, end this black and aching anguish
Soon, with vivid crimson agonies of death
End it in mist-pale sleep."

"Daughter of Zeus," when first published in *The Egoist*, was dedicated, directly beneath the title, "(For J.C.)," and below this the epigraph from Marinetti was printed. In *Images of War* the epigraph was dropped but the dedication remained. The lack of the dedication in the final version is in line with Aldington's practice of omitting these in his *Complete Poems*. The "J.C.," probably, is John Cournos. When the poem was originally published in *The Egoist* of May 1917, the present last line consisted of two lines which read: "Still a tall lady in austere garments/ Comforting our human despair."[7] In *Images of War* the phrase "in austere garments" was deleted and "still a tall lady" printed after the dash in line nine; in the final version this phrase drops down into the final line: "Still a tall lady comforting our human despair."

The two poems which are now listed under the single title "Two Epitaphs" were originally two separate poems with only the initials as titles. Beneath the initials was, in the case of "H.S.R.," the added line "Died of wounds, April, 1917," and in the case of "E.T.," "Died of wounds, May, 1917." In the final versions "Epitaph" is printed above each poem and they are numbered "1" and "2"; the "Died of wounds" becomes the harsher "Killed."

The final poem, of those originally printed in the Beaumont edition and undergoing any noteworthy change, is "Terror." Stanza five of this poem now reads:

Yet because, though we faltered and wept,
We held fast, clung close to our love,
Scorned hate even as they scorned us,
Some god has lightened our lives
Given back the cool mouth of song,
The mouth crushed like a flower.

Originally there was an added line after the last: "Which unpetals in marvelous ways."

As noted earlier, the revision of the poems in the "Images of War" section of *The Complete Poems* was considerably less extensive than in the previous "Images" section. Also, only three of the poems published in the 1919 Beaumont, the 1919 Allen and Unwin, and the 1921 Four Seas editions of *Images of War* do not find their way into the "Images of War" grouping: "Sorcery of Words," "Fatigues," and "Our Hands." Since all three are prose poems (they are reproduced in Chapter 3 of Part II), their omission from the final collection follows the pattern discussed in connection with the earlier section. The "War" section of *War and Love*, the 1919 Four Seas edition which combined poems from the British *Images of War* and *Images of Desire* editions and added others, contains two poems, in addition to the three above, that were not collected in either the "Images" or "Images of War" sections of *The Complete Poems*: "Genius Loci" and "The Faun Complains" (also to be found in Chapter 3, Part II).

In discussing the arrangement of the "Images of War" poems, an important consideration is the fact that from the very beginning Aldington arbitrarily segregated his war poems and his love poems. The result is that this section of *The Complete Poems* does not show quite the subtle psychological development that the previous section did.

The basic arrangement of the Beaumont *Images of War* is retained, the added poems being interspersed. Aldington, however, has not hesitated to move even the original poems around to suit his purposes: "Picket," for instance, the twenty-fifth of the twenty-seven poems in the first edition, becomes the sixteenth poem here. This shifting about of the original poems and weaving in of the added poems seems to have accomplished two purposes.

In the first place, it provides a basic chronological sequence of events. The poet leaves civilian life in poems like "Leave-taking" and "Bondage." Then there is the long central section that is devoted to life in the trenches on both physical and psychological levels, and that contains poems like "On the March," "Misery," "Picket," "Trench Idyll," "Machine Guns," "Barrage," and "Terror." Finally, there is the return to civilian life and the attempt to accommodate to it in poems such as "Resentment," "Apathy," and "The Blood of Young Men."

The structure of the section also illuminates the psychological history of a sensitive idealist brought face-to-face with the drastic reality of war. In "Bondage" the poet considers how he has lived in the past and the life he must now adjust to. In poems like "On the March" he juxtaposes the beauty of nature with the oppression of military duty. Poems like "The Wine Cup" seem to despair of life, only to be confuted by poems such as "Misery" in which the poet promises not to lose his love for life. There is a longing for home and the beloved there, but also, in other poems, a love of the hurt nature which surrounds the poet even in the trenches. Finally, there are the closing poems, which show the damage that the war has inflicted on the soldier-poet and the doubt about his recovery.

The "Images of War" section is nicely framed between "Proem" and "Epilogue." In the first poem the poet expresses the hope that "out of this turmoil" he may "gather something of repose." In the final poem he seems to have found it:

CHE SON CONTENTI NEL FUOCO

We are of those that Dante saw
Glad, for love's sake, among the flames of hell,
Outdaring with a kiss all-powerful wrath;
For we have passed athwart a fiercer hell,
Through gloomier, more desperate circles
Then ever Dante dreamed:
And yet love kept us glad.

The wrenching experience of the war was over, although Aldington was never to forget it. The strength he found in love remained a sustaining support for the rest of his life; in the next section of *The Complete Poems* he paid a powerful poetic tribute to it.

"Images of Desire"

The composition of this section of *The Complete Poems* is very simple: these poems are all from the 1919 Elkin Mathews edition of *Images of Desire*. There are no additional poems and only one poem is omitted here.

The revisions made in the individual poems are minimal. Roman numerals are used throughout in the first edition; these have been changed to arabic, with some loss in appearance. There are a few punctuation changes, including the switch that was made in the collected poems from double to single quotation marks to conform to British usage. (In quoting these poems throughout this text, I have used double quotation marks.)

Even in those poems which we know to have been published earlier in periodicals, there are few if any differences among any of the versions. "Epilogue," the final poem in the section, was originally published in *Arts and*

Letters, New Series Vol. 2, No. 1 (Winter 1918-1919) on page 4. Line thirteen there reads, "We know the clearest light is fed by love" instead of the present "shed by love." Since the image for human life in the previous line is Shakespeare's candle, it seems to me that the original "fed" was the better choice. A life that is "fed" by love will, in Aldington's view, shed the clearest light.

The only poem not carried over from *Images of Desire* was the first poem of that volume, "Dedication," which was set in italic type. It is reproduced in Chapter 3 of Part II; since it is a prose poem the reason for its deletion is self-evident. This same poem was left out of the American publication *War and Love*, as were a number of the other poems that were published in the British *Images of Desire*. On the other hand, the "Love" division of *War and Love* contains four poems that do not appear in either *Images of Desire* or the "Images of Desire" section of *The Complete Poems*; these are: "Song," "Song for Her," "Nights of Love," and "Epilogue." These poems will all be found in the uncollected poems in Chapter 3, Part II. This "Epilogue," it will be noticed, is not the same poem as that which closes the "Images of Desire" section. That poem, in *War and Love*, is titled "Postlude," and the title poem of *Images of Desire* is there called "I Do Not Even Scorn . . . ."

While it is true that Aldington, when making up the final collection, did not disturb the arrangement of the poems in *Images of Desire*, nevertheless his approval of the original arrangement is worth considering. The framing poems are "Prelude," which asks "How could I love you more?" and "Epilogue," which asks "Have I spoken too much or not enough of love?" Even though all of the poems are love poems, there is a consciousness of the war in them. They are not, as a sonnet sequence might be, a rising pattern of passion culminating in union with the beloved. They have, rather, a wave-like rising and falling of passion, which is a natural pattern since the soldier-poet's long tours of duty at the front were broken by occasional leaves.

It is obvious that these poems were written at the same time as the "Images of War" poems and then separated from them. The first ten of the twenty-three poems celebrate the poet's mistress, and here the reader is not conscious of the war. Then abruptly, close to the middle of the section, in the poem "Reserve," which is the shortest of all of the poems, there is a shocking reminder that these are not ordinary love poems:

> Though you desire me I will still feign sleep
> And check my eyes from opening to the day,
> For as I lie, thrilled by your gold-dark flesh,
> I think of how the dead, my dead, once lay.

Following "Reserve" is the title poem, which is a series of nine epigrams praising the poet's mistress; but quickly thereafter follows a large group of poems which deal with parting, fear of separation by death, and even the possibility of the beloved's infidelity. In the final poems of the section the lovers are about to be rejoined permanently, as "Meditation" suggests, but in the poem "Odelette" there is the hint, as toward the close of the previous section in "Apathy," that the war has dealt harshly with the returning lover, and that time will be needed for healing:

> Now I regret
> The fervour that has gone from me,
> Stolen by circumstance,
> Leaving me lassitude—
> A deserted temple with no god.

But from the period of war and love the poet has learned

> That when we kiss with life-blood in our lips,
> Then we are nearest to the dreamed-of gods.

The next section of *The Complete Poems* might be thought of as a convalescent period during which the war is slowly put behind him and his philosophy of love is worked out.

"Exile"

The "Exile" section of *The Complete Poems* is composed of the sixteen poems of the 1923 *Exile and Other Poems*, arranged exactly as they were in that earlier volume, plus the poem "The Parrot," which is inserted just before the last poem. As pointed out in Chapter 2, "The Parrot" first appeared in the 1929 Allen and Unwin British edition of *Collected Poems* almost simultaneously with its inclusion as part VIII of "Passages toward a Long Poem" in the 1930 *Imagist Anthology*.

The revisions that Aldington made in the poems of this section, from the time of the first edition through the various earlier collections to the final *Complete Poems*, are very minor and are concerned strictly with punctuation. Even a comparison of these poems with those first periodical publications which I have been able to locate shows only two changes worthy of note.

The title poem, when it was first printed in *The Dial*, Vol. 75 (October 1923), pp. 323-324, contained an extra line after line twenty-two: "Whose vice is most stupid, most foul." The "vice" referred to belonged to the "whore" of line twenty-one. The point of the lines, it will be remembered, is to compare the goddess worshipped by idealism with that of materialism. In line thirty-nine the addition of the adjective "fluttering" is removed from the line "And gaze through fluttering leaves."

"Rhapsody in a Third-Class Carriage," as originally printed in *The Chapbook: A Monthly Miscellany*, No. 35, March 1923, had the word "men" rather than "workmen" in line ten, and in line twenty-three the word "beetroots" instead of the present "beets." The first change provides more of a contrast for the "heavy cunning men" of the previous line, and the second substitutes the more general term for one that is chiefly British.

In the two collections that followed the 1929 *Collected Poems* "The Parrot" is printed last in the "from Exile" sections. Its switch in *The Complete Poems* is, therefore, one of the latest revisions that the poet made. Now that it has been made, the change seems very logical. The poem follows "Truth" and, one might say, acts as an antidote to it. In the last line of "Truth" the poet says, "I here renounce you and your verminous tricks," while in "The Parrot" he says he plans to buy a parrot that will show him the truth when he fails to see it.

Since the arrangement of the poems in the section remains, except for "The Parrot," as it was in the 1923 volume, we can consider only whether there was any pattern originally. It seems that these poems move from a low point of despair to a quiet center and finally toward what, if it is not hope, is at least a seeing of things as they are; in this last stage is implied the promise of future affirmation. The nine poems up to "Freedom" are concerned with horrid memories of the war, complaints about what it has done to the poet, and observations on the drab life of postwar England. In "Freedom" the poet begins by saying,

> At last, after many years, I am saturated
> With pity and agony and tears;
> At last I have reached indifference;

and he concludes,

> I have passed through hate and pity,
> Desire and anguish to this:
> I am myself,
> I am free.

While Aldington seems to feel in "Freedom" that he has cast off the effects of the war and of the immediate postwar years, we know that he never did so completely. In any event, in the remaining poems of the section, such as "Nightingale," "Truth," and "The Parrot," he seems to be preparing himself for a more affirmative view of life; and in the short section which comes next he clearly indicates the direction this affirmation will take.

"Words For Music"

The "Words for Music" division of *The Complete Poems* is made up of the poems of the second part of *Exile and Other Poems*. There are no added poems and only one poem is omitted. The arrangement of the poems is also the same: the ten "Songs for Puritans" are followed by four of the original five "Songs for Sensualists," and then the two long poems of "Metrical Exercises."

"From Tasso," the one poem missing, was probably omitted on the familiar grounds that it was a translation; it imitated a particular poem, while the other poems in this series were more generally patterned after the styles of various Cavalier poets. The excision was made in all of the earlier collections as well.

There are practically no differences between the poems as they appear here and as they appeared in the 1923 edition. I was able to trace most of the poems in this section to their periodical publications, but even when all the versions are considered, there are, for the most part, no important variations. The "Songs for Puritans" are virtually identical throughout their several printings except for spacing changes. In the four remaining "Songs for Sensualists" there had been two title variations: when printed in *The Living Age*, Vol. 316 (17 March 1923) on page 670, "Words for Music" (the title poem) was called "Delia's Faith"; and when "A Garden Homily" was printed in the same periodical, Vol. 316 (27 January 1923), p. 199, it had the title "The Earth." Both poems, incidentally, are credited by *The Living Age* to *To-Day*.

A much more interesting kind of change takes place in the first poem of "Metrical Exercises," "The Berkshire Kennet." This is the poem that was published in a limited edition of only fifty copies for Holbrook Jackson by The Curwen Press. The following six lines appear in the limited edition of the single poem but are deleted from the same poem as it appears in the 1923 *Exile and Other Poems*:

> If grief come with revolving years
> Grant me the saving gift of tears,
> Yet as you sparkle on the morrow
> Teach me to joy in spite of sorrow,
> Send me peace as only wise gods can
> To the inner and the outer man.[8]

These lines follow line ninety-eight of the poem as it appears now, and form part of the general plea to the river that the poet makes. Perhaps they were too reminiscent of Swinburne's "Time, with a gift of tears;/ Grief, with a glass that ran" in that same *Atalanta in Calydon* that Aldington had defended from Alice Meynell's criticism years earlier.

The general arrangement of the section, which is a carry-over from the early edition, is arbitrary, since the poems do not lend themselves to the type of meaningful design that the poet seemed to be striving for in the earlier sections. The ironically titled "Songs for Puritans" is opposed to "Songs for Sensualists," of course. One might also recall what Aldington said of the last two poems in the Introduction to his 1933 *Collected Poems, 1915-1923*:

> The rhymed pieces at the end were really metrical exercises, arising partly from the conviction that I needed to steep myself in English poetry again after so long an exile—the choice of Waller and Marvell as models was quite fortuitous—and partly from the fact that short poems were no longer adequate to express what I wanted to say.[9]

While the short poems represent that steeping in English poetry of which the poet speaks, the long poems convey the feeling that he was drawing the strength and calm he needed in part from the English countryside. In this sense, the "Words for Music" section of *The Complete Poems* has pattern too.

Because "short poems were no longer adequate to express what I wanted to say," Aldington produced, during the fifteen-odd years after *Exile* when he continued to write poetry, five long poems. The first of these constitutes the next section of his *Complete Poems*.

"A Fool i' the Forest"

This division of Aldington's final collection is a reprint of the 1925 Allen and Unwin first edition of *A Fool i' the Forest*. The sequence of thirty-four poems remains unchanged and very few changes are made within the poems themselves.

The original edition contains one sentence in the author's "Note" (quoted previously) which does not appear in the final collection. On the contents page of the first edition the poems are numbered in roman numerals, and the corresponding page numbers are given to the right of the poem numbers. "A Phantasmagoria" appears on a separate page before poem I, rather than on the title page as it does in *The Complete Poems*; the epigraph is also printed on a separate page.

Most of the changes made in the printing of the individual poems involve the elimination of extra leading or breaks between the lines. These changes were probably made in order to save space. The second largest number of changes was in punctuation, including the usual substitution of single for double quotation marks. The textual revisions that were made do not seem important enough to require comment, but are listed in the paragraph which follows.

In poem II, line eight, "people's" was "peoples' "; a short line, "The New Epiphany," followed line nineteen's "Because we'll have all houses made of glass—," but is now omitted. In poem VII, line thirty-seven—"Nine million hearts beat on to Kensal Green"—"Kensal Green" was originally "Bethnal Green." In poem VIII, line forty-six's "char-a-bangs" has been changed in the final version to "char-à-bancs." In poem XXII there was the following note to the sentence "I replied: 'Lorenzo Valla' " of line sixty-seven:

> "Un humaniste, Laurent Valla (1467) démontra la fausseté de la donation de Constantin. de la correspondance de Jésus avec Abgar d'Édesse." Albert Houtin: *Courte Histoire du Christianisme.*

In poem XXV "Haig" has been substituted for "Kitchener" in line three, which read in the first edition: "Most unbecoming men who strove with Kitchener." Finally, in poem XXXI, the original line four's "Gave me good advice unquenchably" has been revised to "Gave me good advice unquenchable."

In collating the versions of a long poem such as this, it is possible to overlook some of the revisions; but if I have missed any, they are of a minor nature and similar to the changes pointed out above. More interesting revisions were made in Aldington's next long poem before it was reprinted as a section of *The Complete Poems*.

"A Dream in the Luxembourg"

The sixth part of the 1948 collection reprints, with only a very few spacing and punctuation changes, the 1930 Chatto and Windus edition of *A Dream in the Luxembourg*. But while the poem as it finally appears shows little revision from the English edition, there is considerable change from the American edition which was printed in the same year by Covici, Friede, Inc., under the variant title *Love and the Luxembourg*.[10]

Although the title varies, the epigraph, "*Si vis amari, ama*," and the dedication, "For B." (Brigit Patmore), are the same except that they are printed in different order. In the original American edition the epigraph followed the title and the dedication was placed after the numeral "I" of the first poem.

The last three lines of "I" (in the first edition the poems are numbered in roman numerals rather than arabic) are now:

> I scarcely know where and how to begin;
> So hard is it to be truly Reasonable
> When you are a little crazy with a Romantick love.

In *Love and the Luxembourg* two additional lines appeared between the first line I have quoted (line thirteen) and the next line: "Therefore try to forgive me, Euterpe,/ If all this is confused and verbose." Possibly the poet felt an appeal to the Muse of music and lyric poetry to be too formal for the tone he was setting.

A part III appears in the American first edition which is not in the version of the poem in *The Complete Poems*. This very short section consists of the following five lines:

> Be patient with all this long preamble,
> It is all telling you why I sat day-dreaming
> As I watched the fountain under the trees in the Luxembourg,
> Dreaming of the love which might have been mine
> And which somehow I had always missed.

Lines twenty-five to thirty-one of the present part 3 (part IV in the 1930 edition) now read as follows:

How many yellow dead men have I seen?
Carried how many stretchers?
Stood by how many graves—of young men, too?
Reported how many casualties?
But one gets used to it, quite used to it,
And it seems nothing for men to die,
Nothing for one to die oneself.

In the earlier edition the following eleven lines, now omitted, appeared after line twenty-eight:

It's a queer feeling, that gets you at the heart,
To walk back over the battle-ground
And see the men you knew and liked
Lying out there with the dew on their yellow faces,
Odd battered figures in muddy khaki.
And a queerer thing yet to see, as I once saw,
A dead soldier still kneeling upright,
Holding his rifle in his stiff clenched hand,
With a long ghastly black-red stalactite of clotted blood
Frozen from his mouth to his knee—
An odd sight to come on in the pure November dawning.

These original lines, removed before the poem was printed in the first British edition, serve to illustrate how far the poet was from forgetting the horrors of the war, even a dozen years after he had been demobilized.

Part 6 of this poem in *The Complete Poems* (part VII in the Covici, Friede volume) begins:

Here, for a moment, I must pause,
For, as you see, I've come to the core of my dream;
There is so much to tell
And I don't know what I ought or ought not to tell. . . .
And another thing troubles me about all this--
Did it really happen?
Was it only a dream in the Luxembourg?

In the Covici edition the line "And I am afraid of being verbose and tedious . . . ." appears after line four.

The part numbering in *Love and the Luxembourg* is in error. This may or may not have anything to do with part III's being excluded from the British edition and *The Complete Poems*. In any event, through VIII the difference in the numbering of the editions is maintained—for instance, VIII is 7—but then the Covici, Friede edition repeats the numeral VIII, thus putting the remaining numbering in line with the British edition and *The Complete Poems*.

The last five lines of the poem as it appears in *The Complete Poems* are:

I stooped to the ground
And with my finger-tip
Took a tiny pinch of dust
And put it to my lips—

It had a very bitter taste.

Following the line, "And put it to my lips," *Love and the Luxembourg* has the added line "A last sacrament." I think that deletion of this line was not wise, because it added an interesting ambivalent allusion to the close of the poem. As in the Christian sacrament one takes the wafer and the wine as the body and blood of Christ, so the dust of the Luxembourg was the dust of the fallen fountain, of the crumbled Venetian glass, of the dream of love.

A Dream in the Luxembourg is a very subjective love poem; the poet's next long poem, which makes up the following section of *The Complete Poems*, also deals with love but more objectively.

"The Eaten Heart"

As noted earlier, "The Eaten Heart" was printed alone in 1929 in a limited edition by The Hours Press, was included in the 1930 *Imagist Anthology* as one of Aldington's contributions, and was published with "Short Poems" in a 1933 Chatto and Windus edition. As it appears in *The Complete Poems*, where it is in a section by itself, "The Eaten Heart" appears to be identical (except for a line break following line twenty-seven in part four) with its printing in the 1933 Chatto and Windus edition. There were some revisions made, however, between the two earlier printings and the 1933 edition.

In the Hours Press printing of "The Eaten Heart," lines fourteen to eighteen read as follows:

A man or woman might die for love
And be glad in dying;
But who would die for sex?
Would you die for an appetite?
Die for food and drink?

The next to last line above, "Would you die for an appetite?" does not appear in the final version.

The short second part is printed in italics in the 1929 edition, and there is the usual use of roman rather than arabic numerals to divide the poem into parts. Double quotation marks are used throughout, and ellipses appear in sets of three rather than four. In the whole poem there are four punctuation differences and four spacing differences from the final version. In line twenty-eight of part VIII the older version has the word "nasty" instead of "mortal" in the line "Then this is one of those mortal dreams."

The *Imagist Anthology 1930* version shows the same minor differences including "nasty" in line twenty-eight of part VIII. In the American edition in line twenty-four of the same part there is an obvious typographical error in the substitution of "isle" for "aisle." Probably to the typesetter it sounded reasonable to be buried "in a single tomb in the southern isle."

In *The Complete Poems* Aldington made the "Short Poems" of the 1933 *The Eaten Heart* into a separate section, just as he did with the "Words for Music" part of *Exile and Other Poems*.

"Short Poems"

By the time of the 1933 edition of *The Eaten Heart*, the untitled poems of its "Short Poems" section had all reached essentially the same form in which we now find them in *The Complete Poems*. The use of roman and arabic numerals was reversed in the earlier edition; in poem 2 of part II there was a break between lines two and three; and in poem 3 line fifty-three was followed by a break. The title of "In Memory of Wilfred Owen," which was the last poem in the 1933 *Eaten Heart* book, was printed in italics. Otherwise, all of the eleven poems were identical with those of the final collection in wording, punctuation, and order of appearance.

The final poem of the "Short Poems" division of *The Complete Poems*, "Epilogue to 'Death of a Hero,' " does not appear in any of the earlier editions or collections (not even the 1934 *Poems of Richard Aldington*), but comes directly from Aldington's first novel, *Death of a Hero* (1929).[11] It is, in all respects, identical with the printing there.

I have previously mentioned the complicated way in which the "Short Poems" of the 1933 *Eaten Heart* grew out of "Passages Toward a Long Poem," which was one of Aldington's contributions to the *Imagist Anthology 1930*. To recapitulate: the first seven poems are transferred intact; poems VIII and IX are omitted; poem X becomes poem VIII; and the last three poems are new and did not appear in the anthology, although they were previously printed in *Movietones*.

I have also been able to trace a few of these poems back to periodical publication. Poem 3 was published under the title "Gold Grape-Black Grape" in *The Nation and Athenaeum*, Vol. 44, No. 23 (8 March 1930), p. 764, in exactly the form in which it appears in *The Complete Poems* except that there was a break before line thirty-seven and none before line twenty-one. In *The Yale Review*, Vol. 19, No. 3 (March 1930), on pages 489-490, there were six small poems of Aldington's printed under the general title "Inscriptions."[12] The first of these poems is identical with poem IV of part 5 in the "Short Poems" section of *The Complete Poems*, and the fourth with poem II of part 5. The other four poems from *The Yale Review* were not collected and may be found under the title "Inscriptions" in Chapter 2 of the second part of this book.

"Life Quest"

The ninth section of *The Complete Poems* consists of Aldington's long poem *Life Quest*. This was printed in 1935 in England by Chatto and Windus and in the United States by Doubleday, Doran and Company, Inc. Except for a few very minor punctuation changes the poem is reprinted in the final collection exactly as it appeared in the first editions.

"New Poems"

This next to last section is the only one of the eleven parts of *The Complete Poems of Richard Aldington* whose composition does not depend on an earlier "first edition." Instead, the nine poems of this section are reprinted from a previous collection, the 1934 volume *The Poems of Richard Aldington*. In his "Acknowledgements" the poet credits seven of these poems to individual magazines; these are poems published during 1933 and 1934 which he was not able to include in the 1933 edition of *The Eaten Heart*. Since he specifically does not mention the two others, "Death of Another Hero" and "1933" (and since I have been able to find no trace of magazine publication for them), it seems safe to presume that they were published in the 1934 collection for the first time.[13] Because the 1934 edition was as American one only, most of Aldington's British audience did not see any of the poems in this section until the 1948 final collection.

There are no important textual revisions between the 1934 collection and the "New Poems" section of *The Complete Poems*. The only noteworthy change is the removal of the dedication, "For Eric Remarque," from the title of the poem "1933." This is in conformity with the poet's practice throughout *The Complete Poems*.

Some changes, however, had been made earlier in the seven poems that first appeared in periodicals. "A Place of Young Pines" was published in *The Forum and Century*[14] and differed slightly at that time from its final form in the two collections. Line twenty-five, which now reads, "Where all sounds are hushed," had the added words "all conflict still." The "myself" of line thirty-four's "And sorrowfully and in dismay I question myself" did not appear, and in the final line "under" was used in place of "beneath."

"A Grave," probably intended for D.H. Lawrence, was published in *Queen's Quarterly*.[15] The second stanza now reads:

> How many thousands in the years to come
> Will pass indifferently these common tombs,
> Led by the memory of your glowing spirit
> To gaze upon the stone above your bones.

In the periodical publication the second line above read, ". . .those common tombs"; the third line, "Drawn by the passion of your fiery fame"; and the fourth line ended in a question mark.

"To One Dead" was printed in *The Forum and Century*[16] and is reprinted without any revisions. "Dilemma" appeared in the periodical that published Aldington's first poems in 1912, *Poetry*;[17] there are seven punctuation changes in this poem as it is printed in *The Complete Poems*, besides the addition after line twelve of the line "In any case I am sick of words and talk."

"January Aconites" appeared with a bad misprint in the *Saturday Review of Literature*.[18] The fourth line read, "Among the grey clouds under the stark snaky vines," substituting "clouds" for "clods." The lovely "Morning in the South" was printed both in the United States in *The North American Review*,[19] and in England in *The Fortnightly Review*,[20] in one month. The latter printing was identical with that in the "New Poems" section; the former substituted "pouring" for "pour" in line fourteen. "Life Goes On" was printed in *The Yale Review*[21] with only spacing differences.

From the publication evidence and the poet's own letters to John Gawsworth, we can guess that these "New Poems" of the 1934 collection were almost the last poems that Richard Aldington wrote, except for his final long poem of 1937.

"The Crystal World"

The final section of *The Complete Poems* reprints the 1937 William Heinemann, Ltd., first edition of *The Crystal World* without appreciable change. There are a few instances in which foreign words were not originally italicized as they are now; and in the earlier volume the individual poems were numbered in arabic. In addition, the poems were printed each on a separate page, a style which enhanced their appearance.

The over-all arrangement of *The Complete Poems* is, of course, chronological. One might argue that the "Eaten Heart" section should precede "A Dream in the Luxembourg," but this would be logical only if the former section were based on the 1929 Hours Press edition. Actually, it is based on the 1933 Chatto and Windus edition, which also contains the "Short Poems" that should follow the dream poem. Any internal logic that the arrangement may suggest is, therefore, simply the development that took place in the poet himself between those earliest poems of 1912 and the last long poem of 1937.

NOTES

1. Introduction to *The Complete Poems of Richard Aldington* (London: Allan Wingate, 1948), p. 13.

2. New York: Modern Library, 1957, p. 171.

3. "Lesbia" was first published in *Poetry* but only after Aldington had explained its meaning in detail to Harriet Monroe. He also noted that the last line was from Shakespeare's *Antony and Cleopatra*, and defended the word "rotten." He offered her a number of substitutes for the word "Christ," to the use of which in this context she had evidently objected. (Letter of 6 October 1913, in the University of Chicago *Poetry Magazine Papers*.)

4. *Literary Essays of Ezra Pound*, ed. T.S. Eliot (Norfolk, Conn.: New Directions, 1954), p. 14.

5. As noted in Chapter 2, "The Faun Captive" did appear in the 1919 Egoist, Ltd., edition of *Images*, which is almost identical with the "Images" section of *The Complete Poems*. In one sense, therefore, a description of the make-up of a section of *The Complete Poems* is often a description of an earlier "expanded" or "collected" edition.

6. Could this be the poet's "flower whose name I will not tell,/ The symbol of all love to us" which he mentions in "Reverie"? See Chapter 2, above.

7. The poem was in this form when Aldington sent a pencil copy to John Cournos. This copy is in the Houghton Library at Harvard University with the Aldington letters to Cournos.

8. These lines also appear in the original publication in *To-day*, Vol. 10, No. 55 (September 1923), pp. 27-29; otherwise there are only minor punctuation changes between the text there and the version in *The Complete Poems*.

9. Introduction to *Collected Poems, 1915-1923* (London: George Allen and Unwin, 1933), p. xii.

10. The limited American edition published by the Overbrook Press in 1935 (and described earlier) probably was derived from the British edition, because its text is identical with that in *The Complete Poems* except for a few minor punctuation and spacing changes.

11. On 13 April 1955, Aldington wrote to his second wife, Netta: "The BBC have discovered the Epilogue to Death of a H., and have been using it—on overseas broadcasts *only*! They deduct only 45% from their miserable fees. The Irish radio used some of my poems recently and paid 7 guineas direct to Montpellier, [where Aldington was living at this time] with no chi-chi and no deduction!" (Unpublished letter in the collection of the British Museum.)

12. The Lockwood Memorial Library of the State University of New York at Buffalo has a typescript and two corrected proof sheets of "Inscriptions."

13. There is a newspaper clipping of "Death of Another Hero" in the Aldington collection of The Morris Library of Southern Illinois University. It seems to be from a California paper, although Aldington was not in California prior to the publication of the collection in 1934.

14. Vol. 90, No. 6 (December 1933), p. 329.

15. Vol. 41, No. 1 (Spring 1934), p. 20.

16. Vol. 91, No. 2 (February 1934), p. 111.

17. Vol. 43, No. 4 (January 1934), pp. 188-189.

18. Vol. 10, No. 7 (September 1933), p.77.

19. Vol. 327, No. 3 (March 1934), p. 238.

20. Vol. 141, No. 3 (March 1934), p. 296.

21. Vol. 33, No. 2 (December 1933), p. 232.

PART II

UNCOLLECTED POEMS

Introduction

Part II is devoted to reproducing a very large number of poems that were not, for one reason or another, included in *The Complete Poems*. Many of these poems were published in periodicals only and never collected into book form; a substantial number remained in manuscript and were not published at all; and quite a few of them had appeared in earlier editions of Aldington's volumes of poetry but were not retained in the final collection. In previous chapters I examined the first editions and the way in which *The Complete Poems* was built up from the early books, taking note of those poems that were discarded; but here I also noted that two classes of poems were invariably omitted from the final collection—prose poems and translations.

Sometime between the period when he wrote his early poetry and the period when he came to select from his total work the poems he wanted to include in his final collection, Aldington had what might seem to be a change of heart about prose poetry. As can be seen from the gathering that follows this introduction, he wrote quite a number of prose poems, including the two *Myrrhine and Konallis* volumes,[1] but decided against including any of them in his 1948 collected edition. Glenn Hughes points out that originally the difference in the attitudes of Aldington and Eliot toward prose poetry lay in Aldington's "willingness to accept the term, 'prose-poem,' and to recognize it as standing for a definite art form."[2] As early as 1915 Aldington praised the prose poetry of Paul Fort,[3] and as late as 1955 he discussed what he described as a "prose poem" which was left in manuscript by T.E. Lawrence.[4] In August of 1920, in "The Art of Poetry," he said, "Normally it is considered necessary to draw a distinction between prose and poetry. I am not at all sure that any such distinction is possible. . . ."[5] But other critics and poets (in addition to Eliot) vehemently took the opposing view. Harold Monro, for instance, said: "We will uphold a positive distinction between prose and verse; we do not admit that poetical prose can be poetry; and we assert that poetry which leaks over all the boundaries of form becomes prose."[6]

What seems to have happened, therefore, is not so much that Aldington changed his ideas about prose poetry as that he bowed to the opinion of others. It is interesting to note, however, that while carefully excluding his early prose poems from all of his collections, he preserved a number of them in the 1926 volume *The Love of Myrrhine and Konallis and Other Prose Poems*, which, in addition to the prose poetry describing the love of the goat-girl and the hetaira, has a separate section entitled "Nineteen Prose Poems." Furthermore, in 1930, after he had compiled the 1928 American edition and the 1929 British edition of his *Collected Poems*, both of which omit all prose poems, he published a collection of short stories, *Roads to Glory*, in which one story, "Farewell to Memories," includes about half of the "Nineteen Prose Poems." His attitude seems to have been ambivalent: he may not have wanted prose poetry to be included in his collections, but he did want to preserve those prose poems, many written in France, that he considered valuable.[7]

Aldington also excluded from *The Complete Poems* any poetry that he felt could be considered as translation of another poet's work. But he did publish several separate volumes devoted to translations. The Myrrhine and Konallis cycle of love poems, therefore, did not reach the final collection, but was permitted to stand as a separate volume in the 1926 Pascal Covici edition. The first fourteen poems of this cycle, when originally published by The Clerk's Press, were listed as "translated," and the next sixteen, when they appeared in *The Little Review*, were identified on the contents page as "translations." Only the last two poems had no indication that they were not simply written "after the Greek manner." It seems probable that, because he had criticized Eliot and Pound for using other poets' lines in their own work, Aldington may have felt that he could not claim these poems as entirely his own. He rigidly omitted from *The Complete Poems* all prose poetry or poetry that could be considered in any way as translated. The Myrrhine and Konallis poems were excluded on both counts. Nonetheless, I consider them to be original poems, rather than translations, and have included them as such in this collection.

One other class of poetry receives, for the most part, similar treatment: those poems that I have called "joking" poetry. There are quite a number of such poems, particularly from the early magazines. Often Aldington wrote just to amuse himself or others; some poems, such as *Hark the Herald*, were never intended for general circulation.

It is difficult to generalize about previously published poems, outside these categories, that were omitted from *The Complete Poems*. Many of them have already been discussed in connection with the early editions; the rest could only be approached on an individual basis. The fact remains that many good poems were left out of *The Complete Poems*.

I have collected here two hundred and sixteen poems. Included are poems that were never published and works that Aldington published at least once, some twice or more often, in either periodical or book, but which he omitted from *The Complete Poems*. Two hundred and seventeen seems to me a large number. The total number of Aldington's poems, including these, is three hundred and eighty-seven of which five were long enough to publish in separate volumes. In comparison, Dr. Alspach found fifty-eight Yeats poems "not included in the definitive edition"; the total number of Yeats's poems, including these but omitting the narrative poems and verse dramas, was four hundred and thirty-seven.

Of the poems gathered here that have not been previously published in book form, many came to light in the course of a careful search through all the periodicals that Aldington mentions in his acknowledgments in the first editions, and further search through other periodicals known to have published poetry during the years when Aldington was actively writing. It is probable that other poems not included in *The Complete Poems* are buried in obscure "little" magazines and remain to be recovered. This is especially so since Aldington habitually published in French and American periodicals as well as in those of his own country. Aldington says in his autobiography and also in his unpublished letters that some early poems were printed in newspapers.[8] While I have been able to locate a number of these, there are surely others that I have not recovered.

Since this collection is intended to be redemptive—to make available in one place as many as possible of the scattered and almost "lost" poems of Aldington—I have reproduced even those poems of *The Love of Myrrhine and Konallis* which, though long out of print, are still available in one volume, as well as the poems of the exceedingly rare *Movietones*, which, with few exceptions, were not reprinted elsewhere. It seemed better to include *all* of the poems from individual volumes that do not appear in *The Complete Poems* rather than try to set up guidelines as to which should be excluded and which admitted. Furthermore, the best proof of the validity of my earlier argument as to the worth of the Myrrhine and Konallis poems lies in an examination of the poems themselves.

Finally, there are poems included here that have remained until now in manuscript form. These were located among manuscript holdings of various libraries. Most of these poems were written early in the poet's career, but a few date from a period long after that of his last published poetry. I believe that this collection includes the bulk of Aldington's unpublished poetry. However, it is possible that some more may come to light in due course—for instance, among the papers of the poet's friends. I have divided the poems in this anthology into three chapters: those from manuscripts and notebooks, those from periodicals and newspapers, and those from previous editions. The order of the poems in the first chapter is alphabetical. In the last two chapters the poems are arranged according to the dates of first publication, except for the poems from the 1926 *Myrrhine and Konallis* edition. These are grouped together, although some of them had been published earlier.

In transcribing the poems—especially those in the first chapter— from the sources, I have followed exactly Aldington's spelling and punctutation, except for substituting "and" where Aldington in his manuscripts and typescripts used an ampersand and for correcting obvious typographical errors.

NOTES

1. On 22 June 1917 Aldington wrote to Charles C. Bubb, who privately printed the first *Myrrhine and Konallis* volume: "Do you know that although they were published obscurely I received quite a number of reviews & letters & someone wrote a long article in the New Statesman gravely pointing out that they were less rhythmical than poetry (less rhythmical than prose)—a fact with which I am quite cognisant. Indeed it was the effect I aimed at!" (Unpublished letter in the University Research Library, The University of California, Los Angeles.)

2. *Imagism and the Imagists: A Study in Modern Poetry* / Stanford, Calif.: Stanford University Press, 1931), p. 77.

3. "The Poetry of Paul Fort," *The Little Review,* Vol. 2 No. 2 (April 1915), pp. 8-11.

4. *Lawrence of Arabia: A Bibliographical Enquiry* (London: Collins, 1955), p. 367.

5. *The Dial* (New York), Vol. 69, p. 167.

6. "The Bookshop," *Poetry Review,* No. 11 (November 1912), p. 498. The question of poetry in prose is argued out in three essays by T.S. Eliot, Fredric Manning, and Aldington in *The Chapbook,* No. 22 (April 1921), pp. 3-24.

7. At one point Aldington wrote to John Cournos from the trenches in France suggesting that Cournos and H. D. put together a new volume of his poems. He thought they might consider two sections of prose poems: one his poems of the Middle Ages (reproduced below, in Chapter 2, as "Associations") and the other the best of "those pseudo-Hellenic fantasies I have fastened upon Myrrhine & Konallis." As a title he suggests "Despairs & Reveries" or just "Reveries." (Letter dated 14 February 1917, in The Houghton Library at Harvard University.)

8. *Life for Life's Sake: A Book of Reminiscences* (New York: The Viking Press, 1941), p. 84. Also see his letter of 20 November 1917 to Amy Lowell, replying to her request that he give her his background and early history: "My first poem was printed in some obscure journal when I was 16. By the time I was eighteen, I had printed quite a number of poems & translations in papers like The Evening Standard, The Westminster Gazette, The Pall Mall, etc." (Unpublished letter from the Amy Lowell collection in The Houghton Library at Harvard University.) There are poems in the present collection from these newspapers. A number of them are translations but have been included because of their very early date.

1

Poems from Manuscripts and Notebooks

AD CATULLUM

"Catulle frater," if so I dare call you,
I am horribly tired of the fog and the frost,
And the "ultimate Britons"
Bore me to suicide.
Leave for an hour
The exquisite asphodel
And the breasts of Lesbia,
And pay me a visit.

We will talk of Sappho;
You shall read me your verses.
We will avoid any mention
Of Virgil the tedious,
And restrain our discourse
To the Hellenes and women.

I will read you de Régnier.

But, O Catullus,
Best of the Romans,
Save me, I beseech you,
From the fat barbarians
Of New York and London,
From unlimited cant,
From the stink of the streets,
And the sterile stupidity
Of lawyers and clergy.

Let us spend a week-end
In your villa at Sirmio,
Catulle frater!

A corrected typescript of this poem is in The Morris Library of Southern
Illinois University. No record of publication has been found.

ADDITIONAL FILINGS OR HOUR-GLASS GRAINS

1

It is a sorry thing to live too long.
Speak not of hope. I say there is no hope.
You raise the dead? but not the living-dead.
You'll not rehang fall'n petals on the stem
Nor remould ashes into that lost face.

2

Be unto me as sunlight revealed
    And revealing the infinite life-spaces,
Hitherto darkly guarded by death-dragons;
    Pour upon me influx of light,
And in beautiful radiance
    Touch me alive with slender rays.

3

Through you I have inherited a world—
Myself.

And another mysterious and enchanted world,
So mysterious and lovely and beckoning
In the dew and the pure gold dawn.

I tremble, standing in awed silence
On the verge of these worlds.

4

"I loved thee once, Atthis"—
But no,
Pale, beautiful face,
Cool silver moonlight of love,
Through you I learned
To seek for the noonday
And its golden ecstasies.

5

    It is so easy
    To express pain and grief and sorrow;
But who shall find words for joy,
For happiness, for fulfillment?

6

We seek for words;
And words may be beautiful;
But what are words to me
Who remember your touch?

7

Lips that never lost their sweetness,
Nor formed a bitter line,
Delicate frail face and forehead,
Eyes of pain,
Eyes of a sweet, hurt child,
Eyes that touch me to the heart —
O that for long and long
I might feel your presence,
Eyes with a dawn in them.

8

What I write for you is nothing;
What I say to you is little;
What I feel to you is —
Your name!

9

I had thought of immortality
With indifference and cool scepticism
Until I gazed long and long
Into your soft shining eyes
As you loved me.

10

It seemed that the dawns were more exquisite,
The world more mysterious, purer,
The sea and sky more tenderly light-flushed
When we awoke together.

11

When you forget me,
O golden one, petal of Love's rose,
I shall deserve to be forgotten.

12

I am untroubled
When I think you might find
Many lovers better than I.

But when you tell me you have found one
More tender, more perfectly yours,
I shall whisper:
"Go to him, my love."

13

About me are strident lights,
Sharp mirrors, clatter of voices:

A dream, a muttering vision —
Reality is your voice,
Your touch,
Your gaze.

14

Alone I
Re-enter her vacant soundless bedroom.

All was as we had left it
Down to the torn paper-scraps
And the empty bed
So wildly tumbled.
A room left lifeless —
The exquisite "something" departed.

These foretastes of death
Come bitterly upon one.

15

I hold gently between quiet fingers
A small square of folded paper —
Her first love-letter.

Before I had opened it
Unawares there came upon me
A faint silver echo
Of her golden touch
As it glows upon me.

The fragrance of life
was sweet in my mouth.

Enclosed in a letter of 21 December 1928 to Crosby Gaige. The typescript of
this poem is in the Beinecke Rare Book and Manuscript Library at Yale
University. No publication has been located for the entire poem, but stanza 2
(which curiously Aldington sent to Gaige a few weeks later as a separate
poem) appears, with line four omitted, as "V-2" and stanza 7 as "V-1" of
"Passages Toward a Long Poem." Stanzas 3, 4, 9, and 10 were published as
stanzas 2, 3, 5, and 6 of "Inscriptions" in *The Yale Review*, Vol. 19, No. 3
(March 1930), pp. 489-490 and also appear in the next section.

   The title of this poem, as well as references in other letters to Gaige to a
group of poems titled "Filings," suggests that Aldington considered these
poems as belonging to the earlier group. For further information on the
"Filings" poems, see below, Part I, Chapter 1, note 6.

ANY WOMAN TO ANY SOLDIER

What is there left to say
    This side of hell,
What word to speak or pray
    Except "farewell"?

But, ere that bitterest sigh
    Pierces my brain,
Lift your bowed head on high,
    Kiss me again.

Lift up once more your head
    And let me taste
The last of many kisses shed
    On lips and breast.

Kiss my writhed lips again
    This side of hell,
Kiss dumb the sob of pain
    And then—farewell.

Enclosed in a letter of 2 February 1918 to Amy Lowell. On the reverse of
this was handwritten the original version of the poem "An Old Song." From
The Houghton Library of Harvard University. No publication has been
located.

AVE

A hawk swings in the gale:
Up—a shred of paper;
Down—a falling knife.
The wind sweeps at him—he yields;
The wind recoils—he darts at it.

Impalpable waves of air
Break across slate blue rocks;
The gorse, trimmed by interminable winds,
Hisses.

The waves leap underneath—
Echoes of ocean beats
Torn into small white peaks
And scurries of foam,
Breaking endlessly on blunt rocks.

A rabbit scuttles by,
Turns in a fright,
Vanishes under a bank.

A tramp-steamer ducks to the gale.

Two sea-gulls, tossing morsels of white silk,
Rise, like toy monoplanes,
Against the hurrying gusts.

The hawk sweeps away;
The gulls disappear;
The old "tramp" labors and wallows.
A gleam of sun
Stalks over the far hill,
Leaps the valley,
Rushes by in a slow gleam.

Old hawk, old sea, old hills,
Keen, inscrutable, vast,
You claw off follies,

Salt clean insipid disgusts,
Dwarf vanity and praise—
I salute you!

Typescript from the files of *Poetry: A Magazine of Verse* (in the University of
Chicago *Poetry Magazine Papers*) with the note: "Wrote to H.S. about this
May 18, '18 author says discard all these S.W. likes all but *Ave.*" Above
this note are listed "Ave, Beauty Unpraised, Pompeii, Moods—Waking,
Afternoon, Night." No publication located for "Ave."

BALLAD OF SOUTHERN SKIES

Italia, land of sun and song,
    Dreaming of Art (not money),
Oh, tell me, do I do you wrong
    To say your climate's funny?

I sought you in October's glow,
    As Baedeker advises;
And how the stormy winds do blow!
    And how the rain surprises!

November passed in frost and fogs;
    December went one better,
The night-winds howled like hungry dogs,
    The days were even wetter.

In January came the sun;
    "Winter has gone!" we chanted.
Alas! It hadn't yet begun,
    Although it wasn't wanted.

The "lovely southern spring" was rain
    And wind and snow and shivers,
The "azure founts" of Tasso's brain*
    Were nasty muddy rivers.

So March went by in storm and stress;
    "Just wait till April comes" they said,
"With brilliant skies and flowery dress,
    You'll both be quite enchanted."

Eight suns of April now have glowed,
   (But not on us,) in glory—
The sky looks like a muddy road,
   The days are chill and hoary.

"Just wait till June—" I'd rather not,
   I fear I must be going,
For though I've learned to bear a lot,
   I can't stand Summer snowing.

E.N.I.T., return my cash—
   No! Keep it, with my greeting:
Just cut a real climatic dash,
   And put in central heating.

*He was mad, poor man.

A corrected typescript of this poem is in The Morris Library of Southern
Illinois University. No record of publication has been found.

[Untitled]

The basalt is broken, the body split,
The wide head hacked by spears;
Fragments worn by slow drift of sand,
Inert, miserable, defaced.

Where the sun is lighter on a further stone
Morsels of shaped marble—
Bared breasts of the Amazon,
Firm thighs of Apollo,
Dancers, centaurs, fauns,
Broken.

The sharp bronze pitted with verdigris
Blistered with hot ashes.

Might there be an end to anguish—
Some sanctuary unprofaned
Where the gods stand untroubled
In marble cells beyond the violet hill;
About the shrine a land and race unpolluted. . .

Basalt and marble are broken,
Desecrated the once holy earth—

Myriads of faces averse and bestial.

With an envelope addressed by Aldington to F. S. Flint, 23 November 1922.
This holograph poem is in the Humanities Research Center of the University
of Texas at Austin. No publication has been located.

[Untitled]

"Black shore" and "night" and "little waves". . . .

Venice
With the clear moon on the Guidecca,
San Giorgio, the lapping of water
On the gondola. . . .

Ah Venice,
I have loosed a silver ring
Of love into your waters,
And I must come back to you
Because you have taken my silver ring.

A carbon typescript of this untitled poem is in The Morris Library of
Southern Illinois University. No publication has been found.

BLIZZARD

The wind hurls snow against the hills,
Piles it in hollows, against crags:
The ice wind rattles like dying breath.

The rush of hard white flakes blinds me;
I am stunned by the whirring air.
Yet I forget it for a moment
And think of your limbs in the firelight,
The point of your breast
Crushed under my cheek.

Snow, wind, frost assail me;
I am numb and desperate;
But I grow warm—my face flushes—
Remembering our keen forbidden caresses,
The cleft of your body,
Your closed eyes.

A carbon typescript of this poem was enclosed with an undated letter to
Frank Stewart Flint from Aldington. The typescript is now in the Humanities
Research Center of the University of Texas at Austin. No publication has
been located.

[UNTITLED]

1.
The desire of lover for lover,
Flushed cheek by cheek,
Hand gripping trembling hand,
Lip upon lip. . .

2.
Through the dark pine trunks
Silver and yellow gleam the clouds
And the sun;
The sea is faint purple:
"My love, my love, I shall never reach you."

3.
You are beautiful
As a straight red fox-glove
Among green plants;
I stretched out my hand to caress you:
It is blistered by the envious nettles.

4.
I have spent hours this morning
Seeking in the brook
For a clear brown pebble
To remind me of your eyes—
Last night I gnawed the flesh of my arms,
Yearning for your naked body.

5.

Your kisses are poignant
Yet I have to leave you.
Alone here I scribble and rescribble
The words of a long-dead Greek poet:
"Love, thou art terrible;
Ah love, thou art bitter-sweet."

6.

At every step upon the road
I start from my book and listen:
"It is she!"
Wearily I turn back, murmuring
"Surely she will come soon
And kiss peace into my tired eyes."

7.

As I walked in the garden
At the end of the cool rainy evening
I felt sick from the beating of my heart,
The violence of my desire.
Yet the song of a bird comforted me,
Singing:
"You shall have her; you shall have her;
You shall have her."

8.

Tomorrow I will go to her
And take her in my arms,
And she will soothe my hurts
With her lips, kissing me.
And I shall touch her body.
And all that day and night
The memory will beat in my blood
And I shall be happy,
Happy again.

Enclosed with a letter from Aldington to Frank Stewart Flint dated 26 May
1916. This holograph poem is in the Humanities Research Center of the
University of Texas at Austin. No publication has been located.

DUSK AT THE LOUVRE

Princes laid pallid in their marble mail,
Spectres Sleep shadows to eternity?
Those pillars, ivy-crusted like a tree,
Fountains where Beauty smiled without a veil?

Those waxen mitred Bishops laid to rest,
Mothers who dread the Cross in the Child's clasp,
That anguished slave and ironic asp,
Diana, anger swelling her proud breast?

That woman, with her writhen hands, who moans?
Those noble heads of bronze, those luminous stones
Which weep an unsuspected love, like me?

No. In this tear-dim shadow where I stand,
Crushed by desire, yet charmed, I only see
A naked foot clasped by a broken hand.

Remy de Gourmont
Translated by Richard Aldington

This poem, with the subtitle "Sonnet translated from the French of Remy de Gourmont," and three other poems— "Journalism in the Seventeenth Century," "Regrets," and "The Silent Age"—are accompanied by a note by Derek Patmore: "Richard Aldington sent me these poems—some still unpublished when I was living in New York. . . ." They are dated (apparently in Patmore's hand) 1928-1929 and are in typescript in the Humanities Research Center of the University of Texas at Austin. No record of publication has been found. Although a translation, this poem is admitted here because of its association with the other poems, and because of Aldington's close connection with de Gourmont.

FANTASTIC ANACREONISING
(For Mr. Aldous Huxley)

Alcibides, exiled by the indignant Athenians,
retired to the satrapy of the Great King. No more
banquets of philosophers; the attic olive had been gnawed
to the stone. Life was a continual if over-opulent
festival. Disdaining meer silver, Alcibides had his silky

beard combed every morning by the fingers of hetairai.
 All virgins prohibited by order of the satrap.
 Naturally, women adored his rule.
Now he scarcely looked at the newspapers and he abandoned
 Archilochus
for the story of Solomon and the indecent portions of Ezekiel.

He ordered that the works of Crébillon le fils and Pierre Louys
should take the place of other bibles. He had them bound in pink
skin, torn (under protest) from the companions of Cunygonde,
and powdered with silver phalli.
 Persia was amazed.
 "Tu fais une consumation inouïe de femmes," remarked
Critias, companion of Alcibides.

 The festival continued, not without music.
 Outside Rabelias and Lucian.
 "Since you brought a 23 instead of a 35, then it
I refuse." Thus Rabelais.
 "Why?" the Samosutran "You are a Christian: the Pope
shall absolve you."
 The handle flew off.
"One-two-three-hup!" They crouched expectantly.
 The oblong serrated orb described an awkward
hyperbola, spinning clumsily on its longer axis.
 The festival, absorbed in copulation, noticed nothing.
 Crash.
 Abolition of the scene.
 "Are you safe?" Rabelais removed his thumbs from his ears.
 "Something wet hit me in the face."
 "Pick it up. What is it?"
 A palpitating morsel of flesh, sole relic of this reign of
Alcibides.

The holograph manuscript of this poem is part of the Manuscript Collection,
Temple University Library. It is written in pencil and much revised so that
the author's intentions are not always clear. No record of publication has
been found.

THE FLUTE-PLAYER

Why do you follow me, Nymph and Bassarid,
Over Rhodope down into Thrace?
Why do you follow me yew-wreathed Maenads
Wanton with wine?

Why do you follow the moods of my syrinx?
Am I Iacchus or Demeter or Pan?

I have nothing and yet you follow me
Over Rhodope down into Thrace.
Even with kisses I have not kissed you
For I love another over in Thrace.

I go seeking the sun in a pool
Over in Thrace.

A corrected, signed typescript of this poem with the annotation "8 Church
Walk, Kensington" is in The Morris Library of Southern Illinois University.
No record of publication has been found.

[Untitled]

"For your sake I will take up an old measure
    And blow its lean skin bright with healthful blood,
    Set vigour in its wasted bones and hood
Its skull with tresses of gold pleasure!

For love, new love, your love is so great treasure
    I can be prodigal, as a green June wood
    Of leaves; can waste, as ever the sea could,
Waves of my love-song for your dreaming leisure."

That was my boast; but the measure unended
    Japed to my face the folly of foolish verses.
        There's no music like the murmur of kisses;

I'll burn my books, leave poetry untended:
    For one night of you and your naked blisses
I'd tear to threads the wide-stretched universe!

Enclosed with a letter from Aldington to Frank Stewart Flint dated 2 June 1916. This holograph poem is in the Humanities Research Center of the University of Texas at Austin. No publication has been located.

GHOSTS
(Aldington Churchyard, Sussex)

All night, all night waiting;
Wandering; through the tall grass—
Meadowsweet—shall I forget the scent?
Wandering; down to the black pond;
The trees droop in the still dusk
Like banners, like black banners;
Over them the pennons of the stars.
All night, wandering;
All night, waiting;
By the damp gravestones,
By the cold dusty road—
The scent of meadowsweet from the fields—
The church like a great grey banner
Draped on a tomb—
Wandering; waiting
For the banners, the bright banners;
What do the banners mean?

Waiting
For the banners.
Are they the King's? The Duke's?
St. Edmund's? St. George's?
Rustling creatures of the night,
Tell me,
Whose banners are they?
The King's? The—

Wandering; waiting.

Unpublished poem from the Amy Lowell collection in The Houghton Library of Harvard University. Probable date, 1914.

HAPPINESS

It seemed if we might be elsewhere
We might be happy. . . .

A year ago to-night
I lay in a small damp hole
Dug in the brown mud of a sunken road
And shivered (for I had no coat)
Through long cold hours,
And watched the misty stars
And listened for the shells.

What did I feel that night
Beside the cold and a few shells?
Something, something that was good to have,
Something that struggled in my weary mind
Like a child in a tired womb.
Nothing that could be made into philosophy
But just a happy mood.

It was not because the battle was over
Or because I had come through safely,
Or because it was rumoured
That the general said I had done my work well,
Or even because the shells stopped
And the dawn was getting near.
It was none of those things;
And I was too cold and hungry and sleepy
To think clearly.
It came somehow from the stars,
And the slice of moon over the hill,
The black autumn wood in the distance
And from the dark bodies of sleeping men
Who looked, in the thin moonlight,
As if all were dead but the sentries and myself.

I went up the road
(They were still shelling my part)
And looked at the mist in the valley,
Lying flat between the two hills
Like cream in a rough brown bowl.

I went down the road
And talked to the doctor who was awake;
We told each other lies about the battle.

That night I think I was happy
Because I was so aware of beauty,
So sure that what we do matters so little,
So certain I loved and was worth loving,
Certain, for the first time, that I was no exile
But quite friendly with life, especially the stars
And the deep valley and the sleeping men;
Certain I had a right to live.

This poem is handwritten in an Aldington notebook in the Humanities
Research Center of the University of Texas at Austin. Although this poem
was never published in this form, a much shorter poem with the same title
and some similar lines, as well as the same general theme, was published in
The Living Age. A slash through the manuscript seems to indicate that
Aldington was aware of this. For details see Chapter 2, below, of the
Uncollected Poems.

HYMN TO APOLLO

I

O frail sweet dawn, whose first wan beauty glows
    In silent pulse majestical
To lordlier gold and flecks and jets of rose,
As o'er swift harps the prelude grows,
    Until the sun, fronted-imperial,
Throbs heart-like o'er the morn's repose—
    How leaps my soul to thine primordial!
How all my life seems molten into light
    Thrilling intense out towards the eastern sky
        Where shattered night
    Falls smitten to eternity!
How all my days were lost and nothing worth,
    And this sea-cinctured earth
Whelmed in the dusk of direst cataclysm,
    If thou at our first birth
Laved'st not our brows with luminous chrism
Of thine antique and pagan baptism!

II

And thou, O stateliest day-fall—dazzling-hued
   As the voluptuous chamber of a queen,
Heavy with silken colours and imbued
      With sea-reft dyes—
    Which from this shore terrene
      Fling'st back in sighs
    Translucent surges on the glowing skies
To silence and the deep night's solitude!
Thee too I praise, albeit a token of death,
   Hanging dim shrouds about my choking soul,
      And with thine aureole
Gilding the hair of one who perisheth!

III

Wherefore, O Lord Apollo, at this hour
   Of hottest noon, when northern days
   Thou makest tropic with thy burning gaze
     And feet fire-sandallèd,
   To Thee I turn, as from the shower
     Turneth the sun-flower
     When flame-apparellèd
Thou shak'st the clinging clouds from off thine head!
For by the splendour of thy steeds gold-shod
   Trampling a way athwart the fervid blue,
   And by thine evening melodies which strew
Sleep on our heavy limbs, as Hermes' rod
   Shutteth the tear-burnt eyes of woe—
     By these I know
That of all gods Thyself art mightier god;
That Thou art Lord of healing and of light
   And of all things that flow
Betwixt the opposèd portals of the night!

IV

O Lord of harping and of passionate song,
   Whether by some Castalian fount
     In the hushed even-tide
Pellucid chords about thy silence throng;
   Or on the Aonian mount
    Thou call'st the morning from her bed, a bride
Clad in the saffron veil desired so long;

Incline thine ear to me—the youthfullest voice
  Uplift before thy desolated shrine—
  Whom drunken with Thy fire as with new wine
    All fair things bid rejoice,
Who recking naught of trivial blame and praise
    And love or human or divine
Long only for the flowerless crownal of thy bays;
Hear me this once, and with thine aweful breath
    Fulfill my nostrils with inspirèd life
      That out of strife
May spring the songs untouched of any death!

V

"Who recketh naught of love"? Nay, Lord, full well,
  Full well Thou knowest that all my heart (dream-clad
As in a raiment of white poppies—or as a shell
Unheedful of the roaring ocean-swell)
    Beateth with thine and in thy joy is glad,
      When with thy god-like hands
Thou scatterest white flakes of the dawn's clear fire,
      Or with high-flaring brands
    Lightest thy western funeral-pyre!
And one there is, slim, white and maiden-lipped,
      Unkissed of any god save thee,
      Whose eyes are chaster than the sea,
    Whose cool hand never dipped
In the Lethean waters of desire—
      She, even she
Holdeth the barren kingdom of my life in fee!

VI

Thou also, Lord, in thine Hellenic days
  All-amorous of white limbs and purple hair
    And breasts most fair
And cold eyes subtle as an autumn haze,
Didst yearn for love; but as the pale star flees
    The rubious lightnings of thy mounting fire,
      So through the tangled trees
    Fleet Daphne fled the flame of thy desire;
And all thy love was as a sobbing hymn,
    And sorrow was the mistress of thy lyre,
And with fierce tears thy luminous eyes were dim.

This Love hast thrust me backward by the throat—
   Ev'n as the angel bowed the sinful king—
And lo! he plucked me by the hair, and smote,
    And mocked me, threatening;
He tore Life's garland from mine humbled head,
    Crushing the laurel in his hand,
(But all the roses quivered, and fell dead
    In that tear-misty land)
And with the bitter leaves he filled my mouth,
   Made harsh mine eyelids with the acrid fume,
And bade me seek a spring to slake my drouth
    Beneath the tomb.

VII

Where is thy son Asclepios to make whole
   With healing fragrance my woe-smitten mind?
    Or canst Thou find
Cool cassia for the red wounds of my soul?
For lo, my Father, Love waxed wroth with me
    And scarred me with a curse:
From the dusk depths of that tempestuous sea—
   Whose springs are fed with tears,
    Whose waves immerse
   The generations of the phantom years,
   Whose refluent waters lap eternity—
Rose the implacable fierce monster of despair;
   And from the gorgeous chariot of my youth
Hurled me, as chaste Hippolytus was hurled,
   And bruised me without ruth
   Upon the crags of Time, and tare
My limbs upon the sharp rocks of the world.

VIII

Here where I sing the very day stands still,
   Hushed, drooping with excess of heat,
   Like roses over-blown at summer's feet:
Far off the grey-blue glimmer of the hill
    Shines like romance,
    And with Thy gleaming lance,
   Thou, errant monarch of the day,
Gold-huest the trackless azure of Thy way—
And moulder at my feet the sinking stones

Of this grave-garth,
And in the earth
Moulder in dust men's unprotected bones.
O God, the pain of love may find some balm,
Some kind sweet eyes the dear earth holdeth yet,
But canst Thou hush Death's sombre-cadenced psalm?
Canst Thou forget
The unregarding silence of that dark
When no thrilled lark
Shall greet the morning music of Thy train;
When all Thy fire shall sicken with despair;
When tettered stain
Shall steal the damasked glory from Thy cheek;
When all the light shall vanish from Thy hair;
When darkening pain
Shall rend Thy radiant limbs; when weak
With over-mastering anguish of Thy fall
Thy steps shall falter down those skies;
And all the beauty tremble from thine eyes;
And like a leaden ball—
Grim token of her dreadful sovereignty—
Night holds Thee in her hand
In that dim land
Flowed over by her ebon-flooding sea?

IX
Lo, the black rood upon yon mossy spire
Thou crownest with the mockery of Thy light,
But canst Thou smite
This sudden serpent, Death, whose fierce desire
Ravisheth Life of her virginity?
Lord, Thou didst slay the Python in thy youth—
Have Thy corrosive shafts lost fire,
Or dost Thou fear Death's immortality,
Or wilt Thou spare in ruth
This mightiest foe of all things and of Thee?
Ah, who shall trust in gods
Or put his faith in Thy supremacy,
If Thou deny the sobbing of my soul?
Ah Lord, fair Lord, whose lightning breaks like rods
The adamantine pillars of the dusk,

Yet dowers the rose with musk,
Whose breath is in the rattling thunder-roll
Yet in the lightest fragrance of the spring—
Consume this deadlier Python with Thy flame
And overthrow him with Thy whirlwind breath;
Come, Lord, with lightnings round Thee as a ring,
And free our souls from this relentless shame,
Death.

This undated, signed typescript is in the Beinecke Rare Book and Manuscript Library of Yale University. No record of publication has been found.

[Untitled]

I am tired of so many things
I am too tired to count them.

God is a wearisome object;
He seems to lack distinction.
I like a little variety;
I know all about last year's butterflies,
Next year's will be exactly like them.

I contemplate myself with awe,
Having expensive tastes
And no commercial ability.

Allah truly is great,
But he needs the culture of Hellas.

A typescript of this poem is in The Morris Library of Southern Illinois University. No record of publication has been found.

I. M. COVENTRY PATMORE

Wives of great men all remind us
We can treat our own like swine,
And departing leave behind us
Lessons for Frank Waldo Trine.

A corrected typescript of this poem is in The Morris Library of Southern

Illinois University. The number "17" is placed above the title. No publication of this poem has been found.

INSCRIPTION

There was a poet dreamed and droned and rhymed
Fifty years long of buried queens and kings,
Picking old tales from books and garrulous peasants
Whose slant-eyed cunning knows the picturesque
Buys beer and tips. . .

                Why, if he was a poet,
Did he praise the violent predatory men
And all those ignorant women? Why
Slip from the bitter iron strife with truth
To play his parlour tricks with petty words
Laureate of the unearned income world?
Is this our leader?

                I'll not praise fools
Nor flirt by proxy with imagined queens.
I can take harsher wounds than a feigned sorrow.
Give the wit to scorn what merits scorn,
To hate what's hateful, let me break myself
Against the steel and concrete of our days,
Bleeding to bring a newer life to birth.

A typescript of this poem, with "Richard Aldington" typed at the bottom, is in The Morris Library of Southern Illinois University. No record of publication has been found.

[Untitled]

It is bitter, watching the bright leaves fall,
To think: "Now I shall not see her ever,
Never once, never hear her soft voice call
My name, and clasp her hand in mine never."

As the leaves fall I dream that you sit alone,
With hands empty and resigned, and the light
Gone from your eyes and hair, still as a stone,
And a dream face haunting your inward sight.

Time drifts with the leaves, and murmurs: "Too late."
If we met, we could but turn with a sigh:
"Too late," O lost love hidden by Fate
And haunting my bitter heart till I die.

A corrected typescript of this poem is in the The Morris Library of
Southern Illinois University. No record of publication has been found.

JOURNALISM IN THE SEVENTEENTH CENTURY

On Monday, His Majesty hunted from Windsor to Hampton Court, and supped
right merrily with divers lords of good repute. The tables being drawn and His
Majesty seated under a canopy of state upon the dais in the Great Hall, there
entered two fair women fantastically habited in garments of a rare conceit,
whereof one bearing a branch of coral figured Thetis, and the other holding a
pearly conch, Amphitrite. After due reverence made to His Most Excellent
Majesty, they most melodiously tuned their voices and sang to a sweet con-
cert of viols, flutes and recorders:

Thetis: From those pearly bowers that be
           Hid in the deep-bosom'd sea,
           Mighty Emperor! we are come.
           But this Presence strikes me dumb;
               Amphitrite,
               Speak for me.

Amphitrite: Monarch of the western main!
           Loyal hearts know not to feign;
           Pardon, Sire, thy virtues may
           E'en a goddess sore dismay.

           Where translucent breakers run
           Underneath an orient sun;
           Where the swaying sea-plants twine
           Leaves as bright as new-spilled wine
           With olive-tinted fronds; and where
           Sea-moss soft as Venus' hair
           Plumps us beds on Ocean's floor:
           There we dwell and there adore
           The mighty king Oceanus;
           There in sequence murmurous
           The everlasting tides go by. . .

Chafing with perpetual roar
Smooth flat sand and ragged shore;
There the uncouth Triton feeds
Neptune's wild two-footed steeds;
Thence he rises up at morn
To blow his loud upbraiding horn;
There amid encircling rocks
Proteus shepherds home his flocks;
There, as white as wind-blown seas,
Dance the Oceanides,
Whom by Neptune's royal command
We summon to this happy land!

Thetis: You, who wept for my Achilles dead,
Chaunting strange funeral songs,
Mourning my unforgotten wrongs,
Shearing long tresses o'er his bloodless head;

Amphitrite: You who on my spousal day
Danced so merrily, and sang,
Laughing till the hoar cliffs rang
And even Pluto's bride was gay;

Thetis: You who love the gloom of adverse skies,
Dancing more fleet and higher
As the storm-beat mariner
Sinks with the shattered plank and struggling dies;

Amphitrite: You who love sparkling morns,
Ripples on a sunny strand,
Gems and dyes and glittering sand,
Strains from sea-gods' pearly horns;

Thetis: Whether by some perilous reef ye range
Or in the middle deep
On weed-fringed pillows sleep,
Or plot some shipwrack horrible and strange;

Amphitrite: Or by Trinacria's warm beach,
Careless in your moonlit games,
Ye forget your maiden shames
To learn what wanton shepherds teach:

Ambo: Come! White as those frail streams of mist
              That mount the ridged Tyrrhenian hills,
              Clad in your garments ta'en from Neptune's treasure,
              Bright with his gems and rich with all his dyes;
              Come swiftly hither, tread a perfect measure.

Then entered masked divers ladies of the Court, habited as Neptune's
daughters, bearing gifts from the Sea God, which, after they had danced a
measure, they presented to His Majesty in dumb show, as a token that
Neptune abandoned to His Majesty the lordship of all the oceans and the
new lands lying beyond them. These gifts His Majesty was graciously pleased
to accept, swearing pleasantly (as his royal wont is), by the soul of his body,
that the gifts liked him exceedingly well. And upon prayer made by His
Grace the Duke of Buckingham, His Majesty did presently bestow upon his said
Grace by letters patent all those undiscovered lands lying to the north and
west of His Majesty's plantations in Virginia. And His Grace of Buckingham
did bestow upon the poet, one Anthony Hornbook, three broad pieces of
gold, one of His Grace's own cast-off doublets, and three double pottles
of sack.
    (From His Majesty's Court at Hampton, this 15th day of December,
1618.)

This work, in addition to "Regrets," "The Silent Age," and "Dusk at the
Louvre, Sonnet translated from the French of Remy de Gourmont," is
accompanied by a note by Derek Patmore: "Richard Aldington sent me these
poems— some still unpublished when I was living in New York. . . ." They are
dated (apparently in Patmore's hand) 1928-1929 and are in typescript in the
Humanities Research Center of the University of Texas at Austin. No record
of publication has been found.

A LOST DAY

All day the summer wind blew
White clouds, grey foam
About the sky and sea.
All day I waited for you,
Straining my eyes across the hill
For one flash of your bright gown. . .

Now it is evening
And my eyes ache;
My head is dull and hot,
My lips and hands, cold.
Every noise, every word, stabs me.

My thoughts cling to you
Desperately, patiently.

My yearning is a sharp thirst,
Keen as acrid smoke.

The white hours of twilight seem black.

Until you touch my hand
Until you bring me kisses,
Only more beautiful than Christ,
I am as a man dead.

Included with a letter from Aldington to Frank Stewart Flint dated 2 June
1916. This holograph poem is in the Humanities Research Center of the
University of Texas at Austin. No publication has been located.

MEDITATIONS

3

Sometimes it seems that I have really attained you,
That my patient opening of veil on veil
Of darkness which hides us from each other
Has at last been successful,
That the essential you lies naked
Against the essential me.
Sometimes in a flash I perceive you,
Mysterious and friendly and passionate,
Reaching towards me as I towards you,
And this sudden stab of illumination,
This vision which leaps out and fades
Like a distant gun-flash at night,
Is as lovely, as unendurably exquisite
As those longer minutes of delight
When our two bodies
Are fused and welded into each other
By an intense glow of sensation.

Yet I remember once in a sudden ecstasy
A twin possession of body and spirit.

Since then I have lived partly in a dream,
Remembering this strange divination
And, like a watchful beast, my spirit
Couches, waiting to leap out again
Upon a new, even completer possession.

Enclosed with a letter of 17 June 1920 to Amy Lowell which is in The Houghton Library at Harvard. Covering note schedules publication in the *Monthly Chapbook* for July (1920) but, although another poem with the title "Meditation" appeared there, this poem did not.

MEDITATIONS

4

If I could put you from me,
Divest my spirit of you
As the body puts aside its garments before sleep;
If I could be free of you entirely,
As I have freed myself from memories
Of the brutality of men,
Be free from the uncertainties of desire,
Repossess all that I have abandoned to you,
Stand alone with no longing—
Would I do this?
Would I put you aside, even if I knew
I should suffer no regret, no pain, no loneliness?

(I will accept no pretence,
No negative tolerance,
No sham for form's sake.)

Now I am sure I would not leave you,
Sure that the wounds and bitterness
Are worth the recompense.

What is given must be given freely,
Like rain-fall and the grass in spring;
But somewhere within me there must be
A pinnacle of solitude,
Some tract of me no one has seen,

Some ultimate refuge, some escape, if need be.
Then I shall be sure of myself,
Sure that we are unfeigned and spontaneous.

Enclosed with a letter of 17 June 1920 to Amy Lowell which is in The
Houghton Library at Harvard. Covering note schedules publication in the
Monthly Chapbook for July (1920) but, although another poem with the title
"Meditation" appeared there, this poem did not.

THE MIST

Out there beyond the lonely reeds,
Beyond the beech-trees and the briars,
The fog is drifting through the pines.

The wind is quiet.
The faint grass is tipped with drops;
The smell of the pine-leaves and of the earth
Drifts with the fog.

If I were out in the woods there,
Out amid the fog,
I would sit on a red pine stump
And whistle on my wooden flute
Till the ghosts came out of the wood;
I would play till the desolate ghosts
Came gliding by, and touched my face
With white soft lips like fog.

A carbon typescript of this poem, with "Richard Aldington" typed below it,
is in The Morris Library at Southern Illinois University. No record of
publication has been found.

MR. KLAMP ADDRESSES HIS SOUL

Well, you got through. That's that. . . .

What next? Some tedious months
In a rain-logged Belgian village,
Then out you go—a hundred quid
To pay for three years of your life. . .

And after that?
Do you return to the old vomit,
The "literary life"—
Eunuchs of either sex discoursing
Over weak tea and sugary buns?
Ten hours a day of work
For some abuse and a hall porter's pay?
Culture on fifty bob a week?. . .

Well, what? Trade? You'd fail,
You know you'd fail.
A clerk? Hell, why not office boy?
What then? The Colonies?
You'd sooner die and add to Bethnal Green
One other inconspicuous stone?. . . .

Cheer up! You're "one of England's heroes". . .
There, don't be sick. Keep still,
Say what you do want. . .
Silent? I'll answer.
You want something worth while,
Something without the smirch of humbug,
Something a man who's looked on love and death
Can reverence, can die for if need be.
That's what you seek?. . .

Good friend, it were better for you
To lie at Ypres with the million dead
Than take such ancient homespun trash
To London, that great city. . . .

Take my advice,
Lie, humbug, scuffle with the rest,
Scratch for your pelf in the gutter,
Follow the Preacher that was king in Israel
And eat and drink and buy you women slaves
For all is vanity. . . .
No good?
Well, go and help the poor. . .

You're tired of vermin?
Well, I merely try
To find an issue for you.
If you spent your life, now,
In educating England's youth;
Educing from its urchins, shall we say,
Love of Greek verse?. . .

No?
Go in for politics,
You have a sort of supple back
And a gift of eloquent wind;
You might achieve—who knows?—
A half assistant-under-ushership. . .

Still restive?
Then turn Bolshevik
And wreck the world you can't possess
And lose the beauty you have never had. . .

Not even that?
Then go to hell, my soul,
And leave me to my piddling pursuits.

The typescript of this poem is a part of the Manuscript Collection, Temple
University Library. No record of publication has been found.

[Untitled]

My spirit,
she breathed upon our life
        like a rich summer wind
that shakes a silent tree
        to glittering turmoil.

Like a god she passed
unknown, unworshipped
        through the roaring streets,
yet one heart knew
        the goddess by her gait.

The sunlight clasped her
    and the shining clouds
crowded together to behold her,
    the river with its thousand lips
wafted her wavering kisses,
the great trees trembled as she passed.

(O vile concetti,
worn to a rag by herds of amorists,
Gongora's and Tasso's bastards!
Is your mind so dull,
    Bolognese pedant?)

A carbon typescript of this poem is in The Morris Library of Southern Illinois University; it is untitled but a page number (21) and the roman numeral "IV" at the head of the poem seem to relate it to the unpublished poem "To D. H. Lawrence." No record of publication has been found.

NIGHT FANCIES

I

The wide-lipped foxgloves pout across the room,
The watch ticks swiftly and the lamp aspires;
The crumpled "Times" lies with Theocritus—
The thousand years beside a single day.

Deep, deeper the June night blackens,
The owl's shrill note flies through the air,
A gliding star of sound; the night-jars churr.
The watch ticks on, numbering the innumerable.

This, this and this are life—
A dusty cloud of hours, dry rain of time.

II

If I could witch my minutes into marble,
Metamorphose them into durable stone,
And day and night, and night and day, build up
A towering timeless monument?

(So many fancies reeling through my thought,
Loves, gaieties and griefs—all wasted.)

III
Build it up then!
What lives within your mind
Lives somewhere in the world.

IV
First, underneath, a heavy sunken crypt,
Round-arched and echoing, bulk of gloomy truths,
Of chilly thoughts that wiggle through dead queens—
This the foundation, fittingly inscribed:
"To all forgotten gods."

Above it, break forth my splendid house:
Tall doors embossed with painted fruits
And pilasters that leap like springing wheat,
Pillars that spread to glittering leafage,
Windows that twinkle with a myriad lightnings—
Huge flower-petals pierced by starlight—
Wide vaults that strain—huge wombs—
To bring the light to birth;
Floors wide as wealthy gardens,
Let my walls leap up—
No classic girth and weight,
No tampering with Ictinus
And hard Euclidean rules,
But crude northern Romance.
Walls, columns, portals, windows, roof
Towering into the white air
Flecked with the sombre swallows,
Spouting white crests of marble spires,
Foaming into wave-tops of thin stone;
Blossoming in flowered finials, tufted crockets,
Bright-painted corbels, branched cornices . . .

V
The fox-glove drops a flower,
Some unseen hand touches and flutters
The half turned pages of Theocritus.
I have come back. No sound,

Not even a throaty frog-song
Has earth to curse the immortal stars:

Louder ticks the inexorable watch.

Enclosed with a letter of 17 June 1920 to Amy Lowell. Covering note
indicates that no publication was made or scheduled. From The Houghton
Library at Harvard University.

NOSTALGIA

They ask for songs.

How can we grow white violets
Who have but dust and brick and steel and stone
To grow our flowers?
Lycidas indeed might drink beside the firelight,
Crowned with soft flowers, singing across the sea.
But we?

They ask for songs.

At dawn and noon and evening
The dark town screams about us like a wheel;
If they must have the roaring of their engines,
The clanging of their anvils and their cars,
How can we hear the singing of the stars?

They ask for songs.

Alas, alas, we are paupers,
Beggered in song; ah once
The oat-straw may have moved the gods
To walk and speak with men,
Crowned with white ivy by the violet sea.
But we?

Unpublished poem from the Amy Lowell collection in the The Houghton
Library of Harvard University. Probable date, 1914.

OBLIO DOLCE DE' MALI. . . .

In a dream I saw my own grave
lying askew among tumbled mounds
with tufts of harsh coarse grass
on a bleak sullen hillside.

(Horrible reality of Sleep!)

I found I could sit by my grave
and thrust my right hand through the earth
to grasp my rusty brittle bones.
Then, in a frozen horror,
I found another chrysalis self
inhabiting those nasty relics—
a dreary not-quite-dead thing.

At our horrified recognition
occurred a still more dreadful metamorphosis.
Slowly, and with a bleak despair,
bleak and sullen like coarse tufted grass,
these two became one;
then, with a yet more hideous despair,
I lay dry brittle bones
in a dim fantastic agony of horror
which faded slowly, hideously,
to Nothing.

Thou sick men's balm,
Thou baiting place of wit,
Thou knitter of the ravelled slieve of care,
Most Gentle Sleep!

A corrected carbon typescript of this poem is in The Morris Library of
Southern Illinois University. The roman numeral "X" above the title of the
poem may connect it with others in this collection; possibly Aldington
planned a grouping of some sort. No publication has been located.

[Untitled]

Once when I sang of roses,
And Stars, and gardens, and leaves,
And the beauty the world uncloses
To a heart that loves and conceives,

Words came that will come no longer,
And rhyme—that I now despise;—
My art and heart may be stronger;
But my muse is silent, though wise.

Both a holograph copy with revisions and a typed copy of this poem are
included with a letter from Aldington to Frank Stewart Flint dated 29
October 1913, in the Humanities Research Center of the University of Texas
at Austin. No publication has been located.

PETIT MANIFESTE NECESSAIRE

Messieurs dames
LA PATRIE n'est pas
precisément en danger mais j'vous
fiche ma parole qu'y a
partout de petits salauds
salaudants et de gros
bougres bougrants qui brûlent d'envie
de vous fourrer une poire
d'angoisse au cul sauf
vot' respect mesdames

DONC CONSPUONS DIEU
et tout sa kyrielle
d'anges oiseaux agneaux
boucs vierges cochons de Gadara
saints saintes docteurs
bienheureux patriarches poissons en rébus
martyres cendres os sacrés coeurs
mères-de-dieu pleurnicheures chiffons
sadisme et masochisme inconscients
crânes pourritures célestes
enfants de Marie avaleurs de Dieu POETES CONVERTIS

A R R I V I S T E S
qui calculent pour "sauver" leurs
pales et sales petites âmes
et pour "GAGNER" le ciel avec
une Eternité de saloperies
entre les nichons de Marie pet-à-main

A BAS	VIVE
Aquinas	Antichrist
Bossuet	Boccacce
Cocteau	Casanova
Deutéronomie	Dioclétian
Eliot	Ezra (Pound)
Francois d'Assise	Faustus
Grégoire de Tours	Gargantua
Huysmans	Helvétius
Isaac	Irene (con d')
Jeanne d'Arc	Julianus Imperator
Kant	Kant
Lactantius	Leda
Massis, Maritain, Marie,	
Maurras, Manning, Mercier	
jusqu'a Merde	Montaigne
Novalis	Néron
Onuphrius	Onan
Pape (le)	Pan
Quakers	Queen Anne
RR. PP.	Révolution Française
Susanna	Satan
Thomas	Titus (qui brûla Jerusalem)
Unigenitus	Ubu
Vierge	Voltaire
Wenceslas	Wotan
Xmas	Xéres
Yesterday	Youth
Zacharie	Zebb

Two corrected carbon typescripts of this poem are in the collection of The
Morris Library of Southern Illinois University. The one reproduced here
seems to have superseded the other, since its alphabetical listings are complete
while the other has some blanks. No publication of this poem has been found.

THE POETS
(To A.L. on her new book)

Well, I suppose we shall go on with this damnable business, but it would be much better fun at the moment to have a girl to kiss and get tea for than to be racked for hours over a single word.

Good Lord, it is absurd.

And where do you suppose our works will be stored in the year of our Lord ten thousand and fourteen? Do you suppose there will be any more men to read our trash then than there are now?

That was a queer, queer curse put on us when we were born: a worse I can't think of—to have to hunt and hunt by the streams of madness and passion and despair for the word to utter our dreams—the dreams almost too sweet to bear. How absurd it all is.

And what is the end of this search for perfection—this end which was to be a crowning of gold and laurel and purple? Just dejection!

And yet if we were offered all the jobs in the world—from that of a daffodil-curled Sicilian goat-herd to that of the Pope—well, I hope, I know that we would rather be what we are—rather occupy a tenth-rate star in an inconspicuous part of the poetic heavens than control the earth with a word.

But it is, it is absurd.

Unpublished poem from the Amy Lowell collection in The Houghton Library of Harvard University. Probable date, 1914.

P O M P E I I
(February 1913)

To-day the wind is cold in Naples;
The rattling streets are gusty;
Beggars moan at every half-sunned corner;
The Mergellina chokes with driving dust
And the alleys reek.

I wish we could lie here for days and days.
It is so good to lie on the short grass
And lean against the old house wall,
To watch the green-flanked lizards,
To hear a bee or two
Humming around the stunted tiny flowers.

It would be so good
To lie here under the blue sky,
Below the red-seamed cone
With its wisp of white smoke
To remind us of death and of the gods—
For days and days and days
In the warmth and the silence.

Typescript from the files of *Poetry: A Magazine of Verse* (in the University of Chicago *Poetry Magazine Papers*) with the magazine's date stamp of 29 April 1915. No publication located.

[Untitled]

Presque chaque fois que
je
pisse
je fais aussi des réflections
habitude futile
           malsaine
                inutile
                    fâcheuse.
Combien de fois ai-je fait cela?
Combien de fois le ferai-je?
La première fois—
           ah! le sale petit bébé
et ma pauvre mère qui souffrait encore
(mais si les femmes ne savent pas
prendre des precautions
il faut bien que cela arrive.
Il faut etre bien rusée, tu sais,
pour lutter avec la Nature—
ah! La Nature, mes amis, La Nature.)
Et la dernière fois?
Je me dégoute

horriblement
haineusement
avec une répugnance fraternelle
du vieillard ennuyeux
et vicieux
et pleurnicheur
que je serai.

Ah! bon, c'est enfin fini
n'y songeons plus.

(Mais il serait très agréable
ne ne pisser
plus
jamais
rien.)

A corrected typescript of this untitled poem is in The Morris Library of Southern Illinois University. No record of publication has been found.

PROLOGUE

You that take up this book, be warned in time.
'Twas bred by fancy and 'tis writ in rhyme
Mere nonsense, therefore, moonshine, nay 'tis less
Than dry leaves shaken out of autumn's dress.
More valueless to broad cloth folk like you
Than Rhodocleia's garland washed in dew
But, though it jumps not with your shopman's sense,
Brings you no trade and gathers me no pence,
Sneer gently, masters, at that paltry thing—
Court jester in an age that lacks a king.

From a letter dated 3 October 1922, to Harriet Monroe of *Poetry: A Magazine of Verse*. No publication located. (In the University of Chicago *Poetry Magazine Papers*.)

REACTION

A classic dulness—anything but that, anything but the mock-simple lisping of self-conscious Übermensch, the offensive intonations fostered by the twin snob-factories.

Give us the jangling tunes of green-sided barrel-organs laboriously cranked by pandars to Euphrosyne; let us watch and take part in—why not?— the gambols of young females gracelessly displaying inharmonious shins and doubtful under-linen. Give us anything that has life, however squalid, rather than ineffectiveness and starched imbecility.

The street howls colour—clustered flowers in Oxford Circus, red sliding ribs of motor-busses, shrieking puncture holes of flags in the grey-brown batter of brick trenches, silk petticoats kicked over transparent stockings by velvet heels, raucous posters interrogating space with shrill incoherence. Oh, horrible to arctic pinch-nosed defenders of sobriety, but life to the crowd, to us.

Sterility to this pining false refinement, this mass of insipidities, this imitation of the vices of the class next above: link arms, imitate the gambols of Hercules, celebrate the imperishable spirit of human beings seeking a non-existent happiness.

The corrected typescript of this poem is a part of the Manuscript Collection of Temple University Library. No record of publication has been found.

REGRETS
"Je plains le temps de ma jeunesse."

We should have many lives—
Who plucks a shattered rose to give his love?
How we squandered youth,
How the world betrayed us,
How the bright fruit turned to dust!
Yet the same sun lightens above us,
And the same sea laps the cliffs;
Still the blue crocus studs the Roman hills
And in the nooks of southern crags
Still the wild cyclamen springs up,
Still in those echoing halls
Stand the tall gods of Greece,

Still there is bronze and colour,
Still sounds the poets' thrilling speech
And the world's music is not mute.
All is the same and all has changed;
For, as we change, we blame the unchanging world.

Aulis as lovely now
As when Odysseus' prow
Plunged through the virgin sea,
Young heart-blood runs as fleet,
Feigned sorrow of youth still sweet—
But not to the dead, not to me.

What should the dead say to the dead?
Can there be mingling of bodies
And blinding kisses
And trembling hands and wildly beating hearts,
And that long interchange of eyes with eyes
Which is the very core of love?
What should the dead do with love?
What should the dead say to the living?

We should have many lives
To give and give again.
Who can give twice?
What's dead is dead,
And what have I to give?
A dream and a regret.

This poem, "Journalism in the Seventeenth Century," "The Silent Age," and
"Dusk at the Louvre, Sonnet translated from the French of Remy de
Gourmont" are accompanied by a note by Derek Patmore: "Richard
Aldington sent me these poems—some still unpublished when I was living in
New York. . . ." They are dated (apparently in Patmore's hand) 1928-1929 and
are in typescript in the Humanities Research Center of the University of
Texas at Austin. This poem has "Richard Aldington" typed after the final
line. No record of publication has been found, but see the unpublished poem
"What the Dead Say in Spring" which seems to be a slightly different version
of this poem.

SESTINA; FOR ASTRAEA

Back to the desolation of the sea,
Surge of slow waters curled by no fleet winds,
And melancholy of grey sleeping sands;
Back to the wild ways and to austere gods
Whom chaplets honour not, nor blood nor wine
Nor violet nor any dusky flower;

(But pluck thou sea-wrack and the palest flower
Bared at the saddest ebbing of the sea,
And scatter these in lieu of salt and wine;
And of thy tresses dank from moist-lipped winds
Shear one above the cold tombs of these gods
To mourn the dead lords of the drifting sands.)

Back to the pale dunes, where across the sands,
Barren of any save the lowliest flower,
About the unserved altars of dead gods
Murmur the supplications of the sea,
With wailing from the breasts of sombre winds,
With sea-spray for the sacrificial wine.

How then, Astraea? Sayest thou life is wine
Not to be spilt upon these thirsty sands,
Nor blown upon by breath of unglad winds?
Nay, for thy life is fragrant as a flower
Which blossoms in the waste lands by the sea
As in the golden meadows of the gods;

For thou art all as changeful as the gods,
Bitter perchance, yet mirthfuller than wine,
And I should have thee wholly by the sea
Beneath the clouds and gleams that mock the sands,
Yea, I should have thee wholly, flickering Flower,
And share thy beauty only with the winds.

Love laughs, and changes with the changing winds;
Love murmurs, with the speech of slumberous gods;
Love passes, with the passing of a flower;
But thou, whose mouth is brighter than bright wine,

Shalt be at least mine own amid the sands
In this my dream, the frail gift of the sea.
O fresh spring winds, that stir my blood as wine,
Despite the gods I would that by your sands
I had this Flower indeed, beside the sea.

A corrected typescript of this poem is in The Morris Library of Southern
Illinois University; it is signed and beneath the signature is the address: "4
Russel Chambers, Burg St. W.C." No publication of this poem has been
found.

THE SILENT AGE
"We have no great poets." (The Press)

There might have been a time for speech,
But what is music to a throng,
   And in the blare and crash
   Who hears, who heeds?

If there were grassy loneliness
Where men might wander among yews
   To pluck a spray, and think
   What feeds the roots;

Or if in mid-June's ripest fields,
Or where the river pours its flood,
   The hours trod softly by
   In solitude;

Then, from long meditation, speech
Might rise to touch another's mood;
   But have you time to hear
   Another speak?

They who have suffered, who aspired,
Who in mid highway saw the end,
   Who were not duped by noise,
   Can hold their peace.

Those happier yet unborn (perhaps
Less happy) will exclaim: "It seems
 That age was void and base,
 And had no song."

When our proud hearts are still, and dust
Chokes the free mouths, for all your noise
 Your wiser sons will judge
 The silent age.

This poem, "Journalism in the Seventeenth Century," "Regrets," and "Dusk at the Louvre, Sonnet translated from the French of Remy de Gourmont" are accompanied by a note by Derek Patmore: "Richard Aldington sent me these poems—some still unpublished when I was living in New York. . . ." They are dated (apparently in Patmore's hand) 1928-1929 and are in typescript in the Humanities Research Center of the University of Texas at Austin. "Richard Aldington" is typed below the last stanza of this one. No record of publication has been found.

[Untitled]

So sweet is thy discourse to me,
And so delightful is thy sight,
As I taste nothing right but thee.
O why invented Nature light?
Was it alone for beauty's sake
That her graced words might better take?

No more can I old joys recall:
They now to me become unknown,
Not seeming to have been at all.
Alas! how soon is this love grown
To such a spreading height in me
As with it all must shadowed be?

This poem was written on part of the menu for the Café Royal dated 2 March 1933. It was probably written on the spot as a graceful tribute to Brigit Patmore. It may be found among the Aldington letters at the Humanities Research Center of the University of Texas at Austin. No publication (or further revision) has been located.

SPRING MOODS

Waking

After grey sleep the yellow day.

The sky, a great blown sail of blue,
Puffed full with wind,
Strains taut from hill to hill.

The sunlight creeps, a slow gold tide,
Into the shadowed valley.

Keen scent of moistened earth,
New leaves and gillyflowers. . .

If life and sense were always sharp,
Primal, intense as now,
Then how contemptuously,
With our immortal feet
We'd spurn the bony rump of death!

Midday

We have set ourselves a wilder task
Than snatching bodily food
From other men;
Than scrambling in their foolish games.

For us it is enough to live.

Afternoon

The heavy low white-blossomed pear-tree
Lives with its thousand leaves
Gladly as we.
Yet its trunk is gnawed and rough
With moss and orange mould;
Its boughs are stiff with blue lichen;
Little rose and lemon snails
Have tattered all its leaves
And all its flowers.

And we, the strong and glad,
Who love, not own, the earth,
Are gnawed and stifled by accursed fools.

Night

We do not know the gods of life and day;
Indifferent to us their clay simulacra.

It may be that they watch us
And are pleased with gifts,
With bloody corpses and praise.

We stand before them with empty idle hands,
Sunburned with leisure hours, serene,
Contemptuous only of contempt;
Offering nothing.

For us it was enough to live.

Typescript from the files of *Poetry: A Magazine of Verse*, in the University of
Chicago *Poetry Magazine Papers*. The poem bears the magazine's date stamp
of 31 August 1916. No publication has been located. These poems originally
had roman numerals I-IV above their titles. The numerals and the poem
"Midday" have been penciled out on the typescript. "Richard Aldington"
is typed after the last poem.

STORM

Dimmed by thick rain the headland rises black
     Above the hurtling foam; out of the deep
     Cold sea the huge storm drives agianst the steep
Edge of the land, plumed with a mighty rack
Of heavily tossing clouds; wild thunders crack
     The concave sky and trees and bushes leap
     Like mad things in the wind and cattle creep
Humbly for shelter to some sunken track.

Now while disasters threaten, lightnings burn
     And all is noise, my mind dwells on the cool
     Moon slowly climbing to her tranquil height,

> While through the gathering twilight stars return
>> And all is quiet as a placid pool
>>> That ripples gently in her tender light.

Enclosed with a letter from Aldington to Frank Stewart Flint which is dated 27 October 1921. This holograph poem is in the Humanities Research Center of the University of Texas at Austin. No publication has been located.

SUBURBAN LOVE

> A fine dirty rain
> Prints on the window pane
>> Patterns in soot;
> A smoky coal fire
> Furiously puffs dire
>> Whirlwinds of soot;
>
> Above, a pianola
> Rattles, like a steam-roller
>> A vaudeville tune;
> And the children in the court-yard
> Finding life damned hard
>> Bellow a worse tune;
>
> And Mr. Porter (of Lloyds' Bank) seeks amid the din
> 'Mongst ill-washed petticoats the region Epicene.

Included in a letter from Aldington to Frank Stewart Flint dated 8 February 1915. This holograph poem is written beneath the letterhead of *The New Freewoman* (later *The Egoist*), of which Aldington was literary editor. The poem is among the F. S. Flint papers at the Humanities Research Center of the University of Texas at Austin. No publication has been located.

TO D.H. LAWRENCE

> To me also, O Lawrence,
> England seems dead
> now that I come back to it
> excited, urgent with new plans,
> eager to touch live people;
> even London seems moribund.

I came back to England
filled with an ecstasy,
creative,
as if I had risen from the dead.
My vital processes were running at top speed
like a good motor on a smooth road,
I felt that at any moment
I might say or do something interesting,
something with an enormous life-value
for me at least.
I was ready to sell my library
and start on any adventure.

And ever since I returned
the machine has been running down,
slackening down,
in spite of my desperate efforts.

It began at Newhaven.
I didn't mind the ugliness—
ugliness can be very stimulating—
nor even the dull cloudy day
and the soft gentle drizzle.
(But those bare little Sussex hills
looked so dismal and depressing
as we came into harbour—
snug nooks for placid ennui.)

What oppressed me was a curious softness,
a decorous non-vitality,
a genteel resignation and complacency.
The policeman's voice was so reassuring,
as if he said:
"Have no anxiety, Sir,
all is well, Sir,
your investments are quite safe, Sir,
the motor-roads are perfectly safe, Sir,
not the slightest cause for worry, Sir,
this way, Sir, mind the step, Sir,
thank you, Sir,
thank you very much, Sir."

Reassuring the anxious rentier.

And it went on in London.
Everyone was so kind, so kind,
all about my health,
and had I had a good time,
what had I seen and done,
so gentle, so reassuring,
but never a look, a hint, a glance
to question me about what I really was,
to elicit any vital response.
And all the time I went flatter and flatter,
and the machine went on running down,
until it flopped with a groan,
and I flopped with it.

What is wrong with our people?
Why do they smother one?
Why is this gentle unexpressed disapproval
so deadly to one's inner vitality?
Why does life seem impossible here?
Why do these soft gentle people
(yet they're not so gentle either
when it comes to the point)
and this soft gentle country,
smother one
until one wants to shriek aloud
for some rackety place
where people are alive inside?

Turn that bright blue eye of yours
on to this agonizing problem.
I can't see into peoples' minds
as you are able to see.
All I know is that I gradually become alive
when I go away from them,
and rapidly go dead again
when I come back to them.
Yet I like them so much,
I love England so much
when I don't hate it—
Gee, how my Oedipus
sometimes hates this smothering Jocasta.

I wish you would answer these questions.
It is no use asking Americans.
They either loathe England
and depart immediately,
or they have a cult for it,
because it pleases their snobbery
and love of quaintness.

I went down to the City and looked at it.
That was alive all right
with an immense exterior life,
but still I felt the people were dead inside.

Is there anything to be done about it?

This poem was evidently a part of a larger project, since the corrected typescript of it in The Morris Library of Southern Illinois University is numbered pp. 25-27, and the title of the poem is preceded by "VII." No record of publication has been found.

TO MY DAUGHTER ON HER 16TH BIRTHDAY
(6th July 1954)

I was a poet once, but now no longer
    The vivid words throng burning in my brain;
Age chills them all; but love for once is stronger
    And for your sake I feel them burn again.

Scarred from the battle, grim with hopes frustrated,
    What can I bring your glorious youth but this
Last feeble murmur of a Muse belated,
    My love, my anxious care, a father's kiss?

May all your life to come be gay with laughter,
    May love be true, and all your friends sincere!
Whatever comes in all the years hereafter,
    Be sweet, be brave! And there'll be naught to fear.

A typescript of this poem, with "Richard Aldington" below the last line, is in the Humanities Research Center of the University of Texas, Austin. No publication has been located. If not the last, this is one of the last poems that Aldington wrote.

TO ONE JEALOUS, AND TO MYSELF, AND TO ALL MEN

Friend, in whatever sort of weather,
However the wind may blow,
Beautiful women
Will have had lovers before we knew them,
Men will desire them as they pass with us,
And after us may come better men than we.

It's like the nightingale — stand still, and she will sing;
Stand very still and tense — maybe she'll flutter to your arm.
But raise your voice or stretch a hand to grasp —
Both bird and voice are gone.

Stand still; unclasp your hands.

Enclosed in a letter of 9 January 1929 to Crosby Gaige. This typescript
poem is in the Beinecke Rare Book and Manuscript Library at Yale
University. With it are two other poems one of which was later published in
Movietones and the other in the "Short Poems" section of *The Complete
Poems of Richard Aldington.*

THE VIGIL FOR THUIAS

I have stayed long in the darkness
By this river.
By this gray deep river.

Under bare knees
I feel cold hyacinths
And moss.

I am chilled
With a great pleasure,
And I have whispered
To the river.

*O gray river of Semnos,
She will come at dawning,
Thuias, daughter of the Wind.*

I have stayed long
In the darkness.
The owl called and the night-jar;

A bassarid touched the water
With delicate lips;
And two Fauns came;
And one white hound.

She will come at dawning,
Thuias, daughter of the Wind!

A corrected carbon typescript of this poem is in The Morris Library of
Southern Illinois University. The revisions are extensive and the author's final
intentions are not entirely clear. No record of publication for this poem has
been found.

LE VOIX DE LONDRES

Je m'ennuie;
Je m'ennuie prodigieusement;
En effet, je me suis si ennuyé
Que je ne veux plus s'être ennuyé.

Cependant, je m'ennuie.

A corrected typescript of this poem is in The Morris Library of Southern
Illinois University. No record of publication has been found.

VOYEZ NOS PRIX

Nous vendons de charmants
petits Bonsdieu à 3 sous
vous y soufflez dedans et ils
font pipi par les yeux en
gueulant "mais arrive donc"
puis ils vous mettent dans
la main la clé du coffre-fort
et un pain bénit
c'est drôle c'est rigolo

ESSAYEZ NOS DERNIERS MODÈLES MUSSOLINI

A corrected typescript and a finished typescript of this poem are in The Morris Library of Southern Illinois University. No record of publication has been found.

WAR IS AN ANACHRONISM

(Sir Toby: Here's an overweening rogue!
Fabian: O, peace! . . . .)

The American ladies
Decide war is an anachronism
And that there is no war
The American ladies are amazed
At their own magnanimity
The American financiers
Want to squeeze the last drop of Europe's blood
Before they have another war
So they praise the American ladies
And the ignorant and barbarous Europeans
Wish vaguely that the American ladies
Had made their decision in 1914.

In the next (American) war
What will the American ladies do?
Will they defeat the enemy with resolutions
Will they engulf the rebellious Senate
Will they produce Peace like able conjurers
From short-sleeved shirt waists?
On the contrary
The pacific American ladies
Will intrigue safe jobs in uniform for their lovers
And hand white feathers to other men
(especially if they fought in the German war
And became fed up in the process)
And make wonderful speeches about the cowardice
And cold-blooded neutrality of the British
Who care about nothing but money
And the well-known ferocity of Oriental races
Who are worse than savages and Huns.

And thus shall the wisdom of the New World
Reign supreme and secure o'er Chaos.

Typescript from the files of *Poetry: A Magazine of Verse*, in the University of
Chicago *Poetry Magazine Papers*. The peom is dated 1 September 1922 and
marked: "Kept as a curio." "Richard Aldington" is typed below the last
line. No publication located.

WHAT THE DEAD SAY IN SPRING

We should have many lives—
Who plucks a shattered rose to give his love?

How we squandered youth,
How the world betrayed us,
How the bright fruit turned to dust!
Yet the same sun lightens above us
And the same sea laps the cliffs,
Still the wild crocus studs the Roman hills
And in the nooks of southern crags
Still the wild cyclamen springs up,
Still in those echoing halls
Stand the white gods of Greece,
Still there is bronze and colour,
Still sounds the poets' thrilling speech
And the world's music is not mute.
All is the same and all is changed,
Because we are dead we think the world's gone out.

> *All is as lovely now*
> *As when Odysseus' prow*
> *   Plunged through the virgin sea,*
> *Young heart-blood runs as fleet*
> *Young love is just as sweet—*
> *   But not for the dead, not for me.*

What should the dead say to the dead?
Can there be mingling of bodies
And blinding kisses
And trembling hands and wildly beating hearts
And that sweet interchange of eyes with eyes
Which is the very core of love?

What should the dead do with love?
What should the dead say to the living?

We should have many lives,
We should renew our youth—
We should have youth and life
To give and give again.
Who can give twice?
What's done is done,
And what have we to give?
A dream and a regret.

Enclosed in a letter of 31 May 1927 to Crosby Gaige. This typescript poem is in the Beinecke Rare Book and Manuscript Library at Yale University. No publication has been located, but see the unpublished poem "Regrets" which seems to be a slightly different version of this poem.

A WINTER-SCENE BY AERT VAN DER NEER (1603-1677)

This delicate winter-sky,
This rose and citron flush
Of the freezing air,
(The red like a girl's cheek)
The dark pattern of the boughs,
The glimmer on the ice of passing figures—
In these is the beauty
I have sought,
The chaste fragility
As of hoar-frost on laurel-leaves
And sparse snow-flakes.

A corrected carbon typescript and holograph rewrite of this poem are in The Morris Library of Southern Illinois University. No record of publication has been found.

WITH THE HERDS OF ADMETUS

Horror of my exile! How exclude
Brute faces and their dull obscenity
From the gold shadow of my solitude?

My soul is tarnished silver. Must it be
Corroded by this foul desuetude
From the sharp glitter of its purity?

Never shall I pierce this slimy amplitude
Of brutishness which wraps and stifles me,
Never set free my lovely from their lewd;

No olive-tinted frond of the hoar sea,
No wave of all that lustrous multitude,
Can cleanse me back to my integrity.

Gone the austere poise, marble attitude,
Gone the free grace and Doric gaiety
And marred the song of a god's plenitude.

A signed manuscript of this poem is in the Griffith O'Neil collection of the
University of Washington Libraries, Seattle, Washington. No record of
publication has been found.

2

Poems from Periodicals and Newspapers

SONG OF FREEDOM

From the South have bloodily started the
    purple blossoms of war;
Like blood is the smell of their petals, and
    the savour is smelled afar.

And the kings of the South are captive, and
    they that were great are naught,
And lo! with a sword for his wailing people
    the Lord of Hosts hath fought.

And the kings of the North have trembled,
    for the seat of their thrones is shook;
And the seals of the doom of their glory are
    set in a bitter book.

But out of the oceans of striving, where the
    slaves have died with the free,
There hath risen a puissant goddess, and
    her voice is the voice of the sea.

And like Aphrodite, the fair one, she hath
    come from the mist of the waves,
And him that is mighty she smiteth, and
    him that is weak she saves.

And they that have fed upon plenty must cry
    for a morsel of bread,
And they that have fainted for hunger with
    honey and milk are fed.

She hath risen, the puissant goddess! and
    the heart of the world is hers,
For she stalks like a famished lion, and the
    monarchs snarl like curs.

She hath risen, the puissant goddess! and
    the sound of her name is called;
For the excellent balm of her beauty the
    high priest's heart is galled.

O, Freedom, goddess and mother, we have
    cried to thee passing long,
But thou hear'st, and slay'st with thy
    puissance the dragons of wrath and
    of wrong.

Grant now that the priests and the rulers
    shall trouble the people no more;
For the sins of their bodies have troubled
    the hearts of the people sore.

Thou hast fought for us, mother Freedom;
    for the sake of thy love men have died,
O, stay with us now for ever that the sun-
    light of peace may abide.

We are sick of the war and the striving,
    we are pained for the deaths of men,
And Lust and the God of Battle have
    couched in the earth as their den.

We are tired of the cry of the hungry, of
    the noise of the harlot's feet—
O, grant we be deft and courageous, and
    cunning and wise and fleet!

O, grant that the sorrow of riches may fade
    from the eyes of the world,
And we set safely and happy in sight of thy
    banner unfurled.

Justice, 29 October 1910, p. 5. This poem, written when Aldington was eighteen, is the earliest published poem that I have been able to find. Aldington wrote of it: "Somewhere about this time a revolution occurred in Portugal, Dom Manoel was deposed from the throne, and a republic was proclaimed. At that time I knew rather less than nothing about Portugal. . . . All I went on was an abstract and unfounded belief that monarchies are corrupt and republics perfect *per se*. So I celebrated this tremenduous victory of good over evil in a poem. I sent this to a leftish journal called *Justice*. . . . *Justice* printed my poem conspicuously. This filled me with joy, about seventy-five per cent of which was gratified vanity and about twenty-five per cent conviction that this finally clinched the whole matter for happy Portugal" *(Life for Life's Sake*, pp. 92-93). Surely, Swinburne's "Hymn to Proserpine"—"Thou hast conquered, O pale Galilean; the world has grown gray from thy breath"—lies behind these lines.

IN MEMORIAM
ARTHUR CHAPMAN
Born September 27th, 1891
Died August 26th, 1911

Through what mysterious paths abrupt and steep
   Wanders thy helpless spirit to that land
Where no light is, nor any god but Sleep,
   Where Silence soothes thee with caressing hand,
And nothing moves save time's relentless deep
   Upon the strand?

O friend, I cannot touch thee any more;
   I know not if thou know'st these tears of mine,
Or hear'st my singing on that endless shore
   Whose sombre waters cleave my soul from thine,
Or if thou seest me, as thou saw'st of yore
   The sunbeams shine.

Hast thou found harbour in the seas of space?
   Or dost thou linger on the gentle earth
To make the flowers more lovely with thy grace
   And lend thine ardours to the summer's birth?
Or hast thou seen thy life-days face to face
   To know thy worth?

Was God thy god? or are the lands of death
   Kingless as we who strive against the skies?
O dreams we dreamed! O body void of breath!
   Are ye so soon lost to my yearning eyes?
"Could'st thou not leave me him, O Time," Life saith,
   "So young, so wise?"

Alas, I cannot reach thee, O my friend;
   Empty and sad my words return to me;
Unheard and useless are the sighs I spend;
   Not all my grief can ever waken thee;
And there thou liest sleeping to the end—
   Eternity.

Union Magazine, Vol. 5, No. 3 (December 1911), p. 254. This was one of Aldington's earliest published poems. It appeared in University College's magazine over the initials "R.A."; it commemorated the death by drowning of one of the poet's college friends.

CHANSON OF WINTER
(Charles d'Orleans—1391-1465)

Winter, thou art but a knave;
   Gentle Spring is fair and fain—
   May and she down ev'ry lane
Dance like ripples on a wave.

Spring doth clothe the fields and woods,
   Decks them in a robe of pride;
Yea, with many a hue she floods
   All the flow'ring countryside.

Winter, thou art dull and grave—
   Hail and snow and wind and rain—
   Would thou might'st not come again!
   I flatter not; I tell thee plain,
Winter, thou art but a knave.

The Evening Standard, 6 February 1912, p. 3.

VILLANELLE

I swear I love her passing well
   As she rode by so debonair,
That fascinating damozel!

She was the faery of a dell;
   And oh! the ripples in her hair!
I swear I loved her passing well.

No reason can my passion quell,
   She had me in her cunning snare,
That fascinating damozel!

Yet why I loved I cannot tell;
   But ah! she was so very fair,
I swear I loved her passing well!

Let Spenser sing of Florimel,
   He never saw that beauteous—rare
That fascinating damozel!

She was the goddess of a shell,
   A very pearl beyond compare;
I swear I loved her passing well,
That fascinating damozel!

The Evening Standard, 8 February 1912, p. 3.

AT PARTING

As one who stands upon the hill of death
   And sees the sun of life deep sunk in cloud,
Then turns, with dizzy brain and failing breath,
   Down the long valley to his silent shroud;

So did I part from thee, O thou my sun,
   Sweet luminary of my boyhood's night,
Whose deep ineffable radiance doth stun
   My dazzled sense with effluence of light:

His dark is everlasting; but for me
   Shine the clear moon of hope and far above
The undiminished stars of memory:

And though time lag, upon the morning's crest
   Shall gleam the argent heraldry of love,
Token of thee, O loveliest and best.

Pall Mall Gazette, 4 March 1912, p. 6.

GREEK EPIGRAM
(Rufinus)

I send thee, Rhodocleia, for thy hair
This garland, twined from blossoms by my hand—
Rose-buds, and dewy wind-flowers, lily-cups,
Narcissus, and dusk-gleaming violets.
Make thee a crown, and of thy loveliness
Vaunt not: As flowers thy beauty blooms and dies.

Pall Mall Gazette, 21 March 1912, p. 6.

GREEK EPIGRAM
(Meleager)

Now blossoms sweet the violet; and now
Blooms the narcissus amorous of the rain
And mountain-haunting lily; now the rose,
Blossom of blossoms and belov'd of lovers,
Dear unto Zeus, flowers in her splendid prime,
O meadows wanton with fresh buds, why smile,
Why laugh ye radiant, seeing that my love
Is fairer than your fragrance-breathing crowns?

Pall Mall Gazette, 1 April 1912, p. 6.

RONDEAU OF SPRING
(Charles d'Orleans. 1391-1465)

Summer's messengers are here
    To deck her house right featly,
    Hanging forth her tapestry
Of buds and grasses green and clear.

Lo, her tapestries appear
    Spreading far and sweetly;
Summer's messengers are here
    To deck her house right featly.

Hearts with grief made chill and sere,
    Praised be Jesu, wax full merry;
    Hence, thou Winter, hence and flee,
Boast thyself no more my fere;
Summer's messengers are here!

The Evening Standard, 4 April 1912, p. 3.

SPRING AND THE SEA
(Leonidas of Tarentum)

Fair sailing days! For in the spring return
The twittering swallows and the blithe West-wind;
The green meads blossom and the great sea calms
Wild waves that once the driving storms aroused.
Weigh anchor, then, and cast the ropes ashore,
Sailor, with every sail stretched to the winds!
These days the harbour-god, Priapos, gives
That ye may bring your sails to any land.

Pall Mall Gazette, 10 April 1912, p. 6.

SOPHOKLES' TOMB
(Simmias of Rhodes)

Gently, above the tomb of Sophokles,
Oh, gently, ivy, trail thy pale green sprays;
Let the rose-petal fall and fruited vines
Twine lithesome shoots about, for he,
The honey-tongued, the musical, the wise,
Learned of the Mousai and the Karites.

Pall Mall Gazette, 22 April 1912, p. 6.

A SONNET OF LOUISE LABE

While yet mine eyes may overflow with tears
    Of sweet regret for dead days passed with thee,
    And while my voice of bitter sobs is free
So that its music may delight thine ears;
While yet to tell thy beauties and my fears
    The lute obeys my hand; and while I see
    My mind desire no knowledge that may be
Save that which in thy soul's demesne appears;

I shall not wish for death. But when mine eyes
    Withhold their tribute weepings, when my hand
Plucks not the lute, and when my singing dies,
And my sad spirit can descry no way
    To testify of Love at his command—
Then let Death darken my serenest day!

Pall Mall Gazette, 26 April 1912, p. 6.

SONNET

As on a bastioned shore the winter sea,
    Shattered in seething floods foam-laced with white,
    Quenches the chanting of the winds of night
With organ-throbs of thunderous harmony,
So the gold chimes of musing's melody

Which lull the heart to slumberous delight
By soul-heard cries are oft-times put to flight—
Cries from some far pre-natal memory.

Such aeon-dimmed and inchoate tones I mark
In the sad fading of the sunset's red,
And in the rippled music of the lark;
These are the muted voices of the dead,
Who, tongueless else, float through the chilling dark
Like shrivelled leaves or words we wish unsaid.

The Westminster Gazette, 19 June 1912, p. 2.

ONEIRODOTES

Tell me of Eos and of her wine-stained fingers
Plucking the yellow fruits of the sky.
Tell me of silence,
Where Hylas stood
By the slow dripping fountain-head;
Where sharp drops gleam
On moss, on orange lichen, and on ferns.

Tell me of the scarlet prows
And the silver trumpets at Salamis.

Silver and ivory,
Tell me your dreams.

The New Freewoman, Vol. 1 (15 September 1913), p. 132.

PENULTIMATE POETRY
Xenophilometropolitania

I
Tenzone Alla Gentildonna

Come, my songs.

II

Cantata

"Men pols lois puelh voys."
        — Arnault of Marvoil

Come my songs,
Let us observe this person
Who munches chicken-bones like a Chinese consul
Mandilibating a delicate succulent Pekinese spaniel.

III

Elevators

Come my songs,
Let us whizz up to the eighteenth floor,
Let us present our most undignified exterior
To this mass of indolent superstition,
To this perverted somnambulistic age;
Let us soar up higher than the eighteenth floor
And consider the delicate delectable monocles
Of the musical virgins of Parnassus:
Pale slaughter beneath purple skies.

IV

Ancora

Rest me with mushrooms,
For I think the steak is evil.

V

Convicted

Like an armful of greasy engineer's-cotton
Flung by a typhoon against a broken crate of ducks' eggs
She stands by the rail of the Old Bailey dock.
Her intoxication is exquisite and excessive,
And delicate her delicate sterility.
Her delicacy is so delicate that she would feel affronted
If I remarked nonchalantly, "Saay, stranger, ain't you dandy."

VI

Gitanjali

Come my songs,
(For we have not "come" during three of these our delectable canzoni)
Come, my songs, let us go to America.
Let us move the thumbs on our left hands
And the middle fingers on our right hands
With the delicate impressive gestures

Of Rabindranath Tagore. (Salaam, o water-cress of the desert.)
O my songs, of all things let us
Be delicate and impressive.
I implore you my songs to remain so;
I charge you in the name of these states.

VII

Altruism .

Come my songs,
Let us praise ourselves;
I doubt if the smug will do it for us,
The smug who possess all the rest of the universe.

VIII

Song of Innocence

The wind moves over the wheat
With a silver crashing,
A thin war of delicate kettles.

IX

The apparition   of these poems   in a crowd:
White faces   in a black   dead faint.

The Egoist, Vol. 1, No. 2 (15 January 1914), p. 36.

GLAUCOPIS

O maidens, whom I loved
And now love not at all,
Nor even the memory of your shadowy faces,
Who loved me also,
Striving with delicate and sensuous days
To thrall my soul,
Behold!
From the hush and the dusk
Come, like the whisper of dawn,
Her frail, her magical feet.
From the desert she blossoms,
A flower of the winds,
Tremulous, shaken by love.

Ah Gods!
And I may not harken
Nor stoop to the flower.

Poetry: A Magazine of Verse, Vol. 3, No. 4 (January 1914), p. 136. This is
the fifth poem printed under the general title "Poems."

ENNUIES
To a Poet

May we not be spared—
I beseech you—
This insistent cult of "Nature,"
This pitiless reiteration?
May we not accept
The facts of vegetation and florescence
Without these reminders?
I grant you that hyacinths
Are blue, and that olives
Are green in their season,
That berries are juicy and vine-leaves delightful.
But may we not leave them to Wordsworth
And caterpillars,
And ourselves make merry
With our own particular
Unvegetable artifices?   June, 1913

Les Ennuyes Exquis

Our immaculate boredom
Must have no stain of emotion,
And even our *amours*
Must be fragile and curious.
We would languidly fashion
The features of Nero
From emerald and basalt.

Let us be indolent
But very remarkable.
The clots of people
About Piccadilly
Are sordid and sweaty;
We suspect them of vices
Like marriage and business,
And we know they are ignorant
Of Hokkei and Rufinus;
But we cannot be troubled
To protest, or instruct them;
Our immaculate boredom
Must have no stain of emotion.   November, 1912

Verona

The heat is over the land
Like thick gold petals of a rose
That has the sun for heart;
It is spread out
Like three blankets too many
On a summer bridal couch.

When they splash water
On the hot flag-stones
Of the Piazza delle Erbe
The old women laugh with pleasure.

The young women complain;
They buy perfumes.

O England, my dull England,
I am glad to be away from you,
And in a joyous city
Where it is actually too hot.   June, 1913

A Liver

You say "This is not *my* lover!"

Ah, dear little mistress,
You strive vainly to goad my soul into gaiety;
It lies inert and bored, masculine,
With a sick horror of eternal disgusts.   July, 1913

Solemn Meditation

I am a-weary of this fecundity,
This monstrous clamour of babes,
This prodigious animality;
For if I love Woman
It must be as the frail stars
And the light of crystal waters,
Not as two rabbits
In a domestic den.

By Zeus,
I had liever be an eunuch!

Sweet God,
Keep me unwed
And sterile!
Eileithuia,
Be thou a goddess
Unknown in my house,
Neither be thou summoned
By howling of women.   April, 1912

Stodge

Decency,
Reverence,
The home,
The school,
The university,
The church,
The law (especially),
Property,
The leisured classes,
Kensington,
The bible—
O phallus of the Lampsacene,
O Nero, Cybele, Isis, Atys,
O ithyphallic deities,
Have mercy on us.
Kurioi eleïsate.

September, 1913

The Egoist, Vol. 1, No. 9 (1 May 1914), pp. 161-162. These are from a series of eight poems. The first of the series, "At Mitylene," was collected in *The Complete Poems*, after being reprinted in several of the earlier editions. The second, "A Farewell," was never collected or reprinted; it is given below. The remaining six were set originally, as they are here, under the general heading "Ennuies."

A FAREWELL
(For a few men of Poseidonia; for a few of to-day.)

Many have wounded you with evil praise,
O most high gods,
Many have spoken against you;
Many have uttered your names.

And you lie upon golden Olympus—
Aphrodite, Apollo, Heré—
And you muse of love or of fate,
And you watch the gold thin mist
As you lean by the golden cups.

O most high gods—
Artemis, Hermes, Zeus—
We have Até or Isis for queen.

Persephone has left us, has left us. . . .

Many men have wronged you,
O most high gods;
Our praise is as dust in your wine-cups;
The voice of Apollo is still,
O most high gods;
We give you for garlands,
We give you for wine and for salt,
We give you for paeans and hymns, our tears,
Our silence.

O most high gods,
We bring you our silence.

The Egoist, Vol. 1, No. 9 (1 May 1914), p. 161. See note on previous poem.

WAR YAWP

America!
England's cheeky kid brother,
Who bloodily assaulted your august elder
At Bunker Hill and similar places
(Not mentioned in our history books),
What can I tell you of war or of peace?
Say, have you forgotten 1861?
Bull Run, Gettysburg, Fredericksburg?
Your million dead?
Tell me,
Was that the greatest time of your lives
Or the most disastrous?
Who knows? Not you; not I.
Who can tell the end of this war?
And say, brother Jonathan,
D'you know what it's all about?
Let me whisper you a secret—we don't!
We were all too fat with peace,

Or perhaps we didn't quite know how good peace was,
And so here we are,
And we're going to win. . . .

It's fine to be a soldier,
To get accepted by the recruiting sergeant,
Be trained, fitted with a uniform and a gun,
Say good-bye to your girl,
And go off to the front
Whistling, "It's a long way to Tipperary."
It's good to march forty miles a day,
Carrying ninety-one pounds on your back,
To eat good coarse food, get blistered, tired out, wounded,
Thirst, starve, fight like a devil
(*i.e.*, like you an' me, Jonathan),
With the Maxims zip-zipping
And the shrapnel squealing,
And the howitzers rumbling like the traffic in Piccadilly.

Civilization?—
Jonathan, if you could hear them
Whistling the *Marseillaise* or *Marching Through Georgia*,
You'd want to go too.
Twenty thousand a day, Jonathan!
Perhaps you're more civilized just now than we are,
Perhaps we've only forgotten civilization for a moment,
Perhaps we're really fighting for peace.
And after all it will be more fun afterwards—
More fun for the poets and the painters—
When the cheering's all over
And the dead men buried
And the rest gone back to their jobs.
It'll be more fun for them to make their patterns,
Their word-patterns and color-patterns.
And after all, there is always war and always peace,
Always the war of the crowds,
Always the great peace of the arts.

Even now,
With the war beating in great waves overhead,
Beating and roaring like great winds and mighty waters,
The sea-gods still pattern the red seaweed fronds,
Still chip the amber into neck-chains

For Leucothea and Thetis.
Even now,
When the *Marseillaise* screams like a hurt woman,
And Paris—grisette among cities—trembles with fear,
The poets still make their music
Which nobody listens to,
Which hardly anyone ever listened to.

The great crowds go by,
Fighting over each other's bodies in peace-time,
Fighting over each other's bodies in war-time.
Something of the strife comes to them
In their little, high rock-citadel of art,
Where they hammer their dreams in gold and copper,
Where they cut them in pine-wood, in Parian stone, in wax,
Where they sing them in sweet bizarre words
To the sound of antiquated shrill instruments;
And they are happy.

The little rock-citadel of the artists
Is always besieged;
There, though they have beauty and silence,
They have always tears and hunger and despair.
But that little citadel has held out
Against all the wars of the world—
Like England, brother Jonathan.
It will not fall during the great war.

There is always war and always peace;
Always the war of the crowds,
Always the great peace of the arts.

Poetry: A Magazine of Verse, Vol. 5, No. 2 (November 1914), pp. 78-81. In
the original, stanza one is printed in italics.
     D. H. Lawrence mentions this poem in a letter he wrote to Harriet
Monroe dated 17 November 1914: "I hate, and hate, and hate the glib
irreverence of some of your contributors—Aldington with his 'Do you know
what it's all about, brother Jonathan? We don't.' It is obvious he doesn't."
Lawrence continued, "Your people have such little pressure: their safety
valve goes off at the high scream when the pressure is still so low. Have you
no people with any force in them? Aldington almost shows most—if he
weren't so lamentably imitating Hueffer." *The Letters of D. H. Lawrence*, ed.
Aldous Huxley (New York: The Viking Press, 1932), p. 215.

ON A MOTOR-BUS AT NIGHT
(Oxford Street)

The hard rain-drops beat like wet pellets
On my nose and right cheek
As we jerk and slither through the traffic.

There is a great beating of wheels
And a rumble of ugly machines.

The west-bound buses are full of men
In grey clothes and hard hats,
Holding up umbrellas
Over their sallow faces
As they return to the suburban rabbit-holes.
The women-clerks
Try to be brightly dressed;
Now the wind makes their five-shilling-hats jump
And the hat-pins pull their hair.

When one is quite free, and curious,
They are fascinating to look at—
Poor devils of a sober hell.

The shop-lamps and the street-lamps
Send steady rayed floods of yellow and red light
So that Oxford street is paved with copper and chalcedony.

The Little Review, Vol. 1, No. 9 (December 1914), p. 1.

TO THE SUPREME BEING IN WAR TIME
(Adapted from A. Chénier)

Still you don't fear lest at your feet
        Spinoza's words again may fall:
"Between ourselves, O Lord, I fear
        You never did exist at all."

The Egoist, Vol. 1, No. 23 (1 December 1914), p. 443.

ON THERSITES

Your last distempered works are such
   As you, too, shall deplore—
I'd not despise you quite so much
   If you would write no more.

The Egoist, Vol. 2, No. 1 (1 January 1915), p. 14.

SYNTHETIC SONNETS
I Classic

Thee, Smintheus, with plectroned lyre we sing—
   The golden mean—Priapus—thund'ring Jove—
   The pale white violets of the queen of Love
Would that I were a halcyon on the wing!—
The pipes of Pan—kisses that bite and sting—
   Softer than sleep or the breast of a dove—
   Where the high gods sit on their thrones above
There comes no hail, rain, wind, no anything.

Hymettus honey—Aetna's snowy peak—
   The lips of Lesbians hissing hot desire—
   (Caesar's emetic leaves him rather gruff)—
O fields of asphodel—O maidens sleek!—
   Pour your libations on the funeral pyre—
   Odd that the public scorns this sort of stuff!

II Dantesque

When first I saw thee—those on whom she gazes
   Are dumb—when Love doth seize the gentle heart—
   Turn, turn thine eyes; withhold, O Love, thy dart—
Paler than pallid lillies—whose praises
My lady's gentleness, him straight Love raises—
   Tears are but fire not balm unto my smart—
   O warrior Love, how passing fierce thou art—
See, where she sits among th'admiring daisies!

The Spirit of Love hath sent an emanation
   Whose distillation poisons all my life—
      Would I were dead, nay, would she were in heaven—
Madonna mine—Love's bitter deep damnation
   Within my piteous heart holds deadly strife—
      This sort of rot was damned in fifteen seven.

III Francis Thompsonian

Like swift concatenated loops of time
   Her tendrilled tresses fold my minutes up—
   A mammoth drinking from a primrose cup—
("Mary" and "hairy," these be parlous rhyme)
O Paraclete, my hesitant feet to climb,
   Teach Thou—ye ministrants who inter-sup
   With Christ, O purple hierophantic group,
With ye I festinate and haply swyme.

O Lord, when I address Thee as a child
   In monosyllables I make my prayer—
      When as my gibbous self I cantilate
In rubious ecstasy, in wassail wild,
   I hale the planets by their horrent hair!
      Marino, Crawshaw, Donne, behold your fate!. . . .

IV Cosmic
(Sonnet in vers libre)

When I behold Chicago I behold the universe—
   The Stars, the Stars, the Stars! (Where's F. S. Flint?)
   The Milky Way—Arcturus—Peter Doyle—
Where God is Love and Love is God, how then?
The old order changes; Kings and Emperors pass—
   Behold Columbia in her Cosmic robes—
   Illimitable Eros weds Osiris now—
Dagos and niggers, Polacks, Dutchmen, Jews.

Most every Cawsmos has a Soul, I guess,
   Least so they tell us down Springfield way—
      Wild cataclysmic Cosmos, cosmically
I strive across the Void to grapple Thee!
   (I dare not speak; I whisper: "Amy Lowell,
      Ask me to Boston when the last Cosmic poet's dead.")

V Realistic

The clattering tram of workers wan and tired—
    A little child born in a London slum—
      "I'll break your bleedin' 'ead I will, by gum!"—
You leave that pianola, it was hired
By my poor dead old mother—sad, bemired,
    A tattered woman barters life for rum—
      "Well, Bill, yer needn't look so b——y glum,
You ain't the only bastard what's bin fired."

"This is my child; his father was a Lord.
    What matter if I've lost my marriage lines?"—
    See how that private soldier hugs his girl!—
London is sad for old folk—yes, I've wh——d,
    Pretty nigh everywhere—those bloomin' mines—
      Newbolt's a knight; Masefield will be an earl.

The Egoist, Vol. 2, No. 2 (1 February 1915), p. 23.

PALACE MUSIC HALL—*(LES SYLPHIDES)*
To Nijinsky

The little white lambs frisk
And flirt their woolen panties;
In meek and sleek sweet patterns
They group about their shepherd.

Hola!
An elegant shepherd!

He trips like a young princess;
He has curls like a real Madonna.
And there he goes prancing
And dancing, and entrancing
A little pastoral lady.

But perhaps he is really a Panisk,
Running through tall white flowers
After a white mademoiselle butterfly.

He does not do it for money
As they other here have done;

He likes to jump and feel his legs.

And after all I think he is a fairy prince,
And the dance means that he has lost his kingdom
But that he will marry a king's daughter.

Poetry: A Magazine of Verse, Vol. 5, No. 5 (February 1915), p. 221. This poem, along with "Interlude," appeared under the heading "Dancers." "Interlude" was later included in *The Complete Poems*.

JULY SUNDAY
(From a Back Window)

The sky was the colour of a field of cornflowers,
Which are hidden and revealed by the wind,
As it billows the corn into waves
Rolling over the hill-side.

Towards evening
There came a little flicker of rain,
Grey gauze, a thin web of water,
Which settled like shining gossamer on the slates
And the greasy flag-stones.

And on the other side of the courtyard
In the queer darkness of the basement kitchen,
With its smell of food and dishes,
An old man sang to the children,
Dolefully, with a harsh old voice,
In the twilight.

The Egoist, Vol. 2, No. 3 (1 March 1915), p. 45.

EPIGRAMS

Blue

(A Conceit)

The noon sky, a distended vast blue sail;
The sea, a parquet of coloured wood;
The rock-flowers, sinister indigo sponges;
Lavender leaping up, scented sulphur flames;
Little butterflies, resting shut-winged, fluttering,
Eyelids winking over watchet eyes.

The Retort Discourteous

They say we like London—O Hell!—
They tell
Us we shall never sell
Our works (as if we cared).
We're "high brow" and long-haired
Because we don't
Cheat and cant.
We can't rhythm; we can't rhyme,
Just because their rag-time
Bores us.

These twangling lyrists are too pure for sense;
So they chime,
Rhyme
And time,
And Slime,
All praise their virtuous impotence.

Christine

I know a woman who is natural
As any simple cannibal;
This is a great misfortune, for her lot
Is to reside with people who are not.

The Little Review, Vol. 2, No. 4 (June-July 1915), pp. 4-5.

EASTER
(Golders Green Park)

A cinder path, sowed with chips of earthenware, leather, rusty tin, meagrely fringed with trodden mud and pale grass:

This path leads to the pond.
On one side of the pond

Oozes a brownish cataract in three falls, choked and malodorous with dirty straws, creased paper bags, a faded blue matchbox, shreds of pink soiled paper.

On the other side
A small group—a workman, an old clerk, some nursemaids and women with children—watch an urchin thrust his boot through the wooden railing to be pecked at by a seigneurial swan. Alas, oblivious of dignity, like an exasperated poet insulted by a mob, the swan writhes his neck in a white agony of rage and stains his breast against the muddy bank.

Bruno Chapbooks, Special Series No. 5 (between August and September) 1915. This poem and "London (May 1915)" accompanied Aldington's article "The Imagists," and were used, with a poem by H.D. and one by F.S. Flint, to illustrate points Aldington made. "London (May 1915)" appears in Aldington's *Complete Poems* and was one of the poems in his first volume of poetry, *Images (1910-1915)*.

A PLAYNTYVE BALLADE

When Sappho sang "In the Isles of Greece,"
    When Ibycus founded a new free verse,
And Pindarus spun his golden fleece
    Of words that were golden and keen and terse;
What said the critics—race perverse—
    "These fellows have no more bones than a squid,
The race of poets grows worse and worse:
    Why don't they write as Homer did?"

Virgil snivelled of delicate bees—
    That was great, for it filled his purse—
But the world grew sick with a strange disease
Which the Christians claimed they were sent to disperse;

They invented rhymes and rhythms diverse,
In queer acrostics their God they hid:
  Quoth the critics: "Poetry's on its hearse,
Why in hell don't they write as Virgil did?"

The devil take 'em, gabbling geese,
  May he take 'em cunningly in reverse,
Plague 'em with boils and bees and fleas,
  In a seething cauldron their heads immerse!
  Pot-bellied pedlars, hear them rehearse
The old gibes, false as a Brummagum quid:
  "The Imagists' faults are like thorns on furze,
Why, WHY don't they write as Tennyson did?"

Envoy

Prince, in the nineteen ninety three
  When the young men pen a rebellious screed,
Their critics will boom like the booming seas:
  "Now why don't they write as the Imagists did?"

The Egoist, Vol. 2, No. 10 (1 October 1915), pp. 161-162.

EPIGRAMS

Replies
I

When I was hungry and implored them, they said: "The sun-beetle eats
dung: imitate him."
I implored them for my life's sake and they replied: "Last year's roses
are dead; why should you live?"

II
(Three years later)
They came to me and said: "You must aid us for the
sake of our God and our World."
I replied: "Your god is a beetle and your world a ball of dung."
But they returned and said: "You must give your life to defend us."
And I answered: "Though a million of you die, next spring shall not
lack roses."

Happiness

(To F.S.F.)

Cease grumbling, brother!
All men are wretched;
Some too rich,
Most too poor—
Happiness eludes them.

We have books and talk,
Women (not many)
And rich imaginings.
Let us pardon the gods
Who made us men
For they have made us poets!

Beauty

Those who would write great poems
Without the love of beauty
Are like men who desire strong children
Without the love of women;
And like a man who should give a feast
Without wine;
And like a country that goes to war
Without great armies.

The Egoist, Vol. 3, No. 2 (1 February 1916), p. 26. ("Happiness" is probably
dedicated to F. S. Flint.)

FANTASIES

Religious Landscape

"Panting red pants into the West"
        —Francis Thompson

How it fluttered on the line in the Convent Garden—how the good sisters'
white and red washing danced!
        This was in a very windy seaside village of Kent and as I rode to

school on my bicycle I could see it leaping and fluttering in the wind.

The Convent had been driven from France by the narrow-minded "Free-thinkers" of the Third Republic, but the Mothers were very gentle and kind, and the serving sisters big, coarse peasants. . . .

How it fluttered on the line in the Convent Garden—how the good sisters' white and red washing danced!

The Curé and my father were bibliophiles; they used to talk about books—about Pascal and "Meelton." One evening we all went to hear Complines, which they chanted in darkness. Neither their Latin nor mine was very good; I heard only two phrases: "Rose of the World" and "Tower of Ivory." . . .

And at once I saw it fluttering in the Convent Garden—the good sisters' washing dancing and leaping in the wind!

Book Shelves

"Liddell and Scott"; "Rhodigini lectionum antiquarum libri XXX."; "Cowley: Works"; "Hooker: Ecclesiastical Polity"; "Ebermeyer: de Gemmis"; "Appuleii Metamorphoseon," &c., &c., &c. Formidable folios, pell-mell quartos, deserts of type; sixteenth-century printing jostling this year's editions—Euripides beside Ford Madox Hueffer—what a mess! what a bore! what a humiliation!

And is it for this I labour? To be an object of derision to some bibliophile looking at his books as cynically and as disgustedly as I look at mine?

Sloane Street

I walk the streets and squares
Of this lampless war-time London,
Beautiful in its dusk.
On the right an orange moon;
On the left a searchlight,
A silver stream among the stars.

London was a rich young man
Burdened with great possessions—
Now, poor in light,
Menaced, and a little frightened,
At length he sees the stars.

The Egoist, Vol. 3, No. 3 (1 March 1916), p. 39.

BLOOMSBURY SQUARE

I walk around Bloomsbury Square.

Bright sky over Bloomsbury Square;
Bright fluttering leaves
Between the sober houses.

I carry my morning letters,
Some telling of lives spoiled and cramped,
Some telling of lives hopeful and gay,
Some full of yearning for London
And our wider life.

In Bloomsbury Square
The worms of a little moth
Are spinning their Cocoons,
Weaving them out of bright yellow silk
And bits of plane bark
Into strong, comfortable houses.
But hundreds of them
Have wandered on to the iron fence
And go wearily wandering,
Spending a little silk here
And a little silk there,
And at last dropping dead from weariness. . . .

"Our wider life"—
That is our wider life:
To wander like blind worms
Spending our fine useless golden silk
And at last dropping dead from weariness.

Blue sky over Bloomsbury Square;
Bright fluttering leaves
Between the sober houses.

The Little Review, Vol. 3, No. 1 (March 1916), p. 28.

EPIGRAM

Rain rings break on the pool
And white rain drips from the reeds
Which shake and murmur and bend;
The wind-tossed wistaria falls.

The red-beaked water fowl
Cower beneath the lily leaves;
And a grey bee, stunned by the storm,
Clings to my sleeve.

The Little Review, Vol. 3, No. 1 (March 1916), p. 29.

ITALY

You must not tempt us with your beauty;
It is not ours.

For you:
Silver spray of bending olives
Above blue waves,
Music on glittering Venetian waters
At evening,
Carved bronze, old palaces,
And long bright frescoes—
A thousand silent towns
Set upon golden hills.

For us:
Rows of grey bleak houses,
Misery of ceaseless noise,
No sun.

The Egoist, Vol. 3, No. 4 (1 April 1916), p. 53.

A MEMORY: POEM IN PROSE

The river is swift under the old bridge. The town gates are grey and crumbling. Winter sets little plaques of snow all over the cobbled square; summer plants, tufts of grass, and small weeds between the stones. It is very simple and quiet and peaceful in our old forgotten town. It is so old and so many dead people have lived there that the low wooden houses bend over wearily, and the grass-grown winding streets are only happy when there is no step to wake their echoes. It is so quiet that you can hear the minutes slowly moving by. We are so peaceful that we do hardly anything except watch the months pass.

In spring the elm-trees which grow along the town walls—for our town is one of the few in England which still have walls—the elm-trees glint with leaves, and the rushing March wind with its rapid glimmerings of sunlight and cloud whips across our red tiled roofs. But this soon changes, and all along the dykes blossom meadow-sweet and yellow flags; green tall rushes bending in the wind are lighted upon by sharp blue dragonflies; then it is so still that the Tick-Tack, Tick-Tack, Tick-Tack of the church clock sounds right across the empty sun-lit market-place. (Our church clock is two hundred years old; it is almost the newest thing in the town. The newest thing is the Martello tower, which was put up during the wars with Napoleon.)

In the winter, which is very severe in our town, we have sometimes so prolonged a frost that the townsfolk come out in their wraps and skate along the dykes. And the girls are so plump and the young men so serious and the old men so ribald and the children so rosy-faced that you might well imagine you were in some Dutch village of the seventeenth century; it is almost as homey and naïve as a picture by Aart van der Neer. At night everything is so still that you can hear the frost creeping along the dark streets, snapping off a piece of wood from the house where Queen Elizabeth slept, crackling up the thatch of the King's Head, hanging a string of icicles on the eaves of the grammar school, and turning the water in the tanks and dykes and wells, in our jugs and ewers and bottles, into hard clear ice. Only the river under the old bridge is too swift to freeze.

But it is best in early autumn. You lie in a field by a very little stream and the tall poplars shower gold round leaves, like guineas, slowly into the water, while the ducks dibble among the water-weeds. There is a vast yellow glow of sun; blue sky swamped in gold; the air throbs with the whirr of a threshing-machine in the old barn on the other side of the stream; you hear a cow snort as she drinks, and the old people sitting at the doors of their alms-cottages look quiet and happy. Presently the drone of the threshing-machine weakens and stops; the sun goes down in a great wasteful splash of red light; a late bird whistles a few notes; a leaf rustles down; the old people do not move; some one goes slowly along the path.

Yes, it is very quiet in our town.

The Egoist, Vol. 3, No. 4 (1 April 1916), p. 50.

A LIFE

He was a peasant boy
With sharp eyes and beaked nose;
His hair was too long, ragged
And a little greasy.

He was generous, indifferent to comforts,
Lived on bread, onions and apples—
Worked in a shed under a railway arch—
Was very witty and a little violent.
His red shirt was none too clean;
When he got hot he stank.
His hands were mostly filthy
With marble-dust and clay.

In all his sketches and statues
He made you see something fresh—
An unsuspected beauty, a new strength,
The clear line of a naked woman's body,
The lightness of a stag,
A new grotesqueness or hideousness.

He had the blithe intolerance of the very young
But there was nothing petty in him;
He worked hard, had no obvious vices.

Then the war came.
He went off with a joke:
"I'll be back safe in three months:
I'll steal the Picassos from Düsseldorf!"

He was away three months
And another three months;
Was wounded, promoted, went back,
Accepted things cheerfully,
"Without arrogance" (his own phrase).

A few more weeks—
He was shot in the head.
Quenched that keen, bright wit,
Horribly crushed the wide forehead,
Limp and useless the able hands
Of our one young sculptor.
I wish he were not dead;
He was wholesome, his dirt and his genius.
So many "artists" are muffs, poseurs, pifflers.

I sit here, cursing over my Greek—
Anacreon says:
"War spares the bad, not the good."

I believe him.

The Egoist, Vol. 3, No. 5 (1 May 1916), p. 69. (This poem probably refers to Gaudier-Brzeska.)

ASSOCIATIONS

"The Middle Ages"

The middle ages.

Middle? A pause between consciousness and consciousness, between one age of individuals and another—mankind becomes conscious only through individuals. From Tiberius to the Borgia the circle is complete, but a great arc is invisible—the middle ages.

We do not evolve; we gyrate. We do not create; we rearrange. The pessimism of Solomon—the pessimism of Schopenhauer.

The middle ages.

It is misty. There is no moon, no sun; the stars are hidden. There is only grey opaque light, indecisive. It is neither day nor night, neither dawn nor sunset; the year balances, it is either spring or autumn.

The sky is pale, glaucous, flat; the earth dark, thrown up in confused masses.

A line of small ragged trees cuts vague agitated patterns of darkness on the grey heaven. A flock of sheep comes bleating through the mist, running aimlessly down the hill beside the trees.

There is a faint cold wind.

The lambs run with the ewes; they are grey against the dark earth. Behind them on the hill crest, dark against grey, stands, silhouetted for a moment, a tall being, clothed in a garment reaching to the knees.

Male or female? Old or young? All is vague, the mist is impenetrable.

Somewhere near should be a Cross: it is invisible.

What hope?

The being, shepherding the sheep, gives a shrill cry: Anguish or delight? Warning or greeting? Prayer or revolt?

Evening or dawn?

The middle ages.

We also live in the first uncertain twilight of another middle age, a middle age without faith.

The middle ages.

The world does not exist: all is formal, abstract, unnatural. The blue Mediterranean is grey; the marble temples crack, tremble, fall in hopeless ruin; the red fades from the apple and the grape shrivels; scarcely a flower blooms save the wax virgin lily; with candles men put out the sun; great roads become pilgrims' tracks; the arts languish, are proscribed, wither between ecclesiastical violence and military indifference.

Hell is real.

Water exists, but not to bathe in, not to be touched, drunk, worshipped: dirt is holy, and if we drink it must be our own tears with horror and hatred for the snare of the senses.

The middle ages.

From the world colour has flown; beauty is vanished; the gods are dead.

Yet the spirit of man labours. . . .

Grey churches—for the world is grey—but tombs painted crimson and blue, with gold mosaic, for death is desirable; sacred cups of silver studded with large valueless blue stones, heavy pontifical rings and bright coloured priestly robes, for Christ is poor and needs wealth; windows in which are brought together all the colours that have faded from the world, for the heart of man is starving.

Gold and crimson and blue.

That which man is he worships; that which he has not he desires; that which he is ignorant of he believes.

And interminable wars lacerate the earth.

The middle ages.

Pathological aberrations cultivated, worshipped as the symbol of god; the greatest maniac the greatest saint; the most perverted ascetic the most pleasing to god.

The middle ages.

Institutions not individuals. The town, the commune, the empire, the church—interminable wrangling between communal energies. Yet the individual becomes a symbol—pope, king, emperor, bishop. The arts lift their heads and moan.

The symbol outweighs the institution. . . .

Glitter of the new birth—shining Renaissance, dimmed how soon? Leonardo!

The middle ages.

A robed figure in mist, always grey mist.

There are mingled vague voices, light glimmering a moment from royal armour, a bishop's crimson hat, a painted banner—confusion, an endless mysterious host moving confusedly in mist; women sobbing.

A robed figure in mist, always grey mist.

The Egoist, Vol. 3, No. 6 (1 June 1916), pp. 94-95.

THE DAYS PASS

I

Print,
Dirty black marks
Ruining the paper,
Masses of squirming little insects,
I hate you,
What do I care
Though it was Aldus himself made you
In the year of God 1513?

A great flight of pigeons across the sun
Makes the light of my window
Twinkle and flash;
The roses in the blue-patterned jug
Are austere and indifferent;
The trees are not worried with learning.

Let us loaf;
Leave Aldus and his kind on the shelf,
Sooth our eyes and brains
In sunlight and idleness.

II

Useless!
Those who dropped us here,
Like rats in a stone courtyard,
Should know how useless.

A thousand years of youth
Were not enough.

There must be a million
Lovely women in the world—
Can we love them all
In fifty years?

Why, all the summers
And the cities of the world,
All the solitudes of grey hills,
All betwixt sea and sea,
Useless!

The Egoist, Vol. 3, No. 11 (November 1916), p. 169. This is the first of the poems printed under the general heading "Two Poems"; the second, "R.V. and Another," appears in *The Complete Poems* and was also reprinted in *Some Imagist Poets* (1917).

STREAM

I

Pebbles, that gleam dully,
white, faint ochre, drab green:
mosaic under pale sliding water.

II

Foam;
mobile crests leaping, sinking:
thin fingers grasping round cold rocks.

III

Pines, white ash-trees,
black-thorns, winter grass,
mirrored trembling in you, O vagrant,
bending away from you and towards you:
hesitating, importunate lovers.

IV

Small blue waves straining to meet,
never touching, always elusive:
mocking, half-virginal lips.

The Little Review, Vol. 3, No. 10 (April 1917), pp. 12-13. Aldington submitted this poem to the magazine's "Vers Libre" contest. It appears under the note: "The two prizes of $25 each go therefore to H. D. and Mr. Bodenheim. But it may be interesting to print some of the others. For instance, not a single judge mentioned the following." There is also an interesting note after this poem: "Eunice Tietjens mentioned *Flower* and *Foam* with this qualification: 'Provided Richard Aldington wrote them. Otherwise not. My point is that if he wrote them they are authentic as well as lovely, but if he did not so flagrant an imitator ought not to be encouraged even if he is a successful copyist.' "

EVIL MALADY

There are obscene phrases which to hear destroys the soul like an evil malady. . . .
    The soul!
    The soul—the name of the unnameable, of the inexpressible, of our delicacy and our fine sorrows, and our bitter anguish and our frail desires and tenuous happiness.
    For we need not believe in one god, but in many gods; nor in many souls, but a few souls.
    And we may liken the soul to a white beech-tree and to a white butterfly and to a white wave.

    But there are obscene phrases which to hear destroys the soul like an evil malady. . . .

There are clean sorrows which heal the soul, like bitter herbs, and there are foul sorrows which destroy the soul, like heavy poison.

The lightning which cleaves a straight white wound in the gentle beech-tree is a clean sorrow, and the dying tree is lovely as Hylas drooping above the nymph-haunted stream.

And the wind which hurls the fragile white butterfly on to the whipping reeds is a clean sorrow, for the weary butterfly is lovely as Psyche weeping in the hard fields.

And the jagged shore which tears the white wave into fringes and shreds of pale water is a clean sorrow, for the torn wave is lovely as Hippolytus among the high dead.

But there are obscene phrases which to hear destroys the soul like an evil malady. . . .

For the white beech-tree which dies suffocated with soot in a dreary, paved yard; and the white butterfly which is crushed in the cruel, soiled hand of a slave; and the white wave which is killed by filth and refuse and waste—this is a foul sorrow.

For when the soul is cleft with a clean sorrow the immortal gods set rose-wreaths upon their hair and shed gentle tears and the music of many lutes makes prayer to inevitable Fate.

But when the soul is harmed by a foul sorrow, then the immortal gods tear the fresh wreaths of roses from their soft hair, and hide the bright glow of their deathless brows beneath their garments, and the heavenly hosts of the Muses break wildly the strings of their golden lutes, so that with the shrill note a pang of horror strikes into the heart even of inevitable Fate.

For there are obscene phrases which to hear destroys the soul like an evil malady. . . .

The Egoist, Vol. 4, No. 5 (June 1917), p. 70.

DEATHS OF COMMON MEN

Now, while the sun is hot
And they gather the grape-harvest,
And the leaves are gold, and life splendid,
Let me speak once more of the end, the parting—
How simple it is, how natural.

People in cities, perturbed, neurasthenic,
Rushing like futile hogs helter-skelter,
Living as if they would live for ever,
Dread death, shrink and shiver and mumble,
Start at the spectre, evade, palaver,
Till shoved ignominiously
Into the greasy grave.

More of my friends now are dead than living.
I have seen the strong body crumble and wither,
Give at the knees, stumble, crash in the mud,
Groan a little, lie still;
I have seen the good flesh cut, the white bone shattered,
Seen the red face turn like a yellow leaf,
The firm mouth wobble;
Watched it all, taken it in.

I have slept side by side with men
Who are now green corpses
Or bundles of dirty bones.
All of them, dozens, gone, and I only
Left above ground in the hot sun,
Tasting wine, wooing lips, laughing,
Watching the harvest, joking, sweating,
Alive.

Take earth in your hands, common earth,
Moist crumbly loam, dark, odorous—
This is the bodies of our forefathers,
Of long-ago mothers, beasts, insects;
See that you love the common earth,
Press it close in your hands
And murmur: "This is my body."

We are made of the infinite dead,
And, dead, we make the infinite living.
Have no fear of the subtle man,
The man of affected speech and brains;
You and I will make just as good corpses,
Our clay is sweeter.

Have no fear, I say, death is nothing;
I see dead men every week,
Give them a last keen look,
Affectionate, valedictory,
Then cover the face
And turn again to my life,
Serious, but tranquil and cheerful.

Again I say to you, simple folk,
Who, like me, are afraid of the great
And ill at ease with subtle men,
Have no fear;
We are—not the salt—
But the earth of the earth, earth itself,
And we die that life may be richer.

September 1918

The Egoist, Vol. 5, No. 10 (November-December 1918), p. 131.

DÉCOR BANAL

Cinq boutons électriques
Reluisent audessus des têtes
De trois militaires belges;
Un revolutionnaire irlandais
S'en fiche de mes habits guerriers;
Mademoiselle m'apporte du vin,
De la soupe, de la viande,
Mais moi je reste contemplatif,
Hebété par la blancheur de la nappe
En attendant quelq'une qui ne vient pas.

The Little Review, Vol. 5, Nos. 10-11 (February-March 1919), p. 35.

FEAR

Hold to me, take my hand; like two children, suddenly terrified by their loneliness we shrink from the menace of things. Hold to me, let me touch you; if I should lose you!

Hold to me; those who have missed love, seeing our gladness and simple trust, will hate us; they will try cunningly to estrange us.

The world hates lovers, hates those who found the jewel its blindness missed, hates those who are happy. Hold to me close; in the night I am afraid of mysterious presences. We are so utterly alone.

The Anglo-French Review, Vol. 1, No. 4 (May 1919), p. 357. (Printed entirely in italics.)

TWO IMPRESSIONS

I

The colorless morning glides upward
Over the marsh and ragged trees.

Though our mood be sombre
And our bodies angry for more sleep,
This feathered softness of pale light,
Falling negligently upon us,
Delights us.

II

High above the drab barren ground
Three herons beat across the dawn-blue sky.
They drift slowly away
Until they appear
As three horizontal umber brush-strokes
On finely shaded cobalt.
And the mist, driven by the wind
Up and across the distant hill,
Gleams like soft white hair
Brushed amorously backward!

Poetry: A Magazine of Verse, Vol. 14, No. 4 (July 1919), pp. 175-176.
This is the second poem printed under the general title "In France (1916-1918)."

COMPENSATION

As I dozed in a chilly dug-out
I dreamt that Li-Taï-Pé, the sage,
And Sappho, the divine Lesbian,
And Abou-Nawas, the friend of Khalifs,
Came to me saying:
"There can be no death of beauty;
Endure—we also suffered."

And for a token of their love they gave me
A gold chrysanthemum, a fiery rose,
And a cleft-open, dew-wet nectarine.

Poetry: A Magazine of Verse, Vol. 14, No. 4 (July 1919), p. 176.
This is the third poem printed under the general title "In France
(1916-1918)."

BEAUTY UNPRAISED

There is only you.
The rest are palterers, slovens, parasites.
You only are strong, clear-cut, austere;
Only about you the light curls
Like a gold laurel bough.

Your words are cold flaked stone,
Scentless white violets?

Laugh!
Let them blunder.
The sea is ever the sea
And none can change it,
None possess it.

Poetry: A Magazine of Verse, Vol. 14, No. 4 (July 1919), p. 177. This
is the fifth poem printed under the general title "In France (1916-1918)."

MINOR EXASPERATIONS
I The Occultists

Find love so difficult a deed,
Theirs is so pure, so educational.

God! I've been sensual enough,
You can call me beast,
But these, these finger-twitchers, neck-paddlers,
These "souls" with wrists and ankles
But no inwards—!

Spit clean your mouth, Caligula;
At least I'll set my teeth
Deep in the Dead Sea apple,
Not sniff and tongue and pat it
Like an eunuch monkey.

                              Rome, 1912

II Valhalla

The war-worn heroes take their rest
In the mess ante-room . . .

Some sprawl asleep by the stove,
Some play bridge on green tables,
Some read novels,
Mournfully peering through smoky air.

Thus, O Athene, do the high heroes,
Even as Odysseus and the noble Menelaus,
Rest from the toils of war.

                              Newhaven, 1918

III My Colonel

My colonel has several dabs of bright colour
Over his left top pocket;
He walks with harassed dignity;
His gaze of intelligence is deceptive—

There is nothing in his head
But a précis of King's Regs.,
Crime sheets and military handbooks.

Every day he talks seriously to poor fools
Who have stayed out too late at night
Or lost a rifle or forgotten to shave;
Nearly every day he condemns to prison
Some weak-minded son of Cain
For an absurd triviality.

I have never spoken unofficially to my colonel
But I suspect he is even more imbecile than I have painted him.

Newhaven, 1919

IV Breaking-Point

Have I still three friends in the world
Untainted by moral cowardice,
By respect for institutions?

I will dance a solemn war dance,
Crouching down, beating my hands,
Solemnly stamping my feet;
I will dance on the grave of prosperity.
I lust for the scalp of smug security,
To rattle the bones of the bourgeois.

I will make mock of brass hats and brass buttons.
At a serious ceremonial moment
When the hero of a hundred newspapers
(The general who never saw the line)
Is inspecting a motionless brigade,
I will pierce the shocked air
With a laugh of preposterous ribaldry.

I will sneer at this silly war
(I have suffered, I can do as I please),
I will sneer at its bastard pomp,
Expose its flatulent hypocrisy.

O, I could charm the high gods
With a more than Aristophanic levity,
Deploy before their histrionic cachinnations
The biggest fraud in history;
O, I could play hell with this epoch
Had I still three friends in the world
Untainted by moral cowardice,
By respect for institutions.

Newhaven, 1918

Coterie, No. 2 (September 1919), pp. 13-15.

MEDITATION

When at length you come;
When I have caught from a distance
The first murmur of iron wheels,
Have watched through the darkness
The sinuous line of lighted carriages—
One of which holds you—roll nearer;
When I see your uncertain shape
Poised for a second in the glowing doorway,
And feel you coming nearer,
And hear again the sound of your voice,
I shall be happy.
I shall be like a dark unfrequented hill-side
With cold grass and ragged trees and gorse,
Melancholy, hushed and expectant,
Under the soughing wind,
When slowly the heavy broken clouds
Are lighted by distant beams
Of the full moon graciously rising.
Gradually I shall be filled with light
As the desolate hill-side is softened with moon-rays;
Gradually the sensation of your presence
Will be diffused through me;
Each one of my senses, suddenly alert and vigorous,
Will be tremulously perceiving you,
Absorbing you into me;
That which is you I shall snare in my senses,
Possess, exult over.

And I shall know that this is happiness—
To live in the same world at the same time
With you.

The Chapbook, Vol. 3, No. 13 (July 1920), p. 16, and *The Living Age,* Vol. 306 (21 August 1920), p. 493.

INVITATION

Your presence makes interesting the most banal situation, the most somniferous company.

From time to time I glance at your head, its soft cap of dark hair, your profile like a quattrocento medal, your mouth, a voluptuous petal folded inward, frail and exquisite—a mouth whose gift is ecstasy or anguish, never indifference.

What are you? You might be another Heliodora; you might become a 'buveuse d'absinthe' with equivocal eyes.

Lay your hands in mine; I can give you, if not happiness—and perhaps even that—at least self-knowledge.

The Anglo-French Review, Vol. 4, No. 3 (October 1920), p. 235. Printed in italics.

TO FRANCE

If I were Algernon Swinburne, who loved Republics and rhetoric,
I could address you in faultless and mythological verse,
And gloriously praise you with wind, fire, ocean, and blood;
Or if I were Robert Browning, I could tell in singular rhymes
Some heroic story of your past no one had ever heard before;
But as it seems to me indelicate and an anachronism
To liken a republic to a large woman with protruding breasts
And congruous attributes, or to recount obscure anecdotes,
I can only felicitate you in my own indistinguished manner.

Without you the world would have been sadder and narrower,
Without you the sense of Europe, of the world, were incomplete;
You are the brains, the wit, the delicacy of Europe;
Your women are the most charming, your philosophers the most
     indulgent,
Your prose the most polished, your painting the most vital.
I have loved your artists and the gardens of the Luxembourg,
I detest your petit bourgeois and the Tour Eiffel;
I like your food, your fiacres, and your fiction,
But I wish you would catalogue your Bibliothèque sensibly.
I love you but I will not flatter you; you are prone to extremes;
How often have you corrected the errors of one Saint-Simon
By the no less palpable errors of the other!
But with the first you were noble, with the second generous,
Even in your errors you were still *la grande* nation.

May Jeanne d'Arc save you from the clutches of the financiers,
May you remember that the world needs your best
To unfilth it from the infamies of commerce;
May your priests be as enlightened as M. Jérôme Coignard,
May your doctors be as kindly as Benjamin Rathery,
Your philosophers as witty as M. de Voltaire,
Your poets as divine but more fortunate than Verlaine,
Your rulers as brilliant as Colbert but more virtuous,
May you remain enlightened and throw away ambition,
May your valor this time not be a dangerous glory.
And finally, like the good King Henry,
Je vous souhaite tous une poule au pot le dimanche!

The Living Age, Vol. 308 (12 February 1921), p. 417. It is credited over
the title to *The Anglo-French Review*.

SOLEMNITY

Cough up a grin from somewhere.

God's my life! We're sandbagged, choked,
Knuckle-dustered into a swoon
By vile solemnity.

Squeal out, ye bagpipes of the shaken heel,
Halloo, you centaurs of the morning frost,
Be crisp and mirthful, ladies of my choice,
And teach these English bastards to rejoice!

The New Keepsake for the Year 1921, ed. X.M. Boulestin (London: Chelsea
Book Club, 1921), p. 83. Printed in italics.

HAPPINESS

Not that the battle was over,
Not that we had won and I safe,
Not that the last battery was silent,
Not that I was too tired for misery,
Not from these came happiness—
But from the stars, the dusky moon,
The black distant autumn wood,
The dark bodies of sleeping men in the moonlight
As if all but the sentries were dead.

Happiness struggled in my weary soul
Like a child in the strained womb.

The mist lay in the valley,
Flat between two hills,
Like cream in a rough brown bowl.
We talked in whispers of the battle,
And the frost and the casualties . . .

How can I speak it,
How stab you with my certainties?
That night I was at peace,
Sharply aware of beauty,
Poised, confident, tolerant, at ease,
One that had conquered others and himself,
One that had paid full fee for happiness.

The Living Age, Vol. 312 (21 January 1922), p. 182. This poem is credited to
Outlook. Note the much longer version of this poem under the same title in
the previous chapter, "Poems from Manuscripts and Notebooks."

ENGLISH SONGS

In autumn when the air is still
   And leaves hang heavy on the boughs,
How sadly sound from holt and hill
   The echoes English songs arouse.

With old songs, new songs, low songs, slow songs,
Mournfully all the echoes rouse.

But oh! in spring, the merry English spring
   When buds stand light upon the boughs,
How cheerily all the uplands ring
   With the echoes English songs arouse.

With old songs, new songs, gay songs, May songs,
Merrily all the echoes rouse.

The Living Age, Vol. 316 (17 February 1923), p. 428. This poem is credited over the title to *To-Day*.

NATAL VERSES FOR THE BIRTH
OF A NEW REVIEW

Let us resurrect the useful word Dickkopfig,
Let us apply it to those it fits,
Above all let us apply it to ourselves.
But in any case let us apply it to Don Ezra,
Who, having secured at the prime of life
A more than Horatian otium,
And having obtained more applause by his silence
Than ever he obtained by his not always negligible speech,
Now, in the eighth lustre of his career
When the libidinous itch for publicity
Should long ago have subsided into placid indifference
Madly casts away the only true felicity
For the ignominious servitude
And distracting toil
Of Editorship!
Light fall the blows upon his head—

For he will need all its thickness—
And let us regret the fall of this man
For he once had the courage
To be silent for several years.

The Exile, No. 1 (Spring 1927), pp. 86-87.

FILINGS

If man did not exist
It would be—fortunately—
Not necessary to invent him.

New York Herald Tribune "Books" section (Section 11), 2 December 1928, page 5, column 4. On 14 January 1929, Aldington wrote Crosby Gaige, "I got a clipping from N.Y. this morning, showing that at any rate one of my Filings was used by the N.Y. Herald Tribune on Dec 2nd" (Beinecke Rare Book and Manuscript Library at Yale University). For further information on the "Filings" poems, see "Additional Filings or Hour-Glass Grains" and the note appended thereto in Part II, Chapter 1, above.

INSCRIPTIONS

Through you I have inherited a world—
Myself.
And another mysterious and enchanted world,
So mysterious and lovely and beckoning
In the dew and the pure gold dawn.
I tremble, standing in silence
On the verge of these worlds.

I loved thee once, Atthis—
But no,
Pale beautiful face,
Cool silver moonlight of love,
Through you I learned
To seek for the noonday
And its golden ecstasies.

I had thought of immortality
With indifference and cool skepticism,
Until I gazed long
Into your soft shining eyes
As you loved me.

It seemed that the dawns were more exquisite,
The world more mysterious, purer,
The sea and sky more tenderly light-flushed
When we awoke together.

The Yale Review, Vol. 19, No. 3 (March 1930), pp. 489-490. In the magazine there are six poems printed under the title "Inscriptions," of which only two are collected in the "Short Poems" section of *The Complete Poems*. The ones given above are the second, third, fifth, and sixth; these were stanzas 3, 4, 9, and 10 of "Additional Filings or Hour-Glass Grains" which is given in its entirety in the previous section.

LA ROCHELLE

Lightly the land-locked waves slide in the harbor,
Lightly, lightly the wind drifts dust of iron men;
Lightly bare feet pat on sun-warmed flags.
The lime-trees rustle, sweetening the salt air.
Lightly the colored boats ride at the quay—
Patched sails, yellow, brown, red on blue masts,
Patched sailors' clothes, blue, brown, madder and rose,
Nets dyed deep blue.
Men pass with a clatter of wooden shoes. . . .

But who remembers the iron men,
Starving, faces and vitals pinched,
Trusting in a God who betrayed them,
Trusting in the pledged word of the English lords?
Who remembers them as they starved and died?—
And what can men do more than starve and die
For a dream, for a faith, for a pledged word?

Dead men, dead men of iron, let me not forget you!
"Eight months, unsuccored, they held their town,
Held it against a great king's army.
Out of ten thousand there remained a remnant,

One hundred and thirty-six men able to stand.
With rage and tears they surrendered their town."

Dead men of iron, forgive us our cowardice,
Forgive us our treachery,
Forgive us that we broke our word.
Forgive us!

Poetry: A Magazine of Verse, Vol. 38, No. 2 (May 1931), pp. 80-81.

TO: BRIGIT

Another of your *poets*!
Ah! in the years to come they'll say
"The greater poet sang her—well indeed;
The lesser loved her—more than well."

Dear Ezra, take the poet's praise,
Take even my scanty due, take all—
But let me keep her love, and her.

From Miriam J. Benkovitz, "Nine for Reeves: Letters from Richard Aldington," *Bulletin of the New York Public Library*, Vol. 69, No. 6 (June 1965), p. 362.

THE WALK
(For F.S.F.)

In silence I walk beside my friend,
And it seems as if my very flesh
Were aching with remorse and pity
To see how grief has possessed him.
The eyes which should be smiling are dull with tears,
His feet are heavy on the ground,
His neck is bent, his speech troubled.

Together we walk along the empty streets
Between the rows of clipped plane trees
Which look like mangled skeletons;

And I dare not say they look like skeletons
Lest it should remind him
Of terrible images he must try to forget.

How long we have been walking I do not know
Nor how long I have sweated in silence,
Sweated for some word or phrase or thought
Which I could give him—
As one shouted and waved to a friend
In the midst of a barrage—
Not so much to help as to show him
That all comradeship is not dead.

I remember how once before
We walked together, more briskly and rhythmically,
When I seemed the unlucky one,
And how his very silence was an aid;
And I remember how something he wrote
Made a long, almost intolerable struggle
Seem not quite overwhelming.

Oh, if only he can feel my silence
As something beneficent and comprehending
As his was once to me!
If only he understands that I am silent
Because I can find nothing,
Nothing he would not feel trivial. . . .

It is not grief that dares not speak
But pity which can find no words.

Enclosed with a letter of 17 June 1920 to Amy Lowell which is now in
the Amy Lowell collection of The Houghton Library at Harvard Univer-
sity. Covering note indicates that no publication was made or scheduled
by Aldington; the poem has, however, been published in connection
with my essay "Richard Aldington and F. S. Flint: Poets' Dialogue,"
Papers on Language and Literature, Vol. 8, No. 1 (Winter 1972), pp. 64-65.

3

Poems from Previous Editions

TO ATTHIS

(After the Manuscript of Sappho now in Berlin)

Atthis, far from me and dear Mnasidika,
Dwells in Sardis;
Many times she was near us
So that we lived life well
Like the far-famed goddess
Whom above all things music delighted.

And now she is first among the Lydian women
As the mighty sun, the rose-fingered moon,
Beside the great stars.

And the light fades from the bitter sea
And in like manner from the rich-blossoming earth;
And the dew is shed upon the flowers,
Rose and soft meadow-sweet
And many-coloured melilote.

Many things told are remembered of sterile Atthis.

I yearn to behold thy delicate soul
To satiate my desire. . . .
. . . .

Des Imagistes: An Anthology (London: The Poetry Bookshop, 1914;
New York: Albert and Charles Boni, 1914), p. 19.

VATES, THE SOCIAL REFORMER

What shall be said of him, this cock-o'-hoop?
(I'm just a trifle bored, dear God of mine,
Dear unknown God, dear chicken-pox of Heaven,
I'm bored I say), But still—my social friend—
(One has to be familiar in one's discourse)
While he was puffing out his jets of wit
Over his swollen-bellied pipe, one thinks,
One thinks, you know, of quite a lot of things.

(Dear unknown God, dear, queer-faced God,
Queer, queer, queer, queer-faced God,
You blanky God, be quiet for half minute,
And when I've shut up Rates, and sat on Naboth,
I'll tell you half a dozen things or so.)

There goes a flock of starlings—
Now half a dozen years ago,
(Shut up, you blighted God, and let me speak)
I should have hove my sporting air-gun up
And blazed away—and now I let 'em go—
It's odd how one changes;
Yes, that's High Germany.

But still, when he was smiling like a Chinese queen,
Looking as queer (I do assure you, God)
As any Chinese queen I ever saw;
And tiddle-whiddle-whiddling about prose,
Trying to quiz a mutton-headed poetaster,
And choking all the time with politics—
Why then I say, I contemplated him
And marveled (God! I marveled,
Write it in prose, dear God. Yes, in red ink.)
And marveled, as I said,
At the stupendous quantity of mind
And the amazing quality thereof.

Dear God of mine,
It's really most amazing, doncherknow,
But really, God, I *can't* get off the mark;
Look here, you queer-faced God,

This fellow makes me sick with all his talk,
His ha'penny gibes at Celtic bards
And followers of Dante—honest folk!—
Because, dear God, the rotten beggar goes
And makes a Chinese blue-stocking
From half-digested dreams of Munich-air.

And then—God, why should I write it down?—
But Rates and Naboth
Aren't half such silly fools as he is (God)
For they are frankly asinine,
While he pretends to sanity,
Modernity, (dear God, dear God).

It's bad enough, dear God of mine,
That you have set me down in London Town,
Endowed me with a tattered velvet coat,
Soft collar and black hat and Greek ambitions;
You might have left me there.
But now you send
This "vates" here, this sage social reformer
(Yes, God, you rotten Roman Catholic)
To put his hypothetical conceptions
Of what a poor young poetaster would think
Into his own damned shape, and then to attack it
To his own great contemplative satisfaction.
What have I done, O God,
That so much bitterness should flop on me?
Social Reformer! That's the beggar's name.
He'd have me write bad novels like himself.

Yes, God, I know it's after closing time;
And yes, I know I've smoked his cigarettes;
But watch that sparrow on the fountain in the rain.
How half a dozen years ago,
(Shut up, you blighted God, and let me speak)
I should have hove my sporting air-gun up
And blazed away—and now I let him go—
It's odd how one changes;
Yes, that's High Germany.

Des Imagistes: An Anthology (London: The Poetry Bookshop, 1914; New York: Albert and Charles Boni, 1914), pp. 59-61.

DAWN

It is night; and silent.

The mist is still beside the frozen dyke; it lies on the stiff grass, about the poplar trunks. The last star goes out. The gulls are coming up from the sea, crying, and drifting across like pieces of mist, like fragments of white cloth. They turn their heads and peer as they pass. The sky low down glows deep purple.

The plovers swirl and dart over the ploughed field beyond; their screams are sorrowful and sharp. The purple drifts up the pale sky and grows redder. The mist stirs.

The brass on the harness of the plough-horses jingles as they come into the field. The birds rise in scattered knots. The mist trembles, grows thinner, rises. The red and gold sky shines dully on the ice.

The men shout across the thawing clods; the ploughs creak; the horses steam in the cold; the plovers and gulls have gone; the sparrows twitter.

The sky is gold and blue, very faint and damp.

It is day.

Images (1910-1915) (London: The Poetry Bookshop, 1915), p. 29. Reprinted in *Images Old and New* (Boston: The Four Seas Co., 1916).

NIGHT PIECE

I lie awake; and listen.

The water drips musically in the large zinc tank; the little watch beside me ticks away the seconds of my life; and at long intervals the bell of St. Mary Abbot's growls out huskily the quarters: ding, ding, *dang*, dong!

Silence. The water drips slower and more musically; the watch ticks more gently; the window curtain rustles a little in the wind and a faint confused glow of moonlight slips into the room.

Silence. I rise and draw the curtain. The white misty moonlight chequers the houses into blocks and lines and angles of watery silverish white and intense black shadows. There is no movement, no sound in the city.

No sound? A train whistle blows very faint and shrill and clear and far away—clearer than bugles and as shrill as a wandering night bird. A train is running out from Marylebone or Victoria . . .

Very faint and shrill and far away the whistle sounds—more like a wild bird than ever. And my unsatisfied desires and empty wishes and vague yearnings are suddenly set aching by the thin tremulous whistle.

Images (1910-1915) (London: The Poetry Bookshop, 1915), p. 28. Reprinted in *Images Old and New* (Boston: The Four Seas Co., 1916). Compare the passage in *Death of a Hero* written at least fourteen years later: "In the night-silence, water dripped with insistent melody in some hidden tank. From outside came the shrill distant notes of train whistles, rather silvery and exquisite, bringing the yearning for travel, 'the horns of elf-land faintly blowing.' Where had he read that? Oh, of course, Stevenson. Funny how the Coningtons thought Stevenson a good author. . . ." (London: Chatto and Windus, 1929, p. 169).

HYELLA
(From "Acon," written in Latin in the sixteenth century by the Italian, Giovanni-Battista Amalteo.)

See the maiden, the maiden is dying;
And now the glory withers from her rose-red face.

As a dark blue hyacinth flower
In a secret valley,
Fed by the earth our mother,
Received in her breast,
Drawn up by her with dew and happy winds—
If once the heat of heaven or bitter Auster
Fall upon it, straightway,
Spoiled of the joyful pride of beauty,
It droops and dies upon the parched grasses.

Unwonted griefs are in the meadows
And the hay-swathes are rotting;
Christ-thorns grow for violets and the bright lilies
Wither on the drooping stem;
No berries colour the lush river-bank;
Neither grass nor leaf springs in meadow and wood.

Images Old and New (Boston: The Four Seas Co., 1916), p. 26.

A NEW HOUSE

Inside,
A smell of mortar,
Odours of plaster, sawn wood, damp,
Hang in the hollow cold rooms
And taint the breath in one's nostrils.

Outside,
Grey dirty scaffoldings tied with ropes,
Red walls crusted with scum,
Rise from the trampled soil
Among felled trees and naked flowers.

There is a silence, a truce;
The old earth-gods retreat
Sullen, beaten and disconsolate;
London has beaten them,
Swallowed, engulfed their territory,
Crushing their flowers into mud.

Images Old and New (Boston: The Four Seas Co., 1916), p.45.

WHITE ROSE

Here is a white rose. Take it—the sceptre
of Desires and Kharites.

The Love Poems of Myrrhine and Konallis (Cleveland: The Clerk's Press, 1917), p. 20. This is the only poem from this volume not reprinted in *The Love of Myrrhine and Konallis, and Other Prose Poems.*

DEDICATION

How can I reach you? Though I hold you close the essential you escapes me; I cannot pierce to the core of your being.

Though I have given you all myself, what have I gained? Only my own happiness, not yours—so much more precious. Can I be glad seeing the life-weariness in your eyes?

What do you seek from me? Oblivion? Ask it of death, not of me. Happiness? I can only give you happiness if your love is great enough to create it.

To be loved is nothing; to receive is nothing. If you seek happiness, love and give.

Images of Desire (London: Elkin Mathews, 1919), p. 7. The poem is printed in italics and is the only one from this volume omitted from the "Images of Desire' section of *The Complete Poems.*

GENIUS LOCI

This place is evil
Some bitter god dwells here.

For when I think here of my love's face
It is not tranquil,
Nor eager, nor passionate,
Nor flushed with desire,
Nor rejoicing in beauty,
But pale in anger against me
With determined eyes
Thwarting my will
And thrusting upon me langour,
Life-weariness.

Surely, surely, I know
There is evil in this place.

War and Love (1915-1918) (Boston: The Four Seas Co., 1919), p. 30.

SONG

"Lady, let me woo you with song,
        Words choicely got,
With strains intense and long."
        She smiled and answered not.

"Lady, let me sing your praises
        All through the day,
Hymn you with lovely praises."
        She smiled and turned away.

Then I came and caught her hand,
        Saying without fear:
"You are mine—do you understand?"
        She smiled: "How I love you, dear!"

War and Love (1915-1918) (Boston: The Four Seas Co., 1919), p. 75.

SONG FOR HER

Why should love be dumb and go
Hidden in a shroud of lies?
Why should lovers fear to tell
What they see in women's eyes?
What it is all lovers know
And the world should know as well.

Is a woman's heart of ice?
Is a woman's sex of snow?
I've a mistress and I see
Warm desire that moves me so
I would give the whole world thrice
To express it worthily.

Every night that we can steal
Close, as lovers do, we lie,
And the wanton things we do
And the amorous pangs we feel
Told, would make the hard world cry,
"Teach us how to love like you!"

Yet if you would love aright
You must love, like us, with all
Sense and spirit, flesh and breath;
Then indeed it may befall
That you burn with our clear light—
Light that only fades with death.

War and Love (1915-1918) (Boston: The Four Seas Co., 1919), p. 76.

NIGHTS OF LOVE

O the nights of love,
The nights of close long kisses,
Of the passionate clasping of two bodies
So delighted with poignant touch;
O the nights of warm adoration,
Of the meeting of breasts and hands,
Of the joining of flesh with flesh;
O the nights when the world was abolished,
When the city outside was forgotten
When the moon seemed not to shine
And nothing endured but our love;
O the nights of peace after love,
Of sleep with her head on my arm,
Of our breathing mingled as one;
O the nights that were day too soon,
When we hated the light of the sun
That severed our amorous flesh;
O the nights when we needed no God,
When we needed no helper, no friend,
When we needed no good upon earth;
O nights I shall never forget,
You will sweeten the harshness of death,
You will thrill the last beat of my heart,
You will sooth my last moan into praise.

War and Love (1915-1918) (Boston: The Four Seas Co., 1919), p. 91.

EPILOGUE

Back we go to the shell-tossed land,
To the whine of the shells that tears one's nerves
And the crash that's only not near enough;
Back we go to struggle with mud,
To stumble and slip on the greasy boards,
Back we go to the stink of the dead,
Back we go to the sleepless days
And the unwashed weeks and the mouldy months,
Back we go to the thirst and the dust,
Back we go to the grim despair
That holds a man by the heart in France.

We'll go through it all, the fear and pain,
The breaking up of body and soul,
Take our chance of death after all,
Of face or limb or shoulder smashed,
Go through hell again, face it out,
For her, for her love, for her kiss again.

Sneer or snarl, drivel or boast—
What does it matter to us who go
Where they who send us dare not go?
All one to us are the rights and wrongs,
The nations' squabbles, the nations' lies;
Not one land more than another land
Do we love, lovers of love not land—
So it's up the line and hell and pain
For her, for her love, for her kiss again.

War and Love (1915-1918) (Boston: The Four Seas Co., 1919), p. 94. Printed in italics.

FROM TASSO
Dance of Air Spirits

We are those unseen forms that fly
Hither and thither in the sky,
Our home the eternal crystalline
Wide spaces of the pure serene

Where wandering breezes gently stray
And no sun brings too hot a day
And there is never wintery weather
To chill us as we dance together;
Now fate and heavenly grace have brought us
To the sight of you who sought us,
Down we glided from the air,
Young and blithe and light and fair,
To teach you how aerial sprites
Gambol in the starry nights,
To rouse your dull and mortal ears
With the music of the spheres.

Exile and Other Poems (London: George Allen and Unwin, 1923), p. 55.

IDYLL

I, Konallis, am but a goat-girl dwelling
          on the violet hills of Korinthos,
But going down to the city a marvelous
          thing befell me;
For the beautiful-fingered hetaira,
          Myrrhine, held me nightlong
          in her couch,
Teaching me to receive her strange
          burning caresses.

The Love of Myrrhine and Konallis, and Other Prose Poems (Chicago: Pascal
Covici, 1926), p. 17.

MYRRHINE TO HER LOVERS

Beautiful are your names, O young
          men, Lysias and Hermogenes and
          Timagoras, beautiful are your bodies
          and the words you speak are
          hyacinth-sweet.
But lovelier to me is the name of
          Konallis, lovelier her frail body, more
          divine her laughing voice.

The Love of Myrrhine and Konallis, and Other Prose Poems (Chicago: Pascal
Covici, 1926), p. 18.

MORNING

Hierocleia, bring hither my silver vine-
    leaf carved armlet and the mirror
    graven with two Maenads,
For my heart is burned to dust with
    longing for Konallis;
And this is the silver armlet which
    pressed into her side when I held her,
And before this mirror she bound up
    her golden hyacinth-curled hair,
    sitting in the noon sunlight.

The Love of Myrrhine and Konallis, and Other Prose Poems (Chicago: Pascal Covici, 1926), p. 19.

NOON

The doves sleep beside the slow
    murmuring cool fountain,
    red five-petalled roses
    strew the chequered marble;
The flute-girl whispers the dear white
    ode of Sappho,
    and Hierocleia by the pool
Smiles to see the smooth blue
    sky-reflecting water
    mirror her shining body;
But my eyelids are shunned by sleep
    that is whiter than beautiful
    morning, for Konallis is not here.

The Love of Myrrhine and Konallis, and Other Prose Poems (Chicago: Pascal Covici, 1926), p. 20.

EVENING

Hierocleia, weave white-violet crowns
    and spread mountain-haunting lilies
    upon my couch,
For Konallis comes! and shut the door
    against the young men for this is a
    sharper love.

The Love of Myrrhine and Konallis, and Other Prose Poems (Chicago: Pascal
Covici, 1926), p. 21.

THE OFFERING TO PERSEPHONE

We, Konallis and Myrrhine
    dedicate to you, Persephone,
    two white torches of wax,
For you watched over our purple-
    embroidered couch all night;
Was it you who gave the sweetness of
    sharp caresses?
For at midday when we awoke we
    laughed to see black poppies blooming
    beneath our eyes.

The Love of Myrrhine and Konallis, and Other Prose Poems (Chicago: Pascal
Covici, 1926), p. 22.

HER VOICE

Some are lovers of wisdom, some of
    beauty; of Eros and the Muses.
But Myrrhine's voice is more lovely
    than all, even than yours,
    O soul of Plato.

The Love of Myrrhine and Konallis, and Other Prose Poems (Chicago: Pascal
Covici, 1926), p. 23.

PRAYER

O reeds, move softly and make keen
    bewildering music,
For I fear lest Arkadian Pan should
    seize Myrrhine as she comes from
    the city;
O Artemis, shed your light across the
    peaks to hasten her coming,
But do you, Eos, hold back your white
    radiance till love be content.

The Love of Myrrhine and Konallis, and Other Prose Poems (Chicago: Pascal
Covici, 1926), p. 24.

THE STORM

Last night Zeus sent swift rain
    upon the blue-grey rocks,
But Konallis held me close
    to her pear-pointed breasts.

The Love of Myrrhine and Konallis, and Other Prose Poems (Chicago: Pascal
Covici, 1926), p. 25.

MEMORY

When Myrrhine departed I, weeping
    passionately, kissed her knees saying:
"O Myrrhine, by what god shall I keep
    the memory of your caresses?"
But she, bending down like golden,
    smiling Aphrodite, whispered to me;
And lying here in the sunlight among
    the reeds I remember her words.

The Love of Myrrhine and Konallis, and Other Prose Poems (Chicago: Pascal
Covici, 1926), p. 26.

KONALLIS THE EPICUREAN

Nicosthenes, the Stoic, would have
   proved to me the emptiness of life,
   the sweetness of death and
   the force of virtue.
But I looked at your oleander-tipped
   breasts blossoming beneath your
   thin robe, and smiled.

The Love of Myrrhine and Konallis, and Other Prose Poems (Chicago: Pascal
Covici, 1926), p. 27.

THE SINGER

Sappho, Sappho, long ago the dust of
   earth mingled with the dust of your
   dear limbs,
And only little clay figures, painted
   with Tyrian red, with crocus, and
   with Lydian gold,
Remain to show your beauty; but your
   wild lovely songs shall last forever.
Soon we shall join Anaktoria and Kudno
   and kiss your pale shadowy fingers.

The Love of Myrrhine and Konallis, and Other Prose Poems (Chicago: Pascal
Covici, 1926), p. 28.

GIFTS

Fair young men have brought me
   presents of silver caskets and
   white mirrors,
Gold for my hair with long
   lemon-coloured chitons and
   dew-soft perfumes of sweet herbs.
Their bodies are whiter than Leucadian
   foam and delicate are their flute-girls,
But the wild sleepless nightingales cry
   in the darkness even as I for Konallis.

The Love of Myrrhine and Konallis, and Other Prose Poems (Chicago: Pascal Covici, 1926), p. 29.

FESTIVAL

This is the feast of Iacchus, open wide
    the gates, O Hierocleia:
Fill the craters with sweet unmixed
    wine and snow, bring thyrsus wands,
And crowns of pale ivy and violets; let
    the flute-players begin the phallic
    hymn
While the ten girl slaves, drunken with
    the god, dance to the young men.

The Love of Myrrhine and Konallis, and Other Prose Poems (Chicago: Pascal Covici, 1926), p. 30.

THE CHARIOTEER

Eros, charioteer of my soul, why do
    you torment and urge me onwards?
For in her is absolute beauty and
    absolute knowledge and absolute—
"Not Sophrosyne", you say? Ah, but
    Sophrosyne is her captive, even as I.

The Love of Myrrhine and Konallis, and Other Prose Poems (Chicago: Pascal Covici, 1926), p. 31.

JEALOUSY

Said a poet: "Aphrodite seeing her
    statue cried out: "When did the
    sculptor see me naked?"
But I know that he must have lain
    hidden among the laurels to watch
    Myrrhine at the pool.

The Love of Myrrhine and Konallis, and Other Prose Poems (Chicago: Pascal Covici, 1926), p. 32.

THE OFFERING

Women have many gods: Astarte; the
    apple-bearing Aphrodite; the wanton
    Aphrodite of Cyprus; Aphrodite
    Kottyto; the narrow-eyed Isis of
    Heliopolis; the great mother of
    Ephesus.
Some worship the Aphrodite of the
    people; some Artemis, and the violet-
    crowned queen of Athens; some
    home-keeping Hestia and some
    peacock-loving Here.
All the gods are beautiful and to be
    revered but none more than the
    white-fingered daughter of Mytilene,
    to whom I bear these daffodils
    and this bowl of milk as an offering.

The Love of Myrrhine and Konallis, and Other Prose Poems (Chicago: Pascal
Covici, 1926), p. 33.

THE VIGIL

Hedulia now lies with Myrrhine who
    aforetime was my lover,
But seeing Hedulia she forgot me, and
    I lie on the threshold weeping.
O marble threshold, you are not so
    white nor so hard as her breasts,
    receive my tears,
While the mute stars turn overhead
    and the owls cry from the cypresses.

The Love of Myrrhine and Konallis, and Other Prose Poems (Chicago: Pascal
Covici, 1926), p. 34.

UNFRIENDLY GODS

There is a god of Fortune and a god
    of love; they are seldom friends.

The Love of Myrrhine and Konallis, and Other Prose Poems (Chicago: Pascal Covici, 1926), p. 35.

A DIALOGUE

A. O my sister, the lamp of my joy is
    quenched in a black pool of
    sadness. Comfort me.
B. Shall I speak to you of the strange
    loves of Leda among the
    curled hyacinths?
A. The yearning for wild love pours
    deeper sorrow upon me.
B. Shall I speak of Achilles, the young
    fleet-foot slayer of Hector?
A. O my sister, one death awaits
    slain and slayer.
B. But the tall Minyae brought back
    gold and a fair woman.
A. And Medea was the slayer of her
    own children.
B. O my sister, Helen was beautiful—
A. The ruins of Troy are a witness.

The Love of Myrrhine and Konallis, and Other Prose Poems (Chicago: Pascal Covici, 1926), pp. 36-37.

THE PAKTIS

Under your fingers the strings of the
    paktis tremble and cry out shrilly
    and vibrantly of love.
Am I not more beautiful than an
    ivory paktis? Is not my
    voice as sweet?

The Love of Myrrhine and Konallis, and Other Prose Poems (Chicago: Pascal Covici, 1926), p. 38.

ANOTHER GREATER

Here are pines, black against vast blue;
   here the cicada sings; here there are
   sparse wind-flowers.
Above us, Helios; under our feet, the
   breast of the great Mother; far below
   us, the blue curls of Poseidon.
These are great and terrible gods, yet
   in your shape another greater and
   more terrible rules me.

The Love of Myrrhine and Konallis, and Other Prose Poems (Chicago: Pascal
Covici, 1926), p. 39.

ANTRE OF THE NYMPHS

This is the antre of the nymphs—
   sacred, hushed, and dripping
   with white water.
Above the holy spring rustles a
   plane-tree and about the
   sweet-breathing meadows bloom
   many flowers.
River-dwelling narcissus, the rose of
   lovers, white gleaming violets
   and the wind-flowers of Kypris.
I say to them, "Hail!" For these
   things are holy; yet I am sorrowful,
   for this loveliness passes away, like
   the songs of the singing birds
   at evening.
Love also dies and there is none to
   mourn him, none to pour wine or
   thread sombre garlands of grief.

The Love of Myrrhine and Konallis, and Other Prose Poems (Chicago: Pascal
Covici, 1926), pp. 40-41.

THE THREE APHRODITES

It is said that among certain tribes of
   the barbarians the slaves are rulers
   and that among gods they worship
   only Aphrodite Pandemos.
Let them know that a slave's god
   is a slave and that we worship
   Aphrodite Astarte and
   Aphrodite Kottyto.

The Love of Myrrhine and Konallis, and Other Prose Poems (Chicago: Pascal Covici, 1926), p. 42.

THE OLD LOVE

From an old love there is sometimes
   born a new Eros.
It was Akmene, whom I once loved,
   who first brought you to me.
Therefore today, we will hang a
   garland of white violets at her door.

The Love of Myrrhine and Konallis, and Other Prose Poems (Chicago: Pascal Covici, 1926), p. 43.

THE OLEANDER

O lover of flowers, I have brought you
   wind-flowers and the woven
   narcissus, many-petalled hyacinths
   and the blossoms of Aphrogeneia;
Now I bring you one most precious
   blossom you will surely cherish it.

The Love of Myrrhine and Konallis, and Other Prose Poems (Chicago: Pascal Covici, 1926), p. 44.

THE LAMP

Darkness enveloped us; I kindled a
    lamp of red clay to light her beauty.
She turned her eyes away from the
    flame, which glowed gently on her
    arms and the curve of her body.
Lamp! if you are a god, you must be
    broken; if a goddess we will honor
    you; none but a goddess may look
    upon our caresses.

The Love of Myrrhine and Konallis, and Other Prose Poems (Chicago: Pascal Covici, 1926), p. 45.

APRIL

Yesterday we wandered out from the
    town, under the green silver-olive
    trees, gathering the flowers born
    from the blood of Adonis;
Under a sunny wall we found
    a shepherd-lad piping beside a
    red-crested god of gardens;
As he played, the green and gold scaled
    lizards and the many spotted
    butterflies stayed beside him
    to listen:
Eros had stolen the pipes of Marsyas.

The Love of Myrrhine and Konallis, and Other Prose Poems (Chicago: Pascal Covici, 1926), p. 46.

TWO GODDESSES

Artemis has long been our foe,
    Konallis, but even a virgin will not
    despise these scentless virgin
    water-flowers cold from the brook.
Lay them on her altar humbly, without

a prayer, for she has no delight
in us. Our goddess has heavy eyes
and slender fingers and her lips
have grown soft and tired
with many kisses.

The Love of Myrrhine and Konallis, and Other Prose Poems (Chicago: Pascal
Covici, 1926), p. 47.

THE WINE JAR

This is a common wine-jar. The rough
    painter has drawn on it a winged
    Psyche, fluttering in fire. She is
    edged with a black outline, but the
    fire is red.
My soul is black with grief when you
    leave me, but grows red with delight
    when you set your lips on my body.

The Love of Myrrhine and Konallis, and Other Prose Poems (Chicago: Pascal
Covici, 1926), p. 48.

KONALLIS TO MYRRHINE

It is said that Zeus gave wealth to the
    Rhodians and the gift of the Muses
    to the gold-tettinx-bearing dwellers
    at Athens; but his fairest gift was
    to Mytilene when he sent Myrrhine
    thither in a swallow-wing-sailed
    barque of the Kaunians.

The Love of Myrrhine and Konallis, and Other Prose Poems (Chicago: Pascal
Covici, 1926), p. 49.

MYRRHINE TO KONALLIS

Had I been Alexander, son of Priam
    the King, I would have given the
    gold fruit to no goddess but to the
    sweet child of a mortal mother,
    to Konallis whose lips lie so delicately
upon my breast.

The Love of Myrrhine and Konallis, and Other Prose Poems (Chicago: Pascal
Covici, 1926), p. 50.

HOMER AND SAPPHO

The sophists praise above all others
    Homer who sang of battle and
    the deaths of heroes.
But I love the divine sweet-scented
    odes of Sappho.

The Love of Myrrhine and Konallis, and Other Prose Poems (Chicago: Pascal
Convici, 1926), p. 51.

RED AND BLACK

Wine is black, but red are the points
    of your breasts; black are the figures
    of heroes on the tall wine-jars,
    but your lips are red.
Black the frail sea-grass, but flushed
    faint red the curled shells.
Red is your life-blood, but black,
    deep black, the inexorable
    end of all.

The Love of Myrrhine and Konallis, and Other Prose Poems (Chicago: Pascal
Covici, 1926), p. 52.

THE WINE OF LESBOS

The wines of Chios and Samos are
     more esteemed than our heavy wine.
But I mingle your name with the
     draught and the wine is keener
     than the flower-crowned
     drink of the Deathless.

The Love of Myrrhine and Konallis, and Other Prose Poems (Chicago: Pascal
Covici, 1926), p. 53.

AFTER THE ORGY

It is morning; the revellers of last night
     have departed; the music of flutes
     and the voices of girl-nightingales
     are silent now.
Half-filled wine-cups and empty jars
     stand by the couches; your torn
     golden chiton lies by a little pool
     of wine, your broken girdle dangles
     ironically from the Kyprian's wrist.
The flowers of your crown wither
     in my hand, shrivelled with
     the salt of my tears.
Silence and withered flowers and
     the empty wine-cups; Ah, the last
     silence and the last flower-crowns on
     the white stele, the last wine-cup
     poured in the last farewell!

The Love of Myrrhine and Konallis, and Other Prose Poems (Chicago: Pascal
Convici, 1926), pp. 54-55.

THE LAST SONG

Along the shorn fields stand the last
     blown wheat-sheaves, casting long
     shadows in the autumn sunset.
White were the horses of Helios

at dawn, golden at noon, blood-red
    at night—and all too brief the day.
Such was my life and even so brief;
    night comes; I rise from the glad
    feast, drink to the gods of Life,
    cast incense to the gods of Death,
    to Love a shattered rose,
    and turn away.
Hail all! Laugh, this is the bitter
    end of life.

The Love of Myrrhine and Konallis, and Other Prose Poems (Chicago: Pascal Covici, 1926), p. 56.

THANATOS

Myrrhine, we have often sung of the
    sharp end of life, often mocked at
    death in the midst of the fierce
    ecstacy of our embraces.
We have heard of this savage and
    mysterious god from the stately
    words of Homer: and we also have
    mourned for beautiful Bion.
We have seen death graven in bronze
    as a drowsy youth scattering poppies
    from his delicate hands.
But when I saw for the first time the
    pallid shrunken face of a dead girl—
    and that girl our lover Kleone—
    my veins shrank with terror, and
    I feared through all my
    trembling limbs.
Let others sing gayly or yearningly
    of death and deck this sombre lord
    with garlands; we are too timid, too
    frail in hope for that.
Others may dream of the gold islands
    of the happy dead or of the calm
    spirits among the phantom flowers
    in the meadows beyond Acheron;

We can only turn aside, holding heart
   to trembling heart, and number the
   dividing moments with close kisses,
   counting all time lost that is not
   golden with love.
Drink, my beloved; drink from this
   wide silver cup; drink as the
   Maenads in the pine-crowned orgy
   of Iacchus! Drink, drink! And as
   our bodies meet tear the garland
   from my brow and the thin veil
   from my breasts.
Those who are about to die fear only
   chastity and an empty wine-cup.

The Love of Myrrhine and Konallis, and Other Prose Poems (Chicago: Pascal Covici, 1926), pp. 57-59. This poem appears as the first of two headed "Prose Poems" in *The Little Review*, Vol. 3, No. 9 (March 1917), pp. 10-11. The second of the two is "Hermes-of-the-Dead."

HERMES-OF-THE-DEAD

Myrrhine, when I was a girl, I listened
   to the talk of the poets, and of
   philosophers who came to my house
   to buy (as they said) "delicious
   remorse for five minae".
From them, had I been another Aspasia,
   I might have learned wisdom; but
   from the poets I learned only to love
   and to know beauty, and from the
   philosophers nothing except that
   "Death is not to be feared". And
   this I learned no better than they,
   for we are all cowards at the end.
But since I must go from you; since
   already the winged sandals of
   Kyllenian Hermes are rustling the
   Olympian air for me; since in your
   purse now lies the silver obol I
   must drop in the grim ferry-man's
   hand—listen a little to me.

When I am but a cupful of grey dust
   in a tall narrow-throated stone vase;
   when the mouth that sang you and
   the lips that kissed you are withered
   and silent; when the hands that
   touched you have crumbled in the
   funeral flames; when the eyes that
   lighted at your beauty are quenched;
   when the ears that loved your
   beautiful voice are vanished; when
   the frail spirit that leaped and
   mingled with your spirit, like two
   flames, is a tenuous phantom which
   scarcely "is"; when life has left me;
   then you must live, live for yourself,
   but for me also.
For my sake Eos in a cloudless sky
   gliding from the many-isled sea must
   be more tender and more thrilling;
   for my sake the scent of ripe apples
   in the dim gold autumn must be
   keener and more odorous; for my
   sake the music of Pindar and
   Theocritus must be more stately,
   more flower-like, more melancholy
   sweet; for my sake the ecstacy of
   love must be sharper, wilder; for
   my sake you must be more beautiful,
   more alert, more delicate.
I shall be loveless in a scentless land,
   where there is no change of light.
   I shall be desolate and alone and the
   memory of the dear words of poets
   will fade from me. But if you love
   and live fully and serve beauty for
   my sake, then some slight glow will
   lighten the dead sky and there will
   be some faint perfume for me in the
   chill blossoms of asphodel.
Now loose my hand, for Hermes-of-
   the-Dead clasps the other.

The Love of Myrrhine and Konallis, and Other Prose Poems (Chicago: Pascal Covici, 1926), pp. 60-63. This poem appears as the second of two under the heading of "Prose Poems" in *The Little Review*, Vol. 3, No. 9 (March 1917), p. 11; the first of the two is "Thanatos."

EPITAPH

This is the tomb of Konallis; Korinthos
    was her city and Kleobulina bore her,
Having lain in sweet love with
    Sesocrates, the son of Memophiles.
I have lived three and twenty years,
    and then sudden sickness bore
    me to Dis.
So they laid me here with my silver
    armlets, my gold comb, my chain
    with little painted figures.
In my life I was happy, knowing many
    sorts of love and none evil.
If you are a lover, scatter dust, and
    call me "dear one" and speak
    one last "Hail".

The Love of Myrrhine and Konallis, and Other Prose Poems (Chicago: Pascal Covici, 1926), p. 64. This last poem in the cycle is dated 1914-1916. The date appears below the final line at the left-hand margin.

DISCOURAGEMENT

To have passed so close to annihilation
    and (which is worse) to have become
    stained so inalterably with the ideas
    and habits of masses—this leaves me
    immeasurably discouraged, out of
    love with myself.
Now I am good only to mimic inferior
    masters. My thoughts are stifling—
    heavy grey dust from a scorched road.
For me silence; or if speech, then some
    humble poem in prose. Indeed I am
    too conscientious—or shall we say
    too impotent?—to dare the cool
    rhythm of prose, the sharp

edges of poetry.

Nymphes de Parnessse!

Encore un Pégase raté!

The Love of Myrrhine and Konallis, and Other Prose Poems (Chicago: Pascal Covici, 1926), pp. 67-68. This poem is dated "Officers' Camp, Fressin, 1918." A portion of it also appears in the short story "Farewell to Memories" in *Roads to Glory* (London: Chatto and Windus, 1930), p. 258. And the poem is number I in a series of eight prose poems printed under the general title "Prayers and Fantasies" in *Poetry: A Magazine of Verse*, Vol. 13, No. 11 (November 1918), pp. 67-71, and followed by the general dating "France, 1918."

FATIGUES

The weariness of this dirt and labour,
　　of this dirty melting sky!
For hours we have carried great bundles
　　of hay from barge to truck and
　　from truck to train. . . .
The weariness of this dirt and labour!
But look! Last June those heavy dried
　　bales waved and glittered in the
　　fields of England.
Cinque-foil and clover, buttercups,
　　fennel, thistle and rue, daisy and
　　ragged robin, wild rose from the
　　hedge, shepherd's purse, and long
　　sweet nodding stalks of grass.
Heart of me, heart of me, be not sick
　　and faint, though fingers and arms
　　and head ache; you bear the gift
　　of the glittering meadows of
　　England. Here are bundles from
　　Somerset, from Wales, from
　　Hereford, Worcester, Gloucester—
　　names we must love, scented with
　　summer peace.
Handle them bravely, meadow-sweet,
　　sorrel, lush flag and arid knap-weed,
　　flowers of marsh and cliff,
　　handle them bravely.

Dear crushed flowers, and you, yet
   fragrant grasses, I stoop and kiss you
   furtively. No one sees.
Dear gentle perished sisters, speak,
   whisper and move, tell me you will
   dance and whisper for me in the
   wind next June.

The Love of Myrrhine and Konallis, and Other Prose Poems (Chicago: Pascal Covici, 1926), pp. 69-71. This poem is dated "Base Camp, Calais, 1916." It also appears in *Images of War: A Book of Poems* (Westminster: C. W. Beaumont, 1919), pp. 13-14, and, with its last lines slightly changed, in the short story "Farewell to Memories" in *Roads to Glory* (London: Chatto and Windus, 1930), p. 262.

SORCERY OF WORDS

"The poetry of winter"—these words,
   remembered from some aesthetic
   essay, return and return to my
   memory, with an ironic persistance.
   It happened yesterday when the
   ground was sheeted in frost, the sky
   rose upon the pale green coverlet of
   dawn, bare trees silhouetted, frozen
   pools of water.
"The poetry of winter"—yes, that was
   indeed poetry, the breath of the
   gods, light glowing and changing,
   motionless trees, clear air.
Yes, one can be hungry, sore, unshaven,
   dirty, eyes and head aching, limbs
   shivering, and yet love beauty.
From the depths I cry it, from the
   depths which echo with the ironic
   phrase "the poetry of winter",
   from the depths I cry it!
You, who are clean and warm with the
   delicate leisure of a flower-scented
   library, strain your hearing, listen
   across the clamour of the age, for a
   whisper that comes to you so faintly,
   so ironically—"The poetry of winter."

The Love of Myrrhine and Konallis, and Other Prose Poems (Chicago: Pascal Covici, 1926), pp. 72-73. This poem is dated "Base Camp, Calais, 1917." It also appears in *Images of War: A Book of Poems* (Westminster: C. W. Beaumont, 1919), p. 12, and in the short story "Farewell to Memories" in *Roads to Glory* (London: Chatto and Windus, 1930), p. 264.

OUR HANDS

I am grieved for our hands, our hands
    that have caressed roses and
    women's flesh, old lovely books and
    marbles of Carrara. I am grieved for
    our hands that were so reverent in
    beauty's service, so glad of beauty of
    tressed hair and silken robe and
    gentle fingers, so glad of beauty of
    bronze and wood and stone and
    rustling parchment. So glad,
    so reverent, so white.
I am grieved for our hands.

The Love of Myrrhine and Konallis, and Other Prose Poems (Chicago: Pascal Covici, 1926), p. 74. This poem is dated "1917." It also appears in *Images of War: A Book of Poems* (Westminster: C. W. Beaumont, 1919), p. 15, and in *The Egoist*, Vol. 4, No. 8 (September 1917), p. 118.

FANTASY

Touch one again with the lips of
    thought the fair rigid limbs of
    goddesses men imagined beside the
    inland sea. Give the life of our blood
    to one among them, and worship in
    her oval of tremulous gold the beauty
    of that body whose embrace would
    murder us with ecstacy.
Recall from Orcus the Foam-born,
    lady of many names; make for her a
    broidered throne among the dusky
    colonnades of the soul.

Death, a fierce exultation, sweeps from
the lips of the conqueror; but from
hers, gently, a frail kiss, breathes the
savour of life.

The Love of Myrrhine and Konallis, and Other Prose Poems (Chicago: Pascal Covici, 1926), pp. 75-76. This poem is dated "Officers' Camp, Fressin, 1918." It is number II of eight prose poems headed "Prayers and Fantasies" in *Poetry: A Magazine of Verse*, Vol. 13, No. 11 (November 1918), pp. 67-71.

STAND-TO

Slowly, too slowly, the night, with its
noise and its fear and its murder,
yields to the dawn. One by one the
guns cease. Quicker, O dawn,
quicker—dazzle the hateful stars,
lighten for us the weight of
the shadows.
The last rat scuttles away; the first
lark thrills with a beating of wings
and song. The light is soft;
deliberately, consciously, the young
dawn moves. My unclean flesh is
penetrated with her sweetness and
she does not disdain even me.
Out of the east as from a temple
comes a procession of girls and young
men, smiling, brave, candid,
ignorant of grief.
Few men know the full bitterness of
night, but they alone will know the
full beauty of dawn—if
dawn ever comes.

The Love of Myrrhine and Konallis, and Other Prose Poems (Chicago: Pascal Covici, 1926), pp. 77-78. This poem is dated "Loos, 1918." It also appears in the short story "Farewell to Memories" in *Roads to Glory* (London: Chatto and Windus, 1930), pp. 265-266. It is number III of eight prose poems headed "Prayers and Fantasies" in *Poetry: A Magazine of Verse*, Vol. 13, No. 11 (November 1918), pp. 67-71.

IN AN OLD BATTLEFIELD

Life has deceived us. The thoughts we
　　found so vivid and fresh were dull
　　and crass as the prayers muttered to
　　a worn rosary by an infidel priest.
The joy we felt in beauty, our sense
　　of discovery at the touch of some
　　age-green bronze; even the sick
　　horror of some battlefield where the
　　flesh had not quite fallen from the
　　shattered bones—all this was old,—
　　a thousand times felt and forgotten.
And is the kiss of your mouth then
　　but the reflection of dead kisses,
　　the gleam of your breast a common
　　thing? Was the touch of your hand
　　but a worn memory of hands
　　crumbled into cool dust?

The Love of Myrrhine and Konallis, and Other Prose Poems (Chicago: Pascal
Covici, 1926), pp. 79-80. This poem is dated "Loos, 1918." Except for its
last six lines, it also appears in the short story "Farewell to Memories" in
Roads to Glory (London: Chatto and Windus, 1930), p. 266. The poem is
number IV of eight prose poems headed "Prayers and Fantasies" in *Poetry:
A Magazine of Verse*, Vol. 13, No. 11 (November 1918), pp. 67-71.

REACTION

And in the end one comes to love
　　flowers as women and women as
　　flowers. Beauty recoils from excess.
　　Imitate the wise Easterns, and let a
　　few sprays of blossom decorate the
　　empty chambers of the soul and
　　spread their fragrance through
　　its recesses.
Ah! To retain this fragrance, to make
　　permanent this most precious of
　　essences, this mingling of suave and
　　acrid perfumes—something wild
　　and tender and perverse
　　and immortal!

I will make for myself from tempered
    silver an Aphrodite with narrow
    hips and small pointed breasts and
    wide brow above gay subtle eyes;
    and in her hand shall be a perfume
    ball sweet with this divine fragrance.

The Love of Myrrhine and Konallis, and Other Prose Poems (Chicago: Pascal
Covici, 1926), pp. 81-82. This poem is dated "Officers' Camp, Fressin,
1918." It is number V of eight prose poems headed "Prayers and Fantasies"
in *Poetry: A Magazine of Verse*, Vol. 13, No. 11 (November 1918), pp.
67-71.

ESCAPE

Escape, let the soul escape from this
    insanity, this insult to God, from this
    ruined landscape, these murdered
    fields, this bitterness, this agony,
    from this harsh death and disastrous
    mutilation, from this filth and labour,
    this stench of dead bodies and
    unwashed living bodies—escape,
    let the soul escape!
Let the soul escape and move with
    emotion along ilex walks under a
    quiet sky. There, lingering for a while
    beside the marble head of some
    shattered Hermes, it strews the
    violets of regret for a lost loveliness
    as transient as itself. Or perhaps by
    some Homeric sea, watching the
    crisp foam blown by a straight wind,
    it gathers sea-flowers, exquisite in
    their restraint of colour and
    austere sparseness of petal.
There, perhaps, among flowers,
    at twilight, under the glimmer of
    the first stars, it will find a
    sensation of a quiet almost kindly
    universe, indifferent to this
    festering activity.

The Love of Myrrhine and Konallis, and Other Prose Poems (Chicago: Pascal Covici, 1926), pp. 83-84. This poem is dated "Loos, 1918." The first nine lines also appear in the short story "Farewell to Memories" in *Roads to Glory* (London: Chatto and Windus, 1930), p. 268. The poem is number VI of eight prose poems headed "Prayers and Fantasies" in *Poetry: A Magazine of Verse*, Vol. 13, No. 11 (November 1918), pp. 67-71.

PRAYER

The gods have ceased to be truth,
   they have become poetry. Now
   only simple pure hearts and those
   who are weary of doubt believe.
   Why not pray to the gods, any god?
   Perhaps even from the immensity
   of space will come a gentle
   ironic echo.
"Dionysus, Lord of life and laughter,
   from whom come twin gifts of
   ecstacy, hear me.
I pray the noble Iacchus of reverent
   mien and wide tolerant eyes, to look
   kindly upon me and to show me
   the mystery of vineyards,
   the mystery of death.
And I pray the young Dionysus, the
   bearer of the fawn-skin, the
   charioteer of leopards, the lover of
   white breasts, to show me the
   mystery of love.
And grant that nothing ignoble may
   render me base to myself; let desire
   be always fresh and keen; let me
   never love or be loved through
   ennui, through pity or
   through lassitude."

The Love of Myrrhine and Konallis, and Other Prose Poems (Chicago: Pascal Covici, 1926), pp. 85-86. This poem is dated "Officers' Camp, Fressin, 1918." A line from it also appears in the short story "Farewell to Memories" in *Roads to Glory* (London: Chatto and Windus, 1930), p. 270. The poem is number VII of eight prose poems headed "Prayers and Fantasies" in *Poetry: A Magazine of Verse*, Vol. 13, No. 11 (November 1918), pp. 67-71.

LANDSCAPE

The moon, high-seated above the
　　ridge, fills the ruined village with
　　tranquil light and black broken
　　shadows—ruined walls, shattered
　　timbers, piles of rubbish, torn-up
　　ground, almost beautiful in this
　　radiance, in this quiet June air.
Somehow to-night the air blows
　　cleaner and sweeter—the chemistry
　　of earth is slowly purifying the
　　corrupting bodies, the waste and
　　garbage of armies. Sweetness,
　　darkness, clean space—the marble
　　rock of some Greek island, piercing
　　its sparse garment of lavenders and
　　mints like a naked nymph among
　　rustling leaves.
Heavy scented the air to-night—
　　new-mown hay—a pungent exotic
　　odour—phosgene. . . .
And to-morrow there will be huddled
　　corpses with blue horrible faces
　　and foam on their writhed mouths.

The Love of Myrrhine ane Konallis, and Other Prose Poems (Chicago: Pascal Covici, 1926), pp. 87-88. This poem is dated "Loos, May, 1918." It also appears in the short story "Farewell to Memories" in *Roads to Glory* (London: Chatto and Windus, 1930), p. 271. It is number VIII of eight prose poems headed "Prayers and Fantasies" in *Poetry: A Magazine of Verse*, Vol. 13, No. 11 (November 1918), pp. 67-71.

THE ROAD

To have watched all night at the feast
　　where Socrates spoke of love,
　　letting fall from tranquil fingers
　　white violets in the cool black wine;
　　or to have listened while some
　　friend of Bembo talked of the graves
　　of Academe and made golden flesh
　　for us the ghosts of dead Greece—

who would shrink from so exquisite
a vigil? Then indeed not to sleep
would be divine, the dawn—the first
birds among the trees in the misty
park, the first gold flush—would fill
us perhaps with regret, certainly
with exaltation.

But there is no exaltation for those who
watch beside the Road, the Road
some know too bitterly and some
will never know, the Road which is
the Place of Skulls—for it starts
from a graveyard and passes through
graveyards and ends in a graveyard.

By day the Road is empty and desolate;
no boot or wheel marks its mud,
no human figure is reflected in its
deep shell-pools. By day the Road is
silent. But by night it is alive with a
harsh monotonous epic. Along that
muddy trail move the rattling
transport limbers, the field-guns, the
ammunition wagons, the Red-Cross
cars lurch and sway on their springs
over its steep ruts. Down the Road
come the weary battalions, platoon
after platoon, heroic in their
mud and silence. Down that Road
come the dead men on their silent
wheeled stretchers. All that goes up
that Road is strong and young and
alive; all that comes down is weary
and old or dead. Over that Road
shriek and crash the shells; the
sharp bullets strike gold sparks from
its stones; the mortars tear craters
in it. And just before dawn when
the last limber rattles away and the
last stretcher has gone back to the
line, then the ghosts of the dead
armies march down, heroic in their
silence, battalion after battalion,
brigade after brigade, division after

division; the immeasurable forces of
the dead youth of Europe march
down the Road past the silent sentry,
past the ruined house, march back,
march home.

The Love of Myrrhine and Konallis, and Other Prose Poems (Chicago: Pascal
Covici, 1926), pp. 89-92. This poem is dated "Moroc, 1917." It also appears
in *The Egoist*, Vol. 5, No. 7 (August 1918), pp. 97-98, and, with some lines
omitted, in the short story "Farewell to Memories" in *Roads to Glory*
(London: Chatto and Windus, 1930), pp. 269-270.

DAWNS

I am haunted by the memory of my dawns.
   Not those earlier dawns when I saw
   for the first time the bell-towers of
   Florence in the lucid air, of the hills
   of Ravello violet and mist-wreathed
   against the gold sky; not those dawns
   when I rose from some exquisite and
   beloved body, the brain still feverish
   with desire, lips and eyes heavy with
   many kisses, to watch the cool waves
   of light gliding over the silvery roofs
   of London while the first sparrows
   twittered in the heavy plane-trees.
   Not those dawns, but others,
   tragic and pitiful.
I remember those harsh wakenings
   of winter-time in old French barns
   through whose broken tiles at night
   one saw the morose glitter of the
   stars and at dawn the sterile glitter
   of snow, dawns when one's breath
   was frozen to the blanket, and the
   contact of the air was anguish.
I am haunted by sombre or ironically
   lovely dawns seen from some bleak
   parade-ground, by misty spring dawns
   in the trenches, when the vague
   shapes of the wire seemed to be the
   forms of crouching enemies, by

summer dawns when the fresh
immeasurably deep blue was a
blasphemy, an insult to
human misery.

Yet one among them all is poignant,
unforgettable. As the shapes of
things grew out slowly from the
darkness, and the gentle grey
suffusion of light made outlines
visible, little groups of men carrying
stretchers on their shoulders came
slowly, stumbling and hesitating,
along the ruined street. For a
moment each group was silhouetted
against the whitening east: the steel
helmets (like those of mediaeval
men-at-arms), the slung rifles, the
strained postures of carrying, the
useless vacillating corpse under its
sepulchral blanket—all sharply edged
in black on that smooth sky. And as
the groups passed they shouted the
names of the things they carried—
things which yesterday were
living men.

And I forwarded my report through
the usual channels.

The Love of Myrrhine and Konallis, and Other Prose Poems (Chicago: Pascal Covici, 1926), pp. 93-96. This poem is dated "Loos, 1918." It also appears in *The Egoist*, Vol. 5, No. 9 (October 1918), p. 121, and, with a few lines omitted, in the short story "Farewell to Memories" in *Roads to Glory* (London: Chatto and Windus, 1930), pp. 273-274.

SONG

Song—once that meant song indeed:
the voices of Sappho's nightingales,
the exultation of beauty
over-whelming the modesty of silence.
Once it seemed that all life was song:
even trivial or base things becoming
lovely with that passion; even

death becoming less terrible when
hidden by sombre and luxuriously
sad words. For when life was an
ecstasy of discovery—each day with
some new gift of beauty—homely
daily speech became song. To have
loved the world for years, with the
immense vividness of new loves—
that was a gift worthy the
imperishable Olympians.

But now that youth has gone, and the
soul stifles in monotonous captivity,
song has come to have a new
meaning—more common but more
pathetic. It has come to mean now
the expression of the grief and
courage and acceptation of fate of
common, poor men. Song—any cheap
ordinary song—becomes strange and
pathetic, when sung by weary
dispirited men.

I remember songs which might have
moved even rich women to
understanding and compassion:
twenty men huddled in a leaky tent
singing wistfully of the Devon hills;
a weary platoon marching back
through the ruins of Vermelles,
pitiless in frost and sharp moonlight,
singing as they stumbled along; little
parties of men coming down the line
for leave, singing in almost
hysterical gladness.

Only last night, in the midst of a
raid—searchlights, menacing hum of
planes, soft thuds of anti-aircraft
guns, deep rapidly-nearing crashes
of bombs, no cover—I found three
boys sitting in darkness, softly
singing old tunes.

No longer the sharp edge of Attic
song, but the immeasurable pathos
of the song of common men,
patient under disaster.

The Love of Myrrhine and Konallis, and Other Prose Poems (Chicago: Pascal Covici, 1926), pp. 97-100. This poem is dated "Divisional Camp, 1918."

LETHE

Those who have passed through hell
    need only to pass through Lethe to
    become sane once more. When I
    remember those horrible brooding
    years my body shudders; an immense
    discouragement, a brooding weariness
    envelopes me.
Old pain, old terror, old exasperations
    crowd upon me—nights spent in
    shivering anguish shovelling cold
    mud under shell fire; interminable
    marches over pavé roads through
    incredibly insipid country, marches
    when the over-weight of a soldier's
    burden became an exasperation, a
    mad obsession; wet night watches
    in splashy trenches, mud soaking legs
    and feet to a kind of numb pain—
    and always the fierce whine of
    bullets, the nerve-racking detonation
    of shells; exhausting unrefreshing
    sleep in frowsy dug-outs on
    verminous sacks; food muddy and
    impure. And always the menace—
    annihilation. Every second it was
    possible—how did we not go mad?
    We were mad, utterly insane.
Proserpina, Lady of Hell, in whose
    keeping are the great sombre rivers,
    grant me I beseech one draught of
    Lethe to purge my spirit of horror,
    to make me worthy to mingle with
    sane men once more.

The Love of Myrrhine and Konallis, and Other Prose Poems (Chicago: Pascal Covici, 1926), pp. 101-103. This poem is dated "London, 1919." It also appears in *The Anglo-French Review*, Vol. 1, No. 6 (July 1919), p. 512, and in the short story "Farewell to Memories" in *Roads to Glory* (London: Chatto and Windus, 1930), p. 267.

THE RETURN

How I am alien here! How my
    presence troubles the pleasures of
    those who have not lived in hell!
    Like Odysseus, fresh from the bloody
    sacrifice to the cold ghosts, I bear
    with me a flavour of the grave, a
    rebuke from the unremembered dead.
Even in the crowded streets I carry
    repulsion. Even the pale glitter of
    light upon the wet stones exasperates
    me with its tranquillity; even the
    sallow prostitute, trying to speak to
    me, shrinks away. Like foolish
    mannikins the men I knew hunt in
    a ring some purposeless triviality.
    Only from one hand can I gain life—
    and that hand is denied me.

The Love of Myrrhine and Konallis, and Other Prose Poems (Chicago: Pascal
Covici, 1926), pp. 104-105. This poem is dated "London, 1919."

IN THE LIBRARY

There is a strange void in my brain.
    I bend over the black-speckled page
    and try to seize its life. What is it
    I am reading? Greek? What does
    Greek matter?
The rose-crowns of Anacreon, the
    dances of women eager to be taken,
    the sound of the fluid syllables,
    escape me.
I am out again on the muddy
    trench-boards, wearily trudging along
    those chalky ditches, under the rain,
    under the shells. . . .
I am utterly weary now that it is over,
    weary as the lost Argonauts beating
    hopelessly for home against the
    implacable storm.

The Love of Myrrhine and Konallis, and Other Prose Poems (Chicago: Pascal Covici, 1926), pp. 106-107. This poem is dated "London, 1919."

BODIES

Your slight body lies on the coloured
    cushions before the fire; red light
    blooms in its shadows and the higher
    curved flesh glows white and gold.
    Your eyes are half shut, your clear
    red lips just parted; under the small
    left breast I see the beating of your
    heart. I sit and watch you as you
    drowse. You are life.
But the horror will not leave me yet;
    for suddenly my senses are filled by
    ghastly memories. I struggle against
    them. Useless. The beauty of your
    body goes, the room, the silence,
    the perfume.
I stand with an old Frenchman by a
    ruined outhouse in a by-street of
    the village.
"Behind that door, Monsieur," he says,
    "you will find another of them."
The filthy stench of rotten flesh
    assaults my throat and nostrils,
    terrifies the animal in me. I bend—
    as I now bend above you—and note
    the shattered bloody skull, the
    grinning fixed face desecrated with
    dust, blue-grey like the uniform.
    It is a young German officer.
    Someone has taken his boots and his
    stockinged feet stick out ridiculously.
    He was handsome once; how would
    his mistresses like him now?
    Poof! What a stink!
The old man is not moved.
"There is another down the
    street, Monsieur."
"Show me; I will have them buried."

Let me not shriek out—let me hide my
face in your breasts and shudder a
little and try to forget.

The Love of Myrrhine and Konallis, and Other Prose Poems (Chicago: Pascal
Covici, 1926), pp. 108-110. This poem is dated "London, 1919." It also
appears in *The Anglo-French Review*, Vol. 3, No. 2 (March 1920), p. 137.

THE LAST SALUTE

We pass and leave you lying. No need
for rhetoric, for funeral music, for
melancholy bugle-calls. No need for
tears now, no need for regret.
We took our risk with you; you died
and we live. We take your noble
gifts, salute for the last time those
lines of pitiable crosses, those solitary
mounds, those unknown graves and
turn to live our lives out as we may.
Which of us were the fortunate who
can tell? For you there is silence
and the cold twilight drooping in
awful desolation over those
motionless lands. For us sunlight and
the sound of women's voices, song
and hope and laughter; despair,
gaiety, love—life.
Lost terrible silent comrades, we, who
might have died, salute you.

The Love of Myrrhine and Konallis, and Other Prose Poems (Chicago: Pascal
Covici, 1926), pp. 111-112. This poem is dated "London, 1919." It also
appears in *The Anglo-French Review*, Vol. 1, No. 4 (May 1919), p. 333, and
in the short story "Farewell to Memories" in *Roads to Glory* (London:
Chatto and Windus, 1930), pp. 277-278.

THE FAUN COMPLAINS

They give me aeroplanes
Instead of birds and moths;
Instead of sunny fields
They give me mud-holes;
And for my day-long, night-long sacred hush,
(Flutter of leaves, bee-murmurs in the flowers,
Ripe seeded grass just stirring into music)
A hush wherein one seemed to hear
The invisible wheels of burning stars
Echoing upon the tiled paths of heaven—
For this they give me noise,
Harsh clangours of breaking metal,
Abrupt huge bursts of flame.

And for my woodland playmates,
Dryads, yellow subtle fauns,
Naked wanton hamadryads,
And stealthy water-girls
Who stole my honey and fruits
When I lay sleeping by their pools—
For these they give me men,
Odd, loud-voiced, fearsome men,
Who mock my little horns and pointed ears!

Collected Poems (New York: Covici, Friede, 1928), p. 71.

PASSAGES TOWARD A LONG POEM
IX

Ci-gît un homme de paille,
Né; sans avoir de naissance,
Fastueux, quant à la taille,
Heureux, dans les lieux d'aisance;
Il n'avait pas beaucoup d'espoir
Et se fichait bien d'en avoir.

Il n'aimait pas beaucoup Dieu
Qui le lui rendait bien,

Il donnait des torts à c'Vieux:
Et Dieu n'lui donnait—rien.
Ainsi, de saison en saison,
Il perdait jusqu'à la raison.

O Passant, qui lis cest mots,
Inscrits sur une tombe sans croix,
Va ton chemin, mon beau,
Et bénis le Néant, notre roi.
Adieu, mes amis et mes poules,
Adieu, àdieu—tas de moules.

Imagist Anthology 1930: New Poetry by the Imagists (New York: Covici, Friede, 1930), pp. 58-59; also published in London in 1930 by Chatto and Windus. This is the only part of the "Passages" not reprinted in *The Complete Poems*.

SEPADS: A MODERN POEM
(To Walter Lowenfels)

I

Let nothing stand between you
        and water thrills.
Unless you snap the lever
        swank looks like a pin.
So many fascinating possibilities
        fully practical
In individual triangular portions,
correctly planning the miraculous cloth
        and wet sticky sand.

These fellows who cop all
        are as comfortable
as bare feet in amethysts,
alexandrite, kunzite, zircons.

That dark-brown morning taste
        whose four great routes
penetrate and explore
soft-covered elastic threads

(no drain pipe)
highly illustrated without binding or bunching!

Get your shoulders into it,
sparkling windows,
      when orange blossoms are a memory
in yellow and turquoise
    of these smiling sentinels,
your facial loveliness
     without excessive foaming
or liquefying, mile after mile.

Although English in origin
You'll find him of real assistance
until the great round-bellied pot is full.

A procession of wooden horses
     properly buttressed
At the sides with many thousands of miles,
with lustrous chromium bands,
     thundering machinery,
gulf blue, mellow cream, niagara green,
concentrated, homogenized and
     almost unbelievable.

Slash at it murderously.

When trails tough beaches beckon
    off with a leap.
WJZ WBZ WBZA WHAM WREN
KDKA WTMJ KSTP

With the question of body beauty
    uppermost
      all this is natural and logical.
Send that parrot away and
    look to strange corners;
684,000,000 horsepower
     makes the finish last longer—
       finger-tip steering of
to-day's lithe young man and
     slender young woman

very modern, tough, amber-colored,
white and brown,
        completely transparent wrapping.
(It's so good that
        you'll want to hurry.)

Heavy, heavy, hangs over head
the world's dietic urge.

Have you heard it yet?
        The magic mellow melody?
Twenty-eight to thirty-seven dollars!
Even in feminine hands
        the jerks and sudden rebounds
of sinewy cords completely cushioned
        are ductile
and create unusual excitement,
kneading and working together,
        fiery, hot,
pipe and nipple:
fast as a fish,
        dyed forever!
O woman's perpetual search
        for something different!
(Originality in every art
        proclaims the master.)
Hair and skin emanations—
        the lustre dies—
catch on a cellar window.

Are you the type of woman
        conveniently located everywhere now?
Mild, delicious, smooth?
        Super-dynamic speaker, power-pack,
        over a coast-to-coast hook-up?
Staunch under punishment, smartest and snappiest,
        decidedly up to the minute?
Eureka!

Imagist Anthology 1930: New Poetry by the Imagists (New York: Covici, Friede, 1930), pp. 61-64.

dedication
to the pessimist thomist

Well, anyhow, it's something to have had
The glad
Eye from a few bad
Girls, Dad.

Movietones: Invented and Set Down by Richard Aldington, 1928-1929
(privately printed, 1932).

DEBATE

good god he said but why
say good god when god is
neither good nor god well
why seek the absolute in love or
absolute love well you're more
likely to find the absolute in
a woman's eyes or thighs than
in a buggy church steeple yes
but why confound religious and
sexual yearnings they're the same god's
the consoler of lost love thwarted
love the despoiled see how many
women go to church looking for
spiritual lollipops to console
console men are so inexpert so
gross why aren't there more
lesbians on their knees double
mirrors send back infinite
refractions well but it's all
subjective a right angle's no
different geometrically though the
arms are infinite
            but if I have my love
gold chrysanthemum who wants a
papal rose then absolute for
absolute which is best her kiss
your hocussed cup give me my love
and keep your paradise I'll risk
the thing to come she's more
god than god blasphemy

(But here's the secret—promise not to tell—
We shan't meet Maritain or X in hell!)

Movietones: Invented and Set Down by Richard Aldington, 1928-1929
(privately printed, 1932).

[Untitled]

down in the city of
london this morning the
typewriters clickclick shingled
girl typists young men in starched collars
the later you come to the office the
more important you are and the
bank clearings for the day will be over
a hundred millions sterling and
who the devil counts the money but
it all goes on goes on and nobody
seems to hesitate or doubt and
lucky for us they don't for if
they stopped to think our
little paradise would collapse but
it is odd they fancy themselves
so important and believe in themselves and
all that shifting mass of paper which is
supposed to be iron zinc spelter
lead coal oil silk cotton wool ships
copra sugar wheat men's lives
statistics averages percentages
      and do they
know it's all a convention a
phantasmagoria if they had the
wits to see how dangerous we are
to their curious dream they would have
us killed but they only pretend
we don't exist which is all part of
the convention
    and so god
save the kings so long as
the dividends are paid which as
somebody once remarked is the real
miracle

Movietones: Invented and Set Down by Richard Aldington, 1928-1929
(privately printed, 1932).

[Untitled]

unlike mr ezra pound I do not
hum-groan loudly intermittently and
discordantly for hours when
enraged nor is my sluggish british
blood so rapidly made to boil as
the subtler ichor of the american
ibycus nor is my epistolary
style so rich in nitre sulphur
soot and other chemical manures
                             but
When I consider the frank
effrontery and genial rapacity and
hypocritical bonhomie of the
english publisher when picking the
pockets of his authors I
am
    almost
           tempted
                to
                   say
                      something
                          about
                              it

Movietones: Invented and Set Down by Richard Aldington, 1928-1929
(privately printed, 1932).

[Untitled]

the carlylean hero-worship of
these virtuous and cultivated
germans is a little
irritating and should be
discouraged how general bonaparte
would laugh at ludwig's
napoleon olympus is a

molehill and alexander not
fit to command a company and
last century's great poet is
to-day's great bore let
us be our own heroes if we
must crave for the heroic and
when better men that is younger
arrive let them ignore us and
be heroes on their own why
should we paddle in dead men's bones and
call false spectres from the
gigantic grave to frighten us
with bogey greatness being alive
is the true greatness and life is
NOW

Movietones: Invented and Set Down by Richard Aldington, 1928-1929
(privately printed, 1932).

[Untitled]

the first political duty of a
man is to hate his
country indifference is not
enough you must hate your nation
to counterbalance all this
imbecile nationalist hatred which is
making the world unfit to live
in can't you see these nationalist
reactionary governments are all
uneasy and using any means to
coerce us into their foul
policies of hatred hence police
spies passports tariffs journalism prosecutions
gunmen scares repressions moral outbursts
ye have heard an eye for an
eye but I say unto ye
live out of your own country
and think above nationalisms we
are bursting through those old
bonds and the dead-handers want
to drive us back damn the

soviet with its unscrupulous
nationalist use of internationalism and
damn muss of course but that's more
meritorious in russians and
italians we must say damn
the british empire curse the council
for imperial defence damn all
nationalisms especially english
irish and american and
particularly damn the
pope and his fetid cardinals
paltry dago political
intriguers who would murder
the life of the world for
thirty pieces of
peter's pence

Movietones: Invented and Set Down by Richard Aldington, 1928-1929
(privately printed, 1932).

[Untitled]

the second political duty of a
man is to refuse to be a
citizen because the only allegiance
we owe is to the ideal state of
justice and not to the false
democratic states founded on
force and numbers the rules of the
most unjust
                    you are duped by
catchwords and have less real
liberty than a french peasant
in 1780
            the gigantic hypocrisy of
english law and lawyers must be exposed and
the utter death implied by british bourgeois
values must be denounced the
lawyer and the virtuous mother are
as deadly as the priest and the
soldier
            what matters is not your
social self but your individual self

not the causes for which you may be killed but
the men and women for whom you live
your life instinct is
damnably exploited by governments who
in justice are the servants of the
governed and by usurpation have become
the oppressors and natural enemies of
free men

Movietones: Invented and Set Down by Richard Aldington, 1928-1929
(privately printed, 1932).

[Untitled]

all art aspires to the condition of
journalism and movies successful upstarts
abolishing ballad-poets academies moliere
shakespeare opera to require permanent values
timelessness is pure archaism pedantry in
an age of rapid chaos
                        discard all possessions
hence no solid disgustingly indestructible
folk-furniture and classics cluttering the
centuries and perverting the minds of
the amiable rich but cheap
quickly consumed unregretted necessities luxuries

                        books for a season
music more impermanent and capricious than
jazz pictures in synthetic german dyes bound
to fade rapidly sculpture in non-durable
material and buildings to be
destroyed every twenty years
                                let
our art change with our minds and
caprices and 1930 not dress in
mental costumes of 1910-1919

TAKE OFF

your flannel drawers calliope and
wear thin neat

        accessible

            coloured

                artificial

silk ones

*Movietones: Invented and Set Down by Richard Aldington,
1928-1929* (privately printed, 1932).

HARK   HERALD
     THE

why if a girl came to me and
said I'm a virgin only
I'm going to have a baby only
I'm still a virgin a
little bird came down from heaven
and said I forgot what it
said but I got pregnant only
the angel said it was god only
it wasn't god it was the holy ghost
which is the same as god only
it isn't god and the baby
is going to be god too only
he won't be god or the holy ghost
but they're all god and yet only god's god and
my old man Joseph here stand up
Joseph and touch your hat to the gentleman
he's god's putative father
and I'm god's mother POP
I should say vulgarly putting
a finger into my mouth
and popping my cheek
and how these oriental
gods treated their women making
her have the child in an
insanitary stable all dung
and fleas a wonder I think
she didn't get puerperal
fever or some other ghastly

complication it all sounds
rather squalid a sort of
unfunny limerick without a
parrot don't you think so now
really now what do you think?

Noel 1928

TO BRING YOU JOY

Movietones: Invented and Set Down by Richard Aldington, 1928-1929
(privately printed, 1932). This poem had been previously printed in Paris
in 1928 by Nancy Cunard at The Hours Press.

THE POWER AND THE GLORY

of course I'm not a
patriotic american or even an
american at all except by
contact with the best female exiles so the
topic of the pilgrim fathers does not
excite any bad passions in me but
they are a bit of a joke poor old
buggers going off with their
bibles to shoot the indians and their
guns to preach the gospel of love to the
heathen and their hip-flasks of
scotch and not a bath-tub or a
contraceptive device or a copy of
aretino's 36 positions or
anything civilised about them but only
bug-whiskers and snuffling and
bibles and moonshine and hooch and
bibles and bibles and
people like cotton mather and long
fellow and whatshisname who
founded the unitarians and whole
mayflowers of democratic pi-jaws all of
them with coats of
arms and pedigrees and tombs in
westminster abbey philoprogenitively
begetting the great american
aristocracy

              but of course one
must admit they had the sense to
leave england but why they
didn't go straight to
montparnasse or rapallo without
all that fuss I don't know and
another thing I don't know is
who was the bloody fool
who arrested cromwell and pym at
plymouth instead of giving them
ten dollars and a nice new
bible to go play godly tricks on
unfortunate indians and not stay and
murder what civilisation there was in
england
              well paul hath
sowed and apollos hath
watered but the increase is the
federal banks and so god
save the god help the god damn the
pilgrim fathers

FOR EVER AND EVER AMEN

Movietones: Invented and Set Down by Richard Aldington, 1928-1929
(privately printed, 1932).

      to the gentle and corteous reader-critic

of course it is quite
understood that the
preceding pieces have no sort of
merit and that to publish them is
impertinence and that they will be
forgotten in three months just as
the early imagist poems of 1912
have been forgotten through several
editions
              you will be careful to
point out that the satirical poems are
not romantic and that the love
poems are not satirical and
where the rhythm is

broken on purpose you will of course
say it is not regular and where
it is smooth you will say it is
flat and where ideas are expressed
you will say there is no
emotion and where emotion is
expressed you will say there are no
ideas and
            in private you will
insinuate that the large number of my
illegitimate children are only
camouflage for my notorious
sodomy and that the reason I was never a
bankrupt is that nobody will give me
credit
        in short my dear old
friend you will be as honest and
intelligent as ever
            ⸗   and so
godblessyer bertie you always
was a comfort to yer pore ole
mother

Movietones: Invented and Set Down by Richard Aldington, 1928-1929
(privately printed, 1932).

Appendix A
Bibliographical Data on the "Images" and the "Images of War" Sections of "The Complete Poems"

The poems are listed in the order in which they appear in *The Complete Poems*. If periodical publication of the poem was located, the earliest such appearance is given first, together with bibliographical data. Following that is other periodical publication, if any, then the book source or sources. The numeral attached with a hyphen to the symbol or the book source indicates the poem's order in that volume. Data are given for "Images" in order of publication as nearly as it could be determined.

For "Images of War," book publication data are given for the C. W. Beaumont edition of *Images of War* if the poem appeared there, otherwise only for the earliest other edition or Imagist anthology in which the poem was included.

Key to Symbols

A	*The Anglo-French Review*
A 1914	*Des Imagistes: An Anthology*
A 1915	*Some Imagist Poets* (1915)
A 1916	*Some Imagist Poets* (1916)
A 1917	*Some Imagist Poets* (1917)
AL	*Arts and Letters*
D	*Dial*
E	*The Egoist*
ER	*The English Review*
F	*The New Freewoman*
I	*Images*
ION	*Images Old and New*
L	*The Little Review*
LA	*The Living Age*

N   *The Nation*
O   *Others*
P   *Poetry*
R   *Reverie*
S   *The Seven Arts*
W   *Images of War* (C.W. Beaumont)
WA   *Images of War* (Allen and Unwin)
WL   *War and Love (1915-1918)*

"Images"

"Choricos," *P*, Vol. 1, No. 2, 11/'12, pp. 39-41; *A* 1914-1, pp. 7-9; *I*-7, pp. 9-11; *ION* -12, pp. 20-23.

"To a Greek Marble," *P*, Vol. 1, No. 2, 11/'12, p. 42; *A* 1914-2, p. 10; *I*-1, p. 3; *ION*-1, p. 9.

"Argyria," *P*, Vol. 3, No. 4, 1/'14, p. 134; *A* 1914-6, p. 14; *I*-5, p. 7; *ION*-2, p. 10.

"At Mitylene," *E*, Vol. 1, No. 9, 5/1/'14, p. 161; *I*-15, p. 17; *ION*-17, p. 28.

"Stele," *ION*-6, p. 14.

"Lesbia," *P*, Vol. 3, No. 4, 1/'14, p. 133; *A* 1914-4, p. 12; *ION*-8, p. 16.

"Lemures," *A* 1915-7, p. 17; *I*-13, p. 15.

"Hermes, Leader of the Dead," *I*-16, p. 18; *ION*-18, p. 29.

"The River," *P*, Vol. 3, No. 4, 1/'14, p. 133; *A* 1914-8, p. 16; *I*-2, p. 4; *ION*-3, p. 11.

"Epigrams," *A* 1915-5, p. 15. In other editions these are printed as three separate poems: "A Girl," *I*-9, p. 13; *ION*-13, p. 23. "October," *I*-10, p. 13; *ION*-7, P. 15. "New Love," *I*-11, p. 13; *ION*-4, p. 12.

"Beauty, Thou Hast Hurt Me Overmuch," *F*, Vol. 1, 9/15/'13, p. 132; *A* 1914-5, p. 13; *I*-4, p. 6; *ION*-5, p. 13.

"In the Old Garden," *P*, Vol. 1, No. 2, 11/'12, p. 43; *A* 1914-3, p. 11; *I*-3, p. 5; *ION*-9, p. 17.

"June Rain," *I*-19, p. 21; *ION*-10, p. 18.

"In the Via Sestina," F, Vol. 1, 9/15/'13, pp. 132-133; A 1914-7, p. 15; I-6, p. 8; *ION*-11, p. 19.

"Amalfi," *F*, Vol. 1, 9/15/'13, p. 132; I-14, p. 16; *ION-14*, p. 30.

"Bromios," *A* 1914-9, p. 17.

"Images," *P*, Vol. 7, No. 1, 10/'15, pp. 23-24; *I*-8, pp. 12-13; *ION*-14, pp. 24-25.

"The Faun Sees Snow for the First Time," *A* 1915-6, p. 16; *I*-12, p. 14; *ION*-16, p. 27.

"Reflections," *A* 1916-7, pp. 12-13.

"Summer," *I*-17, p. 19; *ION*-21, p. 32.

"Scents," *ION*-23, p. 34.

"The Poplar," *P*, Vol. 3, No. 4, 1/'14, pp. 135-136; *A* 1915-2, pp. 10-11.

"After Two Years," *Poetry and Drama*, No. 8, 12/'14; *A* 1915-2, p. 6; *I*-30, p. 31.

"At the British Museum," *E*, Vol. 2, No. 6, 6/1/'15, p. 96; *I*-18, p. 20; *ION*-22, p. 33.

"At Nights," *I*-26, p. 26; *ION*-26, pp. 37-38.

"Church Walk, Kensington," *L*, Vol. 1, No. 9, 12/'14, p. 2; *ION*-28, p. 40.

"St. Mary's, Kensington," *I*-25, p. 26; *ION*-29, p. 41.

"Evening," *I*-23, p. 25; *ION*-27, p. 39.

"Cinema Exit," *E*, Vol. 2, No. 7, 7/1/'15, p. 113; *O*, Vol. 1, No. 5, 11/'15, p. 83; *I*-21, p. 23; *ION*-31, p. 43.

"In the Tube," *E*, Vol. 2, No. 5, 5/1/'15, p. 74; *O*, Vol. 1, No. 5, 11/'15, pp. 82-83; *I*-20, p. 22; *ION*-30, p. 42.

"Interlude," *P*, Vol. 5, No. 5, 2/'15, p. 222; *I*-22, p. 24; *ION*-32, p. 44.

"Hampstead Heath," *I*-24, p. 25; *ION*-34, p. 46.

"London," *I*-29, p. 30; *ION*-35, p. 47.

"Eros and Psyche," *E*, Vol. 2, No. 8, 8/2/'15, p. 125; *A* 1916-1, pp. 3-5.

"Childhood," *E*, Vol. 1, No. 24, 12/15/'14, pp. 453-454; *A* 1915-1, pp. 3-9.

"Daisy," *A* 1915-4, pp. 13-14.

"Round Pond," *A* 1915-3, p. 12.

"Whitechapel," *E*, Vol. 3, No. 1, 1/1/'16, p. 10; *A* 1916-4, pp. 8-9.

"Images," *A* 1917-7, pp. 12-13.

"Inarticulate Grief," *A* 1917-6, p. 11.

"Fantasy," *A* 1916-3, p. 7. Appears under the title "1915."

"R. V. and Another," *E*, Vol. 3, No. 11, 11/'16, p. 169; *A* 1917-9, p. 15.

"Prayer," *A* 1917-10, p. 16.

"Captive," *A* 1917-8, p. 14.

"Sunsets," *A* 1916-5, p. 10.

"The Faun Captive," *The Nation*, Vol. 25, No. 9 (31 May 1919), p. 265; *The Living Age*, Vol. 302 (9 August 1919), p. 384. Appears under the title "The Captive Faun."

"Images of War"

"Proem," *E*, Vol. 6, No. 2, 3-4/'19, p. 23; *W*-1, p. 5.

"Vicarious Atonement," *W*-2, p. 9.

"Leave-taking," *S*, 8/'17, pp. 468-469; *WA*-2, pp. 11-12.

"Bondage," *A* 1917-2, pp. 5-6.

"Field Manoeuvres," *A* 1917-4, pp. 8-9.

"Dawn," *W*-4, p. 11.

"The Lover," *WA*-7, p. 17.

"A Moment's Interlude," *A* 1917-3, p. 7.

"Insouciance," *P*, Vol. 14, No. 4, 7/'19, p. 175; *WA*-10, p. 20.

"On the March," *R*-5, pp. 18-19.

"In the Trenches," *D*, Vol. 63, 12/6/'17, p. 579; *N*, Vol. 25, No. 5, 5/3/'19, p. 139; *LA*, Vol. 302, 7/19/'19, p. 256; *W*-8, pp. 16-17.

"Ananke," *WA*-12, p. 23.

"Misery," *N*, Vol. 25, No. 5, 5/3/'19, p. 139; *WA*-13, p. 24.

"Living Sepulchres," *W*-12, p. 21.

"Daughter of Zeus," *E*, Vol. 4, No. 4, 5/'17, p. 58; *W*-11, p. 20.

"Picket," *A*, Vol. 1, No. 3, 4/'19, p. 221; *W*-25, p. 40.

"Trench Idyll," *W*-13, pp. 22-23.

"Time's Changes," *A*, Vol. 1, No. 3, 4/'19, p. 221; *LA*, Vol. 302, 7/12/'19, p. 128; *WA*-18, p. 28.

"A Village," *W*-15, pp. 25-27.

"The Wine Cup," *R*-3, pp. 14-15.

"Machine Guns," *W*-24, p. 39.

'Battlefield," *E*, Vol. 4, No. 7, 8/'17, p. 105; *W*-10, p. 19.

"Three Little Girls," *W*-14, p. 24.

"A Ruined House," *E*, Vol. 4, No. 6, 7/'17, p. 92; *W*-9, p. 18.

"Soliloquy 1," *W*-20, p. 35.

"Soliloquy 2," *W*-21, p. 36.

"A Young Tree," *W*-17, p. 29.

"Reverie," *ER*, Vol. 28, 5/'19, pp. 327-374; *R*-2, pp. 7-13.

"April Lieder," *WA*-31, p. 47.

"Barrage," *W*-16, p. 28.

"An Earth Goddess," *A*, Vol. 1, No. 3, 4/'19, pp. 220-221; *LA*, Vol. 302, 7/19/'19, p. 256; *W*-19, pp. 32-34.

"Bombardment," *E*, Vol. 6, No. 2, 3-4/'19, p. 23; *W*-18, pp. 30-31.

"Two Epitaphs," *W*-22,23, pp. 37-38.

"Concert," *AL*, Vol. 2, No. 1, n.s., Winter '18-'19, p. 4; *WA*-36, p. 53.

"Taintignies," *WL*-38, p. 56.

"Terror," *W*-26, pp. 41-43.

"Defeat," *WL*-39, p. 57.

"Doubt," *E*, Vol. 6, No. 2, 3-4/'19, p. 23; *WA*-25, pp. 37-38.

"Resentment," *A* 1916, p. 60. Appears under the title "People."

"Disdain," *E*, Vol. 6, No. 2, 3-4/'19, p. 23; *WA*-29, p. 42.

"Apathy," *E*, Vol. 5, No. 2, 2/'18, p. 25; *W*-27, pp. 44-46.

"The Blood of Young Men," *WA*-40, pp. 60-63.

"Epilogue," *R*-9, p. 25.

Appendix B
Source Guide to the Uncollected Poems

This Appendix is divided into two sections: Poems from Periodicals and Newspapers and Poems from Previous Editions. In each section the publications are listed in alphabetical order and the poems are listed in the order in which they are found in Part II, above.

Poems from Periodicals and Newspapers

The Anglo-French Review
    Fear
    Invitation
Bruno Chapbooks
    Easter
Bulletin of the New York Public Library
    To: Brigit
The Chapbook
    Freedom
    Meditation
Coterie
    Minor Exasperations
        I The Occultists
        II Valhalla
        III My Colonel
        IV Breaking-Point
The Egoist
    Penultimate Poetry
    Ennuies
        To a Poet
        Les Ennuyes Exquis
        Verona
        A Liver
        Solemn Meditation
        Stodge
    A Farewell
    To the Supreme Being in War Time
    On Thersites
    Synthetic Sonnet
        I Classic
        II Dantesque
        III Francis Thompsonian
        IV Cosmic

V Realistic
July Sunday
A Playntyve Ballade
Epigrams
    Replies
    Happiness
    Beauty
Fantasies
    Religious Landscape
    Book Shelves
    Sloane Street
Italy
A Memory: Poem in Prose
A Life
Associations
The Days Pass
Evil Malady
Deaths of Common Men
The Evening Standard
    Chanson of Winter
    Villanelle
    Rondeau of Spring
The Exile
    Natal Verses for the Birth of a New Review
Justice
    Song of Freedom
The Little Review
    On a Motor-Bus at Night
    Epigrams
        Blue
        The Retort Discourteous
        Christine
    Bloomsbury Square
    Epigram
    Stream
    Décor Banal
The Living Age
    To France
    Happiness
    English Songs
The New Freewoman
    Oneirodotes
The New Keepsake for the Year 1921
    Solemnity
New York *Herald Tribune*
    Filings
Pall Mall Gazette
    At Parting
    Greek Epigram (Rufinus)
    Greek Epigram (Meleager)
    Spring and the Sea
    Sophokles' Tomb
    A Sonnet of Louise Labe
Papers on Language and Literature
    The Walk
Poetry: A Magazine of Verse
    Glaucopis

War Yawp
Palace Music Hall—(*Les Sylphides*)
Two Impressions
Compensation
Beauty Unpraised
La Rochelle
Union Magazine
In Memoriam
The Westminster Gazette
Sonnet
The Yale Review
Inscriptions

Poems from Previous Editions

Collected Poems (1928)
The Faun Complains
Des Imagistes: An Anthology
To Atthis
Vates, the Social Reformer
Exile and Other Poems
From Tasso
Images (1910-1915)
Dawn
Night Piece
Images of Desire
Dedication
Images Old and New
Hyella
A New House
Imagist Anthology 1930: New Poetry by the Imagists
Passages toward a Long Poem IX
Sepads: A Modern Poem
The Love of Myrrhine and Konallis, and Other Prose Poems
Idyll
Myrrhine to Her Lovers
Morning
Noon
Evening
The Offering to Persephone
Her Voice
Prayer
The Storm
Memory
Konallis the Epicurean
The Singer
Gifts
Festival
The Charioteer
Jealousy
The Offering
The Vigil
Unfriendly Gods
A Dialogue
The Paktis
Another Greater

Antre of the Nymphs
The Three Aphrodites
The Old Love
The Oleander
The Lamp
April
Two Goddesses
The Wine Jar
Konallis to Myrrhine
Myrrhine to Konallis
Homer and Sappho
Red and Black
The Wime of Lesbos
After the Orgy
The Last Song
Thanatos
Hermes-of-the-Dead
Epitaph
Discouragement
Fatigues
Sorcery of Words
Our Hands
Fantasy
Stand-To
In an Old Battlefield
Reaction
Escape
Prayer
Landscape
The Road
Dawns
Song
Lethe
The Return
In the Library
Bodies
The Last Salute

The Love Poems of Myrrhine and Konallis

White Rose

Movietones: Invented and Set Down by Richard Aldington, 1928-1929

dedication to the pessimist thomist
Debate
"down in the city of"
"unlike mr ezra pound I do not"
"the carlylean hero-worship of"
"the first political duty of a"
"the second political duty of a"
"all art aspires to the condition of"
Hark the Herald
The Power and the Glory
to the gentle and corteous reader-critic

War and Love (1915-1918)

Genius Loci
Song
Song for Her
Nights of Love
Epilogue

Appendix C
Chronological Checklist of Books of Poetry
by Richard Aldington

Images (1910-1915). 1915.

Images Old and New. 1916.

*The Love Poems of Myrrhine and
        Konallis*. 1917.

*Reverie: A Little Book of Poems
        for H. D.* 1917.

Images of War: A Book of Poems.
        1919.

Images of War. 1919.

Images of Desire. 1919.

War and Love (1915-1918). 1919.

Images. 1919.

Images of War. 1921.

The Berkshire Kennet. 1923.

Exile and Other Poems. 1923.

Exile and Other Poems. 1924.

A Fool i' the Forest: A Phantasmagoria.
        1924.

A Fool i' the Forest: A Phantasmagoria.
        1924.

*The Love of Myrrhine and Konallis,
        and Other Prose Poems.*
        1926.

Hark the Herald. 1928.

Collected Poems. 1928.

Collected Poems. 1929.

The Eaten Heart. 1929.

Love and the Luxembourg. 1930.

A Dream in the Luxembourg. 1930.

Movietones: Invented and Set Down by Richard Aldington. 1928-1929. 1932.

The Eaten Heart. 1933.

Collected Poems, 1915-1923. 1933.

The Poems of Richard Aldington. 1934.

Life Quest. 1935.

Life Quest. 1935.

The Crystal World. 1937.

The Crystal World. 1937.

The Complete Poems of Richard Aldington. 1948.

Sources Consulted

WORKS BY RICHARD ALDINGTON
BOOKS

The books of Aldington's own poetry are indicated by asterisks and are confined to first British and American editions and English-language editions from other countries published prior to publication in England or America. Most of these editions may be located in the fine poetry collection of Lockwood Memorial Library of the State University of New York at Buffalo, in The Morris Library of Southern Illinois University at Carbondale, or in The Manuscript Collection Temple University Library at Philadelphia. Up to three locations for each item are shown, however, when that many are known.

Key to Symbols

L   Lockwood Memorial Library
N   The New York Public Library
P   University Library Center, University of Pennsylvania
H   The Widener and Houghton Libraries, Harvard University
Pr   The Firestone Library, Princeton University
R   Rutgers, the State University of New Jersey, Library
T   Temple University Library
M   The Morris Library, Southern Illinois University

A. E. Housman and W. B. Yeats: Two Lectures. Hurst, Berkshire: The Peacocks Press, 1955.
All Men Are Enemies: A Romance. London: Chatto and Windus, 1933.
Balls and Another Book for Suppression. Blue Moon Booklet, No. 7. London: E. Lahr, 1931.
*The Berkshire Kennet. London: The Curwin Press, 1923. (L, H, M)
*Collected Poems. New York: Covici, Friede, 1928. (L, R, Pr)
*Collected Poems. London: George Allen and Unwin, 1929. (L, H, M)
*Collected Poems, 1915-1923. London: George Allen and Unwin, 1933. (West Chester State Teachers' College, West Chester, Pa.)
The Colonel's Daughter: A Novel. London: Chatto and Windus, 1931.
*The Complete Poems of Richard Aldington. London: Allan Wingate, 1948. (L, N, P)
*The Crystal World. London: William Heinemann, 1937. (L, N, P)
*The Crystal World. Garden State, N.Y.: Doubleday, Doran, 1937. (L, N, P)
Death of a Hero. London: Chatto and Windus, 1929.
D. H. Lawrence: An Indiscretion. Number 6, University of Washington Chapbooks, edited by Glenn Hughes. Seattle: University of Washington Book Store, 1927.

D. H. Lawrence: Portrait of a Genius But . . . New York: Collier Books, 1961. Originally
    published in 1950.

A Dream in the Luxembourg. London: Chatto and Windus, 1930. (L, P, R)

The Eaten Heart. Chapelle-Réanville, Eure, France: The Hours Press, 1929. (L, N, Pr)

The Eaten Heart. London: Chatto and Windus, 1933. (L, N, P)

Exile and Other Poems. London: George Allen and Unwin, 1923. (L, N, P)

Exile and Other Poems. Boston: The Four Seas Co., 1924. (L, H, M)

Ezra Pound and T. S. Eliot. Hurst, Berkshire: The Peacocks Press, 1954.

Fifty Romance Lyric Poems. London: Chatto and Windus, 1931. Translation.

A Fool i' the Forest: A Phantasmagoria. London: George Allen and Unwin, 1925.
    (L, N, P)

A Fool i' the Forest: A Phantasmagoria. New York: Lincoln MacVeagh, The Dial Press,
    1925. (H, M, University of California at Berkeley)

French Studies and Reviews. New York: Lincoln MacVeagh, The Dial Press, 1926.

The Garland of Months, by Folgore Da San Gemignano. Poets' Translation Series, No. 5.
    Cleveland: The Clerk's Press, 1917.

Great French Romances. London: Pilot Press, 1946. Translation.

Hark the Herald. Paris: The Hours Press, 1928. (L, N, M)

Images (1910-1915). London: The Poetry Bookshop, 1915. (L, P, H)

Images. London: The Egoist, Ltd., 1919. (L, R, Pr)

Images of Desire. London: Elkin Mathews, 1919. (L, R, P)

Images Old and New. Boston: The Four Seas Co., 1916. (N, P, H)

Images of War. London: George Allen and Unwin, 1919. (L, H, M)

Images of War. Boston: The Four Seas Co., 1921. (L, R, Pr)

Images of War: A Book of Poems. Westminster: C. W. Beaumont, 1919. (L, P, T)

Introduction to Mistral. Carbondale: Southern Illinois University Press, 1960. Preface by
    Harry T. Moore.

Jane Austin. Pasadena, Calif.: Ampersand Press, 1948.

Latin Poems of the Renaissance. London: The Egoist, Ltd., 1919. Translation.

Lawrence of Arabia: A Biographical Enquiry. London: Collins, 1955.

Life for Life's Sake: A Book of Reminiscences. New York: The Viking Press, 1941.
    London: Cassell, 1968.

Life Quest. London: Chatto and Windus, 1935. (L, N, R)

Life Quest. Garden City, N. Y.: Doubleday, Doran, 1935. (Franklin F. Moore Library,
    Rider College, Trenton, N. J. and T, M)

Literary Studies and Reviews. London: George Allen and Unwin, 1924.

Love and the Luxembourg. New York: Covici, Friede, 1930. (L, N, P)

The Love of Myrrhine and Konallis, and Other Prose Poems. Chicago: Pascal Covici,
    1926. (L, N, R)

The Love Poems of Myrrhine and Konallis. Cleveland: The Clerk's Press, 1917. (L, N, H)

Medallions. London: Chatto and Windus, 1930.

Movietones: Invented and Set Down by Richard Aldington, 1928-1929. Privately
    printed, 1932. (M, Galley proofs at University Research Library of the
    University of California at Los Angeles)

Pinorman: Personal Recollections of Norman Douglas, Pino Orioli, and Charles Prentice.
    London: William Heinemann, 1954.

The Poems of Anyte of Tegea. Poets' Translation Series, No. 1. London: The Egoist
    Press, 1915; Cleveland: The Clerk's Press, 1917.

The Poems of Richard Aldington. Garden City, N. Y.: Doubleday, Doran, 1934.
    (N, R, T)

Rejected Guest. New York: The Viking Press, 1939.

Remy de Gourmont: A Modern Man of Letters. Number 13, University of Washington
    Chapbooks, edited by Glenn Hughes. Seattle: University of Washington Book
    Store, 1928.

Remy de Gourmont: Selections from All His Works. Chicago: Pascal Covici, 1928.
    Translation.

Reverie: A Little Book of Poems for H. D. Cleveland: The Clerk's Press, 1917. (L, N, H)
Richard Aldington: Selected Critical Writings, 1928-1960, edited by Alister Kershaw.
        Carbondale: Southern Illinois University Press, 1970.
Roads to Glory. London: Chatto and Windus, 1930.
The Romance of Casanova. London: William Heinemann, 1947.
Seven Against Reeves: A Comedy Farce. London: William Heinemann, 1938.
Soft Answers. Carbondale: Southern Illinois University Press, 1967. Preface by Harry T.
        Moore.
Stepping Heavenward. A Record. Florence: G. Orioli, 1931; London: Chatto and
        Windus, 1931.
A Tourist's Rome. Draguignan: The Melissa Press [1961].
Very Heaven. London: William Heinemann, 1937.
War and Love (1915-1918). Boston: The Four Seas Co., 1919. (L, N, Pr)
A Wreath for San Gemignano. London: William Heinemann, 1946. Translation.

Books Edited And/Or With Introductions

Lawrence, D. H. *Apocalypse.* London: Martin Secker, 1932.
———— . *Kangaroo.* New York: The Viking Press, 1960. First published in 1950.
———— . *Last Poems.* Florence: G. Orioli, 1932. Edited with Guiseppe Orioli.
———— . *The Lost Girl.* Harmondsworth, Middlesex: Penguin Books, 1950.
———— . *St. Mawr; and, The Virgin and the Gipsy.* Harmondsworth, Middlesex: Penguin Books,
        1950.
———— . *The White Peacock.* Harmondsworth, Middlesex: Penguin Books, 1950.
Poetry of the English-Speaking World. London: William Heinemann, 1947.
The Portable Oscar Wilde. New York: The Viking Press, 1946.
The Religion of Beauty: Selections from the Aesthetes. London: William Heinemann,
        1950.
Remy de Gourmont: Selections from All His Works. Chicago: Pascal Covici, 1928.
The Spirit of Place: An Anthology Compiled from the Prose of D. H. Lawrence.
        London: William Heinemann, 1935.
The Viking Book of Poetry of the English-Speaking World. 2 vols. New York: The
        Viking Press, 1958.
Voltaire. London: George Routledge and Sons Ltd., 1925; New York: E. P. Dutton and
        Co., 1925.
Walter Pater: Selected Works. London: William Heinemann, 1948.

Articles

"The Art of Poetry." *Dial* (New York), Vol. 69. (August 1920), pp. 166-180.
"Campion's 'Observations.' " *Poetry: A Magazine of Verse*, Vol. 15, No. 5 (February
        1920), pp. 267-271.
"Free Verse in England." *The Egoist*, Vol. 1, No. 18 (15 September 1914), pp. 351-352.
"The Imagists." *Bruno Chapbooks*, Special Series # 5 (1915), pp. 69-72.
"Le Latin Mystique." *The Egoist*, Vol. 1, No. 6 (16 March 1914), pp. 101-102.
"Letters." *The Egoist*, Vol. 1, No. 7 (1 April 1914), p. 138.
"Modern Poetry and the Imagists." *The Egoist*, Vol. 1, No. 11 (1 June 1914), p. 202.
"A Note on Free Verse." *The Chapbook: A Miscellany*, No. 40 (1925), pp. 36-41.
"Notes from France." *The Egoist*, Vol. 4, No. 3 (April 1917), p. 38.
"The Poet and Modern Life." *Poetry: A Magazine of Verse*, Vol. 17, No. 1ϊ (May 1921),
        pp. 99-100.
"Poetry in Prose." *The Chapbook—Poetry in Prose: Three Essays by T. S. Eliot and
        Frederic Manning and Richard Aldington*, No. 22 (April 1921), pp. 16-24.
"The Poetry of F. S. Flint." *The Egoist*, Vol. 2, No. 5 (1 May 1915), pp. 80-81.
"The Poetry of Paul Fort." *The Little Review*, Vol. 2, No. 2 (April 1915), pp. 8-11.
"Two Poets." *The Egoist*, Vol. 1, No. 22 (16 November 1914), pp. 422-423.

Biographical and Critical Works on Richard Aldington
Books

An Anthology of War Poems. Compiled by Frederick Brereton with an introduction by Edmund Blunden. London: W. Collins Sons, 1930.

Beaumont, C. W., and M. T. H. Sadler, eds. *New Paths, 1917-1918*. Westminster: C. W. Beaumont, 1918.

Bolt, Sydney, ed. *Poetry of the 1920s*. London: Longmans, Green, 1967.

Braithwaite, W. S., ed. *Anthology of Magazine Verse for 1915*. New York: Lawrence S. Gomme, 1915.

Bullough, Geoffrey. *The Trend of Modern Poetry*. London: Oliver and Boyd, 1949.

A Catalogue of the Imagist Poets, with essays by Wallace Martin and Ian Fletcher. New York: J. Howard Woolmer, 1966.

Coffman, Stanley K., Jr. *Imagism: A Chapter for the History of Modern Poetry*. Norman: University of Oklahoma Press, 1951.

Cournos, John. *Autobiography*. New York: G. P. Putnam's Sons, 1935.

————. *Miranda Masters*. New York: Alfred A. Knopf, 1926.

Crowder, Henry. *Henry-Music*. Paris: Hours Press, 1930.

Cunard, Nancy. *These Were the Hours: Memories of My Hours Press Réanville and Paris 1928-1931*. Edited with a Foreword by Hugh Ford. Carbondale: Southern Illinois University Press, 1969.

Des Imagistes: An Anthology. London: The Poetry Bookshop, 1914. New York: Albert and Charles Boni, 1914.

Doolittle, Hilda. *Bid Me To Live (A Madrigal)*. New York: Grove Press, 1960.

Eliot, T. S. *To Criticize the Critic, and Other Writings*. New York: Farrar, Straus and Giroux, 1965.

Guimond, James. *The Art of William Carlos Williams: A Discovery and Possession of America*. Chicago: University of Illinois Press, 1968.

Hoffman, Frederick J., Charles Allen, and Carolyn F. Ulrich. *The Little Magazine: A History and a Bibliography*. Princeton, N. J.: Princeton University Press, 1946.

Howarth, Herbert. *Notes on Some Figures Behind T. S. Eliot*. Boston: Houghton Mifflin, 1964.

Hughes, Glenn. *Imagism and the Imagists: A Study in Modern Poetry*. Stanford, Calif.: Stanford University Press, 1931. London: Bowes and Bowes, 1960.

Imagist Anthology 1930: New Poetry by the Imagists. New York: Covici, Friede, 1930.

Isaacs, J. *The Background of Modern Poetry*. New York: E. P. Dutton, 1952.

Jones, Alun R. *The Life and Opinions of T. E. Hulme*. London: Victor Gollancz, 1960.

Kershaw, Alister. *A Bibliography of the Works of Richard Aldington from 1915 to 1948*. Burlingame, Calif.: William P. Wredon, 1950. London: Quadrant Press, 1950.

———— . and Frédéric-Jacques Temple, eds. *Richard Aldington: An Intimate Portrait*, with a bibliography of Aldington's works by Paul Schlueter. Carbondale: Southern Illinois University Press, 1965.

Lawrence, D. H. *Lady Chatterley's Lover*. New York: Modern Library, 1957.

Longaker, Mark, and Edwin E. Bolles. *Contemporary English Literature*. New York: Appleton-Century-Crofts, 1953.

Lowell, Amy. *Tendencies in Modern American Poetry*. Boston and New York: Houghton Mifflin, 1917.

McGreevy, Thomas. *Richard Aldington: An Englishman*. London: Chatto and Windus, 1931.

MacNeice, Louis. *Poetry: A Personal Essay*. London: Oxford University Press, 1938.

Monro, Harold. *Some Contemporary Poets (1920)*. London: Leonard Parsons, 1920.

Moore, Harry T., and Warren Roberts. *D. H. Lawrence and His World*. New York: The Viking Press, 1966.

Norman, Charles. *Ezra Pound*. Revised edition. New York: Funk and Wagnalls, 1969.

Patmore, Derek, ed. *My Friends When Young: The Memoirs of Brigit Patmore*. London: William Heinemann, 1968.

Pound Ezra. *Gaudier-Brzeska: A Memoir, 1916*. New York: New Directions, 1960.

————. *The Letters of Ezra Pound. 1907-1941*. Ed. D. D. Paige. New York: Harcourt, Brace and World, 1950.

————. *Literary Essays of Ezra Pound*. Ed. T. S. Eliot. Norfolk, Conn.: New Directions, 1954.

Pratt, William, ed. *The Imagist Poem*. New York: E. P. Dutton, 1963.

Smith, G. Eliot. *Human History*. New York: W. W. Norton, 1929.

Snow, C. P. *Richard Aldington: An Appreciation*, with a bibliography of Aldington's works. London: William Heinemann, n. d.

Some Imagist Poets: An Anthology. Boston: Houghton Mifflin, 1915.

Some Imagist Poets 1916: An Annual Anthology. Boston: Houghton Mifflin, 1916.

Some Imagist Poets 1917: An Annual Anthology. Boston: Houghton Mifflin, 1917.

Stead, C. K. *The New Poetic: Yeats to Eliot*. New York: Harper and Row, 1964.

Swinnerton, Frank. *The Georgian Scene: A Literary Panorama*. New York: Farrar and Rinehart, 1934.

Tindall, William York. *Forces in Modern British Literature, 1885-1946*. New York: Alfred A. Knopf, 1947.

Waggoner, Hyatt H. *American Poets: From the Puritans to the Present*. Boston: Houghton Mifflin, 1968.

Wickes, George, ed. *Lawrence Durrell-Henry Miller: A Private Correspondence*. New York: E. P. Dutton, 1963.

Wilkinson, Marguerite. *New Voices: An Introduction to Contemporary Poetry*. New York: The Macmillian Company, 1919.

Winter, Keith. *Impassioned Pygmies*. Garden City, N. Y.: Doubleday, Doran, 1936.

Winters, Yvor. *Forms of Discovery*. New York: Alan Swallow, 1967.

————. *Primativism and Decadence: A Study of American Experimental Poetry*. New York: Arrow Editions, 1937.

Articles

Aldis, Mary. "Some Imagist Poets, 1916." *The Little Review*, Vol. 3, No. 4 (June-July 1916), pp. 26-31.

Baum, Paull F. "Mr. Aldington." *South Atlantic Quarterly*, Vol. 28, No. 2 (April 1929), pp. 201-208.

Benkovitz, Miriam J. "Nine for Reeves: Correspondence from Richard Aldington." *Bulletin of the New York Public Library*, Vol. 69, No. 6 (June 1965), pp. 349-374.

Blackmur, R. P. "Richard Aldington." *The Nation*, Vol. 138, No. 3595 (30 May 1934), p. 625.

"Books of the Fortnight." Anon. review, *The Dial*, Vol. 66, No. 791 (31 May 1919), p. 576.

Bouyssou, Roland. "Dulce et Decorum est Pro Patria Mori." *Caliban*, Vol. 3, No. 2 (1967), pp. 115-124.

Butts, Mary. "Aldington's Images of Desire." *The Little Review*, Vol. 4, No. 4 (August 1919), pp. 35-36.

Colum, Padric. "Egoism in Poetry." *The New Republic*, Vol. 5, No. 55 (20 November 1915), pp. 6-7.

Edwards, Oliver. "Perchance to Dream." *The Times* (London), Thursday, 5 December 1957, p. 13b.

————. "Richard Yea and Nay." *The Times* (London), Thursday, 3 January 1957, p. 11.

Firkins, O. W. "Meteorites in Verse." *The Nation*, Vol. 104, No. 2689 (11 January 1917), pp. 43-45.

Fletcher, John Gould. "Mr. Aldington's Images." *Poetry: A Magazine of Verse*, Vol. 8, No. 1 (April 1916), pp. 49-51.

————. "Three Imagist Poets." *The Little Review*, Vol. 3, No. 3 (May 1916), pp. 30-35.

————. "Three Imagist Poets." *The Little Review*, Vol. 3, No. 4 (June-July 1916), pp. 32-41.

Flint, F. S. "On Richard Aldington." *Coterie*, No. 3 (December 1919), pp. 24-25.

Gates, Norman T. "Richard Aldington and F. S. Flint: Poets' Dialogue," *Papers on Language and Literature*, Vol. 8, No.1 (Winter 1972), pp. 63-69.

―――――. "Richard Aldington and The Clerk's Press." *The Ohio Review*, Vol. 13, No. 1 (Fall 1971), pp. 21-27.

Hueffer, Ford Madox. "A Jubilee." *The Outlook*, Vol. 36, No. 910 (10 July 1915), pp. 46-48.

"Journeyman of Letters." Anon. review, *The Times Literary Supplement*, 26 December 1968, p. 1448.

Kittredge, Selwyn. "Richard Aldington's Challenge to T. S. Eliot: Background of their James Joyce Controversy." *James Joyce Quarterly*, Vol. 10, No. 3 (Spring 1973), pp. 339-341.

Life Quest. Anon. review, *Christian Science Monitor*, 6 September 1935, p. 16.

Life Quest. Anon. review, Boston *Transcript*, 11 September 1935, p. 3.

Lippmann, Walter. "Miss Lowell and Things." *The New Republic*, Vol. 6, No. 72 (18 March 1916), pp. 178-179.

Lowell, Amy. "The Poetry Bookshop: (35 Devonshire Street, London)." *The Little Review*, Vol. 2, No. 3 (May 1915), p. 19.

―――――. "Richard Aldington's Poetry." *The Little Review*, Vol. 2, No. 6 (September 1915), pp. 11-16.

Monro, Harold. "The Bookshop." *Poetry Review*, No. 11 (November 1912), p. 498.

―――――. "The Imagists Discussed." *The Egoist*, Vol. 2, No. 5 (1 May 1915), pp. 77-80.

―――――. "Pathology des Dommagistes (being specimens for a projected Anthology to be issued in the U.S.A.)." *The Chapbook*, No. 23 (May 1921), pp. 21-24.

Monroe, Harriet. "An Imagist at War." *Poetry: A Magazine of Verse*, Vol. 24, No. 1 (April 1929), pp. 42-46.

―――――. "Refuge from War." *Poetry: A Magazine of Verse*, Vol. 12, No. ℾ (April 1918), pp. 44-46.

Pound Ezra. "Historical Survey." *The Little Review*, Vol. 7, No. 2 (Autumn 1921), pp. 39-42.

Quinn, Kerker. "Aldington 1938." *Poetry: A Magazine of Verse*, Vol. 52, No. 3 (June 1938), pp. 160-164.

Rosenthal, Sidney. "Richard Aldington and the Excitement of Reason." In *Twenty-Seven to One . . .*, Ed. Bradford Broughton. Ogdensburg, N. Y.: Ryan Press, 1971, pp. 133-143.

Schlueter, Paul. "A Chronological Check List of the Books by Richard Aldington." In *Richard Aldington: An Intimate Portrait*, Ed. Alister Kershaw and Frédéric-Jacques Temple (Carbondale: Southern Illinois University Press, 1965), pp. 175-186.

Seiffert, Marjorie Allen. "Soldier and Lover." *Poetry: A Magazine of Verse*, Vol. 14, No. 6 (September 1919), pp. 338-341.

Sinclair, May. "The Poems of Richard Aldington." *The English Review*, Vol. 32, No. 5 (May 1921), pp. 397-410.

―――――. "Two Notes." *The Egoist*, Vol. 2, No. 6 (1 June 1915), pp. 88-89.

Smith, Lewis Worthington. "The New Naiveté." *The Atlantic Monthly*, Vol. 117 (April 1916), pp. 487-492.

Thatcher, David S., ed. "Richard Aldington's Letters to Herbert Read." *The Malahat Review*, No. 15 (July 1970), pp. 5-44.

Urnov, Mikhail. "Richard Aldington and His Books." *News*, No. 7 (114) (1 April 1956), pp. 29-30.

"Volumes of Poetry." Anon. review, *The American Review of Reviews*, Vol. 60, No. 4 (October 1919), p. 446.

Wheelwright, John. "A Poet of Three Persons." *Poetry: A Magazine of Verse*, Vol. 45, No. 1 (October 1934), pp. 47-50.

Williams, William Carlos. "Four Foreigners." *The Little Review*, Vol. 6, No. 5 (September 1919), pp. 36-39.

Wolfe, Humbert. "Review of *Fool i' the Forest*." *The Criterion*, Vol. 3, No. 11 (April 1925), pp. 459-463.

Index to the Uncollected Poems

The page on which each poem appears is indicated by italic type.

Index

All works listed are by Richard Aldington unless otherwise indicated.